AMERICAN LIGHTHOUSES

Help Us Keep This Guide Up to Date

Every effort has been made by the authors and editors to make this guide as accurate and useful as possible. However, many things can change after a guide is published—trails are rerouted, regulations change, facilities come under new management, and so forth.

We would love to hear from you concerning your experiences with this guide and how you feel it could be improved and kept up to date. While we may not be able to respond to all comments and suggestions, we'll take them to heart and we'll also make certain to share them with the authors. Please send your comments and suggestions to the following address:

Globe Pequot Press
Reader Response/Editorial Department
P.O. Box 480
Guilford, CT 06437

Or you may e-mail us at:

editorial@GlobePequot.com

Thanks for your input, and happy travels!

AMERICAN LIGHTHOUSES

A Comprehensive Guide to

Exploring Our National Coastal Treasures

Third Edition

PHOTOGRAPHS BY BRUCE ROBERTS

TEXT BY CHERYL SHELTON-ROBERTS

AND RAY JONES

Copyright © 2012 by Morris Book Publishing, LLC

Photo on title page: Eagle Harbor Light, MI
All photographs, unless otherwise credited, are by Bruce Roberts.

Text design: Lisa Reneson
Layout: Casey Shain
Project editor: Ellen Urban

Maps © 2012 by Morris Book Publishing, LLC

Library of Congress Cataloging-in-Publication Data

Roberts, Bruce, 1930-
  American lighthouses : a comprehensive guide to exploring our national
coastal treasures / photographs by Bruce Roberts ; text by Cheryl
Shelton-Roberts and Ray Jones.— 3rd ed.
      p. cm.
  Includes index.
  ISBN 978-0-7627-7960-4
  1. Lighthouses—United States—Guidebooks. I. Shelton-Roberts,
Cheryl, 1950- II. Jones, Ray, 1948- III. Title.
  VK1023.R63 2012
  387.1'550973—dc23
                                           2012006711
Printed in the United States of America

10 9 8 7 6 5 4 3 2 1

For Cheryl, who came with me.
— BRUCE ROBERTS

For Ben and Elsie Jackson,
who have lit the way for so many.
— RAY JONES

For all who keep our lighthouses
healthy and bright, especially volunteers.
—CHERYL SHELTON-ROBERTS

ACKNOWLEDGMENTS

Many thanks to those who supplied photography and other help: Rick Polad, Jeremy D'Entremont, and Kraig Anderson, whose photography enhanced this edition; Mark Riddick, New Light Photography; William G. Kaufhold; Bob and Sandra Shanklin; Ben Russell; John W. (Jack) Weil; Frank Parks; Daniel J. Gruszka; Dave Kramer; Lamar C. Bevil Jr.; Lee Radzak at Split Rock Lighthouse, who was the perfect lighthouse keeper for my picture; Dick Moehl, president of the Great Lakes Lighthouse Keepers Association; Don Terras of the Grosse Point Lighthouse; the late Ken Black of the Shore Village Museum (now the Maine Lighthouse Museum) in Rockland, Maine; James W. Claflin of Kenrick A. Claflin & Son; Cullen Chambers at Tybee Island Light Station; Dave Snyder, former park historian, Apostle Islands National Lakeshore; Jeanne and George Couglar of the Tibbetts Point Lighthouse; Steve Harrison, historian, Cape Hatteras National Seashore; Tim Harrison of *Lighthouse Digest* magazine and Lighthouse Depot, for supplying photographs of isolated Maine lights that supplemented my photography; Candace Clifford of the Maritime Initiative; Dane and Judy Alden and Henry Gonzalez for their advice.

A special thanks to Dr. Robert Browning, US Coast Guard historian, for all his assistance in locating old photos and helping with identification of the lights and many other considerations. And appreciation is given to Dr. Laddie Crisp Jr., whose high-definition digital photography equipment so eloquently illustrates the advance in the art and the upside to technology.

The following websites are some of the available, excellent sources of information on lighthouses. As with all sources, check dates any information was recorded for up-to-date details: Jeremy D'Entremont, www.lighthouse.cc; Bob Trapani, http://stormheroes.com; Lighthouse Directory, http://unc.edu/~rowlett/lighthouse; Kraig Anderson, www.lighthousefriends.com; US Coast Guard, www.uscg.mil/history; National Park Service Maritime Heritage Program, www.nps.gov/maritime; American Lighthouse Foundation, www.lighthousefoundation.org; Bob DaVia, http://seathelights.com; and on North Carolina lights, www.oblhs.org, where questions on lighthouses are fielded and personally answered by the Outer Banks Lighthouse Society; American Lighthouse Coordinating Committee, http://amlhcc.org/research.htm; United States Lighthouse Society, www.uslhs.org; Terry Pepper and the Great Lakes Lighthouse Keepers Association, www.gllka.com. Additionally, many lighthouses are operated by individual groups that have their own websites, and many are listed in this new edition.

Dates quoted for each light station: The year a light station was *established* can vary from one to ten years, depending on how long it took to get a clear deed to the land, construct all buildings, and install the light apparatus. Therefore, dates cited in this edition refer to the year a lighthouse was in service and its light *operative* and are stated as accurately as documentation allows.

We are especially grateful to Erin Turner and Ellen Urban for their invaluable editorial assistance and advice on style.

CONTENTS

PREFACE

Lighthouses Take on New Roles:
From Navigational Aids to Sentinels of History

Lighthouses have been taking on new roles beginning with the time that they were transferred from the US Lighthouse Service to the US Coast Guard (USCG) in 1939 as America prepared for a second world war. The greatest changes have come about during the last two decades as technology introduced some of the most sweeping advancements in the history of mankind. In a very real way, lighthouses have changed from navigational aids to popular tourist destinations steeped in maritime history. Today many are recognized as significant to American history through their listing in the National Register of Historic Places, and at least eleven have been designated National Historic Landmarks.

The digital age has introduced amazing possibilities, exemplified by a computer and a camera tightly bundled into a palm-sized "smart phone." Even the revolutionary optic of its time, the early-nineteenth-century Fresnel lens, is being replaced by high-tech LED lights that can be adjusted for both flash characteristic, or rhythm, and intensity to be clearly visible in areas of intense, urban background lighting. It has been estimated that we are now experiencing a century of change in less than a decade. But as a result of these high-tech changes, people have lost jobs and have been expected to retrain abruptly to serve other purposes to survive.

Similarly, lighthouses lost their jobs as they were outmoded first by radar and then by the global positioning system (GPS), a satellite-based navigation system that in effect made them obsolete as aids to navigation. Thus, our guiding lights became unessential, and in many cases the towers were abandoned, left to deteriorate.

Hundreds of light stations subsequently went up for adoption as coordinated within the National Park Service via the National Historic Lighthouse Preservation Act of 2000 (NHLPA), which created preservation guidelines to ensure that new stewards met mandatory preservation standards set forth by the secretary of the interior. The process begins when a light station is declared surplus property by the USCG to the General Services Administration. Following consultation with the light station's state historic preservation office, a Notice of Availability is published offering affordable ownership of the property. Applications may be made by federal agencies, state and local governments, nonprofit organizations, educational agencies, and community development organizations. Only as a last option does a light station go on the public auction block. At first glance this perhaps sounds unreasonable, but consider that if a light is bought privately, chances are that public access to the historical structure would not be allowed. This places the lighthouse outside its historical context, which is exactly what the NHLPA wants to prevent.

Although the faces of light station owners have changed, rigid preservation standards must be maintained, just as in the olden days when all light stations were under the scrutiny of the US government—the same government that demanded that a keeper turn in an old paintbrush to receive a new one. In response to adopting light stations that have been declared surplus properties, dozens of volunteer groups and chapters of larger nonprofit organizations have formed all around America's coasts and Great Lakes. These groups have taken the opportunity not only to restore these historical sites but also to interpret each light station's legends. Although names and locations may differ, the purpose of these groups remains the same: To breathe life back into these gentle giants and share the rich and varied stories of maritime heritage with visitors. Foremost are the volunteers—to them go the deserved laurels for their efforts to help our lighthouses.

And it bears noting here that working quietly in the background of all this enlivened restoration work is a group known as the American Lighthouse Coordinating Committee. This task group comprises a consortium of organizations and individuals that are experts in every field concerned with lighthouses, standing at the ready to help troubleshoot issues just for the asking.

Like the phoenix rising, some of the best lighthouse preservation efforts to date continue into the twenty-first century. Ownership of and funding for lighthouses have become diversified within the public and private sectors; however, in each case, funds are hard earned and long fought for. As a result of these efforts, at many American lighthouses visitors can now experience what these great structures were like over a century ago when light stations still gleamed under the hands of dedicated keepers. Overnight accommodations are even offered now at several lighthouses for a one-of-a-kind experience.

Herein lies the importance of not only restoring lighthouses but also opening them to the public wherever possible. Modest entry fees generate future maintenance funds—funds that are not dependent on government support. These once-ailing structures have proven themselves *not* to be the invalids they once were thought to be. Restored, many are as strong as when originally completed, if not stronger. Moreover, many have been rekindled, and their comforting lights now shine into the twenty-first century. In summary: Heritage tourism is a hot item—American lighthouses can still work and be productive. When these lights are opened for visitation, people flock to see them, buy tickets to climb them, and take souvenirs home from nearby gift shops while bolstering surrounding community businesses. We salute the efforts of these nonprofit and private groups as well as city, county, state, and federal organizations that are keeping the lights burning.

After all, each of us could do worse than to be like a lighthouse—to stand tall, to be strong in the teeth of a storm, and to shine as brightly as possible. As Ray Jones poignantly stated, "Lighthouses call to us not only across water but also across time."

In all probability at least one of our ancestors who immigrated to this country was greeted by two of the nation's strongest symbols: An American lighthouse and a waving American flag. As representatives of our great nation, lighthouses have remained remarkably the same over the centuries, and many are enjoying a resurgence of popularity in new roles as sentinels of maritime history.

Pictured here is the beautifully restored St. Augustine Light and its first-order Fresnel lens.

Perched on a cliff far above the Pacific, Oregon's Heceta Head Light warns mariners away from this beautiful but extraordinarily dangerous coast.

INTRODUCTION

The Romance of Lighthouses

Very likely tucked away among your most pleasant memories is an evening stroll along a beach, an experience perhaps warmed by the companionship of a friend or a child. Probably you remember the feeling of moist sand under your bare feet, the kiss of a light breeze in your face, or the roar of the sea—in the dark it sounds less like waves striking sand and more like those eternal oceans you hear in a shell. But if there was a lighthouse beacon flashing in the distance, calling to you from the horizon, that part of the memory is especially bright.

Lighthouses and their beacons appeal to our sense of wonder, and as with the ocean itself, we attach a mythological importance to them. Even when we are far inland and away from the shore, the mere image of a lighthouse on a postcard, a stamp, or a company logo will remind us of the sea and of our powerful connection to it.

Nearly everyone, young or old, male or female, sailor or landlubber, is fascinated by lighthouses. And why not? Lighthouses are fun. Lighthouses are filled with meaning and mystery. Among our most historical and romantic structures, they are often located in beautiful places—on spectacular promontories or pristine barrier islands. Many, with their soaring brick walls, intricate steel skeletons, or cozy dwellings covered with Victorian gingerbread, are architectural treasures. Nearly all are more than a century old and some more than two centuries. Most are associated with drama—tragic shipwrecks, heroic rescues, self-sacrifice, and loves lost or found.

Of course, lighthouses have a very practical value for mariners, who still make good use of them. Even nowadays, when radar and satellites make pinpoint navigation possible, seamen are likely to put more faith in what they can see with their own eyes. To understand why this is so, consider that whenever the power goes out at home, we immediately start groping through drawers searching for candles and matches. We need light; otherwise, we'll start bumping into things.

Anyone who has ever experienced total darkness, as sailors do on a moonless, starless night, will know what it's like to feel utterly lost and cut off from the solid earth. The blackness is tangible. It swirls around you like a liquid, making it impossible to tell up from down, let alone north from south or east from west. So it is very easy to imagine the joy a hundred generations of mariners have felt at the sight of a lighthouse beacon on the horizon.

It has been said that men have always made better navigators than they have brothers. The carnage of a thousand sea battles would seem to prove the point. But lighthouses stand as a powerful argument against that view. They save lives, provide direction, and welcome travelers to safe harbor. The people who build or maintain them ask nothing in return.

In this sense the hundreds of lights that extend in a sparkling chain along our coasts represent our very best instincts as Americans. They mark us as an open society, a hospitable people more than happy to welcome others to our shores. For countless thousands of immigrants, the very first glimpse of America was the flash of a navigational beacon—perhaps the Point Bonita Light near the Golden Gate, the Montauk Light at the far eastern end of Long Island, or even of Lady Liberty herself—the Statue of Liberty was, in fact, once a lighthouse.

The magnificent first-order Fresnel lens warms the night sky over Currituck Beach on North Carolina's Outer Banks—just as it has since 1875.

Ironically, the tall sentinels that have welcomed so many to America and have saved so many ships and lives are themselves now in danger of extinction. Over the last half a century, both technical advances in navigation and budgetary concerns have led to the abandonment and destruction of one lighthouse after another. Some have been torn down, others have been permanently scarred by vandals, and a few have collapsed into the sea. But the story of America's lighthouses may yet have a happy ending.

Civic-minded individuals and organizations all over the country are working tirelessly to save our remaining historical lighthouses, and as you'll discover in the pages that follow, they are succeeding. Lighthouses have been guiding ships and sailors for at least three thousand years. Perhaps now they are guiding all of us to a better understanding of our past and of ourselves as Americans.

This guidebook is your invitation to take part in the ongoing lighthouse adventure. This introductory section provides a look at the history of America's light towers, the engineers who built them, and the keepers who, along with their families, lived at the lighthouses and lit their lamps each night.

Following the introduction, we'll take you on an imaginary journey beginning in far Downeast Maine; we'll travel down the Eastern Seaboard, along the Gulf of Mexico, up the Pacific coast from Southern California to the remote Aleutian Islands in Alaska, and finally through the Great Lakes, from Ontario to the far shores of Superior. Through words and breathtaking photography, you'll visit more than five hundred lighthouses, learn their dramatic histories, and see how they work. Ample travel information is included so you can experience and photograph the old towers yourself and, if you like, walk the nearby beaches to watch the lights flashing in the night.

Lighthouses throughout History

The ancient Greeks were a seafaring people, so it should come as no surprise that they included a lighthouse among their Seven Wonders of the World. Along with the pyramids of Egypt, the Hanging Gardens of Babylon, the Colossus of Rhodes, and the other wonders, they ranked the Pharos, history's first great lighthouse, among the most important and spectacular man-made structures of any age. Rising 450 feet into the blue Mediterranean skies, Pharos was the tallest lighthouse of all time. With almost twelve centuries of nearly continuous operation, it was also the one with the longest service record.

Built about 280 b.c. on an island in the bustling harbor of the Greco-Egyptian city of Alexandria, Pharos guided ships to the world's busiest seaport. The light, produced by a fire blazing on the tower's roof, could be seen from nearly thirty miles away. Ancient mariners needed the Pharos light because Alexandria stood on the flat Nile Delta and there were no mountains or other natural features to help them locate the city.

Peoples had long made a practice of banking fires on hills and mountainsides to bring their sailors home from the sea. With Pharos, its artificial mountain, Alexandria pulled in ships from the entire known world. The sight of the Pharos light blazing far up near the dome of the sky must have charged the breasts of countless sea captains with awe. In time the delta city became the busiest and most prosperous city on earth, and it remained so for nearly a thousand years, or about as long as its lighthouse stood—it was eventually destroyed by an earthquake.

Trading ships from Greece, Carthage, and Rome flocked to the city's wharves to load up on the grain that grew in such wondrous abundance along the banks of the Nile. It was for possession of Alexandria and her grain markets that Julius Caesar invaded Egypt and, later, Octavius fought and defeated Antony and Cleopatra. Without Egypt's grain to feed the empire's teeming masses, Rome's conquests would have been meaningless. And without the Pharos light, the lumbering Roman grain ships might never have found Alexandria. Thus, in a very real sense, the Roman empire was dependent on a lighthouse.

Like Rome, the United States of America is a highly commercial nation, part industrial and part agrarian. As with Rome, the growth and prosperity of our country has depended on safe navigation of the waters leading to our busy port cities. Thus, lighthouses have been a major concern for Americans right from the nation's beginning.

Early US Lighthouses

America's oldest light station was located on Little Brewster Island at the outer entrance of Boston Harbor. Built in 1716, the Boston Lighthouse was a cylindrical stone structure with a lantern room at the top. Its design set the pattern for hundreds of lighthouses that would come afterward. Destroyed during the Revolutionary War raids by both Continental and British forces, it was rebuilt in 1783.

Marking the entrance to Nantucket Harbor in Massachusetts, Brant Point Light (1746) was the second lighthouse built in the original thirteen colonies. A rather flimsy wooden structure, it burned or was blown over several times, only to be rebuilt by the island's tenacious whalers and fishermen.

America's third lighthouse, Beavertail Light (1749), marked the passage into Rhode Island's Narragansett Bay. Its square rubble-stone tower anchored the southern tip of sandy Conanicut Island, which the pirate Captain Kidd had used as a hideout during the 1600s. Like the Boston Light, this one was knocked out of operation during the Revolutionary War. By 1790, however, it was repaired and back in service.

Built with the proceeds of a public lottery, New London Light (1760) in Connecticut survived the Revolution intact. During the Revolutionary War continental privateers often used the light to help find refuge from pursuing British warships.

An octagonal brick structure, Sandy Hook Light (1764) stood near the mouth of the Hudson and showed the way to New York City's harbor. New Yorkers had financed and built this strategic tower, but since it was actually located in New Jersey, the legislature of the Garden State laid claim to the facility during the Revolution. This precipitated a protracted legal squabble that was settled only when the federal government took control of this and other light stations in 1789.

Guiding ships into Delaware Bay and the river beyond, Cape Henlopen Light (1765) was one of the most important navigational markers in America. For sea captains caught in a storm, this Delaware light was a particularly welcome sight, as it marked one of the few harbors of refuge along the entire eastern coast. Even in the worst weather, the waters behind the cape were nearly always calm. Burned by British sailors and marines in 1777, Cape Henlopen Lighthouse was repaired and relit in 1784.

Charleston Light (1767), located on a low sandy South Carolina island frequently inundated by tides, pointed the way to the harbor of one of America's oldest and most gracious cities. For decades it was the only significant navigational light south of the Virginia capes.

Serving the famed Massachusetts community founded by the Pilgrims, Plymouth Light (1768) was unique in that it displayed not one but two lights from the same building. The twin beacons set the light apart from ordinary lanterns that marked nearby harbors.

A fanciful depiction of the Pharos Lighthouse in Alexandria, Egypt. Built by Ptolemaic kings about 280 b.c., it stood until destroyed by an earthquake more than a thousand years later.

From an eighteenth-century engraving provided courtesy Department of Rare Books, William R. Perkins Library, Duke University.

During its early years Portsmouth Light (1771) consisted of little more than a lantern hoisted up the flagpole of Fort William and Mary, on the banks of New Hampshire's Piscataqua River. In 1775 the keeper felt free to set aside his duties temporarily and take a wagonload of gunpowder to the embattled Massachusetts Minutemen dug in on Bunker Hill outside Boston. A proper wood-frame lighthouse was eventually built at Portland. During the 1780s it received a pair of famous visitors: Revolutionary War hero General Marquis de Lafayette and his old commander, George Washington himself.

The oldest standing light tower in the United States, the Sandy Hook Lighthouse remains in operation after more than 230 years. Although built by New Yorkers, the station is located in New Jersey.

William Kaufhold

Built to warn mariners away from Thatcher Island, a ship-killing rock off the north coast of Massachusetts, Cape Ann Light (1771) consisted of two separate towers. The island was named for a colonial clergyman and his family, who had been shipwrecked here in 1635. The station's first keeper was a notorious Tory. When the Revolution broke out, a party of Massachusetts militiamen hustled him off the island, plunging the twin lights into darkness until after the war.

Though some large American cities such as Baltimore had no lighthouses during the colonial and early postcolonial period, tiny Nantucket Island had two. The Brant Point Light got a neighbor in 1784, when the Great Point Lighthouse was built on the southern end of the island.

Intended to guide ships safely over the treacherous sandbar at the harbor entrance, the Newburyport Light (1788) in Massachusetts made the first known use of a range-light system. Two lights were displayed, one higher and some distance behind the other. Ships sailing in safe water saw the lights in perfect perpendicular alignment. To mariners straying out of the main channel, the upper light appeared to tilt in one direction or the other.

For most sailors at this time, however, finding a safe channel as they approached the American coastline was a matter of risky guesswork. The lights listed above were the only worthy navigational guideposts along the entire American coast; that is, until the nation's first president took the oath of office in 1789.

The Lighthouse President

A farmer and lifelong landlubber, George Washington had little interest in ships or the sea, but he was always an enthusiastic promoter of lighthouses. The consummate American, Washington had an abiding interest in money and the making of it, and he could see the commercial potential in a well-conceived system of navigational markers. Even before the Revolution, he took note of ports and headlands that might someday need light towers.

In 1789, as president, he urged Congress to make lighthouses a national priority. The Congress responded by passing a "Lighthouse Bill," only the ninth piece of legislation enacted by the nation's fledgling government. This bill placed all existing coastal lighthouses under federal control. It also created the "Lighthouse Established," which would come to be known as the United States Lighthouse Service. In one form or another, the service would survive for more than 150 years, until 1939, when the US Coast Guard took full responsibility for the nation's navigational aids. By that time nearly one thousand fine lighthouses marked the Atlantic and Gulf coasts in the East, the Pacific and Bering Sea coasts in the West, and the shores of the Great Lakes in the Midwest.

A century and a half earlier, however, when the Lighthouse Service was in its infancy, the number of operational lights was pitifully small. Ships and lives were being lost with grim regularity. To remedy this the service undertook an extensive construction program that added a dozen major lights during the 1790s, the nation's first full decade of independence. Lighthouses either completed or under construction by the end of the eighteenth century included those at Cape Henry, Virginia (completed in 1792); Portland Head, Maine (1791); Tybee Island, Georgia (1773); Seguin Island, Maine (1795); Bald Head Island, North Carolina (1795); Montauk Point, New York (1797); Baker's Island, Massachusetts (1791); Cape Cod, Massachusetts (1797); Cape Hatteras, North Carolina (1803); Shell Castle Island near Ocracoke Island, North Carolina (1803); Gay Head, Massachusetts (1799); and Eaton's Neck, New York (1799).

Appropriately, this initial burst of lighthouse construction was nearly complete when George Washington died during the final weeks of 1799. The old general missed witnessing, by only two weeks, the beginning of the nineteenth century and, with it, the opening of a whole new era of expansion and prosperity. Washington had done more than most people to make this new and optimistic age possible. Among his most important contributions, however, was one that is not frequently recognized: his insistence on an efficient system of lights for America's coasts and navigable inland waters.

Lighthouse Engineers

By the mid-1800s the United States had more lighthouses than any other nation on earth. More than two hundred major or minor lights shone from one place or another along its coasts. But though America's light towers outnumbered those of other maritime powers such as Britain, France, and Spain, they lagged far behind in the quality of their construction and the reliability of their beacons. Improvements, such as the use of the advanced, though expensive, Fresnel lenses, designed in France during the early nineteenth century, were delayed by the tight budgets imposed by Congress and by the bureaucratic monovision of treasury auditor Stephen Pleasonton. For more than thirty years, beginning in 1820, Pleasonton lorded over the Lighthouse Service in an imperious—and parsimonious—manner. By 1850, however, Pleasonton's influence began to wane, unleashing a revolution in American lighthouse technology.

In 1852 a Lighthouse Board composed of experienced military officers, engineers, and seamen took charge of the Lighthouse Service. Almost immediately, the Board embarked on an ambitious program aimed at expanding and upgrading navigational aids along all of America's coasts. With the US economy booming and coastal trade on the increase, Congress was willing to foot the huge bill for these improvements. To accomplish its task the board would rely on the skills, energy, and fresh ideas of young military engineers such as George Gordon Meade and Danville Leadbetter.

A Sea Captain's Lamp

Winslow Lewis epitomized the old way of building lighthouses. A former New England sea captain, he represented the age of wooden sailing ships, stone forts, and, naturally enough, stone light towers. About 1810, while suffering through a long stretch of unemployment, Lewis invented a lamp and parabolic reflector system that he said would make America's navigational beacons more powerful. The Lewis system was quickly adopted, and the US government paid him $60,000 to place his devices in all of the nation's lighthouses, a process that would take him seven years. No doubt, Lewis's reflectors were a considerable improvement over earlier systems, but they would prove vastly inferior to the Fresnel lens soon developed by the French. Even so, the Lighthouse Service would keep most of its Lewis reflectors in place until after 1850.

Having found an advocate in Pleasonton, who admired his knack for thrift, Lewis was soon being hired not just to equip lighthouses but to build them. He preferred towers of a conventional, conical design with stout walls of stone or brick, and he built them well. Many of the dozens of light towers Lewis built on sites from Maine to Louisiana still stand to this day.

Perhaps Lewis's best-known success—and failure—came at Frank's Island, Louisiana, where he was hired in 1818 to build an ornate lighthouse and customs office near the primary entrance to the Mississippi. Designed by a government architect who had never visited the site, the absurdly inappropriate structure was far too heavy for the river's delta marshlands and collapsed into a pile of useless rubble only a few days after it was finished. Lewis then contracted to build a sensibly modest tower of his own design, completing it, as we would say nowadays, under budget and ahead of schedule. Although the tower has sunk more than twenty feet into the Mississippi mud, it still stands today, a testament to the workmanship of Lewis's construction crews. But Lewis's outmoded reflectors and stone towers were no match for the challenges that would face the Lighthouse Service in the 1850s.

Two Lighthouse Generals

George Meade could hardly have presented a sharper contrast to Winslow Lewis. Part of a younger, better educated generation of American lighthouse experts, Meade was a trained engineer. In 1835 Meade graduated from West Point at the age of only twenty. After fighting in the Seminole War in Florida, he became a surveyor for the Army Corps of Topographical Engineers, helping to set the boundary between the United States and the then Republic of Texas. In time he developed an interest in marine engineering and lighthouses. His innovative work on light towers in the Delaware Bay convinced his superiors that Lieutenant Meade could help with the seemingly impossible task of marking the Florida Keys.

Arriving at Carysfort Reef in 1850, Meade supervised construction of an iron skeleton lighthouse designed by I. W. P. Lewis, who happened to be the nephew—and harshest critic—of Winslow Lewis. The revolutionary screw-pile technology and open structure of the Carysfort tower appealed to the modern instincts of Meade, the engineer. It was an approach Meade would take—and improve on—again and again over the next several years as he built towers at Sand Key, Sombrero Key, and many other sites. One essential Meade innovation was the use of large metal disks to help anchor

George Meade
Drawing from *Harpers Weekly* from private collection of Jim Claflin

screw piles to an unstable sand or coral base. Of course, Meade always sought to match methods to the designs of the site. For Seahorse Key, located well to the north of Tampa and off the track followed by most hurricanes, he designed a classic brick and wood-frame combination tower and dwelling much like those later built in the Northwest.

Another army engineer building Gulf lighthouses at about this same time was Captain Danville Leadbetter. Although a few years older than Meade, Leadbetter had graduated from West Point one year later, in 1836.

Instead of iron, Leadbetter preferred to use brick, but his often octagonal towers proved as stable and durable as any of the skeleton structures built by Meade. Completed in 1858, his tower at Sand Island off Alabama's Mobile Bay stood over 150 feet tall. Leadbetter's brick tower at Port Pontchartrain was stabilized by a submerged concrete pad. But his most unusual design may have been that of the Sabine Pass Lighthouse, with its extraordinary finlike buttresses. Spreading the weight of the tower over the damp, yielding ground, the buttresses have held the tower in rock-solid plumb for more than 140 years. A Leadbetter design for the Cape San Blas Lighthouse in the Florida Panhandle region was never built but might have been a wonder to behold. His creative plan called for a ninety-foot brick tower set atop screw-pile stilts.

The Gulf of Mexico has swallowed up Alabama's Sand Island, but its abandoned 1873 lighthouse still stands. An earlier Sand Island tower, designed by Danville Leadbetter, was blown up by Confederate forces under his command.

The Architecture of Victory

The outbreak of the Civil War in 1861 changed the professional status and destiny of millions. The same was true of Meade, who quickly rose to the rank of general in the Union Army, and of Leadbetter, who did the same on the Confederate side. But the war had very different fates in store for the two men.

Highly valued for his engineering skills, General Leadbetter was put in charge of Gulf Coast fortifications and, not coincidentally, its lighthouses. With a navy vastly inferior to that of the Union, however, the Confederates had little use for coastal lights, likely only to benefit their enemies. Under Leadbetter's direction Southern troops often removed and carefully hid Fresnel lenses and other useful equipment to keep them out of the hands of the enemy. But some lighthouses thought to be of particular use to Union blockade fleets were marked for

Danville Leadbetter
Massachusetts Commandery Military Order of the Loyal Legion of the U.S. Army Military History Institute

destruction. In a moment of supreme and poignant irony, Leadbetter sent out a raiding party to blow up the Sand Island Lighthouse, which he himself had so proudly built only a few years earlier.

As the war progressed and began to go badly for the South, Leadbetter was recruited to design defensive positions for Confederate infantry. As it turned out, the general had far less skill in creating structures meant to take lives than he had earlier with light towers intended to save them. His entrenchments and other defensive arrangements were thought by some to have been partly responsible for Confederate defeats at Knoxville and Chattanooga.

Following the war, there were few opportunities in the United States for a former Confederate general to work as a lighthouse engineer. To support himself and his family, Leadbetter sought work in Mexico and Canada. Exhausted, he died in Canada in 1866, little more than a year after he returned to civilian life.

Meade, on the other hand, fought in several important engagements while working his way up to the rank of major general. A string of early defeats suffered by the Union Army of the Potomac had led President Lincoln to fire one general after another. Meade inherited this revolving-door command on the eve of the critical battle of Gettysburg. Had Robert E. Lee's Confederates won this battle and surged on toward Washington, the South would likely have won the war. But Meade had learned in Florida how to build a structure capable of weathering a storm. On a series of hills overlooking Gettysburg, he erected his defense, and on the third and final day of the battle, when Lee let loose the thirteen-thousand-man hurricane of Pickett's charge, its foundations held fast.

Lighthouse Keepers

"No man is an island." So said John Donne, the often-quoted British poet and clergyman. But Donne, who died in 1631, never knew any of the lighthouse keepers who for more than two centuries helped make America's coasts safe for navigation. For these brave men and women, life was indeed an island. Surviving on low government salaries, they lived mostly on wild headlands and treeless ledges very far from what most of us would call civilization. Often the closest town was itself a backwater, a remote outpost. In bad weather even the nearest rural church might seem impossibly distant.

When storms rushed in from the ocean, as they often did, lighthouse keepers could not follow the example of the mariners they served and run for some calm harbor. Since their ships had stone foundations and no engines, sails, rudders, or helms, they had to stay and take whatever the sea threw at them. To fight back against gale and gloom, they had only their lights and their wits. The lamps, which more often than not stood at the top of winding staircases with hundreds of steps, were in constant need of attention. But whatever the conditions or the health of the keeper, they had to be kept burning. As a result keepers always worked nights and rarely had a day off.

Lighthouse keepers endured this sort of existence, not necessarily for any high-minded or romantic reason—for instance, because they loved the sea, the wind, or the isolation—but for the same reason most people work: It rewarded them with a place to live and a smattering of pay. It was also a job worth doing, a job that had to be done.

Growing Up on a Rock

The keepers were not the only ones who faced hardship, danger, and punishing weather. Their families usually shared in the heavy work of keeping the lights burning, often displaying the same heroic resolve as the keepers themselves.

On a stormy night in 1856, young Abbie Burgess drew a chair to the kitchen table of the battered keeper's residence on isolated Matinicus Rock off the coast of Maine and dipped her pen into ink. A lonely seventeen-year-old, separated by at least twenty-five miles of turbulent ocean from the nearest country store, barn dance, or church social, she had decided to write a letter to a pen pal on the mainland.

You have often expressed a desire to view the sea out in the ocean when it is angry. Had you been here on 19 January [1856], I surmise you would have been satisfied. Father was away [Keeper Sam Burgess had gone to Rockland to purchase supplies and was trapped there by a sudden nor'easter, leaving his bedridden wife and daughter to weather the storm alone.] early in the day, as the tide rose, the sea made a complete breach over the rock, washing every movable thing away, and of the old dwelling not one stone was left upon another. The new dwelling was flooded, and the windows had to be secured to prevent the violence of the spray from breaking them in. As the tide came, the sea rose higher and higher, till the only endurable places were the light towers. If they stood, we were saved, otherwise our fate was only too certain. But for some reason, I know not why, I had no misgivings, and went on with my work as usual. For four weeks, owing to the rough weather, no landing could be effected on the rock. During this time, we were without the assistance of any male member of our family. Though at times greatly exhausted with my labors, not once did the lights fail. I was able to perform all my accustomed duties as well as my father's.

You know the hens are our only companions. Becoming convinced, as the gale increased, that unless they were brought into the house they would be lost, I said to mother, "I must try to save them." She advised me not to attempt it. The thought, however, of parting with them without an effort was not to be endured, so seizing a basket, I ran out a few yards after the rollers had passed and the sea fell off a little, with the water knee deep, to the coop, and rescued all but one. It was the work of a moment, and I was back in the house with the door fastened, but I was none too quick, for at that instant my little sister, standing at the window, exclaimed, "Oh, look! Look there! The worst sea is coming." That wave destroyed the old dwelling and swept the rock. I cannot think you would enjoy remaining here any great length of time for the sea is never still and, when agitated, its roar shuts out every other sound, even drowning our voices.

A few months after the extraordinary month-long Atlantic storm described in her letter, Abbie Burgess married a young assistant lighthouse keeper. She and her husband eventually became keepers of the Matinicus Rock Lighthouse.

Redcoats, Indians, and Leaky Boats

The wind and weather were not the only dangers faced by lighthouse keepers. Getting to their duty station, especially those on remote points or rugged islands, could place keepers at considerable risk to life and limb. America's very first lighthouse keeper was George Worthylake, a part-time shepherd who tended the Boston Harbor Lighthouse on Brewster Island. Little more than a year after he was appointed keeper, Worthylake's small boat capsized, and he drowned while returning from Boston, where he had gone to collect his pay. Many later keepers would suffer similar fates.

Some keepers kept firearms handy, and for good reason. In 1777 the keeper of the Cape Henlopen Lighthouse was attacked by a landing party of redcoat marines from the British warship *Roebuck*. As it turned out, the *Roebuck* was low on supplies, and the famished marines were far more interested in a nearby herd of cattle than in the lighthouse or its keeper. A burst of gunfire stampeded the animals, however, and as the keeper later boasted to his friends, he gave the British "bullets instead of beef."

In 1836 Cape Florida keeper John Thomas found himself under attack by a war party of Seminoles. Thomas barricaded himself inside the tower, which had fortresslike brick walls five feet thick. Soon a flaming arrow set fire to the station's oil supplies, forcing Thomas to climb the tower steps, which burned away behind him. In the metal lantern room, Thomas managed to keep just beyond the reach of the flames, but even so, he was nearly roasted alive. Later Thomas was rescued by sailors from the US warship *Concord*. Although the tower steps were now gone, they managed to fire a line to him with a musket and then lower him to ground in a basket. After his burns had healed, Thomas returned to his duties as a lighthouse keeper.

Keepers often loved their work, and many remained at it for a lifetime. More than a few ended their days at home in their lighthouses. Like many keepers before him, Emil Mueller, keeper of the splendidly isolated Rock of Ages Lighthouse in Lake Superior, was on duty when he died in 1930. As a storm raged outside, Mueller had climbed the steps of the thirteen-story steel-plated tower to check the station lamps. His assistant, C. A. Mickey, who was asleep far below, was understandably terrified when Mueller came crashing down onto the bunk beside him. Mickey was uninjured, but Mueller lay dead of a heart attack. Mickey's explanation for the tragic incident was a simple one. "Too many steps," he said. "His old heart just gave out."

Ida Lewis, perhaps America's most famous keeper, lived practically her entire life at the Lime Rock Lighthouse in Newport, Rhode Island. Born in 1842, Ida was still a very small girl when she arrived at Lime Rock with her father, Captain Hosea Lewis. A former revenue cutter pilot, Captain Lewis had been forced into semiretirement by illness. Lewis had thought that, despite his failing health, he could handle the duties of lighthouse keeper. As it turned out he could not, and by the time his daughter reached her early teens, she had largely taken over running the lighthouse. In addition to keeping the lamps burning and the Fresnel lens polished and sparkling, young Ida raised two younger sisters and a brother and looked after her father and mother who, in time, both became invalids. Upon her father's death in 1872, she was named official keeper of the Lime Rock Lighthouse.

Ida Lewis might have lived out her life in relatively peaceful obscurity had it not been for her penchant for effecting daring rescues. Whenever anyone fell overboard in Newport Harbor, Ida rushed off to the rescue in the light station skiff. Over the years she single-handedly pulled more than a dozen drunken sailors and careless boys and at least one sheep from the harbor's chilling waters. News of her exploits reached the ears of journalists, and Ida Lewis became the subject of feature articles in newspapers all across the country. Eventually, Ida's story was told in *Harper's Weekly* magazine, for which she became a sort of nineteenth-century cover girl. Some said that for a time Ida Lewis was the most famous woman in America. As such, she received visits—always at Lime Rock, for she never left her station—from some of the country's most famous people. At one time or another, the Astors, Belmonts, and even President Ulysses S. Grant had tea with her in the lighthouse parlor.

Despite her fame, though, Ida remained keeper of Lime Rock to the end of her days. In all she tended the light for more than half a century. When the sad news came that Ida Lewis had died at her post on October 25, 1911, the bells of vessels in Newport Harbor tolled throughout the night.

Although lighthouse keepers faced loneliness and many hardships, some considered their lives idyllic. Surrounded by lush summer growth, a 1940s-era keeper enjoys the company of his wife and family dog at the isolated Cape Flattery Lighthouse in Washington.
U.S. Coast Guard

Lighthouse Lenses

Fresnels: Man-Made Stars That Brighten the Night

The business end of a lighthouse is, of course, at the top. The lighting apparatus is kept in the lantern room as high above sea level as the tower and the elevation of the site can make possible. Height adds to the beacon's range, or distance from which it can be seen. But equally important to the beacon's effectiveness is the strength of the light itself. Usually a lens, mirror, or other optical device is used to concentrate the light, often into a single brilliant flash. For many years the most efficient way of doing this was with a Fresnel lens.

Invented in 1822 by French physicist Augustin Fresnel, these big prismatic glass lenses were designed to snatch every flicker of light from even the smallest lamp and concentrate it into a powerful beam that could be seen from dozens of miles away. Fresnel's elegant lenses did their job so well that they soon became standard equipment in lighthouses throughout much of the world.

The new Fresnel technology, however, was virtually ignored for several decades in the United States, where Winslow Lewis's far less effective parabolic reflectors were employed right up to the middle of the nineteenth century. One reason the United States was slow to adopt the Fresnel system was the considerable expense of the highly polished lenses, which had to be imported from France. Another was the bureaucratic fussiness of Stephen Pleasonton, the US Treasury auditor who served for many years as head of the so-called lighthouse establishment. Displaying undisguised favoritism for Lewis, a personal friend, Pleasonton continued to equip US lighthouses with his outdated reflectors even though they were demonstrably inferior to Fresnel lenses. Following the release of a highly critical report written by Lewis's own nephew, Pleasonton was forced into retirement.

The glass prisms of a Fresnel lens concentrate light into a powerful beam that can be seen from dozens of miles away.

In 1852 stewardship of America's navigational lights passed to a Lighthouse Board, which consisted of military officers, engineers, harbor

At many light stations Fresnel lenses have been replaced with modern plastic optics like this one at East Brother Lighthouse in California. Interestingly, the newer lenses rely on old-fashioned Fresnel technology.

masters, and experienced seamen. The board immediately undertook a complete overhaul of America's ill-equipped and, in many cases, sadly neglected lighthouses. As part of this effort, most lighthouses were fitted with sparkling new Fresnel lenses. Some of these lenses, installed during the years before the Civil War, remain in service to this day.

A Sophisticated Technology

Remarkably, Fresnel lenses are as effective and useful today as they were 150 years ago. This is a claim that can be made for very few devices. Few significant improvements have been made in the design of prismatic lenses since the days of Augustin Fresnel. Unlike so many other technologies—transportation, for instance—this one reached its peak of sophistication very early in the industrial revolution. Long before the development of space rockets, jet airliners, automobiles, or even of large steam locomotives, Fresnel lenses were already shining in lighthouse towers. To fully appreciate the contrast, consider that some early Fresnel lenses were delivered to the light stations where they were to serve—in horse-drawn carts.

Although a Fresnel lens looks like a single piece of molded glass, it is not. The lens consists of individual prisms—sometimes more than several hundreds of them—fitted into a metal frame. This makes them look like giant glass beehives. It also makes them rather delicate.

Fresnels come in a variety of sizes, referred to as "orders." The huge first-order lenses, such as the one that formerly served at the Cape Canaveral Lighthouse (it is now on display at the Ponce Inlet [Florida] Lighthouse and Museum), are six feet

Bodie Island Lighthouse at sunset

or more in diameter and up to twelve feet tall. The smallest lenses, designated sixth order, are only about one foot in diameter.

The larger and more powerful first-, second-, and third-order lenses were intended for use in coastal lighthouses. The smaller fourth-, fifth-, and sixth-order lenses saw use mostly in harbor and river lighthouses. Specially designed three-and-one-half-order lenses—a compromise between the larger and smaller sizes—were frequently used to guide vessels on the Great Lakes.

Although Fresnel lenses are as effective and powerful as any so-called modern optical device, they require considerable care and must be cleaned and polished frequently by hand. The larger Fresnels are quite heavy, sometimes weighing in at more than a ton. As a consequence, the mechanisms that turn flashing Fresnel lenses must be large and cumbersome. Despite their size, the old lenses are quite delicate, easily damaged, and almost impossible to repair. For all these reasons, the efficiency-minded Coast Guard has replaced many Fresnels with plastic lenses or airport-type beacons that are lighter weight and easier to maintain. Many of the old lenses have ended up in museums, where the public can enjoy them. Some Fresnels, however, have been sold off to private collectors by antiques dealers.

Existing Fresnel lenses are practically irreplaceable. When destroyed by storms or vandalism, as, unfortunately, sometimes happens, the Coast Guard must put in their place a modern optic—or a Fresnel previously removed from another lighthouse. The cost of manufacturing new Fresnel lenses is prohibitively high and might run to millions of dollars.

Since 1854 the Tibbetts Point Lighthouse in New York has marked the far eastern end of Lake Ontario and the entrance of the St. Lawrence River.

During the nineteenth century Fresnel lenses were hand-ground and hand-polished by the poorest classes of French laborers, including children, who often worked for pennies a day. It is ironic that the handiwork of these unremembered workers can be counted among the most practical, durable, and handsome devices ever made. No one will ever know how many lives have been saved by these fine old lenses or how many accidents were avoided because their guiding light could be seen on the horizon.

The Sand Key Light, built under the supervision of George Meade, warned of a shallow area in the approach to Key West.

NORTHEAST

Portland Head Light

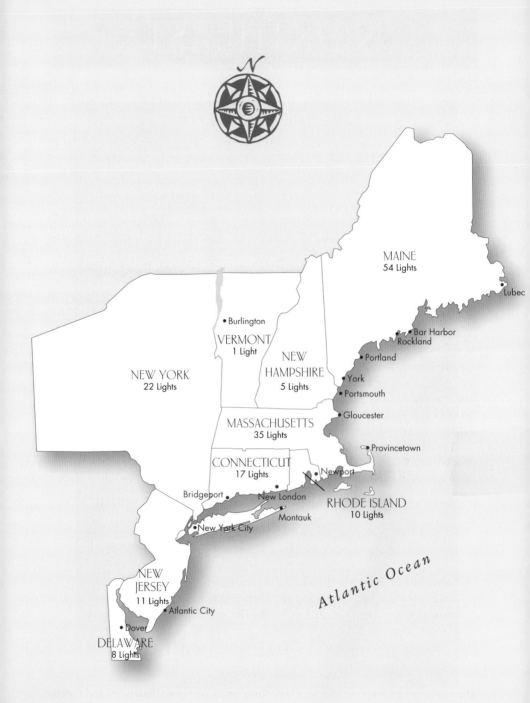

N

MAINE
54 Lights

•Lubec

•Burlington

•Bar Harbor
Rockland

VERMONT
1 Light

NEW
HAMPSHIRE
5 Lights

•Portland

•York

NEW YORK
22 Lights

•Portsmouth

•Gloucester

MASSACHUSETTS
35 Lights

•Provincetown

CONNECTICUT
17 Lights

•Newport

Bridgeport•

New London•

RHODE ISLAND
10 Lights

•Montauk

•New York City

NEW
JERSEY
11 Lights

Atlantic Ocean

•Atlantic City

•Dover

DELAWARE
8 Lights

MAINE

■ WEST QUODDY HEAD LIGHT ■
Lubec (1808, 1831, and 1857)

Looking out across the Quoddy Narrows from its perch on a forty-foot cliff, West Quoddy Head Lighthouse anchors the easternmost point in the United States (East Quoddy Head Light, across the narrows, is on Canada's Campobello Island). Established in 1808, while Thomas Jefferson was still president, this is one of Maine's oldest light stations. The original rubble-stone tower was torn down and rebuilt in 1831, but even this light was of poor construction. Finally, the tower was replaced with a brick one in 1857. At that time the station received the third-order Fresnel lens that

West Quoddy Head Light

still guides ships and fishing vessels into Lubec Channel. The light atop the forty-nine-foot, candy-striped tower flashes white four times each minute and can be seen from a distance of up to eighteen nautical miles.

Equipped with a strobe light and an electric eye that sense moisture in the air, the station's powerful foghorn occupies a separate brick building. Earlier fog signals here included a black-powder cannon, a fifteen-hundred-pound bell, and a steam whistle.

Travel information: From US Highway 1 turn toward Lubec on Route 169; then turn right at the sign for Quoddy Head State Park. The state park offers world-class views of Grand Manan Channel, nature trails featuring real tundra, and a chance to walk the lighthouse grounds at leisure. Contact West Quoddy Head Lighthouse and Visitor Center, located at 973 South Lubec Road, Lubec, ME 04652. The visitor center is run by West Quoddy Head Light Keepers Association and is open generally Memorial Day through Columbus Day; call (207) 733-2180, or see www.westquoddy.com.

■ LUBEC CHANNEL LIGHT ■
Lubec (1890)

Most vessels approaching the St. Croix River ports of Lubec, Eastport, and Calais use the narrow Lubec Channel, which separates Maine from Canada's Campobello Island to the north of Quoddy Head. To make this key passage safer, the US government marked it with an open-water light station in 1890. Built on a massive caisson of concrete and iron, the station's brick-lined, cast-iron tower rises fifty-three feet above the water. When seen from a distance, lighthouses of this type resemble giant spark plugs.

In the past hardy keepers and their assistants lived year-round in cramped quarters on the lower level. The station was automated after a destructive oil fire in 1939.

For nearly eighty years the beacon was produced by a fifth-order, bull's-eye Fresnel lens rotated by a weight-driven clockwork mechanism. A plastic optic replaced the original lens in 1969. Now solar powered, the light remains active, flashing white every six seconds.

Lubec Channel Light
Nick Salata, *Lighthouse Digest*

Travel information: The lighthouse is now privately owned, but the light and fog signal remain active US Coast Guard aids to navigation. The lighthouse can be seen from South Lubec Road, off Route 189 on the way to Quoddy Head State Park.

■ WHITLOCKS MILL LIGHT ■
Near Calais (1909)

One of several small US and Canadian beacons that formerly guided lumber freighters along the St. Croix River to the port of Calais, the Whitlocks Mill Lighthouse dates back to 1909. Its twenty-five-foot masonry tower replaced an early light that was simply a lantern hung on a tree or post. An automated optic replaced the fourth-order Fresnel lens in 1969. The light remains active, flashing green ten times a minute. The **St. Croix Lighthouse,** which at one time stood a few miles downriver from this one, was destroyed by fire in 1976.

Travel information: Grounds are not open to the public because the keeper's house and outbuildings are privately owned. The original fourth-order Fresnel lens is on display at the Maine Lighthouse Museum (see Travel information for **Rockland Breakwater Light**). Travelers can see the tower from the St. Croix View Rest Area on US Highway 1 a few miles east of Calais and about five miles northwest of the St. Croix Island International Historic Site. The lighthouse is maintained by the St. Croix Historical Society, P.O. Box 242, Calais, ME 04619; call (207) 454-3061. For more information on this and other lights in the state, contact the Maine Office of Tourism at (888) 624-6345; www.visitmaine.com.

■ LITTLE RIVER LIGHT ■
Near Cutler (1847 and 1876)

Established during the mid-nineteenth century, the Little River Light Station served mariners for nearly 130 years before being shut down by the Coast Guard in 1975.

Although one of the more attractive lighthouses on the coast of Maine, the forty-one-foot iron tower and L-shaped Victorian dwelling stood empty and neglected for many years. The US Coast Guard put the old light station up for sale during the 1990s, but at first there were no takers. Finally, the deteriorating lighthouse came under the wing of the Friends of Little River Lighthouse. The Friends care for the historical property as a chapter of the Maine-based American Lighthouse Foundation, which acquired the property in 2000. The tower was relighted in 2001, and the lighthouse and 1888 keeper's house have been restored and are open for overnight stays. Overlooking the Bay of Fundy, the setting is idyllic.

Little River Light
Lighthouse Digest

Travel information: Located on an island near Cutler off Route 191 in far eastern Maine, the lighthouse cannot be seen from the mainland. For more information on the Friends of Little River Lighthouse or overnight accommodations reservations, call (207) 259-3833, or see www.littleriverlight .org. For more information on the American Lighthouse Foundation and its wide-ranging preservation efforts contact P.O. Box 565, Rockland, ME 04841, or call (207) 594-4174, or see http://lighthousefoundation.org. Local wildlife and sightseeing cruises offer excellent views of the **Little River Lighthouse** (1876), as well as the **Machias Seal Islands Light Station** (1832) southeast of Cutler and the **Libby Island Light Station** (1848) near Machias; call (207) 259-4484.

■ PETIT MANAN LIGHT ■
Milbridge (1817 and 1855)

During the early nineteenth century, coasting schooners were often forced to heel hard aport to avoid the deadly rocks of Petit Manan Island. A lighthouse built there in 1817 did little to improve the situation. Shining from atop a rubble-stone tower only fifty-three feet tall, its Winslow Lewis lamps were so limited in range that sailors could barely see the beacon until they were almost upon the rocks. For more than a few mariners, the warning came too late.

In 1855 the Lighthouse Board sought to prevent further shipping losses by ordering construction of a soaring 119-foot brick-and-granite tower on Petit Manan. Focused by a powerful second-order Fresnel lens, its flashing light pulsed a warning more than twenty-five miles out to sea. The

Petit Manan Light
Paula Roberts, *Lighthouse Digest*

Fresnel was replaced in 1972 by an automated, solar-powered optic of similar range. The light flashes white six times each minute.

Travel information: From US Highway 1 near Milbridge, turn south on Pigeon Hill Road and follow it to the Petit Manan Wildlife Refuge. A scenic two-mile-long trail leads to the east side of Petit Manan Point, where visitors can enjoy an excellent view of the lighthouse. For information on the wildlife refuge, now known as the Maine Coastal Islands National Wildlife Refuges, see www.fws.gov/northeast/mainecoastal.

■ PROSPECT HARBOR POINT LIGHT ■
Prospect Harbor (1850 and 1891)

Prospect Harbor Point Lighthouse looks much like a fisherman's cottage—except for the thirty-eight-foot conical tower rising from its seaward wall. Its design is appropriate, since its beacon shines out mostly to lobster and sardine boats. Built in 1891, the two-story, wood-frame structure replaced an earlier granite lighthouse that first marked the point in 1850. Ironically, the stone light tower succumbed to the elements after little more than forty years, yet its wooden replacement perseveres, despite weather-

Prospect Harbor Point Light

ing over a century of storms. The light remains active, flashing red and white about ten times a minute.

Travel information: From US Highway 1 follow either Route 186 or 195 to Prospect Harbor. The lighthouse can be seen and photographed from several viewpoints in the village. Although located on a navy base, the tower is licensed to the American Lighthouse Foundation. You can drive up close for a view. From Route 1 head south on Route 195 for about five miles to Prospect Harbor. Turn left onto Main Street. Take an immediate right turn onto Corea Road, continuing straight onto Lighthouse Point Road to the gate of the naval installation. Park on the side of the road.

■ WINTER HARBOR LIGHT ■
Winter Harbor (1856)

Motorists on the perimeter road of Acadia National Park's Schoodic Point often notice a small white-brick light tower and attached Victorian keeper's dwelling. Located on Mark Island, just to the west of Schoodic Peninsula, this is the Winter

Harbor Lighthouse, which served from 1856 until 1933, when its fifth-order Fresnel lens was decommissioned. At present the lighthouse is privately owned and maintained.

Travel information: From US Highway 1 follow Route 186 through Winter Harbor to the Acadia National Park entrance—passes are required during the summer season. Parking areas about a mile south of the entrance afford excellent views of the lighthouse. Be sure to stop at Schoodic Point at the far end of the drive. On most days waves crash into the bare rocks of the point and spew high into the air.

■ EGG ROCK LIGHT ■
Bar Harbor (1875)

The dramatic red flash of Egg Rock Lighthouse in Frenchman's Bay catches the attention of visitors to Acadia National Park. Once described as a "pillar of fire in the Atlantic," the beacon emanates from a barren ledge, which likely got its name from the countless seabird nests found there during mating season. The signal Egg

Egg Rock Light

Rock Light marks seaward approaches to Bar Harbor. Flashing red at five-second intervals, it can be seen from fourteen miles away.

The station's squat, forty-foot tower is far less awe-inspiring than its light. Built in 1875, the squared-off wooden dwelling and brick tower are more functional than scenic. An aeromarine beacon superseded the original fifth-order Fresnel lens when the light was automated in 1976.

Travel information: The light can be seen from several scenic overlooks along the Acadia National Park Loop Road on Mount Desert Island. Thundering surf, panoramic ocean views, and the East's loftiest headland—fifteen-hundred-foot Cadillac Mountain—make this park one of America's must-see scenic wonders. The best time to avoid the summer throngs is before July 4 or after Labor Day. The light remains an active US Coast Guard aid to navigation and is maintained by the US Fish and Wildlife Service as part of the Maine Coastal Islands National Wildlife Refuges. For information contact Acadia National Park, P.O. Box 177, Bar Harbor, ME 04609; call (207) 288-3338. When you go, don't leave without sampling the boiled lobster in Bar Harbor or the popovers and tea at the Jordon Pond House.

■ BASS HARBOR HEAD LIGHT ■
Bass Harbor (1858)

Bass Harbor Head Light

Thought by many people to be the most picturesque lighthouse in America, this compact brick tower and attached wooden dwelling cling to a red-rock cliff near the entrance to Bass Harbor. Located on the western "Quietside" of Mount Desert Island, well away from the tourist throngs of Bar Harbor and Acadia Park Island, Bass Harbor bobs with dozens of brightly painted lobster boats. The station's red light has guided the fishermen of this bucolic village since before the Civil War.

The original fifth-order Fresnel lens was replaced by a fourth-order lens that remains in place. The thirty-two-foot tower has a focal plane at about fifty-six feet above the water. The three-second red beam occults, or goes dark briefly, every four seconds. Panels outside the lens create the light's red color.

> *Travel information:* The light remains an active US Coast Guard aid to navigation, and the keeper's quarters are now used as a residence for personnel. The lighthouse is not open to the public, but visitors can enjoy it nonetheless. To reach the lighthouse follow Route 3 onto Mount Desert Island. At the intersection bear right onto Route 102 South through Somesville and Southwest Harbor. Continue to Route 102A through Bass Harbor; 102A turns left, but continue straight onto Lighthouse Road to the parking area. Open year-round from midmorning until sunset, a small park surrounds the station property with a paved walkway that runs right up to the tower. On the far side of the station, a path connects the parking lot with a wooden stairway that leads down the side of the cliff to the reddish boulders below. The short but strenuous climb rewards the adventurous with extraordinary views of the channel and islands beyond and an unmatched opportunity to photograph one of the nation's prettiest lighthouses.

■ GREAT DUCK ISLAND LIGHT ■
Great Duck Island (1890)

Great Duck Island lies under siege by the Atlantic about five miles to the south of Bass Harbor. In part because of its remoteness, countless seabirds, including rare petrels and eider ducks, call the island home. For nearly a century the island was also home to a tiny colony of lighthouse keepers and their families, who received weekly deliveries of mail and supplies from the mainland.

Established in 1890, the light is now automated. In 1986 a plastic lens replaced the fourth-order Fresnel lens, formerly a fifth-order that crowned its forty-two-foot granite-and-brick tower. The light flashes red every five seconds.

Great Duck Island Light

Travel information: At present, the island and most of the station are a Maine Nature Conservancy preserve; it is a base for field courses for the owner, College of the Atlantic in Bar Harbor, which conducts animal and bird research on the island. For more information see www.coa.edu. The island is off-limits to the public during the summer nesting season, but occasional bird-watching tours are conducted by the Maine chapters of the Nature Conservancy, (207) 729-5181; or the Audubon Society, (207) 781-2330.

■ MOUNT DESERT ROCK LIGHT ■
Mount Desert Rock (1830 and 1847)

Relentlessly pounded by Atlantic waves, Mount Desert Rock surely ranks as one of the least hospitable places in America. Yet, for nearly 150 years, lighthouse keepers and their families lived on this open ocean ledge, which is only six hundred yards long and less than twenty feet above the water at its highest point. So barren was their home that friendly lobster fishermen brought them baskets of soil in the spring so they could make a little garden in some rain-moistened crevasses among boulders.

Mount Desert Rock Light
US Coast Guard

Established in 1830 to warn ships away from this exceptionally dangerous obstacle more than twenty miles from the nearest land, the lighthouse at first consisted of only a two-story wooden cottage with a lantern on its roof. The light, provided by inefficient Winslow Lewis reflectors, often could not be seen in time to prevent wrecks.

In 1847 the Lighthouse Board built a fifty-eight-foot granite tower to replace the original one. In 1858 a new lantern was installed and fitted with a third-order Fresnel lens that exhibited a fixed white light. A one-and-one-half-story wooden keeper's quarters was added in 1876 and then replaced by a double keepers' quarters in 1893. Later, a rotating fourth-order lens took the place of the original third-order lens in 1898. With a focal plane seventy-five feet above the water, the light was visible more than twenty miles away. Its range was sharply reduced in heavy weather, however. During a winter storm in 1902, the crew of the ocean tug *Astral* did not see the light at all, and their vessel slammed into rock. The keeper and his wife managed to save all but one of those on board.

Keepers served at this isolated station until 1977, when the light was automated. At that time the old Fresnel lens was replaced by a plastic lens. The light flashes white four times each minute.

In summer 2000 the station was renamed the Alice Eno Field Research Station. The 220-acre island is shared by the College of the Atlantic with the Nature Conservancy, the State of Maine, and a private summer resident.

> *Travel information:* Mount Desert Rock is, of course, very hard to reach, but whale-watching cruises operating out of Bar Harbor often take passengers within sight of the ledge and its lighthouse. The island is closed to the public. For information contact the College of the Atlantic, which conducts summer Family Nature Camps; call (207) 801-5634. Or contact Acadia Welcome Center, 1201 Bar Harbor Road, Trenton, ME 04605; call (800) 345-4617, or see www.barharborinfo.com.

■ BURNT COAT HARBOR LIGHT ■
Swan's Island (1872)

Burnt Coat Harbor may have gotten its name from a Revolutionary deserter. Seeking refuge from the storm of war then breaking over the country, a soldier named

Thomas Kench symbolically "burned his coat" and fled to the island in 1776. Vessels seeking refuge here from more natural storms have all too often ended up on the island's deadly rocks. To make the harbor—the primary anchorage for lobstermen on Maine's sleepy Swan's Island—easier and safer to reach, a lighthouse was built on Hockamock Head near its entrance in 1872.

At first a pair of range lights marked the safe channel, but these so confused local sailors that wrecks occurred even faster than before. To simplify matters the Lighthouse Board ordered the smaller of the two towers pulled down in 1885. This left the square, thirty-two-foot rear-range tower to guide vessels into the

Burnt Coat Harbor Light

harbor. Perched on a hill, its focal plane—originally a fourth-order Fresnel lens—is a respectful seventy-five feet high. Automated in 1975 with a modern optic, it is still an active aid to navigation. Its white light occults, winking off briefly every four seconds.

Travel information: Swan's Island can be reached via regularly scheduled ferries from Bass Harbor. For information contact the Maine State Ferry Service, P.O. Box 114, Bass Harbor, ME 04653; call (207) 244-3254. Owned by the Town of Swan's Island, the buildings are maintained by the Friends of the Swan's Island Lighthouse. The lighthouse is undergoing restoration, and grounds are open to the public year-round. For more information write to P.O. Box 11, Swan's Island, ME 04685; call (207) 526-4279.

The lighthouse is at the end of the main island road, a little less than five miles from the ferry slip. Services on the island are limited to a few small restaurants open only during summer, a general store open all year, and a bed-and-breakfast, handy for those who miss the last ferry to the mainland.

■ BEAR ISLAND LIGHT ■
Bear Island (1839, 1853, and 1889)

The Bear Island Light tower is only thirty-one feet tall, but it stands on the highest point of a rocky islet, elevating the focal plane of its signal to one hundred feet above the water. From its lofty perch the little lighthouse guides fishing boats and pleasure craft into beautiful Northeast Harbor and ferries out to Acadia's timeless glacial Cranberry Islands. The light station sits about twelve hundred feet offshore from Mt. Desert at the entrance to Somes Sound.

Two other lighthouses preceded the present tower and separate dwelling. The first was a rustic stone dwelling and tower built in 1839. The second, completed in 1853, had a separate brick tower that was apparently removed to make way for construction of the existing station in 1889. A plastic optic replaced the original fifth-order Fresnel lens in 1989. The station is owned by the National Park Service and managed by Acadia National Park; the light is now a private aid to navigation. Although not open to the public, it can be viewed by boat. Visitors can explore nearby islands thanks to pet-friendly ferry service.

Travel information: From the Northeast Harbor Marina, you can see the Bear Island Lighthouse in the distance. To reach Northeast Harbor, one of several extraordinarily scenic villages on Mount Desert Island, follow Route 3 and then Route 189 from Ellsworth. The deck of the Cranberry Island ferry offers a close view of the lighthouse. For information on scheduled service from Northeast Harbor during summer, call (207) 244-3575.

■ BAKER ISLAND LIGHT ■
Baker Island (1828 and 1855)

Vessels plying the rock-strewn waters near Maine's legendary Mount Desert Island have long relied on the Baker Island Light. Since 1828 it has warned them away from the deadly shoals just off Little Cranberry Island and guided them safely into broad Frenchman Bay. The original wood-frame lighthouse was replaced in 1855 by the present forty-three-foot brick tower and separate dwelling.

When William Gilley, the station's first keeper, was dismissed after more than two decades of service, he took the government to court, claiming he owned the island and the lighthouse. Legal squabbling between the Lighthouse Service and the Gilley family went on for more than forty years before the government finally proved its clear title to the property. Baker Island now belongs to Acadia National Park. One-hundred-twenty-three-acre Baker Island is about four miles southeast of Mount Desert Island. It is one of five islands that make up the Cranberry Isles, so named for the bog cranberries that are bountiful each autumn.

The fourth-order Fresnel lens that at one time served here is now superseded by an automated plastic lens powered by batteries. These, in turn, are recharged by solar panels.

Travel information: Each summer national park naturalists lead excursions to Baker Island that include a visit to the lighthouse. Contact Acadia National Park, P.O. Box 177, Bar Harbor, ME 04609; call (207) 288-3338. To make reservations for the lighthouse excursion, call (207) 288-2386. The National Park boat leaves from Bar Harbor at 8:45 a.m. each Tuesday, Wednesday, Friday, and Saturday. Nature cruises and whale-watching excursions as well as narrated tours to Baker Island are conducted by the Bar Harbor Whale Watch Company, 1 West Street, Bar Harbor, ME 04609; for more information, call (207) 288-2386.

■ BLUE HILL BAY LIGHT ■
Green Island (1857)

Since before the Civil War, the Blue Hill Bay Lighthouse has survived wind, weather, and the encroaching sea on tiny Green Island near the entrance to Eggemoggin Reach. Completed in 1857 and exhibiting a light originally by a fourth-order Fresnel lens, it served for almost eighty years before its work was taken over by a more easily maintained light mounted on a nearby steel skeleton tower. In operation since

Blue Hill Bay Light
Jeremy D'Entremont

1935, the new steel light tower's light is now solar powered. The still-standing old brick tower and attached cape-style dwelling are privately owned.

Travel information: One of the hardest light stations in Maine to visit or photograph, the Blue Hill Bay Lighthouse is difficult to approach from the water and is probably best seen from the air. Aerial sightseeing tours that include overflights of this and other lighthouses are available at the Hancock County/Bar Harbor Airport, off Route 3; call (207) 667-5534. Private flights can be arranged via Acadia Air Tours, (207) 667-7627.

■ ISLE AU HAUT LIGHT ■

Isle au Haut (1907)

This lofty, rock-strewn island is often the first land spotted by mariners emerging from the open Atlantic. In 1604 French explorer Samuel de Champlain saw its densely forested hills rising blue above the ocean horizon and gave the place its name, Isle au Haut, or "high island." Despite its beauty and the abundance of food in the rich waters surrounding the island, Champlain found no one living there. The island is still sparsely populated. Only a few dozen hardy islanders live here year-round.

Isle au Haut Light

The Isle au Haut Lighthouse has served the island's scatter of resident watermen since 1907. The forty-foot granite-and-brick tower rises from the rocks at the edge of the tide line on the island's Robinson Point. Still active, its light flashes red for four seconds, with a white sector indicating the clear channel with a focal plane at forty-eight feet above the water.

> *Travel information:* Much of pristine Isle au Haut is part of Acadia National Park. Several ferries from Stonington provide passenger access to the island multiple times each summer day; call (207) 367-6516. Be sure to ask your captain to take you to the island. There is a dock leading toward the lighthouse, about a fifteen-minute walk. The original fourth-order Fresnel lens is on display at the Maine Lighthouse Museum (see Travel information for **Rockland Breakwater Light**).

■ EAGLE ISLAND LIGHT ■

Eagle Island (1839)

First lit in 1839 during the presidential administration of Martin Van Buren, the Eagle Island Light still guides vessels around Hardhead Shoals and into Penobscot Bay. One of a chain of lights near the mouth of the Penobscot River, including

Eagle Island Light

those at Dice Head and Fort Point, it marked a clear path through the rocky bay for a host of nineteenth-century freighters carrying lumber from mills in Bucksport and Bangor.

The short, thirty-foot-tall, whitewashed rubble-stone tower stands on a grassy cliff that helps elevate its light to more than a hundred feet above high tide. A fourth-order Fresnel lens that previously served here was removed in 1963 in favor of an automated plastic lens. The twelve-hundred-pound brass fog bell was decommissioned at the same time, but not in a manner the Coast Guard might have hoped. It broke away, rolled over the cliff, and fell into the sea. A lobsterman later salvaged the huge bell and sold it to noted nature photographer Eliot Porter for use as a dinner bell.

Travel information: Eagle Island Lighthouse, under the stewardship of nonprofit Eagle Island Caretakers, remains an active aid to navigation and is best seen from the water. Summer schooner cruises may pass the island (see Travel information for **Saddleback Ledge**). Keep in mind that Maine had several Eagle Islands. The one in Casco Bay, near Portland, was the home of Admiral Robert E. Peary, the first man to reach the North Pole.

■ SADDLEBACK LEDGE LIGHT ■
Isle au Haut Bay (1839)

Saddleback Ledge, near Isle au Haut, is a bare scrap of rock exposed on all sides to the pounding sea. A forty-two-foot, cone-shaped stone tower has guarded the ledge since 1839, its flashing white light warning sailors in danger of collision with the rock against certain calamity. The lighthouse was automated in 1954, but until that time keepers who had little or no contact with the outside world for weeks or even

Saddleback Ledge Light

months at a stretch kept vigil here. Although the tower still clings precariously to the barren rock, all traces of dwellings and outbuildings have been swept away by wind, water, and time.

Travel information: The Saddleback Ledge Lighthouse is a prominent feature of almost any cruise traversing the eastern approaches to Maine's impressive Penobscot Bay. Both two-day and weeklong schooner cruises are available in Camden, Rockport, and Rockland, Maine; call (207) 310-0998 for a list of available cruise lines. These cruises may or may not pass by Saddleback Ledge, but more than a few lighthouses will be on the itinerary.

■ DEER ISLAND THOROFARE LIGHT (MARK ISLAND) ■
Stonington (1858)

All that remains of this pre–Civil War light station is the twenty-five-foot square brick tower on Mark Island. The light remains active, however, and guides fishing boats and pleasure craft into the thoroughfare that links Stonington to the Atlantic. A plastic lens now serves in place of the original fourth-order Fresnel.

Deer Island Thorofare Light
Lighthouse Digest

Travel information: The lighthouse can be seen from the heights above Stonington, as authentic and hardworking a fishing village as you'll likely see anywhere along the Maine coast. While in town, stop in for some chowder at the Fisherman's Friend restaurant.

■ DICE HEAD LIGHT (OR DYCE) ■
Castine (1829)

One of the oldest and most historical towns in America, Castine had its beginnings as a French fur-trading station established in 1614. Seafaring nations long coveted the rocky heights above Dice Head, which dominates the entrance to the Penobscot River. Over the years the flags of four nations fluttered above forts here, and several battles were fought for possession of the town.

In 1829 the Lighthouse Service built a rubble-stone-and-brick tower high up on the cliffs of Dice Head to guide lumber ships in and out of the Penobscot. The light also welcomed home the clipper ships of Castine captains on the last leg of adventurous trading cruises that took them as far away as China. A colonial cape dwelling, added to the station in 1858, was attached to the tower by a short, enclosed passageway. At the same time the original Winslow Lewis lamp-and-reflector system was replaced with a fourth-order Fresnel lens. Its powerful beacon could penetrate seventeen miles of storm-tossed Penobscot Bay waters. The Coast Guard discontinued the lighthouse in 1956, replacing it with a flashing beacon shining from a small skeleton tower located on the rocks beneath the cliffs. This skeleton tower was nearly destroyed by a northeaster in 2007; subsequently, at the request of the Coast Guard, the town of Castine restored the light to the lighthouse, which is occupied by a caretaker.

Dice Head Light

Travel information: Anyone who appreciates history, old homes, and matchless ocean scenery will love Castine. To get there turn off US Highway 1 at Orland and follow Routes 175 and 166 to the town. The lighthouse is at the end of Battle Avenue.

■ FORT POINT LIGHT ■
Stockton Springs (1836 and 1857)

During the nineteenth century as many as two hundred lumber ships might pass the square-towered Fort Point Lighthouse in a single day. Established in 1836 by order of President Andrew Jackson, the light pointed the way to the Penobscot River and beyond to Bangor, at that time the world's busiest lumber port.

The first granite tower was replaced by the present square brick lighthouse. Although not much taller than the attached keeper's dwelling, the thirty-one-foot tower stands on a high promontory, its light eighty-eight feet above the water. *Fort Point Light*

The lantern still contains the fourth-order Fresnel lens installed when the station was renovated in 1857. A fog-bell house stands nearby, one of the last of its kind. The lighthouse is one of the few lighthouses in America of the old wooden square-tower design that houses a brick circular tower and spiral stairs within.

Travel information: Turn off US Highway 1 in Stockton Springs and follow East Cape Road to Fort Point State Park and the lighthouse. It is one of the more well-preserved light stations in Maine. Resident caretakers occupy the dwelling, but visitors may walk the grounds and enjoy a sweeping view of Penobscot Bay. Nearby are the ruins of Fort Pownall, where British and American forces fought two battles during the Revolutionary War. Nearby is the **Fort Point Ledge Light,** built sometime during the 1800s and subsequently lighted. Originally the lighthouse was just a stone structure marking a dangerous point; later, it was lighted and became a "true" lighthouse. It can be seen from Fort Point Lighthouse; the site is open, but the tower is closed.

■ GRINDLE POINT LIGHT ■
Islesboro (1850 and 1874)

A narrow blade of rock more than ten miles long cleaves the upper reaches of Penobscot Bay. Known as Islesboro, it is a summer home to many wealthy out-

of-staters (people from "away") as well as a community of Maine fishing folk. Most residents travel to and from the mainland via a car ferry that crosses over from Lincolnville several times each day. A small brick lighthouse marks the Islesboro ferry landing.

The square, thirty-nine-foot brick tower, built in 1874, replaced an earlier lighthouse in operation since 1850. The station was decommissioned in 1934. Under pressure from tradition-minded locals,

Grindle Point Light
Lighthouse Digest

however, the Coast Guard reactivated the old lighthouse in 1987. Residents and visitors can see its solar-powered, flashing green light every four seconds from several points along US Highway 1 near Lincolnville. It remains an active aid to navigation.

Travel information: The Islesboro ferry schedule varies, with only two daily round-trip crossings from January through May, up to seven each day during summer, and three or more daily from September through December. The lighthouse stands adjacent to the ferry slip. The Sailor's Memorial Museum, open daily in July and August, is located in the keeper's dwelling. Contact the Maine State Ferry Service, P.O. Box 214, Lincolnville, ME 04849; call (207) 734-6935, or for all state ferries, call the main office in Rockland at (800) 491-4883 or write Maine State Ferry Service, 517A Main Street, Rockland, ME 04841.

■ CURTIS ISLAND LIGHT ■
Camden (1836 and 1896)

During summer, passenger schooners with masts taller and stouter than telephone poles crowd Camden's harbor and lend this charming coastal town a distinctly

Curtis Island Light

nineteenth-century feeling. On their way into the harbor, the schooners pass Curtis Island, with its tiny brick light tower and compact clapboard keeper's dwelling. The squat tower, only twenty-five feet tall, was built in 1896 to replace an earlier structure that had served for sixty years. The original fourth-order Fresnel lens is now on display at the Camden Public Library. Its fixed green light is currently solar powered.

> *Travel information:* Located on the far side of the heavily forested island, the lighthouse is almost impossible to see from land. Harbor cruises often swing around the island so their passengers can glimpse the little tower and dwelling. A range of granite mountains meets the sea at Camden, and visitors should definitely set aside time to enjoy the town and its picturesque setting. Several of Camden's schooners offer extended cruises, with ample opportunities to view and photograph Maine lighthouses. For more information on Camden or its schooners, call (800) 223-5459, or see www.camdenme.org.

■ ROCKLAND BREAKWATER LIGHT ■
Rockland (1888 and 1902)

During the nineteenth century prodigious quantities of lime and construction stone were shipped through the appropriately named port of Rockland, Maine. Freighters lying at anchor in Rockland's unprotected harbor were often at the mercy of high waves rolling in from the sea. To offset this danger the government built a breakwater in 1888, marking its outer end with a small trapezoidal light tower. In 1902 both breakwater and harbor signal were updated. Engineers extended the breakwater to its present length of more than a mile and constructed a more substantial lighthouse to warn mariners of its presence.

The station's square, twenty-five-foot tower rises from the corner of its two-story dwelling. The lighthouse stands on a platform of squared-off granite blocks. A modern optic now does the work of the fourth-order Fresnel lens that formerly produced its flashing white light.

Rockland Breakwater Light

The lighthouse is leased from the city of Rockland by the Friends of the Rockland Breakwater Lighthouse, formed in August 1999 as a chapter of the American Lighthouse Foundation. For more information, see www.newenglandlighthousetours.com.

Travel information: From US Highway 1 in Rockland, follow Waldo Road and Samoset Road to the Marie Reed Breakwater Park. Visitors can hike out the breakwater to the lighthouse. The lighthouse and its light, often stunningly beautiful at night, also can be seen from several points along the Rockland waterfront.

Lighthouse lovers have another treat in store at Rockland. The Shore Village Museum's collection of Fresnel lenses and more is now housed nearby in the Maine Lighthouse Museum. Originally opened as the Shore Village Museum during the 1970s by the late, visionary Ken Black, a retired Coast Guard warrant officer, this delightful and highly informative museum focuses on lighthouse history and engineering. Maine Lighthouse Museum at One Park Drive, P.O. Box F, Rockland, ME 04841; call (207) 594-3301. This museum boasts the largest collection of Fresnel lenses and US Coast Guard lighthouse memorabilia in the United States, several of which belonged to the lights that dotted the quaint island shores of Maine.

■ OWL'S HEAD LIGHT ■
Rockland (1825 and 1852)

Ferry passengers leaving Rockland often scan the headland at the mouth of the harbor, looking for its legendary owl. Anyone with a good imagination can see the old owl sculpted by nature into the rocks. A far more obvious feature of the promontory, however, is the short, white cylinder of its lighthouse that was built in 1852 to replace the original 1825 tower. This little lighthouse is beloved by mariners who, for the better part of two centuries, have followed its fixed white beacon to the safety of Rockland Harbor. The classic fourth-order Fresnel lens that has long served the station remains in place.

The station's especially powerful fog signal has also kept countless ships from crashing on the rocks. Spot, the family dog of a keeper who worked here during the 1930s, is credited with having saved more than a few fog-blinded mariners with his ceaseless barking. What is more, the keeper trained the clever mutt to pull on the fog-bell rope whenever his sharp ears heard a vessel approaching.

Travel information: From Rockland take North Shore Road and follow signs to Owl's Head State Park. From the parking area a short drive along a highly scenic access road leads to the

Owl's Head Light

lighthouse. The lighthouse is licensed to the American Lighthouse Foundation and managed by the Friends of Rockland Breakwater Lighthouse. Be prepared to hold your ears, as the fog signal is so powerful it can damage hearing. The lighthouse can also be seen and enjoyed from the Vinalhaven Ferry.

■ BROWN'S HEAD LIGHT ■
Vinalhaven (1832 and 1857)

The Brown's Head Lighthouse began marking the western approaches to Vinalhaven Island when Andrew Jackson was president. Completed in 1832 at a cost of only $4,000—including the adjacent dwelling—the twenty-foot rubble-stone tower became a prominent feature of the island landscape. A new keeper's quarters and connected cylindrical brick tower were built in 1857 to replace the deteriorated one. A fifth-order Fresnel lens was installed the same year but was changed out for a fourth-order lens in 1902; to this day its fixed white light with two red sectors guides fishing boats and ferries.

Travel information: The Rockland/Vinalhaven ferries make three trips each way daily from April through October and twice daily during the rest of the year. The fifteen-mile crossing takes about seventy minutes. For ferry information contact the Maine State Ferry Service, 517A Main Street, Rockland, ME 04841; call (207) 596-5400. The light station is six miles north of Vinalhaven Village and about a mile off North Haven Road. The century-old dwelling is now a private residence for the town manager of Vinalhaven, steward of the lighthouse. The site is open but not the lighthouse.

While in Vinalhaven don't miss the Historical Society Museum, which features exhibits on local island heritage at 41 High Street, Vinalhaven, ME 04863; call (207) 863-4410. Of particular interest to lighthouse lovers is Armbrust Hill, just south of the village. From here you can see the towers at **Mantinicus Island** to the southwest and **Two Bush Island** and **Saddleback Ledge** to the southeast.

■ HERON NECK LIGHT ■
Vinalhaven (1854)

Heron Neck Light

Among the approximately one thousand hardy souls who live year-round on Vinalhaven Island, a considerable number are fishermen. Just as their fore-fathers have for nearly one and a half centuries, these mariners depend on the lighthouse at Heron Neck to guide them into Carver's Harbor. Its continuous red beacon and white sector to indicate a clear channel marks the entrance to Hurricane Sound as well as the approaches to Vinalhaven. A fifth-order Fresnel lens beamed out from atop the thirty-foot tower until replaced by a plastic lens in 1982. The Island Institute now owns the station and surrounding property, located on Green Island, just off the main island of Vinalhaven. A nonprofit organization, the institute is dedicated to preserving Maine's old maritime culture. For more information on this nonprofit and how it sustains Maine's coastal communities, call (207) 594-9209.

> *Travel information:* This lighthouse is very difficult to reach, but it can be seen from boats approaching Vinalhaven Island or entering Hurricane Sound. Summer cruises from Rockland or Stonington often feature views of the **Heron Neck, Goose Rocks,** or **Brown's Head Lights.** For information and advice on these and other Maine attractions, call the Maine Office of Tourism at (800) 533-9595.

■ GOOSE ROCKS LIGHT ■
Vinalhaven (1890)

Goose Rocks Light
Lighthouse Digest

The Fox Island Thoroughfare separates Vinalhaven Island from the smaller North Haven Island and provides a shortcut for vessels passing between the east and west Penobscot Bay channels. A killer ledge lurks just beneath the surface of this otherwise inviting passage. Since 1890 the ledge has been marked by an open-water light tower built atop an iron and concrete caisson. The fifty-foot cast-iron tower resembles the Lubec Channel "spark plug" Lighthouse, about a hundred miles to the east. It is difficult to imagine that keepers once lived and worked for months at a time in this confined space. Its original fourth-order Fresnel lens was changed out for a modern optic and automated in 1963; the solar-powered beacon flashes red every six seconds with a white sector demarking a clear channel.

Travel information: The lighthouse is now owned by the nonprofit Beacon Preservation, Inc. For group visits or overnight accommodation requests, call (203) 736-9300, ext. 398 (October through May), or (207) 867-4747 (June through September) to discuss your travel plans, or see www .beaconpreservation.org. Also see Travel information for **Heron Neck.**

■ TWO BUSH ISLAND LIGHT ■
Rockland (1897)

Long ago, seamen heading north toward the west side of Penobscot Bay scanned the horizon for a small island, barren except for a pair of scraggly pines. They knew that "Two Bush" Island marked a safe channel leading into the bay. In 1897 the government gave them a more substantial marker by building a forty-two-foot-tall square brick light tower on the island.

For many years a fifth-order Fresnel lens served here, but in 1963 a modern optic was installed, and the station was automated. Later a US Army Special Forces team blew up the old keeper's dwelling as part of a training exercise. The tower still stands, however, and its light remains active, flashing white and red every five seconds. Its beacon can be seen from up to eighteen miles away.

Travel information: Often passengers can see Two Bush Island Light-house or its beacon from the Vinalhaven ferry or the decks of summer excursion boats headed for Matinicus Island or other coastal attractions. For ferry schedules and prices, call the Maine State Ferry Service at (207) 596-5400. For information on cruises call the Maine Office of Tourism at (800) 533-9595.

■ MATINICUS ROCK LIGHT ■
Rockland/Matinicus Island (1827 and 1857)

Exposed to rain, wind, fog, and giant waves, Matinicus Rock seems an unlikely place to build a lighthouse of wood, but that is exactly what the Lighthouse Service did, throwing up two flimsy wooden towers in 1827 about six miles off Matinicus Island. Surprisingly, the wooden towers survived thirty years; not until 1857 were they replaced by a pair of granite towers. A two-story granite and wood keeper's house had been replaced in 1846.

The new towers stood sixty yards apart, and like their predecessors they displayed two lights that appeared quite close together when seen from a distance. The builders hoped mariners could easily distinguish these key beacons from others along this especially dangerous portion of the Maine coast. Unfortunately, the Winslow Lewis lamps and reflectors used in these towers proved too weak for the station to serve its purpose effectively.

In 1857 the Lighthouse Board ordered the station's towers rebuilt and outfit-ted with third-order Fresnel lenses. Built with massive granite blocks, these towers have stood up to the worst the sea could throw at them for nearly one and a half

Matinicus Rock Light

centuries. Although the north tower still stands, it lost its job in 1924, when the Lighthouse Service decided to stop using twin lights and removed its lantern and lens. The south light still shines, warning mariners away from the rock with powerful white flashes, visible every ten seconds from up to twenty miles away. The south tower's old Fresnel was replaced by a plastic lens in 1983, which remains a Coast Guard active aid to navigation.

This is the light station where heroic teenager Abbie Burgess helped save her invalid mother, young siblings, and pet chickens during a tremendous storm in 1856. Her father had gone ashore for supplies but was stranded by the storm and could only watch from afar while daughter Abbie tended to the light and her family's welfare under extreme conditions. (See page 12 [in "Growing Up on a Rock" section of the Intro.])

> *Travel information:* The Fresnel lens from the old north tower can be seen at the Maine Lighthouse Museum (see Travel information for **Rockland Breakwater Light**). The light station is owned by the US Fish and Wildlife Service, and the island is maintained as a bird sanctuary, home to puffins, petrels, and other rare seabirds; therefore, access is very limited. For sightseeing cruises call the Maine Office of Tourism at (800) 533-9595.

▪ WHITEHEAD LIGHT ▪
Thomaston/Spruce Head Island (1804 and 1852)

Established by order of President Thomas Jefferson in 1804, this is one of the oldest light stations in Maine. Although some sources state the light went into service in 1807, Congress appropriated funds in 1803, and the first keeper was appointed in 1804. The forty-foot granite tower and adjacent wooden dwelling seen here today date from the 1850s, when a third-order Fresnel lens replaced an outmoded lamp-and-reflector system. Its green light goes dark briefly every four seconds. A two-thousand-pound fog bell once served here, and for many years it was rung by a mechanical contraption powered by the waves.

Ellis Dolph, one of Whitehead's early keepers, was fired for selling government lighting oil for personal profit. Dolph overstated the station's needs so that he could keep the oil and profits flowing.

Having guarded the southern entrance to Maine's Penobscot Bay for nearly two centuries, the Whitehead Light Station on rugged Pine Island remains an active aid to navigation.

Whitehead Light
Lighthouse Digest

Travel information: The lighthouse cannot be reached from land but can be seen with some difficulty from the south end of Spruce Head Point Road in Spruce Head, reached from Thomaston via routes 131 and 73 and Spruce Head Island Road. Binoculars will help. The keeper's house currently serves as a residence for adult summer courses, including the arts, through its caregiver, Pine Island Camp. For more information write the Whitehead Light Station, P.O. Box 242, Brunswick, ME 04011, or call (207) 594-2402. Also visible from Spruce Head is the **Two Bush Island Lighthouse** (1897), although it is best seen from a boat, since it is several miles offshore.

■ TENANTS HARBOR LIGHT ■
Near Tenants Harbor (1857)

Built in 1857, the Tenants Harbor Lighthouse, southwest of Rockland, Maine, guided fishing boats and other vessels for more than seventy-five years. When the station was closed in 1933, its wooden cape dwelling and attached twenty-seven-foot brick tower were sold to private owners. For years it has been owned by the family of the famous artist Andrew Wyeth, who is said to have painted some of his best canvases while living here. Wyeth's son Jamie, also a well-known artist, now lives and paints in the keeper's dwelling or the reconstructed square pyramidal wood fog-bell tower.

Travel information: Located at the eastern tip of Southern Island, the site and tower are privately owned and closed. But it can be seen from the water as well as from a landing off Route 131 in Tenants Harbor.

■ MARSHALL POINT LIGHT ■
Port Clyde (1832 and 1857)

The small stone lighthouse on Marshall Point serves Port Clyde, one of the loveliest and most bucolic fishing villages in America. Built in 1857, the signal replaced an earlier soap-stone structure that had stood here since 1832. Rising from the water's edge, the thirty-foot tower looks much like the one at Isle au Haut, with its upper section of brick and lower one of granite blocks. A wooden walkway at one time provided access to shore. A fifth-order Fresnel lens served

Marshall Point Light

here until 1980; now a modern optic sends out a fixed white light that can be seen from approximately twelve miles away.

Travel information: This old tower is highly recommended for lighthouse lovers because of its peaceful setting and proximity to the Marshall Point Lighthouse Museum. The demure lighthouse and dramatic walkway appeared in the 1993 movie *Forrest Gump,* as the eastern end of Gump's cross-country run, furthering its popularity. Managed by the St. George Historical Society, this fine little museum displays artifacts and recounts the histories of the **Marshall Point, Whitehead, Tenants Harbor,** and **St. George Lighthouses.** The museum is free and open to the public May through October. Contact the Marshall Point Lighthouse Museum, P.O. Box 247, Port Clyde, ME 04855; (207) 372-6450.

The tower and museum are located at the end of Marshall Point Road in Port Clyde. Reach them via Route 131 from US Highway 1 in Thomaston. On the way to Port Clyde, stop in Tenants Harbor for a look at the (privately owned) **Tenants Harbor Lighthouse.** Decommissioned in 1934, it has served as both a home and an art studio of Andrew and Jamie Wyeth.

■ MONHEGAN ISLAND LIGHT ■
Monhegan Island (1824 and 1850)

About a dozen miles from the Maine coast and about fourteen miles from Pemaquid Point, the near-solid granite mass of Monhegan Island rises out of the Atlantic, its 150-foot cliffs towering over the waves. Since the 1620s the one-and-a-half-mile-long island has been home to a hardy maritime community, and a scattering of lobstering and fishing families still live there. Theirs is a tradition-minded community, and even now some residences have no electric power.

The compact electric generator that supplied power to the modern optic of the Monhegan Island Light tower has been replaced by solar power. Located atop the cliffs, the forty-seven-foot tower emits a white flash every fifteen seconds with a focal plane nearly 180 feet above the waves. From this height it can be seen from more than twenty miles away. The present tower, completed in 1850, replaced an earlier lighthouse that had served the island since 1824. Until 1959 a magnificent second-order Fresnel lens focused the light.

Monhegan Island Light
William Kaufold

Travel information: The Monhegan Museum in the keeper's house is maintained by the Monhegan Historical and Cultural Museum Association. You may write them at 1 Lighthouse Hill, Monhegan, ME 04852 or call (207) 596-7003. Excursions to Monhegan Island are available during the summer from Boothbay Harbor, (800) 298-2284; or New Harbor, (800) 278-3346; and all year long from Port Clyde, (207) 372-8848.

■ PEMAQUID POINT LIGHT ■
Damariscotta/Pemaquid Point (1827 and 1835)

The unusual striated rock formations of Pemaquid Point look like ocean waves turned to stone—more than a few vessels lost in the fog have sailed up onto them, with disastrous results. Established in 1827, the Pemaquid Point Light has prevented many such wrecks.

Built during the administration of John Quincy Adams, the stone tower had walls three feet thick. Despite their bulk the original walls did not stand up to the harsh local weather and had to be rebuilt in 1835. The keeper's stone dwelling also suffered and was replaced in 1857 by the wood-frame cape that nowadays houses an excellent museum.

The thirty-eight-foot tower stands high on the rocks, placing the focal point of the light almost eighty feet above sea level. The station still employs its venerable fourth-order Fresnel lens; its flashing white light can be seen every six seconds some fifteen miles away.

Pemaquid Point Light

Travel information: From US Highway 1 at Damariscotta, follow Route 130 for sixteen miles to the lighthouse. The keeper's dwelling now houses the Fisherman Museum, which contains a fascinating array of nautical and lighthouse exhibits, including a fourth-order Fresnel lens from the Baker Island Lighthouse. The massive bronze fog bell from the old Manna Island station hangs outside. Contact the Fisherman Museum, Pemaquid Point

Road, New Harbor, ME 04554; call (207) 677-2494. Cruises from nearby New Harbor pass by the active **Franklin Island Lighthouse** (1805) to the east of Pemaquid Point; call (800) 278-3346. The grounds and keeper's house are owned and managed by the Town of Bristol, which licenses the tower to the American Lighthouse Foundation. Volunteers of the Friends of Pemaquid Point Lighthouse (a chapter of the foundation) manage the tower only. Volunteers open the tower in season generally from Memorial Day through Columbus Day. Overnight accommodations are available for a cottage apartment at the light station; call (207) 563-6500, or see www .mainecoastcottages.com.

■ HENDRICKS HEAD LIGHT ■
Boothbay Harbor (1829 and 1875)

During an especially severe storm in the late 1860s, the Hendricks Head keeper pulled an ice-encrusted mattress from the waves. Inside, the astonished man found

a crying baby and a note from a sinking schooner's desperate captain who had committed his tiny daughter "into God's hands." The keeper and his wife adopted the little girl, the lost ship's only survivor.

Established in 1829, the Hendricks Head Light no doubt helped prevent many other such losses. The present forty-foot, Federal-style brick tower and connected wooden dwelling were built in 1875 on the site of the original light-

Hendricks Head Light
Ben Russell

house, destroyed by fire earlier that year. The station's automated plastic lens displays a fixed white light with red sectors.

Travel information: From US Highway 1 take Route 27 through Boothbay Harbor to Southport Island. Tower and grounds are not open to the public, but the lighthouse can be seen from a public beach just off Beach Road. Visitors can see the **Burnt Island Lighthouse** (1857), with its flashing red light, from the waterfront in Boothbay Harbor and, in the distance, the **Cuckolds Lighthouse,** dating from the early 1800s. The **Ram Island Lighthouse** (1883), which resembles those at Isle au Haut and Marshall Point, can be seen from roadside overlooks along Route 96 in Ocean Point to the east of Boothbay Harbor. **Cuckolds Lighthouse** can also be seen from here. Some cruises from Bath and Boothbay Harbor pass by Hendricks Head Lighthouse and other area lights. For more information on specific boat tours, contact Boothbay Chamber of Commerce: http://chamber .boothbayharbor.com.

■ SEGUIN ISLAND LIGHT ■

Georgetown (1795 and 1857)

Among the oldest and most significant navigational stations in the eastern United States, Seguin Island Lighthouse stands on a rocky outcropping near the mouth of Maine's Kennebec River. Built by order of President George Washington, the lighthouse had John Polersky, an old Revolutionary War soldier, as its first keeper. The hard work and horrible weather ruined Polersky's health, and he soon died from the strain and exposure.

Seguin Island Light

The lighthouse survived Polersky by many years but finally succumbed to a storm in 1820. The stone tower built in its place stood until 1857, when construction crews completed the present fifty-three-foot granite tower on the island's highest point. The huge first-order Fresnel lens installed at that time still shines from its lofty perch 180 feet above the sea and can be seen from a distance of up to eighteen miles. One of the few original Fresnel lenses still in its original tower and still an active aid to navigation, it has been kept in place by efforts of the Friends of Seguin Island Light Station, Inc., 72 Front Street, Suite 3, Bath, Maine 04530; (207) 443-4808.

Pond Island Light

Travel information: The lighthouse cannot be seen easily from land, but the Maine Maritime Museum on Washington Street in Bath runs regular tour boats to Seguin Island during summer. The museum is a must-see attraction for anyone interested in maritime history, shipbuilding, or lighthouses. Contact the Maine Maritime Museum, 243 Washington Street, Bath, ME 04530; (207) 443-1316. Museum guides can direct you to several small but interesting lighthouses along the Kennebec River. These include

Perkins Island Light

the **Squirrel Point** (1898), **Perkins Island** (1898), **Pond Island** (1855), **Doubling Point** (1898), and **Doubling Point Range** (1898) Lighthouses. Most of them can be seen from Route 209 or side roads between Bath and Popham Beach. Offering views of **Seguin** and **Pond Island Lighthouses** is the Popham Beach Bed & Breakfast, a beautifully restored life-saving station at 4 Riverview Avenue, Phippsburg, ME 04562; call (207) 389-2409 for reservations. The B and B was featured in the movie *Message in a Bottle.*

■ DOUBLING POINT LIGHT ■
Arrowsic Island near Bath (1898)

Rather simply constructed of a wooden tower resting on a granite foundation, this light on Arrowsic Island was built in 1898, the same year the nearby **Squirrel Point** and **Perkins Island Light Stations** were built. Originally equipped with a fifth-order Fresnel lens, it is now lighted by a plastic lens, automated 1988. Located on the east side of the Kennebec River, at the end of Doubling Point Road off ME 127 near the northwest corner of Arrowsic Island, it is upstream from the **Doubling Point Range Lights,** the only active range lights in the state of Maine. The Doubling Point Light remains an active US Coast Guard aid to navigation and is maintained by the Friends of Doubling Point Light, 140 Doubling Point Road, Arrowsic, ME 04530.

> *Travel information:* From US Highway 1 follow Route 127 south and turn right onto Whitmore's Landing Road. At Doubling Point Road turn left and proceed to the station parking lot. While the towers are not open, visitors are welcome to walk along the station boardwalk to view and photograph these unusual structures.

■ HALFWAY ROCK LIGHT ■
Portland/Casco Bay (1871)

An open ocean tower somewhat like the one at **Minots Ledge** in Massachusetts, the Halfway Rock Lighthouse marks a notorious sea hazard about ten miles from Portland, Maine's busiest seaport. Many ships caught by rocks here simply disappeared, the story of their loss never told—or even known. Congress appropriated $50,000 to mark the rocks in 1869, but the station took two years to build. The seventy-seven-foot tower's massive granite blocks dovetail in such a way that the walls grow even stronger when pounded by the waves. Originally, the tower housed a third-order Fresnel lens, and the station remains active, with its automated lens flashing a red warning that can be seen for twenty miles.

Halfway Rock Light
Lighthouse Digest

Travel information: The lighthouse can be seen in the distance from high points in the City of Portland. Perhaps the best view is from the Portland Observatory on Congress Street. Otherwise it can only be viewed from the water. The six-hour Bailey Island Cruise, which leaves from the Casco Bay Ferry Terminal, offers a distant view of the tower. Call (207) 774-7871.

The Portland area is rich in lighthouses, and harbor cruises, available mostly during summer, provide excellent views for photographing them. From cruise-boat decks you may see the **Portland Breakwater Lighthouse** (1875), **Spring Point Ledge Lighthouse** (1895), **Ram Island Ledge Lighthouse** (1905), and **Portland Head Lighthouse** (1791). For more information call Eagle Tours at (207) 774-6498 or the Portland Visitors Center at (207) 772-4994.

■ PORTLAND HEAD LIGHT ■
Portland (1791)

Among its first acts the US Congress created a Lighthouse Establishment in 1789. Constructing the Portland Head Lighthouse became the first major project federal lighthouse officials undertook. Its eighty-foot fieldstone tower was completed in 1791, during George Washington's third year as president. Remarkably, it still stands and, despite numerous repairs and renovations over the years, looks much as it did in the late eighteenth century. A rambling, red-roofed keeper's residence stands beside the tower on a rocky, wave-swept headland. Together they form one of most beautiful and frequently photographed scenes in the East.

Portland Head Light

The Coast Guard removed the station's fourth-order Fresnel lens in 1855 and installed a second-order Fresnel in 1864, a fourth-order in 1883, a second-order in 1885, and finally a modern optic in 1989, the bicentennial year of the Lighthouse Service. Today it continues as an active aid to navigation, with a modern rotating beacon and its powerful flash characteristic of one white flash every four seconds that can be seen for up to twenty-five miles. The dwelling now houses the Museum at Portland Head, where visitors can see an enormous second-order bivalve lens that once served here.

Travel information: The lighthouse is located in Fort Williams Park, off Route 77 near South Portland. Contact the Museum at Portland Head, 1000 Shore Road, Cape Elizabeth, ME 04107; (207) 799-2661, or see www.portlandheadlight.com. Fortunate passengers of airliners landing at Portland occasionally enjoy a stunning view of Portland Head and its two-century-old lighthouse.

■ PORTLAND BREAKWATER LIGHT ■
South Portland (1855 and 1875)

Portland Breakwater Light

Classical Greek styling gives this little thirteen-foot tower the look of a giant chess rook. Despite its rather whimsical appearance, the tower and its beacon were a serious aid to mariners. The light alerted them to the presence of the Portland Breakwater, at one time more than half a mile long. Built in response to a destructive storm in 1831, the breakwater was intended to protect the harbor, but since it was sometimes difficult to see, it posed a considerable threat to shipping. In 1855 a lighthouse was placed at the end of the breakwater to warn mariners. As the harbor was filled in over the years, the mainland marched steadily out toward the end of the breakwater with the result that the lighthouse now stands on dry land. The tower seen here today dates from 1875, when it replaced an earlier structure that was hauled away for use elsewhere as a watchtower. A small sixth-order Fresnel lens provided the beacon until the light was extinguished in 1942. In 2001 it was relighted as a private aid, flashing white every four seconds.

Travel information: From Route 77 in South Portland, follow Broadway, Breakwater Drive, and then Madison Street to the parking area for Bug Light Park and the lighthouse. This tower is one of several lighthouses highlighted in Portland-area sightseeing cruises. One of several cruise companies: Casco Bay Lines with its ferry terminal at 56 Commercial Street, Portland, Maine; call (207) 774-7871 or see www.cascobaylines.com.

■ SPRING POINT LEDGE LIGHT ■
South Portland (1897)

When the Spring Point Ledge Lighthouse was completed in 1897, documentation showed that seven steamship companies had already carried over one-half million passengers past the dangerous ledge. The rocky ledge, as sharp as a knife, extends from the mainland and out to the main shipping channel into Portland Harbor via Casco Bay. Not only were tourists heading for this vacation spot but also fleets of ships carrying cargo that included fish and coal. High-pro-

Spring Point Ledge Light

file shipwrecks occurred over several decades before the Lighthouse Board agreed to build the "spark plug" light to mark the dangerous spot. The ability for vessels to navigate the harbor safely was greatly increased as a result. The light was only several months old when it was darkened for a brief period during the Spanish-American War. The original fifth-order Fresnel lens was replaced by a modern optic after it was automated during the 1960s.

The breakwater connects the light to the grounds of the Portland Harbor Museum; the museum resides within the granite walls of the nineteenth-century Fort Preble.

> *Travel information:* From US 1 turn right on Maine 77 over the Casco Bay Bridge into South Portland. Take a left on Broadway, and travel to the end to the college campus. Continue through the campus via Fort Road to the light. The caisson light is the only one of its kind accessible to the public and can be reached by walking out on the nine-hundred-foot breakwater. Open houses and tours are offered by the light's stewards, the Friends of Spring Point Ledge Light, on summer weekends, thanks to restoration projects since 1998. For more information contact Spring Point Ledge Light Trust, P.O. Box 2311, South Portland, ME 04116; see www.springpointledgelight.com for tour schedules.

■ CAPE ELIZABETH LIGHT ■
Cape Elizabeth (1828 and 1874)

The Cape Elizabeth Light station once guided mariners with two lights—one fixed, the other flashing. The twin lights, shining from towers spaced about three hundred yards apart, allowed navigators approaching from any direction to quickly find their position on a chart. The first towers built here in 1828 cost the government only $4,250 and lasted for almost half a century. Finally, all but destroyed by wind, weather, and the sea, the deteriorated towers were replaced in 1874 by the handsome cast-iron towers that still stand. The Lighthouse Service stopped using twin beacons in 1924; afterward, only the east light was displayed. Although its second-order Fresnel lens was removed in 1994, the beacon remains in service, its flashing white light visible some fifteen miles away.

Travel information: Together with their gorgeous setting, the sixty-seven-foot Italianate Cape Elizabeth towers make this one of the loveliest and most distinctive lighthouses in America. It is located in Two Lights State Park, easily reached from Route 77 via Two Lights Road. Keep in mind that the residence and grounds are privately owned. A visit to Cape Elizabeth can be part of a compact lighthouse adventure including nearby Portland Head and several other lighthouses in the Portland area.

Cape Elizabeth Light

■ CAPE NEDDICK LIGHT "NUBBLE LIGHT" ■
York (1879)

Just off Cape Neddick, near the old colonial town of York, Maine, lies a small, barren island long known to local fishermen as the "Nubble." Imaginative visitors say they can see the ghostly likenesses of people—perhaps sailors shipwrecked here long

Cape Neddick Light

ago—in the fantastic shapes of the island's rock formations. Since 1879 the Cape Neddick Lighthouse, stationed on the island's highest point, has warned mariners of the deadly Nubble. From a forty-one-foot cast-iron tower lined with brick, its flashing red light signals danger. A wood-frame residence connects to the tower by a covered walkway. Delightful miniature lighthouses decorate the balusters of the service gallery.

> *Travel information:* From I-95 take the York exit (exit 7), and bear right at the lights onto Route 1. Take a left at the lights onto Route 1A. Travel one mile to the monument and bear left. Travel six-tenths of a mile and turn right onto Long Sands Road to a stop sign at the intersection with Long Beach Avenue. Take a left onto Long Beach Avenue. The Cutty Sark Motel stands at the end of Long Sands Beach, and Nubble Road is at the corner of the motel. Turn right onto Nubble Road and continue to the Lighthouse Restaurant on your right. Straight ahead is the entrance to Sohier Park and Nubble Light. For more information see www.nubblelight.org. Volunteers run the welcome center. Annually, the light is decorated for the holidays on the first Saturday after Thanksgiving. While in the area don't miss the Lighthouse Depot in Wells, several miles north of York. This extraordinary shop is a treasure-house of information and keepsakes related to Cape Neddick and lighthouses throughout the United States. Write to Lighthouse Depot, P.O. Box 427, Wells, ME 04090 or call (207) 646-0608, or see www.lighthousedepot.com, which includes an educational section.

■ WHALEBACK LIGHT ■
Kittery Point (1830 and 1872)

A scatter of ship-killing rocks and ledges obstruct the entrance to the Piscataqua River and the approaches to New Hampshire's Portsmouth Harbor. Prominent among these is Whaleback Ledge, located just off Kittery Point, Maine, across the river from Portsmouth. The first Whaleback Lighthouse (first called Whale Back in old documents) was built in 1829–1830 by order of President Andrew Jackson. The lighthouse exhibited two fixed white lights in September 1830. A gale destroyed this tower in the 1860s, and a new fifty-foot granite tower that currently marks Whaleback Ledge was completed in 1872. Its fourth-order Fresnel lens retired in 1963 when the station was automated. The light station is currently owned by the American Lighthouse Foundation and is managed by the Friends of Portsmouth.

> *Travel information:* The lighthouse is accessible only by boat and is closed to the public. However, excellent views can be gained. From US 1A in York Harbor, follow Route 103 south for about four miles. Turn left onto Gerrish Island Lane, and follow it to Pochohantas Road and Fort Foster. The park at Fort Foster offers excellent views of the lighthouse. The Isle of Shoals Steamship Company runs cruises offering excellent views of Whaleback and other lighthouses in the area. Contact the Isles of Shoals Steamship Company, 315 Market Street, Portsmouth, NH 03801; call (603) 431-5500 or (800) 441-4620.

NEW HAMPSHIRE

▪ PORTSMOUTH HARBOR LIGHT ▪
Portsmouth (1771, 1784, 1804, and 1878)

Established in 1771, several years before the Revolution, the Portsmouth Harbor beacon has guided ships longer than all but a few lighthouses in North America. Although its light has burned almost continuously for more than two centuries, the lighthouse has evolved and changed substantially. This lighthouse has been known by several names over the centuries: Portsmouth Harbor Light, New Castle Light, Fort Point Light, and Fort Constitution Light. It was initially a fifty-foot-tall, wood-shingled tower that became known as Fort Constitution after the Revolutionary War. In 1784 the light had to be renovated and relighted following the rigors of war,

and President George Washington ordered that the light be continuously attended by a keeper. By 1804 the light shone from atop an eighty-foot octagonal wooden tower, which eventually succumbed to rot and the concussions of the fort's mighty cannon. It was rebuilt in 1878 as a forty-eight-foot cast-iron tower on the same foundation as the previous tower. This lighthouse still stands, its 1851 fourth-order Fresnel lens shooting out a fixed green beam visible from twelve miles away.

Over the years the Portsmouth Harbor Lighthouse has hosted many distinguished visitors, including General Lafayette, Daniel Webster, and Henry David Thoreau. But the most important—and likely the gruffest—personage to knock on the door here was

Portsmouth Harbor Light

President George Washington. He inspected the light station in 1789 and found its upkeep less than satisfactory. Not surprisingly, its keeper was summarily fired.

Early in 2000 the American Lighthouse Foundation leased the tower for preservation and works with a support group, Friends of Portsmouth Harbor Light, for preservation of the historic light station: www.portsmouthharborlighthouse.org.

Travel information: From US Highway 1 in Portsmouth, follow signs to Fort Constitution State Historic Site, or take Route 1B and Wentworth Road to the fort, which is now part of the Portsmouth Harbor Coast Guard Station. Most of the base is off-limits, but this old colonial fort is open to the public. The best views of the lighthouse can be had from its massive walls; contact Portsmouth Harbor Cruises at (800) 776-0915. Also, for sightseeing in the Portsmouth and Portland areas, New England Lighthouse (van) Tours begin in downtown Portsmouth with historian, author, photographer, and tour captain Jeremy D'Entremont; (603) 431-9155.

■ ISLES OF SHOALS LIGHT (WHITE ISLAND) ■
Portsmouth (1821 and 1859)

The Isles of Shoals, consisting of nine islands, barely more than barren scraps of rock a few miles seaward from Portsmouth, New Hampshire, have long attracted the adventurous and hardy of spirit. During the sixteenth century, European fishermen settled the isles to reap extraordinary harvests of cod. Later, Ralph Waldo Emerson, Nathaniel Hawthorne, and John Greenleaf Whittier came to enjoy the soul-expanding scenery and rustic hospitality of the old Appledore Hotel. A lighthouse marked the isles beginning in 1821. The existing fifty-eight-foot brick-and-granite tower has stood since 1859. A second-order Fresnel lens once focused the beacon, but it was replaced in 1987 with an automated optic. The station's batteries are recharged by solar panels.

Travel information: Portsmouth-based tour boats offer excursions to the historical **Isles of Shoals** as well as special lighthouse cruises featuring **Portsmouth Harbor Lighthouse** (1878), **Whaleback Lighthouse** (1872), **Boon Island Lighthouse** (1852), and **Cape Neddick Lighthouse** (1879). See Travel information for **Whaleback Lighthouse.**

Isles of Shoals Light
US Coast Guard

■ LAKE SUNAPEE LIGHTS ■
New Hampshire Lake Country (1893)

For more than a century, Lake Sunapee in western New Hampshire has attracted vacationers who flock here to enjoy the lake's crystal-blue, spring-fed waters. During the nineteenth century visitors arrived by train but traveled from place to place on the ten-mile-long lake by steamboat. A number of small lighthouses were built to make sure these vessels reached their destinations safely. Three of these extraordinary inland navigational aids remain, including the **Herrick Cove Lighthouse** (1893) near the town of Sunapee. Octagonal in shape, the small white tower still displays a modest light. All lights on the lake are owned and maintained by the New Hampshire Department of Marine Control, with supervision by site manager Lake Sunapee Protective Association.

Loon Island Light
Bob and Sandra Shanklin

Travel information: Lake Sunapee Cruises are located at the town dock in Sunapee Harbor; (603) 938-6465. Cruises available offer an excellent view of the lighthouse as well as the **Burkehaven** (1960 reproduction of destroyed 1893 tower) and **Loon Island** (1960, also a reproduction of burned 1893 light) towers.

VERMONT

■ COLCHESTER REEF LIGHT ■
Shelburne (1871)

Many might be surprised to hear of lighthouses in Vermont, but the state once had several important navigational beacons, all of them on Lake Champlain. While not considered one of the Great Lakes, Champlain is nonetheless big enough and sufficiently strategic to have been the site of decisive naval battles. A ragtag flotilla led by Benedict Arnold fought the British here during the early years of the Revolutionary War.

During the nineteenth century Burlington became a key industrial center and shipping point. Vessels moving southward toward the Burlington docks faced an array of three dangerous shoals about a mile off Colchester Point just north of the city. To mark them, workers built a combination light tower and dwelling atop a massive granite pier. A square structure with a mansard roof, it became a familiar sight to commercial vessels and pleasure boaters navigating the middle reaches of the lake. Eleven successive keepers lived with their families in the four-bedroom dwelling.

Decommissioned in 1933, the lighthouse was allowed to deteriorate. In 1952, however, it was brought ashore, restored, and put on display at the Shelburne Museum. Today it stands near the steamer *Ticonderoga*, which plied the waters of the lake for many years. Although inactive, it still houses a sixth-order Fresnel lens.

Nearby is the **Burlington Breakwater Light** that guarded one of the most prosperous communities along the eastern shore of Lake Champlain in Burlington. The lake became a major lumber shipping route after new canals connected it to the Great Lakes and Hudson and St. Lawrence Rivers. Also in the area is the **Juniper Island Lighthouse.**

Travel information: Located off US Highway 7 south of Burlington, the museum is open all year long, but winter hours are limited. Contact the Shelburne Museum, 6000 Shelburne Road, P.O. Box 10, Shelburne, VT 05482; (802) 985-3346; http://shelburnemuseum.org. For cruises that include lighthouse views in the Burlington area, see *The Spirit of Ethan Allen III* that departs from the Burlington Boathouse, at 1 College Street, Downtown Burlington, Vermont; (802) 862-8300; www.soea.com.

Colchester Reef Light
Lighthouse Digest

MASSACHUSETTS

▪ NEWBURYPORT HARBOR (PLUM ISLAND) LIGHT ▪

Newburyport (1788 and 1898)

Newburyport is located on the Merrimack River and became an important port by the late 1700s. However, the entrance to the harbor was dangerous, with shifting channels at the mouth of the river. When this light station was established in 1788 (about the same time the US Constitution was ratified), only ten other lighthouses stood in the entire country. The light station initially consisted of two small wooden lights. Since their inception these two towers served in tandem as range lights; they were situated on movable skids to mark a safe channel in the Merrimac River as it often changed. Originally paid for by local merchants, the light was ceded to the new government in 1790. Damaged by storms, rebuilt, knocked down again, and rebuilt, the range lights eventually would disappear into history, although the Newburyport Harbor Light that we see today

Newburyport Harbor Light
Lighthouse Digest

was built in 1898, possibly from one of the original range lights. In 1981 its fourth-order Fresnel lens was installed, and it exhibits a flashing light that occults four times a minute; it remains an active Coast Guard aid to navigation. Massachusetts's smallest city, Newburyport boasts the title "Birthplace of the US Coast Guard."

Travel information: From US Highway 1 in Newburyport, follow Route 1A and then Ocean Avenue onto Plum Island. The lighthouse is on the north end of the island in the Parker Ridge National Wildlife Refuge. The lighthouse is leased from the owner, the city of Newburyport, by the Friends of Plum Island Light, Inc. For more information write the group at P.O. Box 381, Newburyport, MA 01950. While there, don't miss the Custom House Maritime Museum on Water Street in Newburyport. Among the exhibits is a fourth-order Fresnel lens similar to the one that once served **Newburyport Harbor Light.** Contact the Custom House Maritime Museum, 25 Water Street, Newburyport, MA 01950; (978) 462-8681; or see www.customhousemaritime museum.org. Not far from the museum is a set of range lights that was established in 1873. The old **Newburyport Harbor Front Range** (located on the waterfront between Federal Street and Independent Street about 350 feet east of the rear light) and **Rear Range Light** on Water Street. The Lighthouse Preservation Society offers gourmet dinners at the top of the Rear Range Light as a fundraiser for lighthouses; call (800) 727-2326 for information.

■ CAPE ANN LIGHT
(THACHER ISLAND TWIN LIGHTS) ■
Rockport/Thacher Island (1771 and 1861)

Among the oldest and most historical light stations in America, the twin Cape Ann Lights first beamed out their warnings in 1771, several years before the Revolution. Of the many stories that became legends about this unique light station, one is of Civil War–era and veteran keeper Alexander Bray's wife, Maria, who kept both lights going continuously during a horrific 1864 winter storm. In 2000 a Coast Guard Keeper Class buoy tender was launched bearing her name. Nearly a century and half after the light station was first established, the foghorn here may have saved the life of President Woodrow Wilson by preventing the wreck of his fog-blinded ship as it returned from Europe in 1919, following the Versailles Peace Conference that officially ended World War I. The two 124-foot granite towers that stand here now date from 1861. The south tower remains active with its flashing red beacon produced by a modern optic. Additionally, the recently

Cape Ann Light

restored north tower exhibits a fixed yellow light produced by a modern optic and is cared for by the Town of Rockport and the Thacher Island Association. In 2001, the light station earned recognition by being named a National Historic Landmark. The enormous first-order Fresnel lenses that formerly served here were removed in 1932. The Town of Rockport's Thacher Island Committee has joined in partnership with the Thacher Island Association to maintain the island, including both towers. The Coast Guard continues to service the solar-powered light in the south tower, which flashes red every five seconds and is maintained as a Coast Guard active aid to navigation.

> *Travel information:* Thacher Island is accessible only by boat, but you can see the towers from Route 127A near Rockport on Cape Ann. For information on occasional summer excursions to Thacher Island, contact the Thacher Island Association, Inc., P.O. Box 73, Rockport, MA 01966; call (617) 599-2590; www.thacherisland.org. Also near Rockport are the **Annisquam Harbor Lighthouse** (1897), off Route 127, and the **Straitsmouth Island Lighthouse** (1835), which can be seen from the Rockport waterfront.

■ EASTERN POINT LIGHT ■
Gloucester (1832, 1848, and 1890)

For 180 years three Eastern Point beacons have guided Gloucester fishermen safely home from the sea. The tower and accompanying dwellings were situated on the east side of the town's harbor on a long, rocky point of land that forms a natural breakwater. Eastern Point's first 1832 lighthouse was a simple structure that could hardly bear the weight of wind and waves until it was replaced in 1848 as newly established railroad service allowed the fishing industry to expand exponentially. This second beacon was known as "the ruby light," created by fine

Eastern Point Light

ruby glass around its array of whale-oil lamps and reflectors. A fourth-order Fresnel lens took up residence in 1857 to increase the light's reach to fifteen miles. In 1882, the light was changed from a fixed to a flashing red light. The existing thirty-six-foot brick tower, built in 1890, projects a flashing white light every five seconds that mariners can see from up to twenty miles at sea. The flashing signal helps mark dangerous Dog Bar Reef, near the harbor entrance.

> *Travel information:* Located at the end of Eastern Point Boulevard in East Gloucester, the site is closed to the public, as the keeper's quarters house Coast Guard personnel. Although the road is marked "private," visitors are allowed to drive to the lighthouse. Parking is available, and the stone break-water adjacent to the lighthouse is open all year, which affords good views of the station. The cast-iron **Ten Pound Island Light** tower (1881) and its flashing white light can be seen from the same breakwater. For cruises pass-ing these historical lighthouses and great photographic opportunities, con-tact Harbor Tours at (978) 283-1979 during summer; (978) 804-9575 during winter; or www.capeannharbortours.com. For information on the Gloucester area, call the Cape Ann Chamber of Commerce at (978) 283-1601: www.cape annchamber.com.

■ TEN POUND ISLAND ■
Gloucester
(1821 and 1881)

Having guided generations of mariners into Gloucester's harbor, the Ten Pound Island Light became a movie star as well as a navigational beacon. It was featured prominently in the hit action thriller *The Perfect Storm*, released in 2000; earlier generations may remember the

Ten Pound Island Light
Bob and Sandra Shanklin

lighthouse from paintings by Winslow Homer. A forty-foot stone tower, wood-frame dwelling, and several outbuildings were constructed on the island in 1821. The original tower was replaced by a thirty-foot-tall brick-lined cast-iron cylinder in 1881. A fifth-order Fresnel lens served here for more than a century, but it has given way to a modern optic. The station remains operational, displaying a red light, three seconds on and three seconds dark. The light is a Coast Guard active aid to navigation, and the grounds are managed by the City of Gloucester.

Travel information: Ferries and tourist cruises offer close-up views of the Ten Pound Island tower; call the Gloucester Chamber of Commerce at (978) 283-1979 during summer; during winter months, (978) 804-9575.

■ BAKER'S ISLAND LIGHT ■
Manchester-by-the-Sea (1791, 1798, and 1820)

Established in 1791 by members of the Salem Marine Society during the administration of George Washington, the Baker's Island Lighthouse originally displayed one beacon to guide ships into Salem Harbor. Maritime traffic was brisk in the area and fog a frequent visitor, calling for a second guiding light to be added in 1798. Like the Matinicus Rock Lighthouse in Maine, the station became two separate towers connected to a central keeper's dwelling. Later, the station was altered to only one light, and a shorter one at that; as a result, more ships were wrecked on the island's rocky shore. Thus, a new forty-seven-foot conical stone tower and the refurbished shorter (twenty-six-foot) tower,

Baker's Island Light
US Coast Guard

were lighted in October 1820. Substantial improvements were made to both lights in 1857, including installation of new lantern rooms and Fresnel lenses. In 1878, a new keeper's house was added, which still stands today. The smaller tower served faithfully until its deactivation in 1926, and its fourth-order Fresnel lens removed.

This station, which has witnessed the greatest part of this nation's history, including German submarine threats during World Wars I and II off its immediate coast, received deserved restoration during the 1990s. Ownership of the light station was transferred to the Essex National Heritage Commission (ENHC) in 2006.

Travel information: The island is closed to the general public, but the lighthouse can be seen from Harbor Street or Boardman Avenue, off Route 127 in Manchester-by-the-Sea. For information on cruises passing this lighthouse, contact the Friends of the Boston Harbor Islands at (781) 740-4290. For more information on the lighthouse or an opportunity to visit, contact the ENHC at 221 Essex Street, Suite 41, Salem, MA 01970; (978) 740-0444.

■ MARBLEHEAD LIGHT ■
Salem (1835 and 1896)

Built in 1835 for a mere $4,500, the original Marblehead Lighthouse was not much taller than an ordinary fisherman's cottage. It served effectively, however, until it was replaced in 1896 by the 105-foot steel skeleton tower that dominates the Marblehead beach today. The fixed green light, once focused by a fourth-order Fresnel lens, has been produced by a modern optic since 1960.

Marblehead Light

Travel information: From US Highway 1 take Route 114 to Marblehead; then follow Ocean Avenue to its end near the lighthouse. A small park here provides an excellent view of the tower and of gorgeous summer sunsets. New England Lighthouse tours begin in downtown Portsmouth, New Hampshire, and cover this lighthouse area also (tours are by van). For reservations call Jeremy D'Entremont at (603) 431-9155, or see www.lighthouse.cc.

■ DERBY WHARF LIGHT ■
Salem (1871)

Salem, best known now for its infamous witch trials, was once called "the Venice of the New World." This vigorous maritime community sent whole fleets of clipper ships to China and India. When these vessels returned, spices, tea, and chinaware poured from their holds, bankrolling the fortunes of many an entrepreneur. Salem's cleverest trader was Elias Derby, likely America's first millionaire. Derby built the extensive wharf that still bears

Derby Wharf Light

his name. Marking the far end of Derby Wharf is its small, square brick lighthouse, completed in 1871. The lamp in its small lantern room originally burned whale oil in a fifth-order Fresnel lens, was changed to a kerosene lamp and fourth-order Fresnel in 1906, then a sixth order in 1910, but now a solar panel and batteries power its flashing red signal every six seconds.

Travel information: Old Salem, with its fascinating cemeteries, museums, shops, wharf, and lighthouse, is located off Highway 1A, north of Boston. The lighthouse is in a small park at the end of the wharf off Derby Street. Nearby is the official Visitor Center for the Salem Maritime National Historic Site, a treasury of seventeenth- and eighteenth-century structures. Write to Salem Maritime National Historic Site, 160 Derby Street, Salem, MA 01970; (978) 740-1650; www.nps.gov/sama.

The Winter Island Maritime Park, just north of Salem, features the tiny **Fort Pickering Lighthouse** (1872). The park also provides views of the **Hospital Point Range Lights** in Beverly (1872) as well as the **Derby Wharf, Marblehead,** and **Baker's Island Lighthouses;** call (978) 745-9430.

■ FORT PICKERING LIGHT ■
Salem (1872)

Fort Pickering Light

Since 1872 Salem's Fort Pickering Lighthouse has guided vessels headed for the city's bustling Derby Wharf. The old lighthouse remains in operation, displaying a flashing white light with a focal plane twenty feet above the water. A conical brick tower, sheathed in iron to protect it from the elements, it stands at the water's edge on Winter Island, site of important eighteenth-century fortifications.

Travel information: From Salem, Winter Island Road will take you to Fort Pickering and its lighthouse.

■ BOSTON LIGHT ■
Boston (1716 and 1783)

The oldest navigational station in all of North America, Boston Lighthouse is a national treasure. Built in 1716 on Little Brewster Island at the entrance to the harbor, it helped attract the fleets of trading ships that made Boston one of the world's most prosperous cities. Its light had been shining for almost sixty years by the time Paul Revere saw a different sort of beacon in the belfry of Boston's Old North Church and hurried off on his famous ride. The lighthouse was destroyed by the British during the Revolutionary War but was rebuilt in 1783. That post-Revolutionary tower still stands, its light continuing to guide ships more than 280 years after the station's inception.

The tower's extraordinary longevity is no accident. Aware the lighthouse could face other wars, not to mention fierce battles with Atlantic storms, the Boston masons who built the 1783 tower gave it fortresslike walls more than seven feet thick at the base. In 1853 its height was raised by fifteen feet and its stone walls lined

Boston Light

with brick. Otherwise, except for reinforcing steel hoops added in 1983, the tower remains essentially unchanged.

Nearly as venerable as the tower itself is the second-order Fresnel lens installed here in 1859. It remains in service, producing a flashing white light visible from an impressive distance of more than twenty-seven miles at sea. The nation's last remaining resident lighthouse keepers carefully attend the lens. The US Coast Guard runs this light station the old way, with keepers on-site around the clock, as a sort of living memorial to a centuries-old tradition. It is one of only a few American lighthouses bearing the honorable title of National Historic Landmark.

Travel information: Little Brewster Island is part of Boston Harbor Islands State Park. Call the Friends of Boston Harbor Islands at (781) 740-4290 for information on cruises offering close-up views of the **Boston Lighthouse** and nearby **Graves Ledge Lighthouse.** For private boat owners making the trip to the island, reservations are required. Contact Boston Harbor Islands Park at 408 Atlantic Avenue, Boston, MA 02110; (617) 223-8666; www.nps .gov/boha. Airliners landing at Boston's Logan Airport offer thrilling views of these lighthouses and the **Long Island Head Lighthouse** (1919), near the inner harbor.

■ GRAVES LEDGE LIGHT (THE GRAVES) ■
Boston (1905)

Gray and weather-streaked, the stone tower guarding Graves Ledge looks very old but dates only from 1905, making it a relatively young lighthouse. Some think the ledge received its rather ominous name because of tragedies such as the one that befell the schooner *Mary O'Hara* in 1941. During a blinding blizzard in January of that year, the unlucky vessel rammed a barge and sank,

Graves Ledge Light

leaving nineteen of her crew to drown or freeze. Actually, the ledge is named for Thomas Graves, a prominent sea trader from colonial Massachusetts. Fifteen hundred gallons of fresh water was delivered by boat twice a year and stored in a cistern that was built into the lower level of the tower. Food was delivered on a more regular schedule, but when rations became lean the keepers set up lobster traps. Their skill must have been good, because they wrote of dining on lobster regularly.

Built with massive granite blocks, the 113-foot tower easily withstands the ocean's pounding waves in Boston's Outer Harbor at the entrance to Broad Sound Channel. Providing its keepers with a living space only thirty feet in diameter, it was never a popular duty station. The lighthouse was automated in 1976, and its huge, first-order Fresnel lens was exchanged for a modern lens. Seen from up to twenty-five miles at sea, its two white flashes every twelve seconds, now solar powered, are almost as powerful as that of the Boston Light on nearby Little Brewster Island.

Travel information: See Travel information for **Boston Light.**

■ MINOTS LEDGE LIGHT ■
Cohasset (1850 and 1860)

Few navigational obstacles have snuffed out as many lives as Minots Ledge, a vicious shoal lurking just beneath the waves off Cohasset. Dozens of ships and countless smaller vessels were wrecked on the ledge before anyone seriously considered marking the wave-swept shoal with a light. Finally, in 1850 Lighthouse Service crews completed an iron skeleton tower, built on pilings hammered directly into the ledge. Thought able to withstand any Atlantic storm, the tower stood for less than a year before a mighty gale knocked it down, killing two assistant keepers.

The tower built in 1860 to take its place still stands, however. Its massive granite blocks dovetail, interlocking in such a way that the enormous pressures exerted on the walls by

Minots Ledge Light

Scituate Light

storm-driven waves actually strengthen them. Consisting of more than a thousand carefully shaped blocks, the tower weighs more than 2,300 tons.

Automated in 1947, the tower lost its second-order Fresnel lens, but not its unique one/one-two-three-four/one-two-three flashing sequence. Imaginative Cohasset folks read the flashes as I/L-O-V-E/Y-O-U and have given the Minots beacon the nickname "Lover's Light."

Travel information: The tower and "Lover's Light" can be seen from beaches off Atlantic Avenue in Cohasset.

■ SCITUATE LIGHT ■
Scituate (1811)

Massachusetts has a long history of rescuing its lighthouses. Scituate is no exception: This light was turned on and off over the years, the "on" phases of its life mainly being accomplished by the likes of the Daughters of the American Revolution, Henry Cabot Lodge, and the Town of Scituate. But perhaps the best rescue was by the "Lighthouse Army of Two," the teenage daughters of keeper Simeon Bates. Rebecca and Abigail were home alone while their large family was away on errands. To their astonishment they found themselves staring down a British man-of-war. Brave Rebecca pulled out her fife and proceeded to play as loudly as she knew how, while both sisters stayed out of sight. The British thought the fife music to be a harbinger of Scituate's approaching militia and immediately headed for sea.

Taking second seat to Minots Ledge, which was built and rebuilt between 1855 and 1860, Scituate went dark for a long time. But the town's loyalty never flagged for this twenty-five-foot tower that eventually doubled in height (fifteen feet was added in 1827 and a new lantern in 1930); after purchasing the lighthouse in 1917, the town had restorative measures done to the lighthouse and keeper's quarters over the years. In 1968, although the light had been deactivated for well over a century, care of the historical site was given to the Scituate Historical Society. This tenacious and watchful group continues improvements into the twenty-first century to keep this popular lighthouse an active private aid to navigation.

Travel information: In Scituate head east on Allen Place, take a left on Front Street, then right onto Jericho Road, and, finally, a slight right onto Lighthouse Road to Lighthouse Park on Cedar Point (north side of the entrance to Scituate Harbor); there is a large parking area. The grounds are open year-round, with the tower opened on special occasions. For more information contact the Scituate Historical Society, P.O. Box 276, Scituate, MA 02066; (781) 545-1083; www.scituatehistoricalsociety.org.

■ PLYMOUTH LIGHT (THE GURNET) ■
Plymouth (1768, 1803, and 1843)

One of America's earliest lighthouses and situated on seven-mile-long Gurnet Point, the original Plymouth Light showed two beacons, one each from a pair of small wooden towers only a few feet apart. The lights were not very effective at guiding mariners, but they did attract some unwanted attention from a British frigate that fired on the station during a Revolutionary War battle in 1778.

When the lighthouse accidentally burned to the ground in 1801, its replacement, built two years later, also sported double towers. These were replaced in 1843 by yet another set of twin towers—the double light helped mariners distinguish the lighthouse signal from other nearby beacons. Each tower was thirty-nine feet tall and fitted with its own fourth-order Fresnel lens. One of the towers was dismantled in 1924, but the other still stands. Its light remains active, maintaining a sequence of three white flashes every 30 seconds and a red sector warning of nearby Mary Ann Rocks. As with nearly every New England light station, the fog signal is important. Its characteristic is two blasts every fifteen seconds, because fog is a frequent visitor to the northeastern United States.

Plymouth Light
Bob and Sandra Shanklin

Travel information: The lighthouse is located near the end of the Gurnet, a sandy peninsula reaching several miles into Plymouth Bay. Cruises taking visitors within easy viewing distance of the lighthouse depart from piers along Water Street in Plymouth; call (508) 746-5342. The keeper's residence is open to visitors during the summer, and rooms are available to rent weekly or monthly. Profits benefit Project Gurnet & Bug Lights, Inc. For more information see www.buglight.org.

Also near Plymouth is the still active **Duxbury Lighthouse** (1871), a caisson-type structure located north of the Plymouth inner harbor.

■ CAPE COD (HIGHLAND) LIGHT ■
Cape Cod/Truro (1797 and 1857)

A whorl of sparkling sand deposited by glaciers of the last ice age, legendary Cape Cod is one of the world's most famous geological features. Extending far out into the stormy Atlantic from the southeastern corner of Massachusetts, the peninsula poses a formidable threat to seafaring vessels. Hence, Cape Cod became home to a remarkable array of lighthouses. The oldest and best known of these is the Cape Cod—also known as Highland—Lighthouse, established in 1797. Although its tower was only thirty feet high, the focal plane of its light, shining from atop a high, sandy bluff, was more than 150 feet above sea level. From this height whaling ships and schooners could see it from more than twenty miles out at sea.

Wind and water, the same forces that built the bluffs, also eat away at them and by the 1850s threatened to undercut the lighthouse and dump it into the sea. In 1857 a new sixty-six-foot tower was built more than five hundred feet from the nearest cliff. The erosion did not stop, however, and by the 1990s the cliffs were within 110 feet of the tower's foundation. To save the lighthouse a committee of local preservationists raised $1.5 million to move the lighthouse back from the cliffs and out of danger. An extraordinary engineering feat, the move was completed in 1997.

These days an aeromarine beacon produces the powerful flashes of the Cape Cod Light, but until 1945 a huge first-order Fresnel lens served here. The light has a range of about twenty-three miles.

Travel information: To reach the lighthouse take Route 6 (Mid-Cape Highway) and exit at Highland Road; head east; turn right onto Coast Guard Drive, then left onto Highland Light Road. Anyone interested in lighthouses, history, or beautiful scenery should visit this facility. The Cape Cod Lighthouse offers ample parking, a

Cape Cod (Highland) Light

museum, and a scenic overlook. From US Highway 6 in Truro, follow the Cape Cod Light signs. Contact the Truro Historical Society, P.O. Box 486, Truro, MA 02666; (508) 487-3397. Call the Highland Museum and Lighthouse at (508) 487-1121, or see www.capecodlight.org.

▪ RACE POINT LIGHT ▪
Cape Cod/Provincetown (1816 and 1876)

Hundreds of ships have ended their days on Race Point, which forms Cape Cod's westward knuckle. Vessels must round the point to reach Provincetown Harbor a few miles to the southeast, and over the years more than a few have tried and failed. No doubt, countless others have been saved by the Race Point Light, established in 1816.

Race Point Light

The existing forty-foot-tall cast-iron cylinder replaced the original rubble-stone tower in 1876. Built on a foundation at beach level, the tower elevates its fourth-order flashing white light only forty-one feet above sea level, limiting its range to just over fifteen miles.

Travel information: From US Highway 6 in Provincetown, take Race Point Road to Race Point Beach. Two miles of soft sand separate the parking area from the lighthouse, a hike recommended only for veteran walkers (wear old shoes). Now managed and maintained by the American Lighthouse Foundation, the Race Point Light Station is open to the public and available for overnight stays. If you have overnight reservations, transportation from the beach to the lighthouse can be arranged; call (508) 487-9930. The **Long Point Lighthouse** (1875) and **Wood End Lighthouse** (1873) can be seen from the Provincetown waterfront.

■ NAUSET BEACH LIGHT ■
Eastham (1838 and 1877)

The steadily crumbling cliffs above Nauset were once marked by the **Three Sisters of Nauset** (1838 and 1892), an unusual array of three separate light towers and beacons. Eventually, the Sisters were threatened by erosion and had to be removed. In 1923 the existing forty-eight-foot cast-iron tower was brought to Nauset from Chatham, where it had been part of a twin-tower, two-light system since 1877. In time the replacement tower itself stood in danger of falling over the cliffs, and in 1996 the ninety-ton structure was moved to a safer location away from the crumbling edge. Now owned by the National Park Service and leased to the Nauset Light Preservation Society, the lighthouse is once more displaying its flashing red and white light.

Nauset Beach Light

Travel information: From Route 6 in Eastham, follow Bracket Road, Nauset Road, Cable Road, and then Ocean View Drive to the Nauset Lighthouse parking area. The partially restored Three Sisters towers are in a small nearby park. Contact the Cape Cod National Seashore at (508) 255-3421, www.nps.gov/caco; or the Nauset Light Preservation Society, P.O. Box 941, Eastham, MA 02642; (508) 240-2612; www.nausetlight.org.

■ CHATHAM LIGHT ■
Cape Cod/Chatham (1808, 1841, and 1877)

The large number of navigational beacons beaming seaward from Cape Cod tended to confuse mariners. Maritime officials struggled to give the lights distinctive characteristics. After 1808 a pair of matched towers at Chatham marked the town's busy harbor at Cape Cod's southeast corner with a rare double light, exhibiting two fixed white lights, to distinguish it from the Highland Light. Then in 1838 an even more unusual triple beacon—the Three Sisters—went into service at nearby Nauset Beach. By 1838 the Chatham Light consisted of several oil lamps and reflectors with colored glass before the flames to create green lights.

Built on a high, sandy bluff, the original wooden Chatham towers eventually fell victim to erosion. In 1841 two new brick lighthouses, each thirty feet tall, were completed to replace the old octagonal wooden towers. A new brick keeper's quarters connected both of the new towers via covered walkway. Fourth-order Fresnel lenses were installed in 1857, and the Chatham lights returned to their original fixed white characteristic. Relocated or rebuilt more than once, they finally were replaced in 1877 by two fortyeight-foot cast-iron cylindrical towers on more stable ground across the harbor. In 1923 lighthouse officials moved one of these iron towers to Nauset Beach, where it took the place of the famed Three Sisters Light.

Chatham Light
Lighthouse Digest

Chatham's exceptionally powerful flashing beacon can be seen from up to thirty miles at sea. Its distant twin tower at Nauset Beach displays an alternating white and red light with a range of about twenty miles.

> *Travel information:* Chatham's Main Street leads directly to the lighthouse. The light is open occasionally for tours. Contact the Chatham US Coast Guard Station at (508) 430-0628 or the Chatham Chamber of Commerce and Bassett House Visitors' Center at 2377 Main Street (Rte. 28), South Chatham, MA 02633; (508) 945-5199; www.chathaminfo.com. For the Nauset Beach Lighthouse, turn off US Highway 6 onto Brackett Road and follow signs to the beach. The tower and dwelling are closed to the public but can be viewed from the adjacent Cape Cod National Seashore parking lot. A short, paved walkway leads to the retired Three Sisters towers. For more information on the lights, Cape Cod, or the National Seashore, call (508) 255-3421.

■ NOBSKA POINT LIGHT ■
Woods Hole (1829 and 1876)

At Woods Hole near Cape Cod's far southwestern tip, the Nobska Light warns ships away from a pair of vicious shoals called the Hedge Fence and L'Hommedieu. The first lighthouse built here was a simple stone cottage with a lantern on top, but in 1876 the Lighthouse Board approved a new tower for the Nobska station. Its

Nobska Point Light

iron shell was built in a shipyard and brought to Woods Hole in four sections. Once in place, the forty-foot tower was lined with brick and fitted with the fourth-order Fresnel lens that still focuses its light. Sailors near the shoals see a red beacon, whereas those in safe water see a white one.

Travel information: The Nobska Lighthouse is located off Nobska Road in Woods Hole, south of Falmouth. The keeper's quarters is currently home for the Coast Guard commander of Sector South Eastern New England. Grounds remain open to the public; open house tours are available and conducted by United States Coast Guard Auxiliary Flotilla 11-2. For tour schedules and more information on the Chatham Lighthouse, see http:// a0131101.uscgaux.info.

▪ BASS RIVER (WEST DENNIS) LIGHT ▪
Hyannis (1855)

The Bass River Light is a prime illustration of the changing roles for lighthouses beginning in the late 1930s, when some lights were already being reduced because of advancing radar technology and others were allowed to be bought privately as surplus government property. Established in 1855 with a fifth-order Fresnel lens surmounted in a lantern room atop a two-story wood-framed house, the light served as a guide for local saltworks, fishing, small vessel building, and coastal trade into the Bass River.

When the light was decommissioned in 1880 upon the lighting of the Stage Harbor Lighthouse, a local captain was so disappointed that he took it upon himself to write his cousin, newly elected President James Garfield, to plea for the light's continuance. The wish was granted and the light continued from 1881 until mid-June 1914, when its lens was removed. A prominent Boston family bought and expanded the lighthouse. In 1938 State Senator Everett Stone purchased the property, and his family has run it as an elegant inn. It has survived damaging storms just as have the best of many American lighthouses.

In 1989, in tribute to National Lighthouse Day on August 7, a modern optic illuminated the lantern room once again as a private aid to navigation that operates seasonally, basically from Memorial Day through Columbus Day. The Lighthouse Inn also serves as a place for local third graders to learn more about maritime heritage.

Travel information: Contact the Lighthouse Inn, P.O. Box 128, 1 Lighthouse Inn Road, West Dennis, MA 02670; (508) 398-2244; www.lighthouse inn.com.

▪ BRANT POINT LIGHT ▪
Nantucket (1746, 1759, and 1901)

America's second-oldest lighthouse (after Boston) owes its existence to a town meeting held on Nantucket Island in 1746. Tired of seeing their whaling ships miss the Nantucket Harbor and pile up on nearby beaches, the island folk approved spending two hundred English pounds to construct a small wooden light tower. The little lighthouse burned to the ground several times during its more than 250 years of

Brant Point Light

service, but it was always rebuilt. Shining from a height of only twenty-six feet above the water, its occulting red light has a range of about ten miles.

Much more impressive, although not necessarily as historical, are the lighthouses at Great Neck, on Nantucket's northernmost point, and **Sankaty Head,** near the village of Siasconset. The aeromarine beacon atop the 1850 Sankaty Head Light tower is visible up to twenty-four miles at sea. The **Great Point Light** station dates back to 1748, but the existing rubble-stone tower was built in 1818. Its third-order Fresnel lens is still in use, its signature red light eclipsed every four seconds.

Travel information: A popular summer tourist destination, Nantucket Island can be reached by ferry from Hyannis. For fares and schedule contact Hy-Line Cruises, Ocean Street Dock, Hyannis, MA 02601; (508) 778-2600; http://hylinecruises.com. While on the island, don't miss the Nantucket Historial Society Whaling Museum; (508) 228-1894; www.nha .org. Although Nantucket mariners no longer hunt whales on the high seas, local shops and restaurants may turn you into one with their luxurious and delicious lobster, ice cream, and pastries.

■ SANKATY HEAD LIGHT ■
Nantucket Island (1850)

Perched atop a line of soaring cliffs, the seventy-foot brick tower of Sankaty Head Lighthouse dominates Nantucket Island's southeastern shore. Built in 1850, the tower was fitted with a Fresnel lens, the first in Massachusetts. For years this large second-order lens was rotated by a clockwork mechanism: as weights fell in yield to gravity, gears below the lens turned a table in the lantern room on which the lens rested. In 1950 the historical lens was replaced by a smaller modern optic. During the 1880s numerous improvements and repairs were done, including new iron watch and lantern rooms.

Great Point Light
US Coast Guard

But things started going downhill when in 1950 the Fresnel lens was removed and aerobeacons were installed. When the lantern room was removed during the 1960s, residents protested, and it was replaced. However, over the years, the very cliff that gave it easy recognition eroded out from under the tower; a storm in 1991 forced a "move it or lose it" situation. The 'Sconset Trust raised funds, and in October 2007 the light was relocated by move experts International Chimney, Inc., approximately four hundred feet back from the edge. The light remains in operation, shining out to sea with a focal plane at over 160 feet above sea level. The flashing white beacon can be seen from up to twenty-four miles away. The tower is not open to the public, but the grounds are open year-round.

Sankaty Head Light
Bob and Sandra Shanklin

Travel information: Nantucket can be reached via ferry from the Hyannis terminal on Cape Cod; (508) 771-4000. The light station is located off Baxter Road on the east side of the island. For more information on the tower restoration, contact the 'Sconset Trust, P.O. Box 821, Siasconset, MA 02564; (508) 228-9917; www.sconsettrust.org.

■ GAY HEAD LIGHT ■
Martha's Vineyard (1799 and 1856)

Of the several lighthouses on Martha's Vineyard, the oldest and most impressive is the one standing atop the color-streaked cliffs at Gay Head (Aquinnah). Built during the final year of the eighteenth century, the first lighthouse here was an eight-sided wooden structure. The existing brick tower was built in 1856. Because its approximately fifty-foot tower rises from the considerable height of a cliff, the lighthouse sends out a beam with a focal plane more than 170 feet above sea level. Mariners can see its alternating red and white beacon from up to twenty-five miles away.

Martha's Vineyard also boasts lighthouses at **West Chop** (1817 and 1891), **East Chop** (1878), **Edgartown Harbor** (1828 and 1881), and **Cape Poge** (1893) on the adjacent Chappaquiddick Island. In 1987 a skycrane lifted the erosion-threatened Cape Pogue Light tower and moved it several hundred feet inland.

Gay Head Light
Bob and Sandra Shanklin

Travel information: Ferries to Martha's Vineyard are available from Falmouth or Hyannis. For schedules and fares call the Woods Hole Steamship Authority at (508) 548-5011; www.steamshipauthority.com. Maintained by a modern-day steward, the lighthouse is open on a seasonal basis generally from June through September; for details, call the Martha's Vineyard Museum at (508) 627-4441; http://mvmuseum.org.

▪ EDGARTOWN HARBOR LIGHT ▪

Edgartown on Martha's Vineyard (1828 and 1881)

The forty-five-foot-tall, cast-iron tower that now marks Edgartown Harbor on Martha's Vineyard originally stood at Ipswich, well to the north of Boston. Constructed in 1881, it was pulled down and shipped to Edgartown in 1939. The relocated tower replaced the station's historic 1828 Cape Cod–style lighthouse, which had been so badly damaged by a hurricane in 1938 that the Coast Guard demolished the entire structure when it took over in 1939. Plans were to replace it with a skeleton tower beacon, but residents protested. Thus, the light from Crane's Beach was broken down and moved to its current location. Since 1856 a fourth-order Fresnel lens served this station and the mariners who

Edgartown Harbor Light
Bob and Sandra Shanklin

depended on its beacon to guide them to Edgartown. The classic lens was removed in 1988 and replaced by a modern optic. It is an active Coast Guard aid to navigation, its plastic lens flashing red every six seconds. Its steward is the Martha's Vineyard Museum.

Travel information: Martha's Vineyard can be reached by ferry from Falmouth or Hyannis; (508) 771-4000; www.steamshipauthority.com. Other ferries go to the Oak Bluff dock and Edgartown; transportation is available from Oak Bluff as well. The Vineyard Transit Authority buses drop off on

Church Street in Edgartown; it is a ten-minute walk to the lighthouse from this location. Major renovations have allowed the tower to be open on a seasonal schedule. For more information contact the Martha's Vineyard Museum at 59 School Street, P.O. Box 1310, Edgartown, MA 02539; (508) 627-4441; http://mvmuseum.org/edgartown.php.

■ BUTLER FLATS LIGHT ■
New Bedford (1898)

New Bedford was known as a huge whaling center in its heyday. Serving the famous maritime area, this spark plug lighthouse is located in the New Bedford outer harbor at the mouth of the Acushnet River. Its claim to fame is that it was designed by F. Hopkinson Smith, the engineer who built the foundation for the Statue of Liberty. The concrete-filled, cast-iron caisson supports a brick cylindrical tower, an anomaly among the caisson-style lighthouses, that was first lit in 1898 with a fifth-order Fresnel lens that still flashes a white light every four seconds. The light was added to the National Register of Historic Places in 1987. Summer was a pleasant time at the light, but winter's ice often shook the tower and everything inside. Riprap was added as a buffer to stop ice damage. Even President Grover Cleveland visited the light. This small but significant light is treasured by New Bedford residents.

Travel information: The light is not open to the public but can easily be seen from points along the New Bedford waterfront, especially from the pier near Fort Taber.

■ CLARK'S POINT LIGHT ■
New Bedford (1797, 1804, and 1869)

If a time-lapsed video could be had of this light, it would have been a very animated one. The original wooden version of this light was built by merchants to answer a need for increasing whaling traffic. That light burned; it was rebuilt in 1799. That tower was ceded to the new government around 1800, but it, too, succumbed to fire in 1803. Congress realized the importance of a light on the point in Buzzards Bay on the west side of the entrance to the Acushnet River into New Bedford Harbor and to the port. Therefore, an octagonal rubble-stone thirty-eight-foot-tall tower was erected in 1804. Improvements were added, including an additional four feet and a new lantern room in 1818.

Other improvements were made over the next four decades; however, Fort Taber, as it is known to locals instead of its later, official name "Fort Rodman," was built around the light so that the lantern barely peeked above the wall's height. To solve this issue a rectangular tower was built on the northerly part of the fort and the lantern from the old rubble-stone structure was transplanted to give it visibility. This final phase of the light's history ended in 1898 when the current Clark's Point Light went into action. Fast forward to 2001, when the light was revived by caring New Bedford residents. The top wooden portion of the light was rebuilt and a new lantern put in place. The light came back to life in an all-out gala celebration that included the New Bedford Symphony Orchestra and cannon fire from the fort.

Travel information: Take Route 18 in New Bedford to a traffic light at its southern end; turn left and continue straight for about two miles to Fort Taber Park and the Clark's Point Lighthouse. Although the fort and lighthouse are not open to the public, the fort's grounds are accessible, where good views of the lighthouse are to be had.

■ BORDEN FLATS LIGHT ■
Fall River (1881)

Set atop a massive, open-water caisson, the Borden Flats Lighthouse points the way to Fall River, home of Lizzie Borden. Because she was a member of the prominent Borden family, the light was named for her on its completion in 1881. Some years later the famous New England spinster was charged with murdering her parents with an axe. Although she was acquitted, her story continues to fascinate murder-mystery fans. The lighthouse is still an active aid to navigation with a four-second white flash, which then goes dark briefly. It was originally equipped with a fourth-order Fresnel lens that was replaced by a modern optic in 1977.

Travel information: Though not open to the public, the light can be seen along the Fall River waterfront, especially from the Borden Light Marina. While in the area, be sure to visit the Marine Museum at Fall River, which has one of the best collections of RMS *Titanic* artifacts and memorabilia.

RHODE ISLAND

▪ NEWPORT HARBOR LIGHT (GOAT ISLAND) ▪
Newport (1823 and 1842)

Two different lighthouses have stood on Newport's Goat Island. Its deep-water port made it a popular part of the Triangle Trade of slaves in the West Indies for sugar and molasses, then used for rum in Newport. The original 1823 tower remained active until after a new tower was completed; it was eventually relocated to Prudence Island (Sandy Point) in 1851 and remains active. A new thirty-five-foot octagonal granite structure was built on the breakwater in 1838 but wasn't lighted until 1842, upon the completion of the bulkhead. Its fifth-order Fresnel lens has been replaced by a modern optic but continues to produce a fixed green light. Many lighthouses have survived gales and high water. This one, however, also survived being rammed by a World War I–vintage US submarine in 1922. This accident destroyed the old keeper's dwelling.

Also in Newport are the **Castle Hill Lighthouse** (1890) and **Lime Rock Lighthouse** (1854). The famous lighthouse keeper Ida Lewis lived and served at the latter station for more than half a century. Having rescued at least half a dozen drowning sailors, children, and even a hapless sheep from the icy waters off Lyme Rock, Lewis found herself on the cover of *Harper's Weekly* in 1869. Later that same year she played host to President Ulysses S. Grant.

Travel information: The lighthouse is on Goat Island and remains an active aid to navigation; owned by the Coast Guard, it is leased to the Friends of Newport Harbor Lighthouse, a chapter of the American Lighthouse Foundation. The tower is near historical downtown Newport; although the lighthouse is closed to the public, it is adjacent to the Hyatt Regency Newport. Visitors are allowed to walk the grounds that are reached by walking through the hotel lobby—it's a good idea to tell the staff that you want to visit the lighthouse. The still-active **Castle Hill Lighthouse** is reached via a short trail from the Castle Hill Cove Marina. The old **Lime Rock Lighthouse,** now home of the Ida Lewis Yacht Club, is located off Wellington Avenue.

From Bristol, north of Newport, one can take a twenty-minute ferry ride across to Prudence Island and see the active **Sandy Point (Prudence Island) Lighthouse** (1852), with its birdcage lantern and working modern optic, originally a fourth-order Fresnel lens. For ferry schedules call (401) 253-9808.

■ ROSE ISLAND LIGHT ■
Newport (1870)

The lofty suspension tow-
ers and bright lights of the
Newport Bridge, completed in
1969, made the century-old
Rose Island Light redundant.
The Coast Guard discontinued it in 1971, and the fine
old combination tower and
dwelling might have been
torn down except for the tireless efforts of Newport preservationists. Located on a
small island just south of the
bridge, the station has been

Rose Island Light

handsomely refurbished and relit as a private aid to navigation. It was built on the
remains of what was planned to become eighteenth-century Fort Hamilton, which
was never finished or garrisoned.

   The architecture of the lighthouse is much like several that were built during
this time. A lighthouse tower rises from the side of the mansard roof on top of a
one-and-one-half-story wooden keeper's quarters. The lighthouse is thirty-five feet
tall, and its focal plane is forty-eight feet above the water.

> *Travel information:* Newport harbor cruises nearly always feature a close
> look at the Rose Island Lighthouse. In summer the Newport and Jamestown
> ferry travels between Jamestown and Newport and will stop at Rose Island
> on request. For ferry information, call (401) 423-9900. For tours or to stay
> overnight in the lighthouse—a unique opportunity to sample the life of a
> lighthouse keeper—contact the Rose Island Lighthouse Foundation, P.O. Box
> 1419, Newport, RI 02840; (401) 847-4242; www.roseislandlighthouse.org.

■ POMHAM ROCKS LIGHT ■
Providence (1871)

No longer active, the combination residence and tower clings to an exposed rock
beside the main Providence shipping channel. Its architecture of an octagonal tower
extending above a mansard roof of the keeper's house is similar to several built
at this time, including Rose Island Lighthouse. Its fourth-order Fresnel lens was
removed when the station was discontinued in 1974. Nowadays the station is owned
by the American Lighthouse Foundation.

> *Travel information:* Unfortunately, this interesting structure is closed to
> the public and very difficult to see from any convenient vantage point in
> Providence. You may catch a glimpse of it from Route 103 or at the East
> Bay Bike Path in East Providence between Washington Road and Narra-
> gansett Avenue. **Warwick Lighthouse** (1826 and 1932), is in Warwick, off

Route 117 southwest of Providence. Its occulting green light every four seconds remains active. However, the station houses Coast Guard personnel and is not accessible to the public. Although views are possible from the end of Warwick Neck Avenue, it is best to find a way to view it from the water.

Pomham Rocks Light

■ BEAVERTAIL LIGHT ■
Jamestown (1749 and 1856)

America's third-oldest light station marks the entrance to Newport Harbor and Narragansett. During the 1600s notorious pirate Captain William Kidd used this area as a hideout. Captured by the British in Boston, he was eventually hanged. A century later the British would treat the Beavertail Lighthouse as roughly as they had Captain Kidd, burning it when they abandoned Newport Harbor during the Revolutionary War.

The existing fifty-two-foot square granite tower dates back to 1856. A modern optic replaced its classic fourth-order Fresnel lens in 1991 and emits a flashing white signal.

Beavertail Light

Travel information: This particularly historical and scenic lighthouse is located in Beavertail State Park, reached via East Shore Road off Route 138. The keeper's dwelling now serves as a museum. Contact the Beavertail Lighthouse Museum, P.O. Box 83, Jamestown, RI 02835; (401) 423-3270; www.beavertaillight.org.

■ POINT JUDITH LIGHT ■
Point Judith (1810, 1816, and 1857)

A crude wooden tower, Point Judith's first light tower was blown over by a gale in 1815. Its replacement, completed the following year, was built with stone. The existing fifty-one-foot octagonal granite-block tower was completed in 1857. One of the earliest of America's flashing beacons, its lamps and reflectors were at one time rotated by a clockwork mechanism powered by 288-pound weights. A fourth-order Fresnel lens installed here before the Civil War remains in service.

Point Judith Light

Travel information: The station can be reached off US Highway 1 via Route 108 and Ocean Road. Visitors are welcome to walk the grounds. A convenient inn with easy access to area historical sites and less than three miles from Point Judith Lighthouse and next to the Block Island ferry is Lighthouse Inn of Galilee, 307 Great Island Road, Narragansett, Rhode Island 02882; (401) 789-9341; www.lighthouse-inn-ri.com.

▪ WATCH HILL LIGHT ▪
Watch Hill, a Village of Westerly (1808 and 1857)

In this old seafaring community, the first tower at Watch Hill was used as a lookout with a simple beacon for possible invasion from the sea during King George's War (1744–48). It was destroyed in a storm in 1781. The first true lighthouse here was authorized by President Thomas Jefferson and came into existence in 1808, when a local carpenter erected a round wooden tower

Watch Hill Light

and fitted it out with whale-oil lamps. In 1857 the Lighthouse Board had a square, fifty-one-foot granite tower and attached dwelling built; they equipped the tower with a fourth-order Fresnel lens. An automated modern lens serves the station now and exhibits alternating white and red flashes every two and a half seconds.

Travel information: From US Highway 1 take Route 1A to Avondale and then Watch Hill Road. The station is located at the end of Lighthouse

Road, actually a narrow, paved drive leading off Larkin Road just beyond the village. There is a small museum on site, containing the station's original Fresnel lens. Contact Watch Hill Lighthouse Museum, Watch Hill, RI 02891; www.watchhilllighthousekeepers.org. Since there is no parking near the light station, visitors must park in the village and walk about fifteen minutes to reach the grounds and museum.

■ BLOCK ISLAND SOUTHEAST LIGHT ■
Block Island (1875)

This red-brick octagonal tower and attached Victorian/Gothic residence built in 1875 looks like the setting for a nineteenth-century romance novel or, perhaps, a vampire yarn. After lording over Block Island's Monhegan Bluffs for more than a century, however, the historical lighthouse became the focus of a different sort of drama. By 1990 galloping erosion had eaten the high, crumbling bluffs away to within a few feet of the structure's foundation. To keep

Block Island Southeast Light
Bob and Sandra Shanklin

it from tumbling into the sea, preservationists raised almost $2 million to have the venerable building moved to safety. Lifted by jacks onto rollers, the two-thousand-ton lighthouse was pushed back several hundred feet and out of harm's way. It has earned the prestigious title of National Historic Landmark.

Although the tower is only sixty-seven feet tall, the height of the cliffs places the light a whopping 260 feet above sea level. This helps give its first-order Fresnel lens a range of more than twenty miles. The lens in use here today at one time served in North Carolina's **Cape Lookout Lighthouse.**

Travel information: Block Island is a page out of America's past. To visit its quaint inns, shops, and lighthouses, you must take a ferry from New London, Connecticut; Montauk, New York; or Point Judith, Rhode Island. Call Interstate Navigation for a ferry from Point Judith at (401) 783-7996; www.blockislandferry.com. From the ferry dock on the island, it is about a thirty-minute walk to the **Block Island Southeast Lighthouse.** Alternatively, you may take a bike or call a taxi. Inside the lighthouse is a small museum/gift shop; tours are offered in summer. The light is an active aid to navigation. Grounds and museum are cared for by the Block Island Southeast Lighthouse Foundation; you may write to the foundation at P.O. Box 949, Block Island, RI 02807, or call (401) 466-5009.

■ BLOCK ISLAND NORTH LIGHT ■
Block Island (1875)

On the opposite side of the six-mile-long Block Island is the **Block Island North Lighthouse** (1867), a fifty-foot-tall granite building on Sandy Point. Three earlier lighthouses stood on the point, two of them rare double-towered structures. The existing lighthouse was decommissioned in 1973, its role of guiding mariners taken over by a nearby skeleton tower. At that time the US Fish and Wildlife Service took over the tower and grounds, which became a wildlife refuge. In 1984 the Town of

Block Island North Light
Bob and Sandra Shanklin

New Shoreham gained ownership of the tower, and extensive renovation work was accomplished by the hard work of the North Light Commission. The fourth-order Fresnel lens has been restored to the lantern room and continues to operate as a private aid to navigation. For more information contact the North Light Commission at P.O. Box 220, Block Island, RI 02807; (401) 466-3213; www.new-shoreham .com.

CONNECTICUT

■ STONINGTON HARBOR LIGHT ■
Stonington (1823 and 1840)

The thirty-five-foot stone tower and dwelling marking Stonington Harbor, completed in 1840, replaced an earlier structure undercut by erosion. The existing station served until 1889, when it was decommissioned. A new twenty-five-foot cast-iron lighthouse had been erected on a breakwater in Stonington Harbor that year, and the old lighthouse became outdated. As all things change with time, a skeleton tower replaced the breakwater light in 1926. Old buildings are venerated in New England, as is this one, which serves nowadays as a historical museum, cared for since 1925 by the Stonington Historical Society, P.O. Box 103, Stonington, CT 06378; (860) 535-8445; http://stonington history.org.

Stonington Harbor Light
William Kaufhold

Not far to the west of Stonington along US Highway 1 is the well-known Mystic Seaport, a living maritime-history museum with its own operating lighthouse—a replica of the Brant Point tower on Nantucket.

Travel information: Stonington and its historical museum are on Route 1A, near the eastern extremity of coastal Connecticut. Mystic Seaport is just off Interstate 95 and US Highway 1 in the town of Mystic. Its old whaling ships, shops, maritime exhibits, and the **Mystic Seaport Lighthouse** (replica) are well worth the admission fee. The museum offers a river and harbor cruise, which provides a glimpse of the distinctive **Morgan Point Lighthouse** (1868), now a private residence.

■ NEW LONDON HARBOR LIGHT ■
New London (1761 and 1801)

When the whale-oil lamps of the first New London Lighthouse were lit in 1761, only three other light towers marked the coasts of colonial America. When the existing structure replaced the original sixty-foot stone tower, nearly two generations later, America still had only a few lighthouses. Now approaching its third century of service, the gracefully tapered eighty-foot-tall stone tower still employs its 1857

Mystic Seaport Light

New London Harbor Light   *New London Ledge Light*

fourth-order Fresnel with its flash characteristic of three seconds white alternating with three seconds darkness, with a red sector. Interestingly, the original station was financed by a public lottery.

 Marking a dangerous shoal near the harbor entrance is the remarkable **New London Ledge Lighthouse** (1909). Its French Empire architecture is more suggestive of an old-money aristocratic townhome than a hardworking lighthouse. This still active station displays a white and red beacon, as does the much older harbor lighthouse. It reputedly has a resident ghost, that of a former keeper who, forsaken by his wife, jumped to his death from the tower.

Travel information: You can see the New London Harbor Lighthouse from Pequot Avenue near Ocean Beach. The dwelling and grounds are privately owned and closed to the public. For more information: New London Maritime Society, 150 Bank Street, New London, CT 06320; (860) 447-2501; www.nlmaritimesociety.org. The **New London Ledge Lighthouse** is difficult to see from the shore. The best view is from onboard a Block Island Express ferry: Block Island Express, 2 Ferry Street, P.O. Box 33, New London, CT 06320; Connecticut Phone (860) 444-4624; Rhode Island Phone (401) 466-2212; www.goblockisland.com. The US Coast Guard Academy, reached via Briggs Street and Monhegan Avenue in New London, is well worth a visit, especially as it contains a fine first-order Fresnel lens. Also worth seeing is the **Avery Point Light** (1944), located on the Avery Point Campus of the University of Connecticut in Groton. The modest Avery Point tower was built by the Coast Guard to honor America's lighthouse keepers. Although it was discontinued in 1967, it was relighted in 2006 and continues as an active aid to navigation, flashing green every four seconds.

■ LYNDE POINT LIGHT (OLD SAYBROOK INNER LIGHT) ■
Old Saybrook/Fenwick (1803 and 1838)

Lynde Point Light
Kraig Anderson

Thomas Jefferson was president when the whale-oil lamps of the Lynde Point Light station were first lit in 1803. The original octagonal wooden structure stood until 1838, then was replaced by the existing sixty-five-foot dressed-stone tower. Although automated today, the station's classic fifth-order Fresnel lens remains in operation, sending out a fixed white light with a range of fourteen miles.

Located about three thousand feet from the Lynde Point Light at the end of a nearby stone jetty extending into the Connecticut River is the **Saybrook Breakwater Lighthouse** (Saybrook Outer Light) (1886). The fifty-foot cast-iron tower resembles a giant chess rook. A plastic lens focuses its flashing green light every six seconds, warning vessels away from a sandbar at the mouth of the river.

Travel information: From US Highway 1 in Old Saybrook, follow Route 154 to the gracious, old-time residential community of Fenwick. Both lighthouses are closed to the public but can be seen from Route 154. Various Connecticut River cruises provide fine views of these and other lighthouses; contact the Old Saybrook Chamber of Commerce at (860) 388-3266; www .oldsaybrookchamber.com. Sunbeam Fleet in Waterford, Connecticut, offers cruises for seeing area lighthouses; (860) 443-7259; www.sunbeamfleet.com.

■ FAULKNER'S ISLAND LIGHT ■
Near Guilford (1802)

Local preservationists are struggling to save what remains of this venerable light station that lies more than three miles offshore, but they face a significant challenge. Ravaged by fire in 1876 that destroyed the keeper's house and damaged the tower, Connecticut's second-oldest lighthouse, and the only one operational on an island, is now threatened by erosion—interestingly enough, made worse by burrowing rabbits. The octagonal fieldstone structure was built in 1802 to guide coasting vessels and warn them away from ship-killing rocks lying just off the mainland.

Travel information: Faulkner's Island, owned by the US Fish and Wildlife Service, is now a bird sanctuary within the Stewart B. McKinney National Wildlife Refuge. The light remains an active US Coast Guard aid to navigation. There is no regular access to the public. Those interested in Faulkner's Island preservation efforts should contact Faulkner's Light Brigade, P.O. Box 444, Guilford, CT 06437; (203) 453-8400; www.lighthouse .cc/FLB.

■ SOUTHWEST LEDGE LIGHT ■
New Haven (1877)

Built in a Baltimore shipyard, the Southwest Ledge tower was exhibited at the 1876 Centennial Exposition before being shipped to Connecticut and put into service one year later. The forty-five-foot steel cylinder stands on a concrete-and-steel caisson at the end of New Haven's east breakwater at the entrance to New Haven Harbor; it was considered an admirable engineering feat. Its flashing red light every five seconds, produced by a plastic lens, remains active.

Southwest Ledge Light
Kraig Anderson

The centerpiece of New Haven's Lighthouse Park is the **Five Mile Point Lighthouse** (New Haven Harbor), built in 1805 and rebuilt in 1847 and decommissioned in 1877 when the Southwest Ledge Light became active. Although out of service for more than a century, the tower has survived the ravages of time and urban growth.

Travel information: From Interstate 95 follow Townsend Avenue and then Lighthouse Road to Lighthouse Park, which is open all year during daylight hours. The Southwest Ledge Lighthouse is more than a mile from shore but can be seen from the New Haven waterfront at Lighthouse Point Park. For more information contact the Lighthouse Point Park rangers at (203) 946-8790; www.cityofnewhaven.com/parks/ranger/eastshore.asp.

Five Mile Point Light
William Kaufhold

■ STRATFORD SHOAL LIGHT (MIDDLEGROUND LIGHT) ■

Bridgeport (1877)

A rocky shoal lurks just beneath the surface of Long Island Sound, about halfway between Bridgeport, Connecticut, and the shores of Long Island. Over the centuries it has claimed the vessels of many unwary seamen who expected to find relative safety in the sound. In 1837 the Lighthouse Service marked the shoal with a lightship and then, in the mid-1870s, with a permanent lighthouse.

Completed in 1877, the Stratford Shoal Lighthouse stands on a concrete-filled caisson built atop a foundation of granite blocks held together with iron staples. The caisson serves as a platform for the Victorian-style dwelling with attached tower. The station's aeromarine beacon displays a flashing white light every five seconds that is easily seen from both shores.

To the north is the now inactive **Stratford Point Lighthouse,** flashing from a thirty-five-foot brick tower built in 1881. A few miles away, marking the Bridgeport Harbor with a flashing green light, stands the diminutive twenty-one-foot tower of the **Tongue Point Lighthouse** (1895). To the west, near Fairfield, is the **Penfield Reef Lighthouse,** an Empire-style combination tower and dwelling built in 1874. Its flashing red light every six seconds warns vessels away from a collection of jagged rocks known locally as "the Cows."

Stratford Shoal Light
Lighthouse Digest

Travel information: The **Stratford Shoal Lighthouse** cannot be seen easily from land but can be viewed from the decks of ferries that link Bridgeport to Long Island (Port Jefferson): (888) 443-3779; www.88844ferry .com. **Stratford Point Lighthouse** is located on Prospect Drive, off Route 113 near the Bridgeport Airport. You can view **Tongue Point Lighthouse** from Bridgeport's Sound View Drive. The **Penfield Reef Lighthouse** can be seen from Calf Pasture Park in Fairfield. Seaside Park in Bridgeport also provides a view of the Penfield Reef station as well as access to the historical, but no longer active, **Black Rock Harbor Lighthouse** (Fayerweather Island Light) (1823). The grounds of this light are accessible. For more information: Fayerweather Island Restoration Fund, c/o Burroughs Community Center, 2470 Fairfield Avenue, Bridgeport, CT 06605; (203) 334-0293; www.burroughscc.org.

■ SHEFFIELD ISLAND LIGHT ■
Norwalk (1827 and 1868)

Established in 1827 and rebuilt in 1868, this handsome, two-story stone dwelling and steeplelike tower served as a lighthouse until 1900. Restored and cared for by the Norwalk Seaport Association, the old lighthouse is now open to the public.

Travel information: Summer excursions to Sheffield Island, now a wildlife refuge, are available. Contact the Norwalk Seaport Association, 132 Water Street, South Norwalk, CT 06854; call (203) 838-9444 or for ferry tickets, call (800) 838-3006, or see www.seaport .org. From Sheffield Island or Norwalk's Crescent Beach, you can see the alternating red and white flash of **Green's Ledge Lighthouse** (1902). To the west is the privately owned **Stamford Harbor Lighthouse** (1882).

Sheffield Island Light
William Kaufhold

NEW YORK

▪ RACE ROCK LIGHT ▪
Near Fishers Island (1879)

Built at great expense and through almost superhuman effort during the late 1870s, this lighthouse marks an extraordinarily dangerous shoal known as Race Rock Reef. Strong currents rushing back and forth between Long Island Sound and the Atlantic make this area a nightmare for seamen. Building a lighthouse over the wave-swept shoal was thought impossible, but the government finally took on the project. Construction crews labored for years to build up an artificial island of concrete and stone. On this they erected a granite dwelling and attached square tower. On Febru-

Race Rock Light
Bob and Sandra Shanklin

ary 21, 1879, eight years and $278,716 after work began, the Race Rock Light split the night for the first time, sixty-seven feet above the water. The flashing red signal still warns mariners away from the shoals; its pulse is visible from a distance of up to twenty miles.

The Gothic-like architecture of this lighthouse is a perfect backdrop to stories of its haunted nature. Coast Guard keepers have reported feeling an old Lighthouse Service keeper brush past them on the stairs to the lantern room.

> *Travel information:* Whereas Race Rock Lighthouse can be reached only by water, you can see it from Watch Hill, Rhode Island, and several points along the Connecticut coast. Ferries operating between New London, Connecticut, and Block Island or Orient Point on Long Island often pass within sight of the station. For schedule and fares call the Block Island ferry, (401) 783-4613; www.blockislandferry.com. The Race Rock Lighthouse Foundation is working for restoration of this lighthouse; see www.longisland lighthouses.com/racerock.htm.

▪ MONTAUK POINT LIGHT ▪
Montauk, Long Island (1797)

President George Washington personally ordered construction of the Montauk Point Lighthouse at the strategic far-eastern tip of Long Island. Washington's successor, John Adams, was in office when the project was completed in 1797. The

Montauk Point Light

sandstone tower and adjacent two-story dwelling cost $22,300, a sizable fortune at the time. The young United States government got its money's worth, however—the still operational seventy-eight-foot tower has now passed its two-hundredth birthday and is the oldest lighthouse in the state.

The station's flashing white light, produced originally by a three-and-a-half-order bivalve Fresnel lens, is now created by an aeromarine beacon that shines out toward the open Atlantic from a height of 168 feet above the water.

Cedar Island Light
Bob and Sandra Shanklin

Its guidance is heartily welcomed by seamen, none of whom want to come near the killing sands and surf of Montauk, where ships have been known to "melt away like butter." Unfortunately, that is not all that has melted away over two centuries: over two hundred feet of the bluff on which the lighthouse rests has been washed to sea. Well-planned erosion control methods have helped to stabilize the situation.

Travel information: The lighthouse is next to Montauk State Park at the end of Route 27. To reach the lighthouse, travel through town and go as far east as possible. Since 1987, when the last resident keepers left the station, the dwelling has served as a maritime museum, where visitors may view fascinating historical exhibits and a marvelous array of Fresnel lenses and other lighting devices. Contact Montauk Point Lighthouse Museum, P.O. Box 112, Montauk, NY 11954; or the Montauk Historical Society, which owns and

maintains the lighthouse, at (631) 668-2544; www.montauklighthouse
.com/society.htm. About 25 miles to the east in Cedar Point County Park,
off Route 27, is the granite block **Cedar Island (Cedar Point) Lighthouse**
(1868), abandoned since 1934. Preservation efforts are ongoing by the
Long Island Chapter of the US Lighthouse Society and the Suffolk County
Department of Parks, Recreation, and Conservation. The Cedar Point
County Park is a nice stopover and on the way to **Montauk Point Lighthouse.** The entire area is known as a birder's paradise. The historical villages
of Sag Harbor and East Hampton are also nearby.

■ ORIENT POINT LIGHT ■
Orient Point (1899)

A caisson-type structure, sometimes described as a "coffeepot"
light, Orient Point Lighthouse
marks Oyster Point Reef on the
western side of Plum Gut, one of
Long Island's most feared navigational obstacles. Completed in
1899 on the farthest point east
on Long Island's North Fork, the
tower took two years to build and
cost $30,000, six times the origi-
nal estimate. Keepers in the past
lived and worked in the cramped
cast-iron tower, only twenty-one

Orient Point Light

feet in diameter at the base. Automated since 1954, the station warns vessels away
from the reef with a flashing white light, visible from up to seventeen miles.

Travel information: You can see the Orient Point "coffeepot" Lighthouse
from the ferry landing at the end of Route 25. The church-and-steeple-style
Plum Island Lighthouse (1869), which is no longer active, is visible to the
east of the landing. The ferry that provides passage to New London, Connecticut, offers an excellent view of both lighthouses. On the way across the
sound, passengers also get a look at the impressive eighty-foot granite-block
Little Gull Island Lighthouse (1869); its second-order Fresnel lens is now
on display at the East End Seaport Maritime Museum in Greenport. For
schedules and fares call (860) 443-5281 or (631) 323-2525, or see www.long
islandferry.com. The North Fork area hosts an array of wineries and other
historical sites.

■ HORTON POINT LIGHT ■
Southold (1790 and 1857)

George Washington identified Horton Point as the likely site of a lighthouse while
still a young military officer serving in the French and Indian War. Years later,

as president, Washington helped fulfill his own prophecy by commissioning a lighthouse for the point. The fifty-five-foot granite tower that stands here today, however, was built in 1857. It remains in service, its flashing green light reaching out across Long Island Sound from a total height of just over one hundred feet above the water.

Horton Point Light
William Kaufhold

Travel information: From Route 48 in Southold, turn north onto Sound View Avenue and follow the signs to Horton Point Lighthouse Museum. The keeper's dwelling houses this excellent museum filled with nautical artifacts; contact the Southhold Historical Society at (631) 765-5500 or www.southoldhistoricalsociety.org/lighthouse .htm. To reach the lighthouse and museum, which are open on weekends, call (631) 765-2101. A few miles east, at the entrance to Orient Harbor, is the **Long Beach Bar Lighthouse** (1993), a replica of the original 1870 screw-pile lighthouse that burned to the ground in 1963. It can be seen from several points in the town of Orient, all in the North Fork area.

■ OLD FIELD POINT LIGHT ■
Stony Brook (1824 and 1869)

This lighthouse marks one of several fingers of land that stretch northward to menace shipping in Long Island Sound. The granite combination tower and dwelling seen here at present was completed in 1869. Its stone churchlike architecture is similar to **Plum Island** and **Block Island North** and others in the New England area. It replaced an earlier, though similar, structure that had served since 1824. The station was deactivated in 1933, but it was relighted in 1991 and remains an active aid to navigation.

Old Field Point Light
Bob and Sandra Shanklin

Travel information: The lighthouse houses the town offices of its owner, the Village of Old Field. Although the tower is closed to the public, it can be reached by driving two and a half miles due north of the village to the light station's gates. Parking inside the gates is allowed, and visitors may walk the grounds. Another good view is from aboard the Bridgeport (CT) to Port Jefferson ferry; for schedules and fares, call (631) 473-0286 or go to www.88844ferry.com.

■ FIRE ISLAND LIGHT ■
Fire Island (1826 and 1858)

In 1850 the freighter *Elizabeth* struck a shoal and sank almost in the shadow of the Fire Island Lighthouse, which had guided shipping along the south shore of Long Island for almost twenty-five years. Sea captains had long complained that the seventy-four-foot light tower was too short to give adequate warning of the shoals. The tragic loss of the *Elizabeth,* along with most of her crew, brought a general public outcry, to which Congress quickly responded. The entire Lighthouse Service was soon under close scrutiny, and a Lighthouse Board was formed to revamp the nation's sadly deteriorated system of navigational lights.

The Lighthouse Board approved the construction of a new brick tower more than twice as high as the original. When completed in 1858, it stood 180 feet above the island sands. Focused by a first-order Fresnel lens, the light could now warn mariners as far as twenty-five miles from the coast. This light is recorded in many immigrants' journals as being their first sight of America.

Long ago the station's flashing white beacon earned it the nickname "Winking Woman." The lighthouse stopped winking in 1974, when the station was decommissioned. Rapidly deteriorating, the abandoned lighthouse was on the point of being demolished when a local preservation society came to the rescue. Happily, it has been restored to its appearance as it was in 1939 and relighted, and it is now a prime seashore attraction. The residence serves as a visitor center and maritime museum. The lighthouse is within the Fire Island National Seashore and is owned by the National Park Service; the Fire Island Lighthouse Preservation Society, in an agreement with the park, took over maintenance and operation of the lighthouse and keeper's quarters in 1996, as well as ownership and maintenance of the beacon, which remains an active aid to navigation.

Travel information: From Route 27A take the Robert Moses Parkway onto Fire Island, and follow signs to parking for the lighthouse. Contact the Fire Island Lighthouse Preservation Society, 4640 Captree Island, Captree Island, NY 11702; call (631) 661-4876, or see www.fireislandlighthouse.com.

■ EATON'S NECK LIGHT ■
Asharoken (1799)

One of only a handful of surviving eighteenth-century light towers, Long Island's Eaton's Neck Lighthouse near Asharoken remains in operation after more than two hundred years of service. Established to guide ships through the western reaches of Long Island Sound, it dates back to the administration of John Adams, the nation's second president. Constructed of fieldstone, it was lined with protective walls of brick during the years following the Civil War. The station's Winslow Lewis Argand

Fire Island Light
William Kaufhold

lamp-and-reflector system gave way in 1858 to a third-order Fresnel lens. That same fine old lens still shines from a height of 144 feet above the waters of the sound. Its fixed white light can be seen from about eighteen miles away.

Incredibly, during the late 1960s, the Coast Guard announced plans to pull down this historical tower. Thanks to the pleas of local preservationists and lighthouse lovers nationwide, it was saved from the wrecking ball.

Eaton's Neck Light
Bob and Sandra Shanklin

Travel information: Despite its historical nature and presence on the National Register of Historic Places, the Eaton's Neck Light station is not readily open to visitors. You can get special permission to visit, however, by contacting the US Coast Guard Station, Eaton's Neck, Northport, NY 11768; call (631) 261-6959. The **Huntington Harbor Lighthouse** (1912) in nearby Lloyd Harbor, New York, can be seen from the Lloyd Harbor Road. To the west, near the terminus of Long Island Sound, are the **Execution Rocks Light** (1850), located off Sands Point on Long Island, and **Stepping Stones Light** (1877), located off Kings Point.

■ CONEY ISLAND LIGHT (NORTON POINT) ■
Brooklyn (1890)

This distinctly blue-collar lighthouse was assigned the task of guiding New York City garbage barges to the watery dumps in the Atlantic. Established in 1890, the light also guided hulking iron freighters to their Coney Island loading docks.

The sixty-eight-foot tower consists of a central cylinder crowned by a gallery and lantern room and braced by four steel legs. Originally, this workmanlike structure operated as the rear member of a pair of range lights. The front-range light was taken out of service shortly before the turn of the last century, but the rear-range light remains in operation to this day, displaying a flashing red light visible more than fifteen miles away.

Travel information: From Interstate 278 follow the Prospect Parkway and Ocean Parkway to Coney Island. The lighthouse is on Surf Avenue between Forty-Sixth and Forty-Seventh Avenues in the community of Seagate. The fourth-order Fresnel lens, which focused the Coney Island Light until the station was automated in 1989, is on display in the South Street Seaport Museum in Lower Manhattan. Another attraction of this famous maritime museum is the lightship *Ambrose* (Number 87), launched in 1907. For more information call (212) 748-8600; or go to www.seany.com.

Coney Island Light
US Coast Guard

Ambrose *Lightship*
US Coast Guard

■ ROBBINS REEF LIGHT ■
New York City (Staten Island) (1839 and 1883)

A coffeepot-style, cast-iron tower, the exist-ing Robbins Reef Lighthouse replaced an earlier stone structure in 1883. Located on a massive stone pier in the middle of the main channel through the Upper New York Bay, the light remains active, guiding vessels in and out of the great city's busy harbor. The original fourth-order Fresnel lens was replaced by a modern optic when the station was automated in 1966. This offshore light-house is famous for keeper Kate Walker, who took over the job from her husband when he died in 1885 and faithfully watched the light for the next thirty-four years. Walker han-dled even the most physically taxing keeper's chores unassisted, and she is credited with saving as many as seventy-five lives.

Robbins Reef Light
Bob and Sandra Shanklin

Travel information: The best way to see this lighthouse is from the decks of the Staten Island ferry; (718) 727-2508; www.siferry.com.

■ STATUE OF LIBERTY ■
New York (1886)

Dedicated in 1886 and commissioned as a harbor light that same year, the Statue of Liberty is probably the world's most famous lighthouse. The light in the bronze lady's torch guided ships in and out of the harbor for many years and is still hailed as a guiding light by many landlubbers. The lady herself is 151 feet tall; she lifts her lamp a spectacular 305 feet above the ground, making this one of America's loftiest navigational lights. Particularly hardy visitors may choose to climb the 354 steps leading to the statue's crown. Those who pay homage to Lady Liberty owe much of their deep attachment to her to Emma Lazarus's famous inscription on the pedes-tal: ". . . Give me your tired, your poor,/Your huddled masses yearning to breathe free/. . . Send these, the homeless, tempest-tossed to me, I lift my lamp beside the golden door!"

Travel information: The ferry to Liberty Island and its statue leaves from Battery Park at the lower tip of Manhattan. Passengers can also view the cast-iron coffeepot-style **Robbins Reef Lighthouse** (1849). Its flashing green light remains in operation. For more information on Statue of Liberty National Monument ticket reservations, call (877) 523-9849, or see www.nps.gov/stli; for ferry schedules, call (201) 604-2800, or see www.statuecruises.com.

Statue of Liberty
Lighthouse Digest

■ JEFFREY'S HOOK LIGHT ■
New York City (1921)

There may be no greater architectural contrast than that presented by New York's
"little red lighthouse" beside the Hudson
and the mighty George Washington Bridge
soaring overhead. Originally, this small
cast-iron lighthouse stood on Sandy Hook,
New Jersey, in 1880. Its flashing red light
guided ships until it was declared outmoded and subsequently dismantled in
1917. It was reconstructed in 1921 on Jeffrey's Hook and became an important navigational aid on the Hudson River for heavy
river traffic. When the George Washington
Bridge opened in 1931, the diminutive
lighthouse's humble flash was overshadowed by the many and bright lights of the
bridge's massive, 3,500-foot central span,
again rendering the lighthouse outdated.
In 1948 the Coast Guard decommissioned
the lighthouse, and its lamp was extin-

Jeffrey's Hook Light
William Kaufhold

guished. The Coast Guard intended to auction off the tower as scrap metal and
would have done so if not for the public outcry, raised in part by publication of
Hildegarde Hoyt Swift's classic children's book *The Little Red Lighthouse and the Great
Gray Bridge*. The Jeffrey's Hook structure still stands as a sort of monument to the
little and forgotten things of this world.

> *Travel information:* The long-abandoned tower, kept painted bright red
> and cared for by a partnership between the New York City Urban Park
> Rangers and the New York Historic House Trust within the New York City
> Department of Parks and Recreation, stands directly under the George
> Washington Bridge on the Manhattan side of the Hudson. Take the Fort
> Washington exit off Riverside Drive. For tours call the city parks depart-
> ment at (212) 304-2365.

■ RONDOUT CREEK LIGHT ■
Kingston (1837, 1867, and 1915)

The Hudson River used to have as many lighthouses as some entire coastal states.
One of the best known marked the harbor entrance at the mouth of Rondout
Creek of the inland port city of Kingston. The Rondout was the point at which vast
amounts of Pennsylvania coal being transported from northeastern Pennsylvania to
the Hudson River were lightered from large canal barges to smaller river barks that
floated the coal to New York City. Boats often left the Rondout with passengers and
cargo headed for the big city.

The first light station was established here in 1837; a simple wooden construction, it didn't last long in harsh elements. A second lighthouse was constructed in 1867 of bluestone with a cut stone base; crumbling, it was razed in 1954. Built on a new site, farther from the river's shore, the current fifty-two-foot square brick tower and attached dwelling date only from 1915. Known locally as Rondout Two, the lighthouse stands on a concrete pier surrounded by the river's swirling waters. Though the lighthouse is owned by the city of Kingston, the Hudson River Maritime Center leases the building for use as a museum depicting the lives of river lighthouse keepers and their families.

Rondout Creek Light
Bob and Sandra Shanklin

Travel information: Reach Kingston via Interstate 87 (New York Thruway) or Route 9. For museum hours contact the Hudson River Maritime Center at (845) 338-0071, or see www .hrmm.org. Tours of the Rondout Lighthouse by the Maritime Center are offered

Esopus Meadows Light
Bob and Sandra Shanklin

on summer weekends. A few miles downriver from Kingston is the **Esopus Meadows Lighthouse** (1879), now undergoing restoration by local preservationists. Located in midchannel, it cannot be reached from land but can be seen from points along Route 9 on the east side of the river.

■ SAUGERTIES LIGHT ■
Saugerties (1836 and 1869)

Floodwaters and ice were always problems for lighthouses on the Hudson. The Saugerties Lighthouse, established in 1836, held up to the annual beatings for nearly thirty years before finally succumbing during the 1860s. Positioned at the mouth of the Esopus Creek along the Hudson, it served as a warning to ships of nearby shallows when Saugerties was a major port serving passenger and commercial vessels. Engineers built the two-story brick dwelling and attached tower that replaced it in

1869 on a massive stone caisson to shield it from the river's destructive floes. This strategy succeeded, and the lighthouse remained safe and relatively dry until the station was decommissioned eighty-five years later.

Saugerties Light
Bob and Sandra Shanklin

Travel information: Handsomely restored by the Saugerties Lighthouse Conservancy, the lighthouse is now a museum open to the public on summer Sundays or by appointment. For overnight accommodations write the organization at 168 Lighthouse Drive, Saugerties, NY 12477; call (845) 247-0656, or see www .saugertieslighthouse.com. The conservancy now works to preserve other lighthouses, too. Well to the north of Saugerties, and more than a hundred miles from the sea, is the **Hudson City Lighthouse** (Hudson-Athens) (1874). Located in midchannel, it cannot be reached from land but can be seen from either the city of Hudson on Route 9 or from Athens on Route 385. It has been restored and is maintained by its steward, the Hudson-Athens Lighthouse Preservation Society; (518) 828-5294; www .hudsonathenslighthouse.org.

Hudson City Light
Bob and Sandra Shanklin

▪ STATEN ISLAND LIGHT (AMBROSE CHANNEL RANGE LIGHT) ▪
New York City/Staten Island (1912)

The ninety-foot octagonal brick tower rises from high ground that lifts its light more than 230 feet above sea level. Built in 1912, the structure is Edwardian in character. It was declared a Historic Landmark by the City of New York in 1968.

Interestingly, its huge second-order bivalve lens was imported from England rather than France. Still in use today, the bull's-eye lens produces a fixed white beacon that is used as a rear-range light. Its companion, the front-range beacon, shines from the **West Bank Lighthouse** (1901), a cast-iron tower built on a concrete caisson more than five miles away.

Travel information: Although the lighthouses are closed to the public, you can approach the Staten Island tower by way of Lighthouse Avenue, off Richmond Road. The West Bank Lighthouse is located in the open waters of the Lower Hudson Bay. The historic **New Dorp Lighthouse** (1856), a wooden combination tower and dwelling, is now a private residence. It can be seen from Altmont Street, off Richmond Road. From the Gateway National Recreation Area and Great Kills Park off Hylan Boulevard, you can spot the "coffeepot-style" **Old Orchard Shoal Lighthouse** (1893), rising on a caisson about three miles to the southeast. Its flashing white and red light remains active.

Staten Island Light
William Kaufhold

NEW JERSEY

■ SANDY HOOK LIGHT ■
Highlands/Sandy Hook (1764)

On the evening of June 11, 1764, a keeper trudged up the steps of the recently completed Sandy Hook Lighthouse and lit its lamps for the first time. Local New York merchants petitioned for two lotteries to be conducted to raise funds for land and the lighthouse. Its need was critical, to warn ships approaching New York Harbor of the "sandy hook" of land that extended seaward. Today—nearly two-and-one half centuries later—the light at the top of the eighty-five-foot stone tower still burns each night, making this the oldest continuously operating lighthouse in America.

Sandy Hook Light
William Kaufhold

The **Boston Lighthouse,** completed in 1716, was blown up by the British during the Revolutionary War and had to be rebuilt. The Sandy Hook tower almost suffered the same fate as its older Boston counterpart when Continental soldiers tried but failed to blow it up to keep it out of British hands. At this time and again during World War II were the only brief periods of darkness that the Sandy Hook Light has seen in its long history of service.

A large, open-panned lamp with forty-eight separate wicks provided the station's light during the eighteenth century. Later, a Winslow Lewis Argand lamp and reflector served here and then, after 1857, a third-order Fresnel lens. The old Fresnel remains in service, displaying a fixed white light with a range of about twenty miles. It is a National Historic Landmark and is now owned by the National Park Service.

Travel information: Take Route 36 to Highlands Beach and follow signs to this lovely and historical light station. Contact the Gateway National Recreation Area, 58 Magruder Road, Highlands, NJ 07732; (732) 872-0115; www.nps.gov/gate. Daily tours are offered by park rangers during summer. For more information contact the New Jersey Lighthouse Society, P.O. Box 332, Navesink, NJ 07752; (732) 291-4777; www.njlhs.org.

■ HIGHLANDS (NAVESINK) LIGHT ■
Highlands (1828 and 1862)

Highlands (Navesink) Light

Henry Hudson first noted the distinctive hills of New Jersey's upper elbow and used them as daymarks during his 1609 voyage of exploration. Mariners have used these highlands for navigation ever since. Perched 246 feet above sea level, the highlands afforded panoramic views of the Shrewsbury River, Sandy Hook, the New York skyline, and the Atlantic Ocean.

In 1828 the US government made the navigator's work easier by placing lights in a pair of fortresslike stone towers atop the hills. In 1838 these towers became the home of America's first Fresnel lenses. An enormous first-order lens sent out its light from the north tower, while a revolving bull's-eye-type second-order lens flashed from its neighbor. This lighthouse is also remembered by thousands of immigrants as their first recognizable confirmation that they had reached America, the "new world."

Rebuilt during the early Civil War years, the twin light towers were relit in 1862. Interestingly, the new south tower was given a square shape, whereas the north tower was octagonal.

In 1898 the north tower was taken out of service and the south tower fitted with an experimental first-order Fresnel lens. One of the largest lenses ever used in an American lighthouse, it weighed more than seven tons and was wide enough (almost ten feet in diameter) to fit a comfortable room inside it. This extraordinarily powerful light could be seen from up to twenty-five miles at sea. The light and station were deactivated in 1953.

In 1899 Guglielmo Marconi used a transmitter and mast located not far from the Highlands Lighthouse to conduct the first practical demonstration of his wireless transmitter. Using the air rather than a wire to carry the dots and dashes of Morse code, he relayed to New York City the results of the America's Cup races being run off Sandy Hook.

After falling into disrepair after deactivation, fund-raising efforts over several years by the New Jersey Park Service, Twin Lights Historical Society, and a local garden club allowed the light station to be restored and a museum opened in several rooms near the north tower. Today visitors may climb the north tower, where a sixth-order Fresnel lens keeps a light shining for all to see.

Travel information: From exit 117 off the Garden State Parkway, follow Highway 36 and the signs to Twin Lights State Historic Site and Museum. The museum recounts the extraordinary history of this light station. Although the museum, tower, and gift shop's public-accessible hours vary, the grounds are open year-round. Contact Twin Lights Museum, Lighthouse Road, Highlands, NJ 07732; (732) 872-1814; www.twin-lights.org.

■ SEA GIRT LIGHT ■
Sea Girt (1896)

With its weathered brick walls, pitched roof, and spacious balustered porch, the Sea Girt Lighthouse looks much like other homes in this seaside community. Unlike neighboring houses, however, this one wraps around two sides of a square, forty-foot tower with a gallery and a small lantern perched on top.

Now operated as a private aid to navigation, this homey-looking lighthouse was built in 1896 to guide fishing boats and other vessels into the shallow Sea Girt Inlet. The light also filled in a dark stretch of coast between the **Barnegat** and **Highlands Lights.** The lantern shone out from its fourth-order Fresnel lens until 1945, when the Coast Guard discontinued the light. During the 1980s the Sea Girt Lighthouse Citizens Committee, which leases the station from the Borough of Sea Girt, raised enough money to restore the structure.

> *Travel information:* From the Garden State Parkway just south of Interstate 95, take the Highway 34 exit and drive south for approximately six miles. Take Route 71 north to Sea Girt. The lighthouse is on the corner of Ocean Avenue and Beacon Boulevard. Regular tours are offered most summer Sundays. For more information or group tours, call the lighthouse at (732) 974-0514, or go to www.seagirtlighthouse.com.

■ BARNEGAT LIGHT ■
Long Beach Island (1835 and 1859)

The original Barnegat tower, completed in 1835, was the work of famed lighthouse contractor Winslow Lewis. Only about twenty years after the station's lamps first burned, however, a government inspector declared the workmanship shoddy and the light woefully inadequate—even though Lewis had designed the lamps and reflectors himself. The inspector was none other than George Meade, a US Army engineer, who some years later would lead the Union Army to victory at Gettysburg. Meade's call for a new and better lighthouse at Barnegat went unheeded, but only a year later a storm knocked down the old Lewis tower. Meade probably smiled at the news.

The soaring, 172-foot-tall brick tower seen at Barnegat nowadays was completed in 1859 under the watchful

Barnegat Light

Sea Girt Light
William Kaufhold

auspices of the Lighthouse Board. With the fate of the original lighthouse fresh in their minds, designers of the new tower gave it two walls, the outer one more than four feet thick. The project cost $45,000, with another $15,000 for a first-order Fresnel lens. The height of the tower and power of its lens gave the light such a boost that it was occasionally seen from as far as thirty miles at sea. The light stayed in service until 1944.

The Friends of Barnegat Lighthouse have helped to preserve and promote the Barnegat Lighthouse State Park. Thanks to this nonprofit group of volunteers and a supportive community, the old veteran was relighted on New Year's Day 2009 and continues to show its signature white flash every ten seconds.

Travel information: From the Garden State Parkway, take Route 72 to Long Beach Island, turn left, and drive to Barnegat Lighthouse State Park at the far northern end of the island. Visitors may climb the tower of "Old Barney," as local residents call it, for a small fee. You may contact the park at P.O. Box 167, Barnegat Light, NJ 08006; (609) 494-2016; www.state .nj.us/dep/parksandforests/parks/barnlig.html. The station's old first-order lens is the primary attraction of the nearby lighthouse park's Interpretive Center. For more information contact the Friends of Barnegat Lighthouse State Park, P.O. Box 167, Barnegat Light, NJ 08006; www .friendsofbarnegatlighthouse.org.

■ ABSECON LIGHT ■
Atlantic City (1857)

The bright lights of Atlantic City's gaming palaces are dim by comparison with the powerful flash of the Absecon Lighthouse in its heyday. Focused by a first-order Fresnel lens with a focal plane almost 170 feet above the ocean, the beacon could be seen from more than twenty miles away.

Congress ignored demands for a light to mark this stretch of the New Jersey coast for decades before finally providing $35,000 for the project in 1854. Flooded foundations and dried-up funding delayed the work for almost three years. It took a $12,000 supplemental federal appropriation and the engineering skills of George Meade to complete the lighthouse. Keeper Daniel Skull first lit the lamps inside the station's big lens in early 1857. The station's name, Absecon, honors an Indian tribe that at one time lived on the New Jersey coast.

On several occasions erosion threatened to undermine the tower's foundation. It survived the Atlantic's worst storms and tides, however, only to succumb to what is often described as progress. By 1933 the beacon could no longer be distinguished from the lights of the burgeoning city that then surrounded it. In 1933 the Coast Guard abandoned the station, deeding it to the city. Better days were to come for this light.

In a modern-day Cinderella story, the lighthouse's recent multimillion dollar restoration by the Inlet Public/Private Association (IPPA) includes a reproduction of the keeper's house, a museum, a gift shop, a Fresnel lens exhibit in the original oil house, and landscaped grounds.

Abescon Light
Kraig Anderson

Travel information: The light is located at the intersection of Vermont and Pacific Avenues in Atlantic City. For information contact Absecon Lighthouse, 31 S. Rhode Island Ave., Atlantic City, NJ 08401; (609) 449-1360; www.abseconlighthouse.org.

■ HEREFORD INLET LIGHT ■
North Wildwood (1874)

With its long porch, delicate balusters, and four-story square tower pushing up through its pitched roof, this fanciful, stick-style lighthouse strongly suggests the Victorian era that produced it. Completed in 1874 at the relatively modest cost of $25,000, the unusual structure proved a solid piece of work. An 1889 hurricane swept away entire nearby communities but spared the little lighthouse, along with eighteen storm refugees who huddled within its surprisingly sturdy walls. The structure was designed by the Lighthouse Service's chief draftsman, Paul J. Pelz. His Victorian-era design was repeated in five near-twin lights. Only Point Fermin and East Brother in California still exist.

Despite numerous storms and a couple of nearly disastrous fires, the Hereford Inlet Light remained in service for ninety years. In 1964 the Coast Guard discontinued the station, replacing it with a far less attractive skeleton tower. With the property restored and maintained with city and state funds by the Hereford Lighthouse

Commission, the station's fourth-order Fresnel lens is now active once more as a private aid to navigation.

Travel information: The lighthouse is located in North Wildwood, just off Central Avenue between Chestnut and First Streets. It is open to the public during summer. Hours vary. For more information call the Friends of Hereford Inlet Light at the lighthouse (609) 522-4520, or see www.herefordlighthouse.org. The Friends continually put on programs and special events.

Hereford Inlet Light

■ CAPE MAY LIGHT ■
Cape May Point (1824, 1847, and 1859)

The 157-foot tower of the Cape May Lighthouse soars above the flat, sandy New Jersey coast and the blue Atlantic beyond. Built in 1859, the distinctive white tower still guides ships along the coast and into Delaware Bay. The enormous tower replaced two earlier structures, dating from 1824 and 1847 respectively.

Exactly 199 steps lead from the ground floor to the lantern room, where an extraordinarily powerful aeromarine beacon flashes its white signal every fifteen seconds. Vessels more than twenty-five miles away can see its light.

Like several other light towers along the New Jersey coast, this one is of double-wall construction. Built on a foundation of stone blocks, the giant tower is twenty-seven feet wide at the base and precisely half that wide at the top. These dimensions give the tower its graceful, tapered appearance.

Perhaps the tower's beauty and the romantic nature of its ocean setting account for its apparent influence on young lovers. Over the years numerous marriage proposals have been offered—and accepted—in the lantern room.

Cape May Light
William Kaufhold

After millions of dollars were raised by the Mid-Atlantic Center for the Arts & Humanities (MAC) for renovation work, the lighthouse is as charming as the surrounding community of Victorian homes.

Travel information: Follow the Garden State Parkway south until it ends in Cape May. The lighthouse is in Cape May Point State Park on Lighthouse Avenue, just off Sunset Boulevard. A visitor center is open daily much of the year but only on weekends during cold-weather months. Contact Cape May Point State Park, P.O. Box 107, Cape May Point, NJ 08212. For lighthouse tours, contact the Mid-Atlantic Center for the Arts & Humanities at 1048 Washington Street, P.O. Box 340, Cape May, NJ 08204, or call (609) 884-5404; www.capemaymac.org. This light is rated one of the best American lighthouse climbs. The park is a protected natural area of considerable diversity and beauty. Step gently here, but enjoy.

◾ EAST POINT (MAURICE RIVER) LIGHT ◾
South of Millville (1849)

Though severely damaged by fire in 1971, the East Point Lighthouse still marks New Jersey's Maurice Cove and the mouth of the Maurice River. Completed in 1849, the station is a two-story brick dwelling with an octagonal tower on its roof. A sixth-order Fresnel lens once served here, but the light is now produced by a modern optic. This very photographic light had its name officially changed from Maurice River to East Point Light in 1912.

East Point (Maurice River) Light
H. Kent Edwards

Travel information:
The station is located on East Point Road in Maurice River Township, about an hour south of Millville, New Jersey. The Maurice River Historical Society leases the property and is restoring the building; call (856) 691-5934. Farther up the Delaware Bay are the historic **Miah Maull Shoal** (1913) and **Finns Point Rear Range** (1877) **Lighthouses.**

◾ TUCKER'S ISLAND LIGHT ◾
Tuckerton (1868 and 1999)

Built in 1868, the Tucker's Island Lighthouse was swept out to sea along with much of the surrounding community during the 1920s. A replica of the original two-story dwelling and tower now serves as a key attraction of Tuckerton Seaport, a fascinating museum complex consisting of sixteen re-created historic structures. The lighthouse serves as an interpretive center.

Travel information: From the Garden State Parkway, take exit 58 and follow Route 539 to Tuckerton; then follow Route 9 to the Tuckerton Seaport. Contact the seaport at (609) 296-8868 or go to www.tuckertonseaport.org.

DELAWARE

■ LISTON REAR RANGE LIGHT ■
Fort Penn (1877)

Range lighthouses operate in pairs to mark channels for shipping. Arrayed one behind the other, with the rear light on a higher plane, the beacons appear in perfect vertical alignment to pilots who steer their ships in the middle of a safe channel. If the upper light appears to tilt either to the left or the right of vertical, the vessel is straying out of the channel in the direction indicated, and the pilot must correct the course.

Over the years, several range lights have served ships moving through the Delaware Bay. Among the most remarkable of these is the Liston Rear Range Light, built in 1877 and still active. It originally served as the Port Penn Rear Range Lighthouse and helped guide ships from Ship John Shoal to Dan Baker Buoy until the US Army Corps of Engineers realigned the shipping channel. Always choosing the most practical of expenditures, the Lighthouse Service chose to disassemble the **Port Penn Range Light,** relocate, and reerect the tower as the **Liston Rear Range Light** in 1906 rather than building an entirely new lighthouse. A 120-foot

Liston Rear Range Light
Mark Riddick/New Light Photography

Fourteen Foot Bank Light
Carole F. Reily

black iron skeleton tower, it houses a second-order Fresnel lens, the only range light on the Delaware River to retain its original lens. The companion front-range light shines from a forty-foot tower near the river's edge seventeen miles away, the longest navigable range in America.

Travel information: From US Highway 13 turn eastward toward Fort Penn on Route 2. The Liston light station is located less than a mile from the turn. From Bowers Beach southeast of Dover, the **Fourteen Foot Bank Lighthouse** (1888) can be seen standing on a huge concrete caisson surrounded by the waters of the bay.

■ HARBOR OF REFUGE LIGHT ■
Lewes (1896 and 1926)

Ships sailing along the northeast coast of the United States are often caught in the grip of powerful storms. As early as the 1820s, government maritime officials planned a harbor of refuge where ships could ride out major gales. They created a harbor at Lewes, near the southern entrance to Delaware Bay, by building an extensive series of breakwaters.

A pair of cylindrical iron light towers built in 1926 mark the harbor breakwaters. The sixty-six-foot Harbor of Refuge Lighthouse replaced an earlier tower built in 1896. It remains active, flashing white and red twelve times a minute. The nearby

Harbor of Refuge Light
Carole F. Reily

Located at the southernmost part of the Delaware Bay, Brandywine Shoal Light was the first screwpile lighthouse ever built in the United States
Carole F. Reily

forty-nine-foot **Delaware Breakwater Lighthouse** was preceded by several different towers and navigational aids, the earliest dating from 1834. No longer an active light, it serves as a daymark.

For many years the **Cape Henlopen Lighthouse,** an old stone colonial tower established in 1767, guided ships into Delaware Bay and pointed the way to its safe harbors. Eventually, erosion undermined the historic structure, and it finally collapsed during a storm in 1926. No trace of it remains.

Travel information: To view or photograph the harbor lights, follow US Highway 9 to its end at Cape Henlopen State Park, just east of Lewes. The park features delightful ocean scenery and is open all year during daylight hours. Harbor cruises are available in nearby Lewes, where one can also visit the lightship *Overfalls* (1838), now designated as a National Historic Landmark. The Overfalls Foundation restored and maintains the light-

The Miah Maull Shoal Light (see page 119) is located southeast of Fortescue, New Jersey, in Delaware Bay. Locals treasure it as one of their favorite fishing spots.
Carole F. Reily

ship, which spent most of its operational life in New England. Contact the Overfalls Maritime Museum, 210 Pilottown Road, P.O. Box 413, Lewes, DE 19958; (302) 644-8050; www.overfalls.org.

Overfalls *Lightship*
Cathy Heronemos, Overfalls Foundation

■ FENWICK ISLAND LIGHT ■
Fenwick Island (1859)

The famed Mason-Dixon Line not only runs right through the light station property, it starts here. The lighthouse, built half in the North and half in the South in 1859, helps guide ships into Delaware Bay with its occulting white signal.

Like the **Barnegat** and **Cape May Lighthouses** to the north, this one has a double-walled tower. The brick structure rises eighty-seven feet above the island sands, placing the focal plane of its light nearly ninety feet above the water. The third-order Fresnel lens is the station's original optic. Eclipser panels roll around the lens on a dolly, causing it to occult, or wink, about four times a minute.

Fenwick Island Light

Travel information: Located on Route 528 at the Delaware border north of Ocean City, Maryland, the lighthouse and its small museum are open to the public, but hours are very limited. For a schedule contact "New" Friends of the Fenwick Island Lighthouse, P.O. Box 1001, Selbyville, DE 19975, or see http://fenwickislandlighthouse.org. The Friends open the lighthouse to visitors on summer weekends.

Cape Hatteras Lighthouse before it was moved

MARYLAND

■ CONCORD POINT LIGHT ■

Havre de Grace (1827)

Two years after he built the original Thomas Point Lighthouse—and botched the job—contractor John Donohoo was hired to erect a light tower on Concord Point at Havre de Grace. Donohoo, a well known and community-minded Havre de

Grace citizen, completed the thirty-two-foot stone tower in less than a year for $3,500. Apparently, he learned from his earlier mistakes. This tower is constructed using local granite and mahogany doors and still stands, no less solid than when its lamps were first lit in 1827.

Concord Point Light

The tower was built as a warning to mariners to beware the dangerous shoals and currents around the mouth of the Susquehanna River. Originally, the lantern held a set of lamps and sixteen-inch reflectors. Later, these were exchanged for a fifth-order Fresnel lens. At present the tower displays a fixed green light as a private aid to navigation.

All the keepers of this lighthouse were members of the same family, that of war hero John O'Neil. During the War of 1812, O'Neil made a quixotic one-man stand against an entire British fleet. Miraculously, he survived and, as a reward, was named keeper of the Concord Point Light. The job passed down from one generation of O'Neils to the next, until the light was automated in the 1920s.

Travel information: The lighthouse, the northernmost on the Chesapeake Bay, sits in a small park beside the Susquehanna River in the town of Havre de Grace at Concord and Lafayette Streets. The tower is open for tours on weekends from April to October. The 1884-period-restored keeper's quarters currently houses exhibits and a gift shop. Contact the Friends of Concord Point Lighthouse, P.O. Box 212, Havre de Grace, MD 21078; (410) 939-3213; www.concordpointlighthouse.org. Be sure to visit historic Havre de Grace and its Maritime Museum, located at 100 Lafayette Street, Havre de Grace, MD 21078; call (410) 939-4800, or go to www.hdg maritimemuseum.org.

■ TURKEY POINT LIGHT ■
Elk Neck (1833)

Turkey Point juts southward into the Chesapeake Bay near its far northern end. A modest masonry light tower has marked the point since 1833, its beacon guiding ships headed for the Susquehanna River. John Donohoo built the conical stone tower and a nearby keeper's dwelling for $4,355. Although only thirty-five feet tall, the tower stands on a one-hundred-foot bluff, making its light far more effective. The bluffs at this point have been navigation landmarks for centuries. The light was established to work in tandem with **Pooles Island** and **Concord Point Lighthouses** marking the way from the bay into the Elk River to the Chesapeake and Delaware Canal.

Turkey Point Light
Mark Riddick/New Light Photography

Several female lighthouse keepers served here, including Mrs. Harry Salter, appointed to the post by President Calvin Coolidge in 1925 after the death of her husband, the previous keeper. She was the last female keeper in the old Lighthouse Service.

Travel information: The lighthouse is located in pristine Elk Neck State Park, a major game preserve. Take the Route 272 exit off Interstate 95, several miles north of the Susquehanna Bridge. Today the lighthouse is owned by the Maryland Department of Natural Resources and is under the wing of the nonprofit Turkey Point Light Station, Inc. Volunteers open the tower on weekends from April to mid-November. Write TPLS, Inc., P.O. Box 412, North East, MD 21901, or see www.tpls.org.

■ SEVEN FOOT KNOLL LIGHT ■
Baltimore (1855)

The oldest of the Chesapeake Bay's surviving screw-pile light towers and the first to be built in Maryland, the Seven Foot Knoll Lighthouse was completed in 1855. Most of the bay's other screw-pile lighthouses had octagonal, cottagelike dwellings, but this one is entirely of iron and looks more like a huge, red cheese-hoop-shaped box.

Built to mark a dangerous shoal near the entrance to the Baltimore harbor at the mouth of the Patapsco River, the lighthouse stood on eight iron piles hammered and screwed into the muddy bottom of the bay. Designed for a third-order Fresnel lens, it received a less powerful fourth-order lens instead.

It appears the first structure was brown and octagonal, replaced by the circular design seen today about 1875. Keepers lived and worked in a round-walled, one-story dwelling. A short cylindrical tower rose from the flat roof of the building.

First automated, then abandoned by the Coast Guard, Seven Foot Knoll served mariners as an active light and daymark for more than 130 years. Eventually, it was donated to the City of Baltimore for use as a museum. In 1988 the 220-ton structure

Seven Foot Knoll Light

was cut from its pilings and barged to its current location at Pier Five in the city's popular Inner Harbor district.

Travel information: From Interstate 95 take the Pratt Street exit and follow signs to the Baltimore Inner Harbor. The lighthouse is at the end of Pier Five, not far from the permanent berth of the lightship *Chesapeake* (1930). The lightship is now a floating navigational museum, part

The Chesapeake *Lightship is owned by the National Park Service and is docked near the Maritime Museum in Baltimore Harbor. Built in 1930, it was the last active lightship on Chesapeake Bay.*

of the fascinating and historical Baltimore Maritime Museum complex, also known as "Historic Ships in Baltimore." It includes the Coast Guard cutter *Roger B. Taney*, the only ship still afloat that survived the attack on Pearl Harbor, and much more. Call (410) 396-3453, or go to www.historicships.org. For Baltimore tourism information contact Baltimore Tourism Association, P.O. Box 2254, Baltimore, MD 21203; (410) 625-7064; www.baltimoretourism.com.

■ THOMAS POINT LIGHT ■
Annapolis/Thomas Point (1825, 1838, and 1875)

Vessels moving through the middle reaches of the Chesapeake Bay must swing wide to avoid a treacherous bank of shoals just off Thomas Point near Annapolis. Since 1825 lighthouses have marked this obstacle. Two of these were built onshore by legendary lighthouse contractor Winslow Lewis. The first Lewis tower proved nearly useless, so he built another some thirteen years later. But the light, provided by a lens-and-reflector system of Lewis's own design, remained too weak to adequately warn ships approaching the shoals.

Thomas Point Light
Mark Riddick/New Light Photography

   In 1875 the Lighthouse Board decided to move the light offshore and place it where it would be most effective—out in the bay, directly over the shoals. The new lighthouse was a small hexagonal building held above the water by iron legs anchored to screw piles. Abandoned, the Lewis tower on the point eventually collapsed, but for more than a century the lighthouse on the shoals has weathered storms, floods, and ice floes. Its flashing beacon still guides ships and has well earned its distinction as a National Historic Landmark. Annapolis is home to the US Naval Academy and is often referred to as the sailing capital of the world.

In 2004 a highly successful public-private partnership formed via the National Historic Lighthouse Preservation Act. The City of Annapolis, the US Lighthouse Society and its Chesapeake Chapter, the Annapolis Maritime Museum, and Anne Arundel County joined efforts to obtain ownership of the lighthouse from the federal government. Tours began in 2007 and continue each summer.

Travel information: The best way to see this open-water lighthouse is from a boat. Sightseeing cruises out of Annapolis, Maryland, often pass the station. Contact Annapolis and Chesapeake Bay Conference and Visitors Bureau, 26 West Street, Annapolis, MD 21401; (410) 280-0445; www.visit annapolis.org. For more information on the lighthouse, write to CCUSLHS, P.O. Box 1270, Annandale, VA 22003-1270, or see www.cheslights.org, or www.thomaspointlighthouse.org.

■ SANDY POINT SHOAL LIGHT ■
Skidmore (1883)

With its mansard roof and pitched dormer windows, the Sandy Shoal Lighthouse looks more like an old Victorian townhouse than a navigational marker. Its loca-

tion is distinctly maritime, however. It rests on a caisson, completely surrounded by the choppy waters of the Chesapeake Bay. The seemingly out-of-place structure and its flashing light mark a troublesome shoal off Sandy Point, near where the Chesapeake Bay Bridge now connects Maryland's eastern shore region with the rest of the state.

The Lighthouse Board established a light station onshore at Sandy Point in 1858, but it was of limited use to pilots trying to avoid the shoal, especially in fog or stormy weather. In 1883 the light was moved directly over the shoal to maximize its effectiveness. A combination tower and dwelling, the structure rises more than fifty feet above the waters of the bay. It remains in operation, displaying a white flash ten times every minute.

Sandy Point Shoal Light
Mark Riddick/New Light Photography

Travel information: The lighthouse is off-limits to the public; it was sold in auction via the Internet and has been privately owned since 2005; however, it can be seen from Sandy Point State Park, accessible from an exit off US Highway 50, just west of the Chesapeake Bay Bridge tollbooths. The park is also an excellent place to have a picnic and enjoy the bay scenery. Contact the park for more information at (410) 974-2149; www.dnr .state.md.us/publiclands/southern/sandypoint.asp.

▪ HOOPER STRAIT LIGHT ▪
St. Michaels (1867 and 1879)

Hooper Strait Light

For more than forty years, beginning in 1827, a lightship marked a crooked channel of Hooper Strait. The last lightship anchored here was built in 1845 and destroyed by Confederates during the War between the States. Because this spot was a critical one to clear for traffic between the Chesapeake Bay and Tangier Sound, in 1867 the Lighthouse Board built a modest screwpile tower to guide shipping. Ten years later a massive ice floe swept the little lighthouse off its piles and carried it five miles down the bay. Two lighthouse tenders, the *Tulip* and *Heliotrope*, were sent to fetch the wreckage and managed to salvage the lens and some of the equipment. Although both keepers were stranded as a result of the incident and suffered severe frostbite, they returned to man the new lighthouse built a couple of years later.

A larger, hexagonal lighthouse had replaced the crushed tower by the autumn of 1879, and it remained in service for three-quarters of a century. Deactivated in 1954, it was eventually acquired by the Chesapeake Bay Maritime Museum in St. Michaels on the Maryland eastern shore. To move the forty-four-foot-wide structure down the Chesapeake to St. Michaels, museum officials had it cut in half, like a giant apple, and loaded onto a barge. Reassembled and restored to like-new condition, the lighthouse now stands on Navy Point beside the museum.

Travel information: To reach the museum and lighthouse, take US Highway 50, then Route 33 to St. Michaels. Signs point the way to Navy Point and the museum. For more information about tours and events, contact the Chesapeake Bay Maritime Museum, P.O. Box 636, 213 N. Talbot Street, St. Michaels, MD 21663; (410) 745-2916; www.cbmm.org.

▪ COVE POINT LIGHT ▪
Solomons (1828)

Among the oldest light towers on the Chesapeake Bay, the Cove Point Lighthouse marks the entrance to the Patuxent River. The conical, fifty-one-foot brick tower is the work of John Donohoo, who built several of the Chesapeake's historical lighthouses. The Cove Point tower is among his best—it has stood intact since 1828.

Erosion threatened the structure almost from the start. During the 1840s retaining walls were built to hold back the eroding tides, which they have managed to do for more than 150 years. The tireless Chesapeake, however, has now cut to within a few feet of the foundation and may yet claim its victim. In 2000 the lighthouse was handed over to the Calvert Marine Museum, which provides public access.

Cove Point Light

> *Travel information:* Although the light is now automated, Cove Point remains an active aid to navigation. Resident keepers live on site. Follow Maryland Route 4 to Solomons, then Cove Point Road to the lighthouse. Helpful information may be obtained from the Calvert Marine Museum, 14200 Solomons Island Road, P.O. Box 97, Solomons, MD 20688; (410) 326-2042; www.calvertmarinemuseum.com.

■ DRUM POINT LIGHT ■
Solomons (1883)

American taxpayers have known few such bargains as the hexagonal, cottage-type Drum Point Lighthouse, which cost only $5,000 to build. Completed in 1883, the little lighthouse served faithfully for nearly eighty years. Its fourth-order Fresnel lens, which likely cost more than the lighthouse itself, warned mariners until 1962, when the station was taken out of service.

During its active years the light marked a sandy spit that threatened vessels passing Drum Point. Now, as part of the Calvert Maritime Museum, it continues to

Drum Point Light

Fresnel lens from Drum Point Light

render useful service by reminding visitors of the important role lighthouses and their keepers have played in the nation's history. It has become the museum's popular and most recognized exhibit.

Travel information: Follow Route 4 to Solomons. The museum and lighthouse are near the bridge across the Patuxent River. The lighthouse has been wonderfully restored and furnished in early 1900s style. Contact the Calvert Marine Museum (see Travel information for **Cove Point Lighthouse**).

From Solomons the **Point Lookout Lighthouse** (1830) can be reached via a half-hour drive across the Patuxent Bridge on Route 4, then southeastward along Route 235 and Route 5 to Point Lookout State Park. Deactivated in 1966, the old lighthouse has become one of America's most famously haunted sites because of all the deaths while it was used as a prison for Confederate prisoners of war; it is under restoration by the state.

From the park, drive back toward Washington, D.C., on Route 5 to the small town of Callaway; turn south on Route 249, and drive to Piney Point, where an authentic John

Point Lookout Light
Mark Riddick/New Light Photography

Donohoo light tower still stands. Deactivated in 1964, the **Piney Point Lighthouse** (1836), the lighthouse museum, gift shop (located a short distance from the tower), and historic park with pier can also be reached by boat. Boaters may dock at a river pier that leads directly to the boardwalk. Call the Piney Point Lighthouse Museum and Park at (301) 994-1471; for more information go to www.co.saint-marys.md.us/recreate/PPL.asp. The **Blackstone Lighthouse** (St. Clements Island) replica has been built by volunteers. Contact the St. Clements Island Museum at (301) 769-2222; www.co.saint-marys.md.us/recreate/stclementsisland.asp. For information on travel along the Chesapeake Bay, go to www.baygateways.net.

VIRGINIA

■ ASSATEAGUE ISLAND LIGHT ■
Assateague Island (1833 and 1867)

In 1831 Congress appropriated funds for a lighthouse a few miles south of the Maryland border on Virginia's portion of Assateague Island. Its chief duty was to warn ships away from a series of shoals that extend seaward like knife blades from the island. But when completed two years later, the forty-five-foot stone tower and its Winslow Lewis lamp-and-reflector system proved far too weak to perform this task effectively.

During the 1850s the Lighthouse Board launched a determined campaign to upgrade lighthouses along all of America's coasts. As part of this comprehensive effort, the board decided to rebuild the Assateague tower, but the Civil War interrupted the project. Hence, the new 142-foot tower was not ready for service until October of 1867. When its first-order Fresnel lens finally began to shine, however, mariners saw an

Assateague Island Light

immediate improvement in the station's beacon, which they were now able to spot from more than twenty miles at sea. An automated aeromarine beacon replaced the old Fresnel in 1961, and it remains an active aid to navigation.

In 2004 the Coast Guard gave the lighthouse to the US Fish and Wildlife Service, which has made the tower more accessible to the public. The island is managed by two other official park agencies: Assateague Island National Seashore, managed by the National Park Service, and the Department of Natural Resources. The trio of caretakers offers visitors opportunities for adventures at the Chincoteague National Wildlife Refuge and a chance to enjoy the beach, wildlife, wetlands, wild ponies, and lots more.

Travel information: Take US Highway 13 and Route 175 to Chincoteague; then follow the signs to the Chincoteague National Wildlife Refuge on Assateague Island. A quarter-mile trail leads from the lighthouse parking lot to the base of the tower. Contact the Chincoteague National Wildlife Refuge, P.O. Box 62, Chincoteague, VA 23336; (757) 336-6122; www.fws.gov/northeast/chinco. For more on the Assateague area and activities available, contact the Chincoteague Island Chamber of Commerce, 6733 Maddox Boulevard, Chincoteague Island, VA 23336; (757) 336-6161; www.chincoteaguechamber.com. This light has been rated as one of the best climbs in America.

▪ CAPE CHARLES LIGHT ▪
Smith Island (1828, 1864, and 1895)

A pair of light stations marks the Virginia Capes. Dating back to 1792, the two-century-old Cape Henry Light on the southern lip of the capes is the elder of the two. The younger, Cape Charles Light, marks the northern side of the capes on Smith Island. Established in 1828, it has shone for 185 years.

The giant, 190-foot steel skeleton tower that stands on Smith Island now is Cape Charles station's third tower. The first, a fifty-five-foot stone structure, was always woefully inadequate. Its light, supplied by outmoded lamps and reflectors, was rarely visible more than a dozen miles away. A 150-foot brick replacement tower was built during the Civil War, despite a destructive assault on the station in 1862 by a Confederate raiding party. Completed in May of 1864, it served for thirty years before coastal erosion forced the government to relocate the station.

Cape Charles Light

The huge skeleton tower that took its place is more than a mile inland. Its pyramidal steel superstructure is intended to protect the tower from high winds. A winding staircase inside a nine-foot-wide steel cylinder provides access to the lantern room. The flashing white light has an effective range of about twenty-five miles.

Travel information: Even the Coast Guard has trouble getting to this light station on remote Smith Island. Not surprisingly, the station is closed to the public. Motorists, however, can see the lighthouse as they cross the seventeen-mile-long Chesapeake Bay (toll) Bridge on US Highway 13.

The first-order Fresnel lens that served here until the station was automated in 1963 is now on display at the Newport News Mariners' Museum, 100 Museum Drive, Newport News, VA 23606; (757) 596-2222 or (800) 581-7245; www.marinersmuseum.org.

▪ JONES POINT LIGHT ▪
Alexandria (1855)

On the south shore of the Potomac, just downriver from Washington, D.C., stands a small rectangular building with whitewashed wooden walls, pitched roof, and raised porch. Except for the tiny lantern perched on its roof, the little building might be taken for a nineteenth-century country schoolhouse. Instead, it is the Jones Point Lighthouse, built in 1855 to guide trading ships, tugs, and barges into the then-thriving port of Alexandria and Washington Navy Yard. Deactivated in 1926, after more than seventy years of service, the lighthouse stood unused for much of the twentieth century. Recently, however, it was handsomely restored and relit as a private aid to navigation in an agreement between the Daughters of the American Revolution and owner National Park Service.

If these walls could talk, there would be volumes to record, including President Washington's placing one of the cornerstones demarking the diamond-shaped Washington, D.C. From the Civil War to the Signal Corps of Engineers and their secret missions

Jones Point Light
Mark Riddick/New Light Photography

during World War II, this small building has seen a great deal of history. Reduced to a mere shell of a structure, it has made a comeback in fine shape to continue sharing its legends.

Travel information: From Interstate 95, exit onto US Highway 1 North (exit 1). Take the first right turn onto Franklin Street. Travel three-tenths of a mile, turn right on South Royal Street, and proceed two-tenths of a mile; watch carefully for the Jones Point entrance. In addition to the lighthouse, the grassy park at Jones Point, ever expanding with new additions, offers sweeping Potomac River views and a stone that marks a corner of the original, ten-mile-square federal district (Alexandria and the southwest side of the district voted to rejoin Virginia in 1846). Grounds are open year-round from dawn to dusk. More information is available on the George Washington Memorial Parkway at www.nps.gov/gwmp; (703) 289-2500.

■ NEW POINT COMFORT LIGHT ■
Mathews (1804)

Completed of sandstone during late 1804, the fifty-eight-foot-tall New Point Comfort Light did not, as its name implies, replace the Old Point Comfort Light. Instead, the two lighthouses, both built at about the same time and of similar design, take their names from the separate headlands where they have stood guard now for nearly two hundred years. Built on a small island

New Point Comfort Light

near the entrance to Mobjack Bay, the New Point Comfort Lighthouse pointed the way up the Chesapeake toward Baltimore. Deactivated during the 1950s, it now serves only as a daymark.

Travel information: Virginia's Mathews County, the Mathews County Historical Society, and the New Point Comfort Preservation Task Force have joined efforts over recent decades to stabilize and restore the lighthouse as a memorial to local mariners who lost their lives at sea. It can be reached only by boat, but a good view can be had from the boardwalk within the Nature Conservancy's New Point Comfort Preserve. For directions, see www.nature .org. Seven miles to the north is the **Wolf Trap Lighthouse.**

■ WOLF TRAP LIGHT ■
Chesapeake Bay (1870 and 1893)

Wolf Trap Light
Frank L. Parks

In 1691 a Chesapeake shoal ensnared the HMS *Wolfe* and has been known ever since as the Wolf Trap. A bright red octagonal lighthouse, built on an enormous concrete-and-iron caisson, now guards the shoal. The light flashing from its fifty-two-foot tower warns vessels against being trapped like the *Wolfe*. A cottage-style screw-pile lighthouse placed here in 1870 had a misadventure of its own when a mighty ice floe swept it down the Chesapeake during the winter of 1893. A lighthouse tender found it bobbing in the waves out toward the Virginia Capes. Protected by its massive caisson, the current structure is far less vulnerable.

Travel information: The Wolf Trap Lighthouse can be reached only by boat. It can be seen from the water, but it is off-limits to the public. When it was offered in a public auction on the Internet, a buyer finally stepped up to take over the familiar daymark. The new owner had a new roof installed and will now turn to its interior restoration, but has subsequently offered it for resale, making its future tentative.

■ OLD POINT COMFORT LIGHT ■
Fort Monroe (1802)

Among the earliest lighthouses constructed on the Chesapeake Bay was the fifty-four-foot tower erected in 1802 at Fort Monroe. The light marked the mouth of the James River and the entrance to Hampton Roads.

Because of its strategic location, the lighthouse has seen plenty of conflicts. During the War of 1812, British troops seized the fort and used the lighthouse as a watchtower. Half a century later, the ironclad *Virginia* steamed past the Point Comfort Light on its way to do battle with the *Monitor*. Following the Civil War, Confederate President Jefferson Davis was imprisoned in a cell not far from the tower.

Fort Monroe remains an active military post to this day. Its lighthouse is still on duty, displaying a flashing red light with a range of about fifteen miles.

Travel information: Fort Monroe can be reached from Norfolk via Interstate 64, Route 169, and Route 143. The sentry at the gate can point the way to the lighthouse. Although the tower is not open to the public, visitors are more than welcome at the nearby Casemate Museum, which celebrates the fort's rich and often somber history. Contact the Casemate Museum, P.O. Box 51341, Fort Monroe, VA 23651; (757) 788-3391. The Fort Monroe Authority assumed responsibility for the complex of army buildings and the lighthouse as of early 2012. This committee, a political subdivision of the Commonwealth of Virginia, will open the area to the public. The President and Secretary of the Interior signed a declaration in November 2011 that established Fort Monroe as a National Monument. The historic fort and lighthouse will become a highly visited urban national park with

Old Point Comfort Light

National Park Service presence. For travel plans or to follow the progress at Fort Monroe, call (757) 637-7778, or go to www.fmauthority.com.

■ NEWPORT NEWS MIDDLE GROUND LIGHT ■
Newport News (1891)

Built on an open-water caisson, this lighthouse warns ships away from the dangerous "Middle Ground," an L-shaped shoal in the heart of Hampton Roads, one of the nation's busiest harbors. Shaped something like a coffeepot without a handle, the fifty-six-foot tower displays a flashing white light as an active aid to navigation. Auctioned in 2005 after being released by the US Coast Guard, a private owner has worked diligently to stabilize the structure and keep it as a vacation home.

Newport News Middle Ground Light
Mark Riddick/New Light Photography

Travel information: The lighthouse is a featured attraction of Hampton/Newport News harbor cruises. Call (757) 245-1533. On Museum Drive, just off US Highway 60 in Newport News, is the excellent Mariners' Museum (see Travel information for **Cape Charles Lighthouse**), which tells the story of humanity's long—and occasionally stormy—relationship with the sea. On display here is the huge first-order Fresnel lens from the **Cape Charles Lighthouse.**

■ PORTSMOUTH LIGHTSHIP ■
Portsmouth (1916)

Portsmouth *Lightship*

Known to the Coast Guard as *Lightship LV 101*, this sturdy vessel served for forty-eight years at stations off the Delaware, Maryland, Massachusetts, and Virginia coasts. As with other lightships, it marked dangerous obstacles and key navigational points where it was impossible or too expensive to build a lighthouse. Among its unusual features is a hollow light mast, allowing internal access to its optic. Retired in 1964, the *LV 101* became the lightship *Portsmouth*, a floating maritime museum. Present-day visitors will find the crew's quarters, galley, and engine room all shipshape, as if the *Portsmouth* were ready to go to sea at a moment's notice. As an added surprise several Fresnel lenses are on display, including a first-order Fresnel in special housing right on the revived waterfront.

> *Travel information:* The lightship *Portsmouth* and its museum are part of the art center complex on the Portsmouth waterfront. Contact the Portsmouth Lightship Museum, located at Water and London Streets in Olde Towne, Portsmouth Waterfront (London Slip). Just one block away is a sister museum, the Portsmouth Naval Shipyard Museum at 2 High Street; for information on both museums, call (757) 393-8591, or go to www .portsnavalmuseums.com.
>
> From Ocean View Avenue in nearby Norfolk, one can see the **Thimble Shoal Lighthouse** (1914). The three-level tower rests on a caisson and displays a flashing white light.

■ CAPE HENRY LIGHTS ■
Virginia Beach (1792 and 1881)

In 1774 the colonies of Maryland and Virginia decided to mark the entrance to the Chesapeake Bay with a lighthouse, a project that had been under consideration for almost a century. Tons of stone were piled up at Cape Henry, the selected site. But before construction could begin, the Revolutionary War brought a stop to all such public works. The effort did not get under way again until 1791, when the now-independent nation's first federal Congress appropriated $24,077 to see it completed.

Hired by Secretary of Treasury Alexander Hamilton, contractor and respected architect John McComb hoped to use the original stockpile of stone for the tower but soon discovered that the large blocks had sunk deep into the sand. Nonetheless, using freshly quarried sandstone, he completed the ninety-foot tower in less than a year. It was a solid piece of work. The McComb tower has stood for more than two centuries, through several wars and countless gales. The Confederates put the

New Cape Henry Light

light out at the beginning of the Civil War, but the Union had its whale-oil lamps burning again by 1862.

During the 1870s cracks appeared in the tower's octagonal walls. Fearing it would collapse, the Lighthouse Board had a second, much taller tower built just south of the original. This cylindrical cast-iron structure, more than 150 feet tall, was ready for service in 1881. Its first-order Fresnel lens, a magnificent optic becoming a lighthouse of such importance, still flashes its white signal every twenty seconds as an active aid to navigation within the working Coast Guard station.

Old Cape Henry Light

Travel information: The Cape Henry towers are located in historic Fort Story, reached off US Highway 60 in Virginia Beach via Atlantic Avenue. To visit the lighthouse you must pass through the security gates of Fort Story; be prepared with picture identification. Visitors can climb the two hundred steps to the top of the old 1792 tower—concerns over the stability of the original lighthouse proved unwarranted. For more information on the Old Cape Henry Lighthouse, call Preservation Virginia at (804) 648-1889, or go to www.apva.org/CapeHenryLighthouse.

Also of interest in Virginia Beach is the Old Coast Guard Station at 2400 Atlantic Avenue. Celebrating the old US Life-Saving Service, it is filled with displays of life-saving equipment. Photographs and displays recount stories of shipwreck and bravery. Call (757) 422-1587.

■ CURRITUCK BEACH LIGHT ■

Corolla (1875)

Near the border between the North Carolina and Virginia coasts, the mighty Gulf Stream sweeps in close to the mainland. To avoid fighting its powerful northeasterly current, captains of southbound ships must steer perilously close to land. Sometimes they come too close—with disastrous results. To warn mariners to keep their ships at a safe distance, the Lighthouse Board erected a series of three tall coastal sentinels along this dangerous stretch of coast: the 200-foot **Cape Hatteras** tower (1870), 162-foot **Bodie Island** tower (1872), and 162-foot **Currituck Beach** tower, completed in 1875.

Currituck Beach Light

Strategically placed about halfway between the Cape Henry (Virginia) and Bodie Island lights, the Currituck Beach Lighthouse illuminated one of the last remaining dark stretches of southern coastline. Stout walls, almost five-and-one-half-feet thick at the base, help the tower withstand Atlantic storms. To distinguish it from neighboring lighthouses, its red bricks were left unpainted, and they remain so. The twelve-foot-tall lantern at the top still holds the station's original first-order bull's-eye Fresnel lens. The automated light flashes white every twenty seconds and can be spotted from up to nineteen miles away.

Travel information: This light is rated one of the best American lighthouse climbs. From Kitty Hawk turn north off US Highway 158 (the Outer Banks Highway) onto NC 12, and drive approximately twenty miles to the village of Corolla. The lighthouse, on the left, can be seen from the road. Visitors may climb the tower's 214 steps for a small fee—the extraordinary view from the gallery is well worth the price. The Outer Banks Conservationists, Inc. (OBC) has been expertly restoring the entire light station; as the lighthouse's permanent steward, it keeps the grounds and tower open from Easter through Thanksgiving. For information write to OBC, 1101 Corolla Village Road, P.O. Box 58, Corolla, NC 27927 or call (252) 453-8152, or see www.currituckbeachlight.com. At one time the lighthouse was surrounded by wild horses, but the Corolla herd has been relocated for safety to Corova. For more information contact the Corolla Wild Horse Fund, 1126 Old Schoolhouse Lane, P.O. Box 361, Corolla, NC 27927; (252) 453-8002; www.corollawildhorses.com. Highway 12 traverses the quaint villages of Duck and Corolla, with their array of art galleries, restaurants, and specialty shops.

■ BODIE ISLAND LIGHT ■
Bodie Island (1848, 1859, and 1872)

It is hard to imagine a contractor being instructed to do a poor job, but that was the case with Francis Gibbons, builder of the first Bodie Island Lighthouse. Despite a thick layer of mud under the construction site, a penny-pinching US Treasury official ordered Gibbons to drive no piles, so Gibbons built on a shallow foundation of brick. Not surprisingly, his tower began to lean out of plumb almost as soon as he finished it in 1848. The leaning tower of Bodie Island was rebuilt in 1859, but its replacement lasted only two years. Confederate troops blew it up during the opening months of the Civil War.

The soaring 162-foot tower seen at Bodie Island today rests on a granite foundation set atop iron pilings and a grillage of pine timbers. This technique (also employed

Bodie Island Light

The shipwreck of the Laura A. Barnes *lies near the Bodie Island Light*

at Cape Hatteras) enables the tower to stand straight, as it has since 1872. Automated in 1932, when its beacon was electrified, the Bodie Island Lighthouse remains vital to navigation. The lantern retains its original giant lens. Its twice-a-minute white flashes shine out to a distance of 19 nautical miles. Restoration work on the tower began in 2009 with plans to finish by 2013, but the grounds remain open year-round. Upon completion the first-order Fresnel lens will resume its work and the tower will be opened to the public. The 1874 Bodie Island Life-Saving Station and the 1912 Coast Guard station have been relocated off the ocean's edge to the entrance to Bodie Island immediately off Highway 12. It will become part of the Bodie Island historical district, complete with nature trails and wildlife observatory decks.

Travel information: Located off Route 12 about seventeen miles north of Rodanthe, the scenic grounds surrounding the Bodie Island Lighthouse (BILH) are open daily to the public. The National Park Service operates a small museum in the keeper's dwelling (1893). Contact the Cape Hatteras National Seashore, 1401 National Park Drive, Manteo, NC 27954; (252) 473-2111; www.nps.gov/caha. For school group tours call BILH at (252) 441-5711.

Visitors to the Bodie Island Lighthouse will want to stop at Rodanthe for a look at the **Chicamacomico Life-Saving Station** (CLSS) (1911), now a fascinating museum dedicated to the old US Life-Saving Service. The station and museums are open weekdays May through November. For more information on summer programs and beach apparatus drills, contact CLSS, 23645 NC Hwy. 12, Rodanthe, NC 27968; (252) 987-1552; www .chicamacomico.net.

Chicamacomico Life-Saving Station

■ CAPE HATTERAS LIGHT ■
Hatteras Island (1803 and 1870)

Two mighty ocean rivers, the cold Labrador Current and the steamy Gulf Stream, oppose each other just off Cape Hatteras. The violent seas and killer shoals thrown up by their interaction have claimed at least 2,300 ships, causing sailors to dub these waters "the Graveyard of the Atlantic."

Congress authorized a lighthouse for the cape in 1794, but political squabbling over selection of a contractor delayed the project for years. Fighting storms, mosquitoes, and outbreaks of yellow fever, construction crews finally had the ninety-five-foot stone tower standing by late 1803. Not tall enough to be seen from the vicious

Diamond Shoals that extend several miles seaward from the cape, this first Hatteras lighthouse was never considered adequate. Reporting to the Lighthouse Board in 1851, a navy inspector called it "the worst light in the world." Following the Civil War, the board replaced it with a new, two-hundred-foot brick tower, and then, three years after its completion, painted it with distinctive spiraling black-and-white stripes in 1873.

Cape Hatteras Light during efforts to save it after Hurricane Fran in September 1996

Built on a granite foundation set atop iron pilings and a grillage of pine timbers, the big brick tower withstood many hurricanes; however, the lighthouse faced a much more serious threat from the sea. Once located sixteen hundred feet from the ocean, after a number of years, the Cape Hatteras Lighthouse teetered at the very edge of the tides. Storm-driven waves threatened to undermine the foundation of the massive tower.

In one of the largest preservation efforts for an American lighthouse to date, the tower and keeper's quarters—all outbuildings—were relocated twenty-nine hundred feet to the southwest, out of harm's way, by expert movers. The lighthouse was cut away from its foundation; next, using hydraulics technology, the National Historic Monument was lifted, supported, and nudged down the steel-beams move track by a three-zone hydraulic jacking system specially designed for this one monumental task. Relighted in November 1999, its light shines

Cape Hatteras Light after relocation in 1999

each night, flashing white every seven-and one-half seconds from an elevation of over two hundred feet above high water. In clear weather sailors can spot it from a distance of almost twenty-four miles. The tower is open for climbing generally from Easter until Columbus Day.

Diamond Shoals Lightship
US Coast Guard

> *Travel information:* Rated one of the best American lighthouse climbs, the lighthouse is located just off Route 12, near the village of Buxton on Hatteras Island. A keeper's dwelling houses a visitor center and museum dedicated to the history of the station and the Outer Banks. Nearby is the Buxton Visitor Center and bookstore. From the top of the lighthouse and with binoculars, visitors may be able to see the **Diamond Shoals Lighthouse** (1967), which rests

on steel pilings directly over the shoal and looks something like an offshore oil rig. The light has been decommissioned. Contact the Cape Hatteras National Seashore, 1401 National Park Drive, Manteo, NC 27954; (252) 473-2111; www.nps.gov/caha. Another excellent source of information on these and other North Carolina lighthouses is the Outer Banks Lighthouse Society, P.O. Box 1005, Morehead City, NC 28557; (919) 787-6378, or see www.outerbankslighthousesociety .org. At the southern end of Hatteras Island at the ferry terminal, housing an exhibit of the Cape Hatteras Lighthouse's first-order Fresnel lens, is the Graveyard of the Atlantic Museum, 59200 Museum Drive, P.O. Box 284, Hatteras, NC 27943; (252) 986-2995; www.graveyardoftheatlantic.com.

■ OCRACOKE LIGHT ■
Ocracoke (1803 and 1823)

The first Ocracoke Lighthouse went up in 1803, the same year the original Cape Hatteras tower was completed. It stood on Shell Castle Island, where British colonial forces cornered and killed the notorious pirate Blackbeard early in the eighteenth century. Until the mid-1800s, Ocracoke Inlet was the only navigable one in that section of the Outer Banks to reach the sounds and rivers leading to business destinations, including ports in Bath, New Bern, Washington, Plymouth, Edenton, and Elizabeth City. Lightning destroyed the Shell Castle Lighthouse in 1818.

On an adjacent island the existing seventy-five-foot conical brick tower near Ocracoke Village was completed in 1823 as a harbor light. Automated in 1955, the Ocracoke Lighthouse displays a fixed white light with a focal plane about seventy-five feet above high water that can be seen from fourteen miles away. In 1988 the National Park Service, US Coast Guard, and North Carolina State Historic Preservation Office preserved this National Historic Landmark. Ownership of the tower transferred from the Coast Guard to the National Park Service in 2000, and restoration was completed in 2010. Its fourth-order Fresnel lens remains an active aid to navigation.

Travel information: Ocracoke Island is accessible only by ferry from Cedar Island, Swans Quarter, or Hatteras Island. Schedules vary. Contact the North Carolina Department of Transportation, Ferry Division, 113 Arendell Street, Morehead City, NC 28557; (800) 293-3779, or see www.ncdot.org/ferry.org. The lighthouse is located off NC 12 on Lighthouse Road, about a mile north of the main ferry. A small, limited parking area allows visitors access to the station grounds and tower. Please be respectful of sur-

Ocracoke Light at sunset

rounding private residences. For additional information contact the Cape Hatteras National Seashore, 1401 National Park Drive, Manteo, NC 27954; (252) 473-2111; www.nps.gov/caha.

For the Ocracoke Island Visitors Center, call (252) 928-4531. Just one of the historic attractions on this idyllic island is the British Cemetery honoring thirty-four British sailors who perished after the HMS *Bedfordshire* was struck by a German torpedo in 1942. Ocracoke Village is perfect for walking and bicycling.

■ CAPE LOOKOUT LIGHT ■
Cape Lookout (1812 and 1859)

Completed in 1812, the first Cape Lookout Lighthouse was of unusual design, with a central brick interior that housed stairs and was enveloped in an outer cocoon of wood, painted red and white. Although it cost $20,678 to build—a small fortune at the time—and stood more than a hundred feet tall, its light was surprisingly weak. It offered little assistance to mariners trying to avoid the cape, long ago nicknamed "Horrible Headland" because of the many shoals just offshore.

To improve the light the Lighthouse Board had the present 162-foot tower built in 1859, fitting it with the first-order Fresnel lens from the old tower. Only two years later, during the Civil War, Confederates removed the lens and took it to Raleigh for storage. In 1864 Confederate raiders aided by local spies tried to destroy both towers, and they nearly succeeded. The old tower was severely damaged, but only the lower part of the wooden stairs of the new tower were put out of order; the temporary third-order lens survived the ordeal. After the war in 1867, the original lens was returned to Paris for repair and later reinstalled in the lighthouse.

In 1873 the new tower received its distinct daymark pattern of black-and-white checkers, now called diamonds. The black diamonds indicate north-south,

Cape Lookout Light

while the white ones point east-west. In 1967, some years after the station was automated, the big Fresnel lost its job to an airport-style beacon and eventually was relocated to the **Block Island Southeast Lighthouse** in Rhode Island. The modern optic flashes white every fifteen seconds continuously and can be seen from up to twenty-five miles away.

Travel information: The lighthouse is located on Core Banks Island, now part of Cape Lookout National Seashore. The island can be reached only by passenger ferry; contact Barrier Island Transportation Service, P.O. Box 400, Harkers Island, NC 28531; (252) 728-3907; http://harkersmarina.com. For other information contact Cape Lookout National Seashore, 131 Charles Street, Harkers Island, NC 28531; (252) 728-2250; www.nps.gov/calo. Volunteer resident keepers stay in the keeper's quarters; to volunteer in the park, call (252) 728-2250, ext. 3008.

A must-see, the Core Sound Waterfowl and Heritage Center is next to park headquarters at the end of the island; see http://coresound.com. An interesting maritime museum in nearby Beaufort houses a fourth-order Fresnel lens and exhibits the treasure recovered from Blackbeard's flagship, the *Queen Anne's Revenge.* Contact the North Carolina Maritime Museums, 315 Front Street, Beaufort, NC 28516; (252) 728-7317; www.ncmaritime museum.org/beaufort.html. A nine-mile-long island adjacent to this lighthouse is home to approximately 135 wild horses on Shackleford Banks. The horses are monitored by the National Park Service and the Foundation for Shackleford Horses, Inc., 306 Golden Farm Road, Beaufort, NC 28516; (252) 728-6308; www.shacklefordhorses.org.

■ BALD HEAD (CAPE FEAR) ISLAND LIGHT ■
Bald Head Island (1795 and 1818)

Although its lantern has been dark since 1935, the Bald Head Island Lighthouse, the eldest of the state's standing lighthouses, remains a majestic structure, its octagonal brick tower rising ninety feet above the mostly flat island. Established in 1795 on Bald Head Island at the mouth of the Cape Fear River, this light station was North Carolina's first.

After a tornado toppled the original lighthouse in 1812, it was replaced by a 110-foot-tall fortresslike octagonal stone tower with brick walls five feet thick and a seven-foot-deep brick-and-sandstone foundation. Unlike many light towers the interior of the shaft was not open but instead consisted of a series of five storage and work rooms stacked one atop the other. The lantern room at the top originally housed whale-oil lamps and reflectors said to produce a fixed white light seen from eighteen miles at sea.

Known to seamen as "Old Baldy," the lighthouse was deactivated in 1935. In 1985 the Old Baldy Foundation (OBF) refurbished the structure and fitted it with a copper dome. The dedicated group continues restoration and grounds improvements today.

Bald Head Island Light

Travel information: The lighthouse is located on Bald Head Island, which can be reached by passenger ferry; contact the Bald Head Island Resort, (800) 234-1666; www.bald headisland.com/contact/ferry_infor mation.aspx. For day tours call Deep Port Transportation at (910) 457-5003. Ferry service is also available from Southport for visits to historic Fort Fisher and the ruins of the **Federal Point Lighthouse** (1837); ruins of **Price's Creek Range Light** (circa 1850) can be seen only from the ferry because the area is not open to the public. For special summer historic tours and events, contact the Old Baldy Foundation, P.O. Box 3007, NC 28461; (910) 457-7481, or see www.oldbaldy.org. In Southport,

Price's Creek Range Light

now at old Fort Johnston, see the North Carolina Maritime Museum, 204 E. Moore Street, Southport, NC 28461; (910) 457-0003; www.ncmaritime museums.com/southport.html.

■ OAK ISLAND LIGHT ■
Caswell Beach (1958)

Built during the late 1950s, this 148-foot reinforced-concrete tower houses a modern optic that produces an extraordinary fourteen million candlepower. Under normal conditions its original eight aerobeacon lights (two banks of four, one atop the other) was the strongest light on the East Coast and could be seen from up to twenty-four miles away. However, the lower bank of lights was decommissioned several years ago, and it lost that distinction, now claimed by the **Sullivan's Island Lighthouse.** Oak Island Light continues as an active aid to navigation for the Cape Fear River and to warn of Frying Pan Shoals, which juts into the Atlantic Ocean, with its four one-second flashes of white light every ten seconds.

Still located near the US Coast Guard Station, the tower and property were transferred to the Town of Caswell Beach in 2004 and are cared for by a nonprofit group that conduct summer tours and continues landscaping improvements and preservation of related oceanfront property. To climb this lighthouse is quite an adventure—its stairs are not circular but comprise multiple levels of ship's ladders. For more information contact the Friends of Oak Island Lighthouse, 1100 Caswell Beach Road, Caswell Beach, NC 28465; www.oakislandlighthouse.org.

Travel information: From US Highway 17 near Wilmington, follow Route 133 to Caswell Beach. Located on an active Coast Guard station, the lighthouse is closed to the public.

Oak Island Light

Reproducing the Past

Illustrating the resurgence of interest in lighthouses, North Carolina alone has one original river light that has been relocated and restored, one reproduction river light, and one reproduction sound light. The original **Roanoke River Lighthouse** (1886) has been stabilized, and restoration is ongoing in Colonial Park on the historic waterfront of Edenton. For more information contact Historic Edenton State Historic Sites, 108 North Broad Street, Edenton, NC 27932; call (252) 482-2637, or see www.edentonlighthouse.org.

On U.S. Highway 64 on Plymouth's historic Roanoke River waterfront is a reproduction of the original 1866 **Roanoke River Lighthouse** and Maritime Museum; call (252) 217-2204, or go to http://www.roanokeriverlighthouse.com.

East of Plymouth via U.S. Highway 64 on Manteo's historic waterfront is a reproduction of the 1857 **Roanoke Marshes Light;** go to www.townofmanteo.com, or call the stewards, Roanoke Island Festival park at (252) 475-1500.

Original 1886 Roanoke River Light relocated to Edenton
Robert DaVia

Reproduction Roanoke Marshes Light in Manteo

Reproduction Roanoke River Light in Plymouth

SOUTH CAROLINA

▪ GEORGETOWN LIGHT ▪
Georgetown (1801 and 1812)

Built for $7,000 on land donated by Revolutionary War patriot Paul Trapier, the original Georgetown Lighthouse consisted of a seventy-two-foot cypress tower, a small, two-story keeper's dwelling, and a tank for storing the whale oil that fueled the lamps. Completed in 1801, the tall wooden tower collapsed in a gale just five years later.

Located on North Island near the mouth of Winyah Bay, the eighty-seven-foot brick tower here today dates back to 1812. Constructed at a cost of more than $17,000—a hefty figure at the time—it was built to last, with 124 spiral steps cut from solid stone, and it has weathered more than two centuries of Atlantic storms. Refurbished in 1857, when it received a fourth-order Fresnel lens, and again in 1867 to repair Civil War damage, the lighthouse still displays its flashing white light. The station's resident ghost reputedly

Georgetown Light
Bob and Sandra Shanklin

climbs up and down the tower's steps on occasion. Thus, in more ways than one, this remains an active aid to navigation, but it is not open to the public.

Travel information: The best way to see the lighthouse, which is accessible only by boat, is via a tour boat from Georgetown. It is under state control and part of a wildlife preserve. For information or reservations write to Captain Sandy's Tours, P.O. Box 2533, Pawley's Island, SC 29585; call (803) 527-4106, or see the state's official tourism site at www.discoversouth carolina.com.

▪ CAPE ROMAIN LIGHT ▪
McClellanville (1827 and 1858)

In 1827 the government established a light station on Cape Romain to warn mariners of threatening shoals some nine miles to the southeast. Noted contractor Winslow Lewis built the first Cape Romain Lighthouse for approximately $7,500, equipping the sixty-five-foot conical brick tower with lamps and reflectors he had designed himself. The Lewis optic proved insufficient, however, and when a new, more powerful reflector system also failed to do the job, officials decided to rebuild the lighthouse.

Completed in 1858, only a few years before the Civil War, the second Cape Romain Lighthouse owns the dubious distinction of being built by slave labor. Its magnificent 150-foot, octagonal brick tower still stands despite a tilted foundation, which causes it to lean queasily out of plumb, like the famed tower of Pisa.

A first-order Fresnel lens cast light at least nineteen miles into the night, more than enough to warn ships away from the shoals. Damaged by Confederate forces in 1861, the lighthouse remained dark throughout the Civil War but was fully repaired and back in operation by 1866. Automated in 1937, the light was discontinued ten years later. Buoys now mark the notorious shoals.

Cape Romain offers a rare glimpse at what an American light station looked like when its early-nineteenth-century light still stood. Traditionally, the old towers were destroyed when new towers were built.

Travel information: Part of a protected coastal wild area, the lighthouse is located six miles east of McClellanville on Lighthouse Island and is accessible only by boat. Contact the Cape Romain National Wildlife Refuge, 5801 Highway 17 North, Awendaw, SC 29429; (843) 928-3264; www.fws.gov/caperomain, or see Travel information for **Georgetown Light.**

■ MORRIS ISLAND LIGHT ■
Charleston (1767, 1838, and 1876)

Among the oldest, most gracious cities in America, Charleston, South Carolina, was the site of one of America's earliest lighthouses, established in 1767. The black-and-white-banded tower now on Morris Island was built in 1876, but a copper plate on its cornerstone reads, "The first stone of this beacon was laid on the 30th of May 1767 in the seventh year of his Majesty's Reign, George III." That first 42-foot tower was replaced in 1838 by a new 102-foot-tall lighthouse. The second tower suffered destruction, as did several Southern lights during the Civil War.

The existing 162-foot brick tower—inactive since 1962, when it was sold to a private citizen—rests on a concrete foundation eight feet thick and is set atop piles driven fifty feet into the mud. This solid underfooting helped save the lighthouse

Morris Island Light

when an earthquake leveled much of Charleston in 1885. Replaced in 1962 by the **Charleston Light** on Sullivan's Island, the abandoned tower was threatened by severe erosion. Fortunately, the nonprofit Save the Light friends group came along, consulted the Army Corps of Engineers, and completed phase I of stabilization by encircling the tower with a cement wall to prevent further weakening of the foundation. Phase II includes adding to the existing foundation support to enable continued restoration plans.

> *Travel information:* Follow US Highway 17 south from Charleston, then East Ashley Street to its end. The lighthouse stands about one hundred yards off the nearby beach. The Charleston Lighthouse on Sullivan's Island can be seen across the harbor. For more information on the restoration process or to offer help, contact Save the Light, P.O. Box 12490, Charleston, SC 29422; (843) 633-0099; www.savethelight.org.

■ CHARLESTON LIGHT (SULLIVAN'S ISLAND) ■
Sullivan's Island (1962)

Unlike the old Morris Island station, which predates the Revolution, the Charleston Light, on Sullivan's Island near Fort Moultrie, is a product of the rock 'n' roll era. Built in 1962, the 140-foot triangular tower is fashioned of reinforced concrete clad in porcelainized aluminum siding. In its youth the tower sported true Coast Guard white and red-orange colors. Coast Guard service personnel travel via the nation's only lighthouse elevator to the station's modern optic, which once generated a sizzling twenty-eight million candlepower; however, it now generates just 1.5 million candlepower. Residents used influence to have the light dimmed and change the daymark to black and white. The flashing white beacon marking the entrance to Charleston Harbor is still visible up to twenty-seven miles at sea.

Charleston Light

The National Park Service (NPS), which has owned the light as part of the Fort Sumter National Monument since 2008, has ongoing plans to improve the once-military complex into a friendlier park for visitors. The NPS owns several American lighthouses, which now include the oldest standing (Sandy Hook) and this, the last lighthouse built in the country, signaling the end of an era.

> *Travel information:* Follow Route 703 through Mount Pleasant to Sullivan's Island and follow the signs toward Fort Moultrie. As you approach the fort, you'll see the tower on the left about two blocks off Middle Street. The tower is closed to the public, but visitors are welcome to walk the station grounds.

While in the area be sure to visit Fort Moultrie National Monument; call the park at (843) 883-3123, or go to www.nps.gov/fosu. The fort took part in Revolutionary War and Civil War battles. Edgar Allan Poe was once stationed here, as was, interestingly enough, William Tecumseh Sherman.

▪ HUNTING ISLAND LIGHT ▪
Hunting Island State Park (1859 and 1875)

The Hunting Island Light had beamed for only two years when the Civil War plunged it into darkness. By the end of the war, the station had mysteriously disappeared. Lighthouse officials assumed it was blown up by Confederates or, more likely, felled by erosion.

With the island's rapidly eroding shoreline in mind, the Lighthouse Board commissioned the station's cast-iron replacement tower—completed in 1875—to be built in sections that could be taken apart and reassembled elsewhere if necessary. When erosion threatened in 1885, the 132.5-foot-tall tower was safely moved about a mile inland. A second-order Fresnel lens served here until the station was decommissioned in 1933. Visitors are allowed to climb the 175 steps to the service gallery. The lighthouse is within Hunting Island State Park, a five-thousand-acre semitropical barrier island.

Hunting Island Light

Travel information: Take US Highway 21 east from Beaufort to Hunting Island State Park. For more information write the park at 2555 Sea Island Parkway, Hunting Island, SC 29920; call (843) 838-2011 or the park's Nature Center (843) 838-7437, or see www.southcarolinaparks.com.

▪ HARBOUR TOWN LIGHT ▪
Hilton Head (1970)

The ninety-foot red-and-white-striped reproduction tower of the Harbour Town Lighthouse is the visual centerpiece of the popular Sea Pines Resort on Hilton Head Island. Its white light flashes every two and a half seconds to mark the Inland Waterway and Calibogue Sound. Completed in 1970, Harbour Town Light was the first privately financed

Harbour Town Light

light tower built since the early 1800s. Visitors who climb the tower steps will find at the top a gift shop and an excellent spot to view Hilton Head.

Travel information: Follow US Highway 278 until it ends at Sea Pines Plantation. Contact Sea Pines Resort, 32 Greenwood Drive, Hilton Head Island, SC 29928; (866) 561-8802; www.seapines.com; or the lighthouse at 149 Lighthouse Road, Hilton Head Island, SC 22928; (843) 671-2810; www.harbourtownlighthouse.com.

■ HILTON HEAD REAR RANGE LIGHT (LEAMINGTON LIGHT) ■
Hilton Head Island (1880)

First marked during the Civil War by a Union Navy lightship, Hilton Head received a pair of land-based range lights in 1880. The lantern room of a tall, cast-iron skeleton tower housed one light, and a second, lesser tower was perched atop a house. Braced iron legs help the ninety-five-foot rear-range tower withstand gales. Keepers climbed the 112-step spiral staircase, winding upward through a central steel cylinder, to reach the hexagonal wooden lantern room, which once held a Fresnel lens. Both lights were retired from service in 1932. A pair of keeper's dwellings built near the rear-range tower during the late 1800s are said to be haunted. According to popular legend, the ghost is that of Caroline Fripp, the daughter of an early keeper.

Hilton Head Rear Range

Travel information: On Hilton Head Island the rear-range tower is located in exclusive Palmetto Dunes on hole 15 of the Arthur Hills Golf Course, a gated and guarded residential community; the lighthouse grounds are generally closed to the public except by permission of Greenwood Communities and Resort; call Security for a special permit at (843) 785-1120. The supposedly haunted dwellings have been moved to nearby Harbour Town, where they house businesses, including a popular delicatessen.

■ HAIG POINT REAR RANGE LIGHT (DAUFUSKIE ISLAND) ■

Freeport (1872 and 1986)

So many battles were fought on Daufuskie Island that locals began calling it the "Place of Blood." During the early 1800s a pair of range lights on Bloody Point guided vessels to the island, where cotton and sugar plantations then prospered. At one time lighted by candles and later by kerosene lanterns, the Bloody Point Range Lights served mariners for more than a century before being extinguished in 1922.

Beginning in 1872, a second pair of range lights was established on the opposite side of the island on Haig Point. One light was fastened on a pole far out in the water, while the rear-

Haig Point Rear Range Light
Daniel J. Gruszka

range light shone from a twenty-five-foot-tall tower atop the keeper's dwelling. The government deactivated Haig Point Range Lights in 1934. Now a private club, the restored lighthouse is corporate-owned and operates as a private aid to navigation.

> *Travel information:* You can reach Daufuskie Island via scheduled cruises from Hilton Head. For ferries or tours contact Calibogue Cruises and Freeport Marina, located at Broad Creek Marina on Hilton Head Island, (843) 342-8687, or see www.daufuskiefreeport.com. Also contact Adventure Cruises, Dock C, Shelter Cove Harbour, Hilton Head Island, SC 29928; (843) 785-4558; www.hiltonheadisland.com/adventure. The Haig Point Lighthouse can be seen from Calibogue Sound but is closed to visitors. The building that formerly served as the **Bloody Point Rear Range Lighthouse** (1883) still stands, but it has been moved away from the water.

GEORGIA

■ TYBEE ISLAND LIGHT ■
Tybee Island (1736, 1742, and 1773)

Shortly after General James Oglethorpe founded the colony of Georgia in 1733, he ordered construction of a ninety-foot-tall, brick tower (with no light, just a landfall marker) on Tybee Island as a daymark to guide ships into navigable channels of the Savannah River. It was completed in 1736 but lasted only five years because of storms and erosion. Rebuilt in 1742, it eventually again succumbed to erosion. A third tower was built further inland in 1773; it was a one-hundred-foot-tall wooden and brick structure. The lighthouse was ceded to the government in 1790 after Georgia ratified the Constitution. The Tybee Island Lighthouse served faithfully until retreating Confederate troops burned it in 1862.

Tybee Island Light

Following the Civil War, in 1867 masons restored the tower by adding brick to the still-strong lower sixty feet of brickwork. The 154-foot octagonal structure's massive twelve-foot-thick brick walls at the base had survived the rebels' explosives. The lantern was fitted with the same first-order Fresnel lens that still serves the station, giving the light a range of about twenty miles. The top two-thirds of the distinctive Tybee Island tower is painted black and the lower third white, reflecting its 1916 appearance. In 1987 the Coast Guard leased the lighthouse to the City of Tybee Island and the Tybee Island Historical Society, which has full responsibility for its maintenance and restoration. It remains an active aid to navigation, and it is one of America's finest restoration projects, under the expert supervision of Cullen Chambers and staff.

> *Travel information:* Follow US Highway 80 from Savannah to Tybee Island. The lighthouse, which can be seen from miles away, is located at the north end of the island in old Fort Screven. Contact the Tybee Island Lighthouse and Museum, P.O. Box 366, Tybee Island, GA 31328; (912) 786-5801, or see www.tybeelighthouse.org.

■ COCKSPUR ISLAND LIGHT ■
Savannah (1849 and 1855)

During the late 1840s the Lighthouse Service established a pair of light towers marking the key north and south channels of the Savannah River. The **North Channel**

Light, built on Oyster Bed Island, was destroyed by storms that buffet the area. Despite being caught in a tremendous artillery duel between Union batteries on Tybee Island and the big Confederate guns at nearby Fort Pulaski, the **South Channel Light** survived the fighting. The forty-six-foot-tall lighthouse served continuously until 1949, enduring storms, earthquakes, and floods, when it was retired at the ripe old

Cockspur Island Light

age of one hundred. The lighthouse is part of the Fort Pulaski National Monument; it is open for public visitation, but the terrain of Cockspur Island is rugged and can be perilous—native American alligators inhabit the area. Watch your step!

Travel information: Located on an islet off the southeastern tip of Cockspur Island, a scrap of semidry land, the lighthouse can be seen from the US Highway 80 bridge twelve miles east of the port of Savannah. Nearby Fort Pulaski, completed in 1848, is well worth a visit. The brick-and-stone fort took eighteen years to build but only a few days to fall to Union forces during an 1862 artillery duel. For information contact Pulaski National Monument, P.O. Box 30757, Savannah, GA 31410; (912) 786-5787. For area historic sites and tours, contact Visit Savannah, 101 E. Bay Street, Savannah, GA 31401, or call (877) 728-6624, or see www.savannah visit.com.

■ SAPELO ISLAND LIGHT ■
Sapelo Island (1820)

Few places along the US East Coast are as wild as Georgia's Sapelo Island, a natural treasure trove of tall marsh grass, pristine beaches, and gnarled coastal forests. An eighty-foot brick-and-stone tower, the first Sapelo Island Light tower was the work of Winslow Lewis, who built so many of America's early lighthouses. Lewis billed the government $17,000, a price that included one of his patented lamp-and-reflector optics. During the early 1850s the government raised the tower by ten feet and installed a fourth-order Fresnel lens.

Sapelo Island Light

In 1905 a giant steel skeleton tower took over the work of the original lighthouse. Deactivated in 1933, the later structure was dismantled and shipped to Lake Superior for use in the Apostle Islands. The earlier light tower still stands; following its 1998 restoration by Georgia State Parks and Historic Sites, it once again became a working aid to navigation.

Travel information: The Georgia Department of Natural Resources maintains Sapelo Island as a wildlife and nature preserve and offers a variety of nature tours, which include tours of the lighthouse; call (912) 437-3224, or see www.gastateparks.org. Privately operated lighthouse tours are available from Meridian, Georgia, reached via Route 99, off Interstate 95; call (912) 638-6732. In addition to the original Lewis tower, Sapelo Island is also home to the tiny, iron-legged **Sapelo Front Range Lighthouse** (1868).

■ ST. SIMONS ISLAND LIGHT ■
St. Simons Island (1810 and 1872)

Built in 1810, the first St. Simons Lighthouse was a white, seventy-five-foot-tall structure, covered with tabby, a stuccolike cement made of crushed oyster shells. Topped by an iron lantern containing an oil lamp suspended by chains—a fire prevention measure—it marked the St. Simons Sound. Confederate troops destroyed the tower and all the station outbuildings as they retreated from the island in 1862.

St. Simons Island Light

Outbreaks of a mysterious illness, probably malaria, that repeatedly decimated work crews delayed construction of a new lighthouse for years. The 104-foot brick tower and adjacent dwelling were finally completed in 1872. The St. Simons Island Lighthouse remains in service to this day, its third-order L. Sautter Company Fresnel lens still in place. The beacon flashes white once a minute and has a range of twenty miles.

According to legend the ghost of a former keeper haunts the station. Killed more than a century ago in a duel with his assistant, the keeper is said to walk the tower steps at night. The Coastal Georgia Historical Society has won numerous national preservation and heritage educational awards for its lighthouse restoration and establishment of unique museums here.

Travel information: Charming St. Simons Island is reached by causeway from Brunswick. On the island follow Kings Way and Beachview; then turn right onto Twelfth Street. The fascinating Museum of Coastal History, located in the old brick keeper's residence, displays a fourth-order Fresnel lens. Contact the Coastal Georgia Historical Society, St. Simons Island Lighthouse and Museum, Maritime Center at the Historic Coast Guard Station, P.O. Box 21136, St. Simons, GA 31522; call (912) 638-4666, or see www.saintsimonslighthouse.org.

■ LITTLE CUMBERLAND ISLAND LIGHT ■
Little Cumberland Island (1820 and 1838)

The coast of Georgia is protected by a line of barrier islands. The St. Marys River lumbers into the Atlantic Ocean between Amelia Island, Florida, and Cumberland Island, Georgia. To the north is a smaller barrier island known as Little Cumberland. The larger of the two barriers received the earlier guiding light, the **Great Cumberland Island Lighthouse.**

Winslow Lewis, America's most prolific lighthouse builder, received a contract in 1819 to erect a light tower and dwelling on the southern tip of big Cumberland Island. For $17,000 Lewis delivered a fifty-foot brick tower, a small brick keeper's dwelling, and a Lewis-style optic for the lantern, all ready for service by July 1820. In 1838 it was broken down, relocated across the mouth of St. Marys River to Amelia Island, and reassembled. It stands today under the care of Fernandina Beach, Florida.

Little Cumberland Island Light
Bob and Sandra Shanklin

In 1838, even before the relocation of the Great Cumberland Island Lighthouse began, the Lighthouse Service decided to build a new tower on Little Cumberland Island's northernmost point to mark the entrance to St. Andrews Sound and the Satilla River. The new sixty-foot tower was sturdily built of brick. In 1857 a sparkling, third-order Fresnel lens supplanted the old Lewis-style lamps-and-reflector optic. During the Civil War Confederate troops damaged the lens and the tower, putting the station out of service until repairs were completed in 1867. The station was discontinued and abandoned in 1915. Today it is cared for by the residents of the private community in which it resides.

Travel information: Little Cumberland Island is a private residential community, and neither the island nor the lighthouse is open to the public. Tour cruises, however, from nearby Jekyll Island pass within sight of the tower. Contact Coastal Expeditions at (912) 265-0392.

FLORIDA

▪ AMELIA ISLAND LIGHT ▪
Old Fernandina Beach (1839)

In 1838 the Lighthouse Service dismantled the tower that had marked Georgia's Great Cumberland Island since 1820 and reassembled it on Amelia Island, near the mouth of the St. Marys River. In 1881 a new lantern room was installed, increasing the tower's height to sixty-four feet. Rising from the pinnacle of a hill, its focal plane is over one hundred feet above the water. Renovated in classic Victorian style in 1885, Florida's northernmost lighthouse is a graceful structure. A gleaming black lantern crowns the white brick tower. The third-order Fresnel lens placed here in 1903 still shines each night, displaying a flashing light. Navigators approaching the dangerous shoals in nearby Nassau Sound see a red flash, whereas others in the safe channel see a white flash.

Amelia Island Light

The City of Fernandina Beach received ownership of the lighthouse from the Coast Guard in 2001. Garnering funding, the city accomplished restoration of the historic tower in two phases, completed in 2008. The iconic lighthouse is open for public tours on a limited basis, and reservations are required.

> *Travel information:* Located within a private residential section of town, the lighthouse is not open regularly to the public. To make reservations for a lighthouse tour or a schedule of times the grounds are open, contact the city's Recreation Center at (904) 277-7350, or see www.fbfl.us. A lighthouse brochure is available from the City of Fernandina Beach, 204 Ash Street, Fernandina Beach, FL 32034. You can see this historic structure from Route A1A in Old Fernandina Beach; perhaps the best way to enjoy the sight is on an evening walk along one of Amelia Island's lovely beaches, with its warm beacon flashing in the distance.

▪ ST. JOHNS RIVER LIGHT ▪
Mayport (1830, 1835, and 1859)

A simple oil lamp hung on a pole was likely the first navigational light used to guide ships into the untamed St. Johns River, now a bustling thoroughfare for warships, commercial freighters, fishing boats, and pleasure craft. The river's first official lighthouse, completed in 1830, was among the first light towers in what was then the

Territory of Florida. The structure cost the government $24,000 but lasted little more than five years. Surging tidal currents quickly undermined its foundation, and it was torn down in 1835. That same year a second lighthouse was built, but by the early 1850s nearby sand dunes had piled up so high that the beacon could no longer be seen from the sea.

Completed in 1859, the river's third lighthouse was a sixty-six-foot brick tower fitted with a third-order Fresnel lens. Its lamps burned regularly until 1864, when Confederate gunners shot out the light in hopes of blinding federal gunboats. The light was quickly restored following the Civil War. In 1887 brick masons added fifteen feet to the tower, raising it to a height of eighty-one feet. The light served until 1929, when a lightship moored seven miles from the mouth of the St. Johns replaced it. The old tower remains in excellent shape, although twelve feet of it is now underground, buried during construction of a runway for the adjacent Mayport naval air station and forcing the first level window to become the new entrance. The Navy and Mayport Lighthouse Association are working together to protect, restore, and interpret the lighthouse.

St. Johns River Light

> *Travel information:* Located on the Naval Station Mayport, the lighthouse
> is closed to the public but may be viewed from nearby streets, especially
> on the road east from the Mayport ferry. Contact the Public Affairs Office,
> Naval Station Mayport, P.O. Box 280032, Mayport, FL 32228-0032 or call
> (904) 270-5226, x1013. Also closed to the public but viewable from a nearby
> naval compound is the **Mayport Light** (1954), just south of the St. Johns
> River Light. The art deco–style sixty-four-foot tower has no lantern room,
> only a modern optic. For more information on these lights, contact the
> Mayport Lighthouse Association, Inc., 4610 Ocean Street, Mayport Village,
> FL 32233; for information on all Florida lighthouses, contact the Florida
> Lighthouse Association, P.O. Box 1676, St. Petersburg, FL 33731; call (727)
> 667-7775, or see www.floridalighthouses.org.

■ ST. AUGUSTINE LIGHT ■
St. Augustine (1824 and 1874)

Shortly after the United States acquired Florida from the Spanish in 1819, a federal customs collector placed a lantern in an old stone tower to guide American ships to St. Augustine. A more conventional seventy-three-foot brick tower soon replaced this rather primitive lighthouse, but its weak reflecting optic projected light only a short distance beyond the harbor entrance.

Although darkened during the Civil War, the St. Augustine Lighthouse survived the conflict—only to be flattened by tidal erosion. Before the tower collapsed, the government established a new light station on nearby Anastasia Island. The keeper lit the lamps inside its first-order Fresnel lens on October 15, 1874. From atop this new 165-foot brick tower, a combination fixed and flashing light shot its beam through some twenty-five miles of darkness. The same lens remains in operation today. Painted in distinctive black-and-white barber-pole stripes, the tower helps guide mariners during the day.

Beginning in 1980, St. Augustine's Junior Service League launched a restoration project for the keeper's house (destroyed by fire a decade earlier) and the tower. The house serves as a museum. In 2002 the US Coast Guard transferred the tower and first-order lens to the St. Augustine Lighthouse & Museum, Inc. It continues to be one of America's most beautifully restored light stations.

St. Augustine Light

Travel information: Follow Route A1A and Old Beach Road to Lighthouse Avenue. The beautifully restored brick keeper's residence houses an excellent museum that celebrates the history of the lighthouse and coastal Florida. For a gull's-eye view of the Atlantic and the old Spanish town of St. Augustine, visitors may climb the 219 steps to the service gallery. Contact the St. Augustine Lighthouse and Museum, Inc., 81 Lighthouse Avenue, St. Augustine, FL 32080; (904) 829-0745, or see www.staugustinelighthouse.com. This light has been rated as one of the best lighthouse climbs in America.

■ PONCE DE LEON INLET LIGHT ■
Ponce Inlet (1887)

The first lighthouse at Ponce Inlet, then called Mosquito Inlet, collapsed in an 1835 storm before its lamps were ever lit. Half a century passed before the government once more attempted to establish a major coastal light here, this time on an Olympian scale. Using red brick shipped south from Baltimore, construction crews erected an impressive 175-foot tower, completing it in 1887. This makes Ponce the second tallest brick lighthouse in the country. In the lantern room a first-order Fresnel lens focused the light provided by a five-wick kerosene lamp designed by none other than George Meade, the famed lighthouse engineer and Civil War general. This lens was traded out for a third-order lens when the light was electrified in 1933.

The Coast Guard discontinued the light in 1970 as an economy measure and removed the Fresnel lens to protect it from vandalism, replacing the grand old brick tower with a simple steel tower at the Smyrna Dunes Coast Guard station. Nearby high-rise construction, however, soon rendered the new light ineffective, and in 1982 the Ponce de Leon Inlet Lighthouse was reactivated with an aeromarine beacon. After decades of restoration by the Ponce de Leon Inlet Lighthouse Preservation Association, the light station earns top ranking as one of the best preserved in the nation and is designated a National Historic Landmark. In 2004 its former third-order rotating Fresnel lens was restored and returned to the lantern room, making the lighthouse a private aid to navigation.

This light station was one of the first great restoration efforts for American lighthouses that began decades ago by the Ponce de Leon Lighthouse Preservation Association. With museum exhibits, interpretive guides, the opportunity to climb Florida's tallest lighthouse, and nearby attractions, this light station is one of America's top destinations.

Travel information: Its tower, dwellings, and other outbuildings beautifully restored, the light-station complex composes one of the finest lighthouse museums in America. A special exhibit building houses several lenses of all sizes, including a fourth-order bivalve Fresnel lens, the first-order Fresnel that once served at Cape Canaveral, as well as Ponce de Leon Inlet Lighthouse's original magnificent first-order Fresnel lens. Contact the Ponce de Leon Inlet Lighthouse Museum, 4931 South Peninsula Drive, Ponce Inlet, FL 32127; (386) 761-1821, or see www.ponceinlet.org.

■ CAPE CANAVERAL LIGHT ■
Cape Canaveral (1848 and 1868)

Thrusting eastward into the Atlantic, Cape Canaveral poses a formidable threat to ships moving along the Florida peninsula. Yet when the Lighthouse Service marked the cape with a sixty-five-foot brick tower in 1848, it perhaps did more harm than good. The light proved so weak that captains often ran their vessels aground on nearby shoals while searching for the signal. The Civil War cut short efforts to correct this unhappy situation.

After the war the Lighthouse Board gave the Cape Canaveral station high priority. They constructed a cast-iron cylinder tower fitted with a first-order Fresnel lens. Shining from atop the 145-foot brick-lined tower, the light could be seen from eighteen miles away, a distance sufficient to keep ships away from the shoals. In 1893 beach erosion forced relocation of the lighthouse to a new site about a mile inland.

A modern, automated beacon replaced the massive glass Fresnel lens in 1993. Sailors still use the light to navigate safely around the Canaveral shoals, but nowadays they often see other bright lights on the cape—rockets rushing skyward from the Kennedy Space Center.

Cape Canaveral Light
NASA

The lighthouse was transferred from the Coast Guard to the Air Force in 2000. An ongoing restoration project is being done by the Cape Canaveral Lighthouse Foundation, Inc.

Travel information: Owned by the US Air Force, the Cape Canaveral lighthouse is open to the public via tours through Patrick AFB Public Affairs. The 45th Space Wing is offering tours of the air station the second Wednesday of each month; for reservations call in advance of your visit (321) 494-5945, or see http://canaverallight.org.

No visit to the area would be complete without a visit to the Kennedy Space Center. Contact Spaceport USA/Visitors Center, Kennedy Space Center, FL 32899; call (321) 449-4444 or see www.kennedyspacecentertours.net.

■ JUPITER INLET LIGHT ■
Jupiter (1860)

Robert E. Lee surveyed the site for the Jupiter Inlet Light station. George Meade designed and supervised construction of the 125-foot Jupiter tower. The two army engineers would eventually square off against each other as commanding generals of opposing armies at Gettysburg, Pennsylvania, with General Meade emerging as victor.

Juniper Inlet Light

The Jupiter Inlet Light also played a role in the Civil War. Established just prior to the fratricidal conflict that plunged much of America into darkness, the Jupiter Inlet Light was snuffed out by Confederate raiders after burning for little more than a year. Following the war, keeper James Armour found the station's first-order Fresnel lens hidden in a nearby creek. He soon restored the lens to its proper place and had the light back in operation by the end of 1866. The big lens still remains in use, its flashing white light visible from twenty-five miles away.

Nature as well as war has battered the structure. A 1928 hurricane knocked out both the primary and emergency electric power, forcing keeper Charles Seabrook to reinstall the station's old mineral lamps. When the keeper fell ill from exhaustion, his sixteen-year-old son climbed the swaying tower's steps to rotate the lens by hand and keep the light burning.

Maintenance and educational tours of the Jupiter Inlet Lighthouse are the sole responsibilities of the Loxahatchee River Historical Society. A museum on area heritage is in the newly restored World War II building.

Travel information: Now open to the public as a key attraction, the bright red tower and museum are located in Lighthouse Park, reached via Route 707 off US Highway 1; turn east on Beach Road. Contact Jupiter Inlet Lighthouse and Museum, 500 Captain Armour's Way, Jupiter, FL 33469; call (561) 747-8380, or see www.lrhs.org.

■ HILLSBORO INLET LIGHT ■
Pompano Beach (1907)

Located on the north side of Hillsboro Inlet, the light marks the northern limit of the Florida Reef, an underwater coral formation on the lower east coast of the state. Looming dramatically above Hillsboro Inlet near Pompano Beach, this cast-iron skeleton tower fits right into the local scenery but is not a Florida native. A Chicago foundry fabricated the 132-foot tower and barged it down the Mississippi to St. Louis, where it delighted crowds at the 1904 Exposition. After the fair the government bought the lighthouse, took it apart, and reassembled it on faraway Hillsboro Inlet. The second-order bivalve Fresnel lens, purchased by the government in 1907 for $90,000, still functions, displaying a flashing white light with an impressive range of twenty-eight miles.

   Travel information: This striking lighthouse and immediate area are used by the Coast Guard and are not open to the public but can be viewed from the A1A bridge over Hillsboro Inlet or from the beach on the south shore.

Hillsboro Inlet Light

■ CAPE FLORIDA LIGHT ■
Key Biscayne (1825)

A Seminole war party attacked the Cape Florida Lighthouse in 1836, killing the keeper's assistant and torching the tower. Keeper John Thomson survived by retreating to the lantern room sixty feet above the ground as the tower steps below him went up in flames. The fortuitous arrival of a US Navy warship saved the badly burned Thompson from certain death by starvation or exposure.

Cape Florida Light
Mark Riddick/New Light Photography

   The threat of Indian attack made repair of the lighthouse impossible for nearly ten years. Despite the fire and a decade of neglect, the original hollow-walled brick tower remained standing. It is noteworthy to state here that hollow walls were not an engineering technique used until after US Army Corps engineers started tower construction about three decades later. In this case a parsimonious contractor skimped on the number of bricks used and made the walls hollow. By the mid-nineteenth century, it would become the preferred engineering design. After raising the height of the tower to ninety-five feet, the Lighthouse Service restoration crew had the station back in operation by the end of 1856.

   Its light was extinguished in 1878 when the **Fowey Rocks Lighthouse** was completed, and the Cape Florida tower languished dark and empty for more than twice as long as it had served as an active aid to navigation. At present, however, the tower is handsomely refurbished, thanks to $1.5 million in privately donated and

Fowey Rocks Light
Bob and Sandra Shanklin

state-matching funds raised by the Dade County Heritage Trust. Given a fresh coat of stucco and white paint, the gleaming tower was relit during the Miami Centennial celebration in July 1996. The light's first-order Fresnel lens was removed in 1974 and is on display at the Aids to Navigation Museum at the National Aids to Navigation School in Yorktown, Virginia.

Travel information: The lighthouse is located on Key Biscayne, southeast of downtown Miami. From Interstate 95 follow the Rickenbacker (toll) Causeway and Crandon Boulevard. Contact the Bill Baggs State Recreation Area, 1200 South Crandon Boulevard, Key Biscayne, FL 33149; for the sundry activities available at this beautiful state park, call (305) 361-5811. Rising from open water more than ten miles south of Cape Florida, the **Fowey Rocks Lighthouse** (1878) cannot be seen from land. The iron skeleton tower marks a shoal named for the British frigate *Fowey*, lost here in 1748. For more information, see www.key-biscayne.com.

■ CARYSFORT REEF LIGHT ■
Key Largo (1852)

When completed in 1852 the 110-foot iron skeleton Carysfort Reef tower represented a completely new approach to lighthouse construction. Legendary contractor Winslow Lewis, who built so many of the nation's early masonry light towers, submitted a bid to erect this one, using familiar stone-construction techniques. Officials opted instead for a more radical plan put forward by the contractor's own nephew—and harshest critic—I. W. P. Lewis.

Carysfort Reef Light
US Coast Guard

George Meade, the US Army engineer who later led Union forces to victory at Gettysburg, supervised construction of the lighthouse I. W. P. Lewis envisioned. Built in open water directly over the reef, the tower stood—and still stands, almost a century and a half after it was built—on eight cast-iron legs arranged in an octagon some fifty feet wide. A screw pile, stabilized with massive iron discs four feet in diameter, anchors each leg to the sea bottom. Braced by iron girts and tie bars, the legs hold aloft a twenty-four-foot-wide platform supporting a two-story keeper's dwelling. The lantern rests on a second platform about one hundred feet above the water. Keepers climbed a staircase rising through a cylinder centered between the outer piles to reach the first-order Fresnel lens, installed in 1855.

Keepers formerly lived here year-round, but now the old lighthouse stands guard over the reef alone, as it has since 1962, when a third-order Fresnel lens replaced the original one. That lens was also removed by the Coast Guard and a solar-powered modern optic was put to work in 1982. The once-flashing white and red beacon became a fixed white light with a fifteen-mile range as always.

Travel information: The red skeleton lighthouse is visible from County Road 905 on Key Largo. To see it up close, however, you must charter a boat in Key Largo; visitors are not allowed on the structure. The lighthouse is now part of John Pennekamp Coral Reef State Park; call the park at (305) 451-1202, or see www.pennekamppark.com. It is used by the National Oceanic and Atmospheric Administration as a Sanctuary Preservation area; see http://floridakeys.noaa.gov.

■ ALLIGATOR REEF LIGHT ■
Matecumbe Key (1873)

Affectionately known as "Old Gator," the Alligator Reef Lighthouse is as tough as a reptile. Built during the early 1870s on a wave-swept shoal off Matecumbe Key, the 136-foot iron skeleton tower has withstood dozens of major hurricanes. Even the 1935 Labor Day superstorm that slammed the tower with a twenty-foot wall of water could not topple it.

Alligator Reef Light
Kraig Anderson

Despite its playful moniker neither Old Gator nor the ship-killing reef on which it stands is named for the American alligator. Instead, the names honor the US Navy schooner *Alligator*, sunk here in 1822. Over the years countless vessels have followed the USS *Alligator* to their doom on the reef's jagged coral. To stop or at least slow the losses, in 1870 the Lighthouse Board launched construction of a light tower here. Ironically, the project headquarters and workers' barracks were on nearby Indian Key, also inhabited by wreckers who made their living salvaging vessels caught by the reef.

Blows from a two-thousand-pound hammer drove twelve-inch iron pilings ten feet into the coral to support the tower. Iron discs help anchor the pilings to the coral. Completed in 1873 at the then phenomenal cost of $185,000, Old Gator still stands tall, but its original first-order bivalve Fresnel lens that once focused a white and red flashing light is now a modern optic powered with batteries recharged by solar panels. The automated beacon remains a Coast Guard active aid to navigation and has a range of about twelve miles. Its starch-white middle keeper's quarters and iron bracings are capped by a pitch-black lantern and lower support pilings, which make it an impressive resident of the emerald waters of the Keys.

Travel information: Driving the unique 126-mile Overseas Highway is a bit like motoring across the open ocean. Near Islamorada look to the southeast anywhere from Mile Marker 80, near the north end of Lower

Matecumbe Key, to Mile Marker 77 to see the venerable Alligator Reef Lighthouse. To view or photograph the lighthouse at leisure, turn off the road at Mile Marker 79.

■ SOMBRERO KEY LIGHT ■
Marathon (1858)

Although scheduled for construction in 1854, storms and funding shortages delayed completion of the Sombrero Key Lighthouse until 1858. Army engineer George Meade, later to earn glory and fame as the Union commander at Gettysburg, saw the project through to its end. The tower he and his work crews built here cost the government $150,000, a considerable fortune at the time. But the tower proved well worth its hefty price, standing up to gales and hurricanes for more than 140 years.

Meade placed the 142-foot tower atop eight galvanized iron pilings (iron dipped in molten zinc) and placed them at the corners of an octagon with a central piling and cross-bracing connecting the sturdy frame. This was an innovation that may account for the lighthouse's extraordinary longevity. The station's original first-order Fresnel lens, which cost $20,000, produced a fixed white light visible up to fifteen miles away. In 1931 the light

Sombrero Key Light
Bob and Sandra Shanklin

was made to flash by fitting the lens with revolving opaque screens. The light was automated and personnel were removed in 1960 following the death of a returning coastguardsman who died of injury while attempting to go aboard the lighthouse. This site had long earned a reputation for being accident prone. In 1982 a modern optic powered by solar cells replaced the huge Fresnel.

> *Travel information:* You can view the lighthouse from Sombrero Beach State Park near the town of Marathon on Vaca Key and its family park. Turn left at Mile Marker 50. The station's old first-order Fresnel is on display in Key West. Contact the Key West Lighthouse Museum, 938 Whitehead Street, Key West, FL 33040; (305) 295-6616, or see www.kwahs.com/lighthouse.htm.

■ AMERICAN SHOAL LIGHT ■
Sugarloaf Key (1880)

The killer reef off Looe Key, about twenty miles northeast of Key West, has torn open the hulls of numerous ships—the exact number may never be known. Early attempts to stop the carnage included placing daymarks on Looe Key and erecting a tall, unlighted piling atop the shoal. But vessels caught in the tricky currents near the shoal often saw these markers too late, and at night, of course, they were of no use at all. Finally, in 1878 Congress appropriated $75,000 to place a lighthouse directly over the shoal.

Fabricated in a New Jersey shipyard, the 109-foot Victorian octagon tower was shipped nearly fifteen hundred miles south and installed atop a massive underwater platform. The final cost of the station, including the tower, the octagonal keeper's dwelling resting on a platform about forty feet above the water, and the first-order Fresnel lens in the lantern room at the top, came to $125,000—$50,000 more than the original estimates. A reluctant Congress finally coughed up the extra funds, and the station's lamps shone out for the first time on July 15, 1880.

American Shoal Light

The Coast Guard automated the light in 1963, removing the original rotating first-order Fresnel lens. The modern optic currently in place is powered by batteries recharged daily by solar cells. Its flashing white and red light has a range of about thirteen miles but this time more to protect Looe Key, now designated a marine sanctuary.

Travel information: Near Overseas Highway Mile Marker 17 on Sugarloaf Key, turn left on Sugarloaf Boulevard (County Road 939), then right on County Road 939A. The lighthouse can be seen from out in the ocean to the southeast of a bridge across a small inlet.

■ SAND KEY LIGHT ■
Near Key West (1827 and 1853)

On October 9, 1846, a hurricane devastated Havana and moved on the following day to blast the Florida Keys. Joshua Appleby, the old New England sea captain who kept the Sand Key Lighthouse, not far from Key West, must have seen the swirling black clouds coming and known that he was in trouble. Mistakenly believing the hurricane season was over, Appleby had invited his daughter Eliza, her three-year-old son Thomas, and some friends to the island. No doubt the visit was a joy for the lonely keeper, but it ended tragically. By the time the storm clouds passed, the light tower and keeper's dwelling had disappeared. So, too, had Appleby and his visitors—their bodies were never recovered, and Sand Key had vanished.

Sand Key Light

Built in 1827, the sixty-five-foot brick tower on Sand Key weathered many harsh storms before succumbing to the 1846 hurricane. For more than twenty years, its fourteen whale-oil lamps and twenty-one-inch Lewis reflector guided ships along safe channels south of the Keys. After Sand Key drowned, a lightship took up this duty until a new lighthouse was completed in 1853.

Designed by I. W. P. Lewis and built under the supervision of George Meade, the new iron skeleton tower rose 105 feet above what was now open water. Perhaps with the 1846 disaster in mind, Meade gave the tower a solid underfooting of twelve hefty iron pilings and heavily braced legs sloping inward toward the lantern. Fitted with a first-order Fresnel lens, its flashing light could warn mariners up to twenty miles away. The grand old Fresnel was removed when the station was automated just before the United States entered World War II in 1938. Nearly destroyed in a 1989 fire that started in the abandoned keeper's dwelling, the lighthouse recently underwent a $500,000 restoration.

Travel information: For information on boat charters from Key West or flying services offering overflights of Sand Key, contact the Key West Chamber of Commerce, 510 Greene Street, Key West, FL 33040; call (305) 294-2587, or see www.keywestchamber.org.

■ KEY WEST LIGHT ■
Key West (1825 and 1847)

Once a stronghold for pirates, Key West became a thriving commercial center soon after the United States bought Florida and its Keys from the Spanish in 1819. After 1825 a sixty-five-foot brick lighthouse on Whitehead Point served the bustling Key West harbor, which attracted vast quantities of goods salvaged from shipwrecks in the Keys. Some people considered the notorious wreckers who did most of the salvaging little better than the pirates only recently expelled by the US Navy.

Key West Light

The 1846 hurricane that swallowed up Sand Key swamped hundreds of vessels, generating plenty of business for the wreckers. But it also destroyed much of the town, along with its lighthouse. By 1847 a new tower stood on a more secure site farther from the water. A third-order Fresnel lens, placed in the lantern in 1872, improved the range of the beacon. So, too, did the twenty feet added to the height of the tower in 1892. The station was decommissioned in 1969 but was restored to active service in 1972 as a private aid to navigation. Presently, the lighthouse serves as one of many attractions in this sunny, water-besieged and margarita-soaked tourist mecca.

Travel information: The lighthouse and the Key West Lighthouse Museum (housed in the station's old keeper's bungalow) are located at the intersection of Truman Avenue (US Highway 1) and Whitehead Street in the Key West Historic District. Among the wide array of fascinating museum exhibits is a fourth-order Fresnel bull's-eye lens. Contact the Key West Lighthouse Museum, 938 Whitehead Street, Key West, FL 33040; (305) 295-6616, or see www.kwahs.com/lighthouse.htm.

■ GARDEN KEY LIGHT ■
Dry Tortugas (1826 and 1876)

About 120 miles west of the Florida peninsula, a scatter of small islands and reefs known as the Dry Tortugas rise out of the Gulf of Mexico. Unpredictable currents combine with a jumble of ship-killing shoals to make this one of the most dangerous places in all the world's oceans. To warn mariners the Lighthouse Service established a light station here in 1826, but not without considerable difficulty. Dramatizing the need for the light, one of the ships carrying materials for the seventy-foot brick tower wrecked on the very shoals the light was intended to guard.

Garden Key Light
Florida Department of Commerce, Division of Tourism

By 1846 the tower's lantern barely peeked above Fort Jefferson, an impressive structure with walls fifty feet high and eight feet thick and containing more than forty million bricks. Fort Jefferson's 450 smooth-bore cannons were capable of pummeling an entire enemy fleet but were never once fired in anger. Instead, the fort served as a prison, its most notable inmate being Maryland physician Samuel Mudd, thrown into a stinking cell here for having—innocently enough—set the broken leg of Lincoln assassin John Wilkes Booth. President Grant pardoned Dr. Mudd in 1869 for his humanitarian efforts during a yellow-fever epidemic.

A hurricane ruined the original Garden Key Lighthouse in 1873. Its replacement, completed three years later, consisted of a thirty-seven-foot cast-iron tower positioned atop the walls of the fort. Its fourth-order Fresnel lens, illuminated by kerosene lamps, gave the beacon a range of approximately sixteen miles. The light was decommissioned in 1912.

Travel information: Garden Key and its lighthouse are part of Dry Tortugas National Park, encompassing nearly 65,000 acres of coral reef and churning surf, but only forty acres of dry land. Attractions include historic Fort Jefferson and a one-hundred-square-mile naturalist's paradise where ocean mammals, sharks, fish, and seabirds of every variety abound. Charter boats, ferries, and scheduled seaplane service are available from the Key West Chamber of Commerce, 510 Greene Street, Key West FL 33040; call (305) 294-2587, or see www.keywestchamber.org. Contact Dry Tortugas National Park, P.O. Box 6208, Key West, FL 33041; call (305) 242-7700, or see www.nps.gov/drto/index.htm.

■ DRY TORTUGAS LIGHT ■
Loggerhead Key (1858)

In 1836 the *America* ran aground in the Dry Tortugas. Instead of preventing the wreck, the weak navigational light on Garden Key may very well have lured the ship to its ruin. The controversy generated by the loss of the *America* persisted for decades, leading finally to funding of an entirely new Dry Tortugas light station. Built on Loggerhead Key for $35,000, the 157-foot tower was completed in 1858. Its considerable height and state-of-the-art first-order Fresnel lens gave the beacon a range of at least twenty miles, more than enough to keep ships away from the shoals.

Severely damaged by the same 1873 hurricane that destroyed the lighthouse on neighboring Garden Key, the tower was at first thought to be a complete loss. Masons sent to do emergency repairs, however, did their work so well that the tower still stands, survivor of at least a dozen additional major hurricanes.

Dry Tortugas Light
Bob and Sandra Shanklin

Because of its remote location, in 1925 the station was outfitted with an automatic acetylene lamp to replace its full-time crew. A modern optic superseded the original Fresnel lens in 1986. It displays a flashing white light seen from up to twenty-five miles.

> *Travel information:* Loggerhead Key and its lighthouse are located within the 65,000-acre confines of Dry Tortugas National Park (see page 175). For advice on charter boats, ferries, and seaplanes providing access to the park, contact the Key West Chamber of Commerce, 510 Greene Street, Key West, FL 33040; (305) 294-2587, or see www.keywestchamber.org.

■ SANIBEL ISLAND LIGHT ■
Sanibel Island (1884)

In 1883 a ship carrying iron to build the Sanibel Island Lighthouse struck a shoal and sank only a few miles short of its destination. Salvagers from Key West managed to pull most of the materials off the sandy sea bottom, and crews completed the tower in time to have it in service by August 1884. Afterward, its light guided ships in and out of the port of Punta Rassa, past the same shoals that sank the construction-supply ship.

An iron skeleton structure designed to withstand hurricane winds, the tower stands on four legs braced by girts and tie bars for lateral support. A central metal-walled cylinder provides access to the lantern via a winding staircase of 127 steps. Soaring one hundred feet above the low, sandy point, the lantern room at one time housed a third-order Fresnel lens displaying a flashing white beacon. The old,

French-made glass lens eventually gave way to a modern plastic lens. Built on piles to protect them from storm-driven high waters, nearby keeper's cottages sport steeply sloped pyramidal roofs and wide wraparound verandas.

Sanibel Island Light
Bob and Sandra Shanklin

> *Travel information:* From Fort Myers follow the Sanibel Causeway, Highway 867, and Lighthouse Road to the J. N. "Ding" Darling National Wildlife Refuge administered by the US Fish and Wildlife Service. The refuge visitor center is located on One Wildlife Road, just off San-Cap Road. The lighthouse is open to visitors only by appointment; call the refuge at (239) 472-1100 or see www .fws.gov/dingdarling. The original 1884 Sanibel Island third-order lens is now on display at the Sanibel Historical Museum: call (239) 472-4648, or see www.sanibelmuseum.org. For information on Sanibel, the refuge, and attractions in the Fort Myers area, see www.sanibeltrails.com.

■ BOCA GRANDE REAR RANGE LIGHT ■
Boca Grande (1932)

To boost a hard-pressed Florida economy during the Great Depression, a range-light system was established on Gasparilla Island to guide freighters carrying Florida phosphates to chemical plants along the Mississippi. Originally, this 105-foot iron skeleton tower had been constructed in 1885 to serve as the Delaware Breakwater Rear Range Light; however, erosion forced it out of service in 1918. Exhibiting its adaptability, the tower was disassembled in 1921, taken to Gasparilla Island, and reassembled in 1927. It resumed service in 1932 as a rear-range light for the front-range light, which was a flashing light on a steel structure about one mile offshore in the Gulf of Mexico. By lining up the two lights, a ship's captain knew when to turn into the safe shipping channel leading to Port Boca Grande. The tower's fixed white light, beaming from an aeromarine optic, remains in service to guide ships into Charlotte Harbor.

Boca Grande Rear Range Light

> *Travel information:* To reach Gasparilla Island from US Highway 41, follow Florida Routes 776 and 771 to Placida. Then follow signs to the Boca Grande Causeway and toll bridge leading to Gasparilla Island and the Gasparilla Island State Recreation Area. Contact Barrier Islands GEO Park, P.O. Box 1150, Boca Grande, FL 33921; call (941) 964-0375. The lighthouse can be visited; a public beach is near the light.

▪ OLD PORT BOCA GRANDE (GASPARILLA ISLAND) LIGHT ▪

Gasparilla Island (1890 and 1986)

The Port Boca Grande Lighthouse balances on iron stilts above the erosive surf near the entrance to Charlotte Harbor, its square wooden tower and dwelling supported atop screw piles. Completed in 1890 at a cost of $35,000, the tower shot out its fixed white beacon from a three-and-one-half-order Fresnel lens similar to those frequently used in the Great Lakes region. Red flashes warned mariners of nearby shoals.

Old Port Boca Grande Light

From the first, erosion threatened the structure. By 1970 seawater lapped at supports that held up the lighthouse. Construction of a 265-foot granite jetty helped saved the historic building. So, too, did the Gasparilla Island Conservation Association, by raising funds to restore the lighthouse when the Coast Guard abandoned it in 1967. The station was relit and returned to service in 1986. The lighthouse is located on Gulf Boulevard at the far southern tip of the island in the center of Gasparilla Island State Park. The lighthouse has been restored by the Barrier Islands Parks Society and has a maritime museum within.

Travel information: From Placida follow signs to the Boca Grande Causeway and toll bridge leading to Gasparilla Island. Contact Barrier Islands Parks Society, 880 Belcher Road, P.O. Box 637, Boca Grande, FL 33921; call (941) 964-0060, or see www.barrierislandparkssociety.org. For more information on Gasparilla Island State Park, 880 Belcher Road, Boca Grande, FL 33921; call (941) 964-0375, or see http://floridastateparks.org.

▪ EGMONT KEY LIGHT ▪

St. Petersburg (1848 and 1858)

In 1848 contractor Francis Gibbons completed a lighthouse on Egmont Key to serve the rapidly developing Tampa Bay area. Gibbons would later build the first lighthouses on the coasts of California, Oregon, and Washington State, many of which still stand. The lighthouse he built for $10,000 on Egmont Key—a small island named for an eighteenth-century British admiral—lasted only ten years. Repeatedly pounded by hurricanes so powerful they frightened one keeper into early retirement, it had to be torn down and rebuilt in 1858.

Egmont Key Light
Bob and Sandra Shanklin

Masons reinforced the new eighty-five-foot masonry tower with brick walls more than three feet thick. These stout walls have stood up to more than 140 years of hurricanes and gales. Located at the north end of the island, the structure still proudly stands. Its automated light remains active.

Travel information: Egmont Key and its lighthouse are accessible only by boat, but you can see and enjoy the signal from nearby Fort De Soto State Park. To reach the park follow Routes 682 and 679 south from St. Petersburg. For information on the Egmont Key Light, contact Florida State Parks information at (850) 245-2157.

■ CEDAR KEYS LIGHT ■
Seahorse Key (1854)

Used in the manufacture of pencils, Cedar Keys hardwood attracted such an endless parade of lumber ships that the government established a light station in 1854. Built under the watchful eye of US Army engineer George Meade, the lighthouse stands on Seahorse Key, about three miles southwest of Cedar Key, the largest island in the chain. Unlike his iron skeleton-type towers, Meade constructed this lighthouse as a one-story brick dwelling with a squat tower perched on its roof. The entire project cost a mere $12,000.

Cedar Keys Light
Bob and Sandra Shanklin

Although only twenty-eight feet high, the little Cedar Keys Lighthouse stands on a hill, placing the focal plane of its beacon some seventy-five feet above the water. The fixed white light from its fourth-order Fresnel lens was visible from fifteen miles away.

During the last years of the nineteenth century, the economy of the Cedar Key area fell onto hard times, and the Cedar Keys Lighthouse was permanently darkened in 1915. Seahorse Key is now part of a wildlife refuge.

Travel information: Located in an environmentally sensitive wildlife refuge, Seahorse Key is closed to the public except on one day in spring and another in fall, but it can be seen from the water. For excursions contact the Cedar Key Chamber of Commerce, P.O. Box 610, Cedar Key, FL 32625; call (352) 543-5600, or see www.cedarkey.org. Known for its great fishing and seafood, the Cedar Keys area can be reached from US Highway 19 or Interstate 75 via Florida Route 24 South.

■ ST. MARKS LIGHT ■

St. Marks (1831, 1840, and 1867)

The workmanship of the first St. Marks Lighthouse, built in 1831, proved so shoddy that officials ordered it torn down, lest it fall of its own accord. Rebuilt that same year, it lasted only until 1840, when erosion forced relocation of the station. A third St. Marks tower fell victim to a gunpowder explosion set off by Confederate raiders during the Civil War. The conical tower seen here today dates back to 1867. Built atop a twelve-foot-deep limestone foundation, its four-foot-thick walls rise eighty-two feet into the Florida skies. Its automated light shines more than twenty miles out to sea.

St. Marks Light

Travel information: The St. Marks Lighthouse is located in a pristine coastal game refuge. Although the station is closed to the public, visitors are welcome to walk the grounds and enjoy the unmatched scenery. Follow Route 363 from Tallahassee to the St. Marks National Wildlife Refuge, then County Road 59 to the lighthouse. Call the refuge at (850) 925-6121, or see www.fws.gov/saintmarks.

■ CROOKED RIVER LIGHT ■

Carrabelle (1895)

On September 18, 1873, a major hurricane struck the Florida Panhandle, blasting the Dog Island Lighthouse, which had guided vessels into St. George Sound and along to Apalachicola since 1838. The storm swept away the tower and keeper's residence, but miraculously, the keeper and his assistant survived. Perhaps wisely, the Lighthouse Board decided not to rebuild the exposed Dog Island station, and the area was left without a lighthouse for more than twenty years.

During the 1890s lumber freighters flocked to the Crooked River just north of Dog Island to take on loads of hardwood. To guide them a lighthouse was built near the mouth of the river, this time on the more stable ground of the mainland. Its designers took into account the special geology and weather conditions of the Gulf Coast. Hurricane-force winds pass through the open

Crooked River Light

iron skeleton, doing little damage. The 115-foot tower has stood now for more than a century, but it was deactivated in 1995 and its fourth-order Fresnel lens removed.

In 2001 the Carrabelle Lighthouse Association had the deed for the tower and grounds turned over to the City of Carrabelle. Their efforts have renovated the keeper's house, which is now a museum and gift shop. The association also opened the lighthouse for climbing on weekends.

> *Travel information:* Located roughly five miles south of the eastern end of the seven-mile bridge near Marathon, the lighthouse can be seen about a mile away from US Highway 98 west of Carrabelle. The tall red-and-white tower soaring toward the sky is an inspiring sight. Contact the Carrabelle Lighthouse Association, P.O. Box 373, Carrabelle, FL 32322; call (850) 697-2732, or see www.crookedriverlighthouse.org.

■ CAPE ST. GEORGE LIGHT ■
St. George Island (1833, 1848, and 1852)

Rivers of cotton once flowed into Apalachicola on their way to distant ports in New England and Europe. To guide freighters into the bay, the government established

a light station on the extreme west end of St. George Island in 1833. Well-known contractor Winslow Lewis built the seventy-foot brick lighthouse for $9,500, fitting it with one of his own patented lamp-and-reflector systems. As was the case with many Lewis lighthouses, the St. George Island beacon proved far less than adequate—its light reached only a few miles out to sea and did not warn ships approaching from the east in time to avoid the southern tip of the island. In 1848 this lighthouse was torn down and its materials were incorporated into a new tower on the southern end of the island.

Bowled over by an 1851 hurricane that leveled several Florida light stations, the Cape St. George Lighthouse was rebuilt in 1852. For more than 150 years this sturdy brick tower withstood hurricanes and pounding Gulf waves—even a Civil War cannonade by Confederates who tried

Cape St. George Light before it fell; it was relocated and reassembled

but failed to destroy it; but, it finally collapsed into the surf in October 2005. With National Archives original tower plans in hand, St. George Lighthouse Association volunteers salvaged this light brick-by-brick and reassembled it, all seventy-nine feet of it, in a central St. George Island park.

> *Travel information:* Contact the St. George Island Visitor Center and Lighthouse Museum, 2 East Gulf Beach Drive, St. George Island, FL 32328, or call (850) 927-7744. Or contact the St. George Lighthouse Association, 201 Bradford Street, St. George Island, FL 32328; see www.stgeorgelight.org.

■ CAPE SAN BLAS LIGHT ■
Cape San Blas (1848, 1856, 1859, and 1885)

The Cape San Blas Lighthouse stood for only three years before the 1851 hurricane that destroyed the Dog Island station knocked it down. Yellow fever delayed construction of a replacement. Masons finally laid the last bricks of the new tower in 1856, just in time to see it toppled by another hurricane. A third tower, completed in 1859, served for less than two years before Confederate forces snuffed out its lamps, removing the third-order Fresnel lens and setting fire to the tower. Renovated following the Civil War, the tower held out against repeated buffetings by gales and flood tides until 1882, when erosion cut the foundation away and it toppled into the Gulf.

Cape San Blas Light
Kraig Anderson

A ship carrying the materials needed to rebuild this hard-luck lighthouse sank off Sanibel island, but the materials were mostly salvaged in the shallow waters; the ninety-six-foot-tall tower was completed in 1885. This time, however, the Lighthouse Board wisely chose an iron skeleton design capable of withstanding hurricane winds. What is more, the tower is put together in such a way that it can be taken apart and reassembled elsewhere whenever threatened by the Gulf's bulldozerlike tides—which is exactly what the Lighthouse Service did in 1919 when it moved the entire light station to its present location. The tower has survived intact for more than a hundred years. Its third-order flashing Fresnel lens, intended to warn ships away from shoals off Cape San Blas, was deactivated in 1996. In 2005 the keeper's house that was in the best condition left on the station was renovated. Efforts on the parts of the Air Force and a friends group have saved this light station.

> *Travel information:* Follow routes 30 and 30E to Cape San Blas. Located about half a mile from a US Air Force radar station, the lighthouse is now open to the public; for more information, contact the St. Joseph Historical Society, 142 Keepers Cottage, Port St. Joe, FL 32456; call (850) 229-1151; the society runs the refurbished lighthouse keeper's quarters as the "Sleeping Beauty" gift shop and museum.

■ ST. JOSEPH BAY LIGHT ■
Port St. Joe (1839 and 1902)

In 1838, delegates gathered in what was then the thriving Gulf port of St. Joseph to frame Florida's first state constitution. That year the federal government acknowledged the town's growing importance by placing a lighthouse on the far tip of the St. Joseph peninsula to guide ships into port. Neither the town nor the lighthouse would last, however. Ravaged by yellow fever brought in by a ship three years after the lighthouse was completed, the town was abandoned and the tower left to deteriorate at the mercy of several storms.

From the ruins of the once-thriving community of St. Joseph, the village of Port St. Joe emerged, but more than half a century passed before the government thought it merited a lighthouse. Finally, in 1902, a square wooden combination dwelling and tower was built on the mainland, directly across from St. Joseph Point on "Beacon Hill." The lantern, situated atop the peaked roof of the main building, held a third-order Fresnel lens. It served as a range light with another beacon situated six hundred feet toward the beach.

In 1960 the Coast Guard closed the St. Joseph Bay station, replacing its light with an automated beacon displayed from atop a steel tower resembling a broadcast antenna. The old lighthouse was sold off for private use including as a barn. Several years ago it was purchased, relocated to St. Joseph Bay, and refurbished as a private residence complete with a reproduction lantern room; the project was finished in 2011.

Travel information: From Port St. Joe, drive northwestward for 10 miles to Beacon Hill. The existing steel tower rises just to the west of Beacon Road. The site of the original station is nearby.

■ PENSACOLA LIGHT ■
Pensacola (1824 and 1859)

Pensacola Light

After the acquisition of Florida from Spain in 1819, President James Monroe ordered the US Navy into the Gulf of Mexico to flush out pirates. With no base on the Gulf Coast, the US fleet might as well have been patrolling foreign waters. Then the navy found exactly what it needed at Pensacola in the Florida Panhandle—a deep-water port for its fighting ships. To this day, the US Navy maintains a significant presence at Pensacola.

To guide navy warships in and out of the new base, the Lighthouse Service established a station here in 1824. Winslow Lewis built the forty-five-foot tower on a sandy spit near the entrance to the harbor, fitting it with oil lamps and reflectors of his own design. Lewis billed the government a modest $5,725 for the entire project. Even so, the station was not worth its cost; for like many Lewis beacons, this one proved far less than adequate.

In 1859 a 160-foot-tall brick tower replaced the old Lewis lighthouse. It cost nearly $46,000, a bargain considering the tower has survived hurricanes, lightning strikes, and 140 years' worth of wear and tear, not to mention a fierce Union cannonade during the Civil War. Moreover, its impressive height and first-order Fresnel lens more than doubled the range of the old Lewis beacon to better than twenty-five miles. Now automated, the old light still guides navy ships and Coast Guard cutters in and out of the harbor.

Today, through a lease with the Coast Guard, the Pensacola Lighthouse Association is solely responsible for the maintenance and public tour operations at the light. Thanks to this group's efforts, this lighthouse and the Richard C. Callaway Museum (and gift shop) in the restored 1869 keeper's quarters are now open to the public.

Travel information: Follow Navy Boulevard (Route 295) to the Pensacola Naval Air Station. The guard at the gate can provide a car pass and directions to the lighthouse. Exhibits at the nearby Naval Air Museum celebrate the history of the light station and the US Navy's strong links to Pensacola. For additional information, call the naval base at (850) 675-5305. To contact the Pensacola Lighthouse and Museum, call (850) 393-1561, or see www.pensacolalighthouse.org.

ALABAMA

■ MOBILE POINT LIGHT ■
Mobile (1822, 1873, and 1963)

A wall of barrier islands and a maze of shoals force ships entering Mobile Bay into the narrow channel that runs past Mobile Point. To guide vessels through this strategic passage, the Lighthouse Service established a light on the point. Completed in 1822 at a cost of $9,995, the station's forty-foot brick tower stood on the grounds of Fort Morgan. A soldier was paid an extra $15 per month to light its lamps each evening.

Mobile Point Light
Bob and Sandra Shanklin

With a limited range of less than ten miles, the beacon gave scant warning of the dangerous shoals that lay up to nine miles south of the point. Hired to improve the light, Winslow Lewis installed a flashing lamp-and-reflector optic that he proudly claimed made the light visible from "thirty miles away." It did not. The Lighthouse Service finally solved the problem in 1838 by placing a lighthouse on remote Sand Island, several miles from the mainland.

Although bristling with cannon, Fort Morgan failed to stop the Union fleet of Admiral David Farragut in 1864, when he issued his famous order "Damn the torpedoes, full speed ahead!" and forced his way into Mobile Bay. During the ensuing battle Union gunners blasted the Mobile Point Lighthouse into a pile of rubble.

In 1873 the broken walls of the fort acquired a thirty-five-foot steel light tower. Its fourth-order Fresnel lens displayed a red light with a focal plane approximately fifty feet above high water. In 1963 this light was discontinued and replaced by a 125-foot, antenna-like tower. Despite the untraditional—some might say ugly—looks of the present tower, its flashing white light efficiently guides ships in and out of Mobile Bay. The fourth-order Fresnel lens and the Sand Island Lighthouse lens are on display at the Ft. Morgan Museum.

Travel information: From Mobile follow Interstate 10 east to exit 44. Then follow Route 59 south to Gulf Shores and turn westward on Route 180. Signs lead the way to the Fort Morgan State Historic Site, which features fascinating Civil War displays and the old first-order Fresnel lens from the nearby **Sand Island Lighthouse.** The 1873 tower and present antenna-style tower, standing near each other beside the walls of the fort, offer a study in contrasting technologies. For Fort Morgan information: Fort Morgan, 51 Hwy 180 West, Gulf Shores, Alabama 36542; call (334) 540-7125; www

.ft-morgan.com; or the Alabama Historical Commission, 468 South Perry Street, Montgomery, Alabama 36130; call (334) 540-7125; www.preserveala .org. For travel information call the Alabama Gulf Coast Visitors Bureau at (251) 974-1510 or (800) 745-7263, or go to http://www.gulfshores .com/conventions-meetings/convention-services. The nonprofit Alabama Lighthouse Association helps all three of the state's lighthouses. For more information, contact them at P.O. Box 250, Mobile, AL 36601; call (251) 626-4743, or see http://alabamalighthouses.com.

■ MOBILE (MIDDLE) BAY LIGHT ■
Mobile (1885)

Mobile Middle Bay Light

The Mobile Bay station consists of a hexagonal cottage perched atop iron pilings screwed securely into the muddy bottom of the bay, a style used frequently on the Chesapeake Bay. But Mobile Bay proved less friendly to screw-pile construction techniques than the Chesapeake, and the structure was completed only with considerable difficulty. Storms repeatedly drove workers off the bay, and the soft mud swallowed up pilings almost as fast as they could be driven. Because of settling, the lighthouse ended up seven-and-one-half feet shorter than planned when finally completed in 1885. The signal, commissioned to mark a key turning point in a recently dredged, deep-water channel, served its purpose, however. Its red light guided ships through the bay for more than eighty years. Concerned Mobile citizens and the Alabama Historical Commission saved the lighthouse, deactivated in 1967, from the scrap heap. The Alabama Lighthouse Association now maintains the lovely bay light.

Travel information: Located in the middle of Mobile Bay, the restored lighthouse is a popular destination for day boaters. Contact the Mobile Bay Convention and Visitors Bureau, One South Water Street 4th Floor, P.O. Box 204, Mobile, AL 36602; call (251) 208-2000 or (800) 566-2453, or see www.mobile.org. Also see Travel information for **Mobile Point Light.**

■ SAND ISLAND LIGHT ■
Mobile (1838, 1859, and 1873)

Abandoned, isolated, and besieged by the waters of the Gulf, the Sand Island Lighthouse now serves only as a monument to its own often violent and tragic past. In 1859 a mighty 150-foot brick tower replaced a smaller lighthouse that had stood here since 1838. In 1861 a Confederate raiding party stacked barrels of gunpowder inside the big tower and blew it up to prevent its use by Union forces. Ironically, the raiders were sent on their mission of destruction by General Thomas Leadbetter, who had designed and built the Sand Island Lighthouse only two years earlier.

Yellow fever decimated the crew sent to rebuild the tower in 1871. Nevertheless, they completed the task and the new light was activated in 1873. Fitted with a first-order Fresnel lens, the new 132-foot tower displayed a white beacon with a range exceeding twenty miles.

Sand Island Light

During the late nineteenth century, Sand Island began to sink. It disappeared altogether after a 1906 hurricane, which also carried away the keeper's dwelling, the keeper, and his wife. An inspector sent to assess the damage sent the following poignant telegram to his superiors: "Sand Island Light out. Island washed away. Dwelling gone. Keepers not to be found."

The lighthouse is now owned by the residents of Dauphin Island where an extensive restoration process is beginning.

Travel information: Deactivated in 1971, the Sand Island Lighthouse is closed to the public. It can be approached only by boat but can be seen from Fort Morgan State Historical Site, about 3 miles away. A museum at the fort houses Sand Island's first-order Fresnel lens, which was badly damaged during Hurricane Katrina. Restoration of the lens is ongoing. For Fort Morgan information: Fort Morgan, 51 Hwy 180 West, Gulf Shores, Alabama 36542; call (334) 540-7125, or see www.ft-morgan.com; or the Alabama Historical Commission, 468 South Perry Street, Montgomery, Alabama 36104; call (334) 242-3184, or see www.preserveala.org.

MISSISSIPPI

■ BILOXI LIGHT ■
Biloxi (1848)

Often located on remote peninsulas or barrier islands, lighthouses are commonly far from the beaten path. Not so the Biloxi Lighthouse. Its white, forty-eight-foot tower stands like a giant traffic signal in the middle of busy US Highway 90.

A cast-iron shell sheathes the brick-and-mortar tower. The metal has protected the light from countless Gulf storms, including the infamous Hurricane Camille, which blasted Biloxi in 1968.

The even more destructive storm of the Civil War ravaged the Gulf coast a century earlier. The lighthouse survived, but following what Mississippians still call the "War Between the States," the Biloxi tower was painted black—some say as a token of mourning for President Abraham Lincoln. Ironically, the so-called memorial could be seen from the porch of

Biloxi Light

Confederate President Jefferson Davis's former home. Maintained by the City of Biloxi, the tower's 1926 fourth-order Fresnel lens, which replaced the 1848 fifth-order lens, still shines today as a private aid to navigation. Miraculously, Hurricane Katrina did not completely destroy the lighthouse, but did deal severe damage to its brick interior in 2005. After the leviathan storm abated, an American flag adorned the city's signature landmark, sending a message to the world that, like the lighthouse, the area would survive. Lighthouse owner, the City of Biloxi, restored the tower and rededicated it in 2009 with its starch-white appearance.

Travel information: The lighthouse is located on US Highway 90 at Porter Avenue. Contact the Biloxi Recreation Department at (228) 435-6294.

Lost Lights
Round Island Light
Round Island (1833 and 1859)

A bank of threatening shoals lies just off Round Island, named by French explorers for its shape. To warn mariners of this danger and guide ships through Mississippi Sound to the bustling port of Pascagoula, the Lighthouse Service established a light station on Round Island in 1833. The entire station, including the tower, keeper's dwelling, lamps, and reflectors, cost the government less than $6,000. The money was well spent, for the forty-five-foot brick tower survived hurricanes, flood tides, and even an invasion of freebooting adventurers bent on throwing the Spanish out of Cuba. The Cuban venture failed, and the lighthouse kept on shining.

Round Island Light before it was destroyed by a hurricane
Bob and Sandra Shanklin

Tidal erosion finally undercut the tower during the 1850s, forcing construction of a new lighthouse on a higher and drier part of the island. Fifty feet tall and fitted with a fourth-order Fresnel lens, it served well until the Civil War darkened lights along the entire Gulf coast. In operation again by 1865, the light remained on duty for the next seventy-nine years. The Coast Guard discontinued it in 1944. Hurricane Georges destroyed what remained of the lighthouse in 1998, so it no longer stands. With great effort, the lighthouse began to rise again with a new foundation and plans to reclaim bricks and the lantern room from the sea. But fate dealt another blow when Hurricane Katrina not only stopped the project but destroyed all progress. Undaunted, in mid-2011, the Round Island Lighthouse Preservation Society and lighthouse owner Pascagoula City obtained funds to rebuild the foundation on the southeast side of US Highway 90 bridge and to re-create the lighthouse with salvaged parts of the tower and lantern during the near future. You can reach Round Island and its historic lighthouse only by boat. For more information on the restoration project, contact the Round Island Lighthouse Preservation Society, P.O. Box 1059, Pascagoula, MS 39568, or see www.roundislandlighthouse.org.

Lost Lights

Ship Island Light
Ship Island (1853, 1886, and 2000)

Before Jefferson Davis became president of the Confederacy, he lobbied fellow members of the US Congress incessantly to secure federal facilities for Mississippi, his home state. His pet project was a fort and naval base to be placed on Ship Island, about a dozen miles from Biloxi. Congress rejected funding the hugely expensive fort but mollified Davis by building the $12,000 Ship Island Lighthouse.

The former Ship Island Light
Lamar C. Bevil Jr.

Completed in 1853, this handsome facility had a forty-five-foot brick tower and spacious keeper's dwelling. Initially, the lantern was fitted with an outmoded lamp-and-reflector lighting system, but this was updated with a state-of-the-art fourth-order Fresnel lens just three years later.

Eventually, Ship Island became home to a substantial military installation as well, but it was definitely not the one Davis had wanted. By 1861 Davis was the Confederate president. Late that year he learned that Union troops, backed by a powerful fleet of warships, had seized the island. Before leaving the island, Confederates removed the lens, packed the tower with explosives, set it ablaze, then stole away with the lens. Union soldiers worked on the charred tower and installed the reclaimed lens and the lantern room from the Bayou St. John Lighthouse, putting the light back into service in late fall 1862.

The Ship Island Lighthouse saw such hard service during the war and the years immediately after that it literally began to fall apart. Declared unsafe, it was pulled down in 1886 and replaced by a pyramidal wooden tower. Covered by protective weatherboarding, the frame structure survived until 1972, when it burned to the ground in a fire accidentally set by tourists. A steel skeleton tower took its place, and its light still guides mariners. A reproduction of the original lighthouse was completed on the old 1886 foundation in 2000 by combined efforts of the Friends of the Gulf Islands National Seashore, US Forest Service, and US Navy Seabees. In 2005 Hurricane Katrina destroyed the new tower. The original fourth-order Fresnel on display at the Maritime and Seafood Industry Museum in Biloxi was damaged in the storm also. The lens was restored at the St. Augustine Lighthouse and is back on display in the repaired museum.

Maintained by the National Park Service, the historic fort is open throughout the year. Contact Gulf Islands National Seashore, 3500 Park Road, Ocean Springs, MS 39564; call (228) 875–9057, extension 100, or see www.nps.gov/guis.

■ TCHEFUNCTE RIVER LIGHT ■
Madisonville (1837 and 1867)

During the Battle of New Orleans in 1815, a ragtag flotilla of American gunboats gathered at Madisonville on Lake Pontchartrain before sailing off to be blasted to splinters by the heavy guns of the British invasion fleet. But defeated by Andrew Jackson on land, the British retreated, leaving Louisiana in relative peace and Madisonville to become a prosperous port.

Tchefuncte River Light

In 1837 the Lighthouse Service made navigation on Pontchartrain easier and safer by establishing a light station near Madisonville. The lighthouse, a squat thirty-eight-foot brick tower at the entrance of the Tchefuncte River, burned during the Civil War. Rebuilt in 1867–68 on the same foundation and using many original bricks, it exhibited a fifth-order Fresnel lens. It was later automated during World War II; its light still guides vessels along Pontchartrain's northern shores.

The lighthouse and property transferred to the Town of Madisonville in 1999. It is now directed by the Lake Pontchartrain Basin Maritime Museum, which is responsible for its restoration as an education center in partnership with Southeastern Louisiana University.

> *Travel information:* After it was damaged by several storms, stabilization of the lighthouse began in 2007, and restoration continues. The tower and grounds are closed during restoration, but views are good by boat at the Tchefuncte River entrance channel or on land at the southern end of Highway 1077. Visit the Lake Pontchartrain Basin Maritime Museum, 133 Mabel Drive, Madisonville, LA 70447; call (985) 845-9200, or see http://lpbmm.org/lighthouse. From Interstate 12 take exit 59, and follow Route 22 to Madisonville. An old fishing village, Madisonville is home to some of the best seafood restaurants in Louisiana. Contact the Greater Madisonville Area Chamber of Commerce, P.O. Box 746, Madisonville, LA 70447; (985) 845-9824, or see http://madisonvillechamber.org.

Lost Lights

Many areas suffered from Hurricanes Rita and Katrina in 2005, but none worse than Louisiana, which lost more than a dozen of her lighthouses.

Chandeleur Island Light
Chandeleur Island (1848, 1856, and 1896)

In January 1815 a British invasion fleet waited at Naso Roads, just inside Chandeleur Sound, while redcoats attacked New Orleans. Eventually, Andrew Jackson's frontier army drove the troops back to their ships.

The lost Chandeleur Island Light
Bob and Sandra Shanklin

To help friendly peacetime vessels take advantage of the same vast anchorage that once attracted the British war fleet, the government established a light station on the northern tip of Chandeleur Island in 1848. A seabreak of sand and shell protected its fifty-five-foot brick tower from gales. Even so, an 1852 hurricane swept over the wall and obliterated the lighthouse. The fifty-foot tower that replaced it in 1856 received a high-quality fourth-order Fresnel lens, enabling the light to mark effectively the dangerous, spreading shoals in Chandeleur Sound.

Along these chains of Gulf barrier islands, nature can be as vicious as she is beautiful. The destructive floodtide of an 1893 hurricane undercut the tower, forcing the Lighthouse Board to replace it once again, this time with an iron skeleton structure better able to withstand high winds and water. Rising 102 feet above mean sea level, it held aloft a third-order Fresnel lens displaying a flashing white light. The Coast Guard automated the light in 1966, replacing the classic lens with a modern optic.

During Hurricane Katrina in 2005, all man-made objects on the island were destroyed—only nature has survived. This light had been a point of stability for all traveling the barrier islands. The Chandeleur Lighthouse site is part of the seven-thousand-acre Breton National Wildlife Refuge, the nation's second oldest refuge, revered by boaters, anglers, and naturalists. The lighthouse site and refuge can be reached only by boat. Contact the US Fish and Wildlife Service, Southeast Louisiana Refuges, Bayou Lacombe Centre, 61389 Highway 434, Lacombe, LA 70445; call (985) 882–2000, or see www.fws.gov/breton.

Pass Manchac Light
Ponchatoula (1839, 1842, 1846, and 1857)

The Pass Manchac Lighthouse marked the western reaches of Lake Pontchartrain, guiding vessels through the narrow passage that connects the enormous lake with the smaller but still sizable Lake Maurepas. Vulnerable to storms, erosion, and Louisiana mud, which repeatedly swallowed its foundation, the tower was rebuilt three times.

The former Pass Manchac Light
Lamar C. Bevil Jr.

The first tower lasted only three years. Its masons had used mud for mortar, which not surprisingly, melted away in the rain. The tower literally fell to pieces. A second, better quality structure succumbed to erosion during the 1840s and the third to the hungry mud in the 1850s. The fourth tower, completed in 1857, was damaged by Union raiders and later vandalized by soldiers during the Civil War, but it was put back into service after the war in 1867; fitted with a sparkling new fourth-order Fresnel lens, this lighthouse proved more fortunate and long-lived. A forty-foot brick tower built atop a stone foundation, it served for 120 years and withstood no fewer than five huge storms. Automated in 1941, it was finally retired in 1987. Although this stout light withstood nature's fury again and again, the combined erosion of Lake Pontchartrain and buzz-saw winds of Hurricane Katrina in 2005 cut the tower in half. The Lake Maurepas Society is planning a rescue and restoration of the light. Follow US Highway 51 north from La Place toward Ponchatoula. The tower's ruins are on the north side of Pass Manchac. The dwelling and other station buildings were removed long ago.

New Canal Light
New Orleans (1838, 1855, 1890s, and 1901)

Now a Coast Guard life-saving station, the New Canal Lighthouse takes its name from a failed 1830s effort to link Lake Pontchartrain with downtown New Orleans by canal. A brick lighthouse marked the lake terminus of the canal, which was never completed. Rebuilt in 1855 and again during the 1890s, the lighthouse endured, despite the defunct canal.

The fifty-foot square wooden tower that stands here today is said to date back to 1901. The lantern and gallery rise through the second-story roof. Originally, the lighthouse stood on piles in open water a quarter of a mile from shore, but landfill projects during the 1930s surrounded it with dry land. A fifth-order Fresnel lens formerly served here; it has since been changed to a modern optic. One hurricane knocked the classic lighthouse off its foundation; a subsequent one finished it off. A nonprofit group salvaged each piece worth saving and is poised to raise the light again. For more information on the lighthouse and its restoration, contact the Lake Pontchartrain Basin Foundation, P.O. Box 6965, Metairie, LA 70009; call (504) 836-2215, or see www.saveourlake.org. Also a victim to Hurricane Katrina was the old **West Rigolets Lighthouse.**

The New Canal Light suffered great damage during Hurricanes Katrina and Rita. Efforts are ongoing to restore the icon of Lake Pontchartrain.

Frank's Island Light
Lower Mississippi Delta (1823)

Having negotiated the Great Lakes and nearly the entire length of the Mississippi, the French explorer La Salle reached the Gulf of Mexico in 1682. He placed a marker bearing his personal coat of arms at the mouth of the great river to help mariners recognize it among the maze of delta bayous and passes. Many years later navigational lights would guide vessels to the river. The first of these was built by the French in 1767 at a place called La Balize (seamark).

After the United States acquired Louisiana in 1803, President Thomas Jefferson ordered a lighthouse built on Frank's Island, near a key river entrance. Noted architect Benjamin Latrobe, who designed the Capitol Building in Washington, drew the plans. His design proved so grandiose and impractical that it was not completed until 1818. Its reluctant contractor, Winslow Lewis, warned officials that the $79,000 granite-and-marble structure could not stand for long in the delta mud. Sure enough, it fell down almost as soon as its last stones were cemented in place. Lewis then contracted to build a far more sensible eighty-two-foot masonry tower for the comparatively bargain price of $9,750. The Frank's Island Lighthouse, in service by 1823, guided mariners until 1856. Its foundation settled twenty feet into the mud, and it finally collapsed in 2002.

Over the years the silt-laden Mississippi changes its primary outlets, opening new passages and filling in others. The Frank's Island Lighthouse ceased operations after the river began to favor the once-secondary **Pass a l'Outre** (meaning "Pass Beyond" or "the Way Out"). The Lighthouse Board constructed the Pass a l'Outre Lighthouse, an eighty-five-foot iron tower completed late in 1852, for the new river outlet. This light, in turn, was discontinued in 1930 after the Mississippi filled Pass a l'Outre with huge muddy lumps, making it almost impassable to ships. Only a small part of the tower remains, because of sinking and storm damage. Light towers marked other Mississippi River outlets as well. These include the **South Pass Lighthouse** and **Southwest Pass Lighthouse,** both completed by Winslow Lewis in 1832, and the **Head of Passes Lighthouse,** first lit in 1836. All formerly served primary entrances to the river, and all survive to this day, though some have sunk down a bit in the muck.

The Coast Guard finally solved the sinking problem in 1962 with construction of the **Southwest Pass Jetty Light.** Built in open water atop large concrete supports, this modern light station resembled an offshore oil rig, a likeness that has earned it the nickname "Texas Tower." Its aeromarine beacon had a focal plane more than eighty feet above the Gulf waters and can could be seen from up to twenty-four miles away. The Coast Guard destroyed it in 2007.

None of the lighthouses mentioned above can be reached by land, and if they survived Hurricane Katrina, each one should be approached from the water only by highly experienced navigators. Contact the Eighth Coast Guard District, Hale Boggs Federal Building, 500 Poydras Street, New Orleans, LA 70130.

Frank's Island Light
Bob and Sandra Shanklin

Pass a l'Outre
Bob and Sandra Shanklin

South Pass Light
US Coast Guard

■ PORT PONTCHARTRAIN (MILNEBURG OR PONTCHARTRAIN BEACH) LIGHT ■
New Orleans (1832, 1839, and 1855)

A privately financed lighthouse marked Port Pontchartrain as early as 1832. The primitive device consisted of a square lantern hoisted between two fifty-foot poles. Under pressure from local business interests, Congress eventually funded an official lighthouse for the port. Completed in 1839 at a cost of only $4,400, its twenty-eight-foot, octagonal wooden tower displayed a flashing white beacon from its iron lantern. In 1855 the Lighthouse Board replaced the rotting structure with a forty-foot masonry tower equipped with a compact fifth-order Fresnel lens.

Port Pontchartrain Light
Lamar C. Bevil Jr.

Many of the keepers who served here were women. Perhaps most notable of them was Margaret Norvell. She kept the light burning throughout the great hurricane of 1903, while playing host to some two hundred refugees.

Although inactive since 1929, the lighthouse still stands. Interestingly, the tower, at one time located half a mile from land, is now well inland. Over the years land-hungry New Orleans developers filled in large areas of the shallow lake, extending usable lands but leaving the little lighthouse high and dry. The land lay unused until 1991, when the University of New Orleans Research and Technology Park took over the site. Although there has been some settling of the tower, it still stands.

Travel information: The lighthouse is now on private land. From New Orleans take Interstate 10 East to Interstate 610 East. Turn onto Elysian Fields to a traffic circle. At the second exit the lighthouse can be seen. The area is gated, and visitors are required to see the guard on duty. Only pictures are allowed. For general visitor information, call the New Orleans Convention and Visitors Bureau at (800) 672-6124, or go to www.new orleanscvb.com.

■ SOUTHWEST REEF LIGHT ■
Berwick, Louisiana (1859)

Built in Louisiana's plantation country to replace a lightship that marked Atchafalaya Bay, this light was completed in 1859. The iron-clad Southwest Reef Lighthouse was built to withstand the fury of hurricanes blowing in from the Gulf. A storm of a very different type, however, put the station out of service little more than two years after it began operating. With the outbreak of the Civil War, local Confederate officials ordered removal of the fourth-order Fresnel lens, lamps, and even the lantern's window glass. Union troops recaptured these items late in the war, and by August

Ship Shoal Light
Bob and Sandra Shanklin

Timbalier Bay Light
US Coast Guard

of 1865 the station's light once more sent out its signal. When it was damaged by a hurricane in 1867 that broke up the tower, repairs were done on site, and the light was brought back to life.

The 125-foot tower stood on screw piles in open water, where its red light warned vessels away from a dangerous reef in the Atchafalaya Bay. The lighthouse served until 1916, when a dredging operation cut through the shoal. Afterward the old tower stood rusting in the bay for nearly three-quarters of a century. Then during the 1980s the southern Louisiana town of Berwick brought it ashore for use as the primary attraction of a city park.

Southwest Reef Light before restoration
Bob and Sandra Shanklin

Travel information: Berwick is on US Highway 90, just west of Morgan City, Louisiana. The tower stands in Everett S. Berry Lighthouse Park, reached via Bellevue Front Street and Canton Street. The Berwick City Hall on Third Street, about two blocks from the Lighthouse Park, displays a beautiful third-order Fresnel lens; call (504) 384-8858, or go to www.nps.gov/maritime/gulflt.html.

Berwick also hopes to make the **Ship Shoal Light** (1859) a part of its Lighthouse Park. For the moment the abandoned iron skeleton tower remains offshore several miles from Raccoon Point.

Lost Light: To the east of Ship Shoal was another open-water light station, the **Timbalier Bay Light** (1917) that was completely destroyed by a hurricane also. To the west, also in open water, was the **Oyster Bay Light** (1904). There are many empty spaces along Louisiana's Gulf Coast where mighty and proud lights once stood.

▪ SABINE PASS LIGHT ▪
Louisiana Point (1856)

Efforts are being made to stabilize and preserve the Sabine Pass Light

Bob and Sandra Shanklin

The finlike concrete buttresses of this pre–Civil War structure give it a surprisingly modern appearance. Army engineer Danville Leadbetter, later a Confederate general, designed the fins to spread the tower's weight over the marshy ground and buttress it against hurricane winds. Leadbetter supervised construction of the lighthouse in 1856 and did such a good job that it still stands after more than 150 years.

The station received a fine third-order Fresnel lens at the time it entered service, but after only four years Civil War fighting snuffed out its lamps. In fact, several sharp engagements between the Confederate and Union forces occurred within sight of the tower. The men in gray won most of these battles.

Relit following the war, the station served until the Coast Guard discontinued it in 1952. Plans to make the lighthouse part of a Louisiana state park eventually fizzled. The tower, which is now privately owned, has been given to the Cameron Parrish Alliance. The Louisiana Preservation Alliance has declared it one of the top ten endangered historic sites in the state; the tower is in a state of collapse, and the alliance continues attempts to aid the lighthouse.

Travel information: Located on private land, the lighthouse is accessible only by boat. It can be seen, however, from the town of Sabine Pass on the Texas side of the Sabine River. Contact Sabine Pass Battleground State Historic Site, 6100 Dick Dowling Road, Port Arthur, TX 77640; (512) 463-7948; www.visitsabinepassbattleground.com. Or contact the Port Arthur

Convention and Visitors Bureau at (800) 235-7822, www.visitportarthurtx
.com: or Beaumont Convention and Visitors Bureau at (409) 880-3749,
www.beaumontcvb.com. While in the area, be sure to visit Sea Rim State
Park just southwest of Sabine Pass. The park's scenery and wildlife offer
a glimpse of Texas as it must have looked 150 years ago. Contact Sea Rim
State Park, P.O. Box 1066, Sabine Pass, TX 77655; call (409) 971-2559, or
see www.tpwd.state.tx.us/spdest/findadest/parks/sea_rim.

■ SABINE BANK LIGHT ■
Gulf of Mexico off Sabine Pass (1906)

By the end of the nineteenth century, increasing numbers of deep-water freighters
visited the docks at Port Arthur and other towns along the Sabine River. To reach
the river entrance safely, however, ships had to steer clear of the Sabine Bank, a
major shoal lurking below the surface about fifteen miles from shore.

   To warn mariners, lighthouse officials decided to place a navigational light
directly over the shoal. A foundry in Detroit assembled a tanklike iron tower and
shipped it to the Gulf, where it was placed atop a massive concrete caisson. Lamps
inside the station's third-order Fresnel lens were first lit on March 15, 1906. An
acetylene lighting system replaced the original Fresnel lens in 1923, when the light
was automated. Today the old lighthouse still stands guard over the shoal, and its
beacon remains in service. This was a rare event because "spark plug" type lights
were not usually built out to sea. Indeed, the cost of maintaining a cast-iron tower
in the open Gulf was unreasonable; therefore, the Coast Guard removed the tower
from above the caisson, to be replaced by a steel skeleton tower in 2002, which
exhibits a quick white flash of light.

   Travel information: Because it remains an active aid to navigation, the
   Sabine Bank Lighthouse is off-limits to the public. Located off the Texas-
   Louisiana border about fifteen miles from the coast, it can be reached only
   by boat. (See travel information for Sabine Pass Light on page 198.) The
   third-order Fresnel lens is on display at the Museum of the Gulf Coast,
   700 Procter Street, Port Arthur, TX 77640; call (409) 982-7000, or see www
   .museumofthegulfcoast.org.

TEXAS

■ BOLIVAR POINT LIGHT ■
Galveston (1852 and 1872)

Built in 1852, Bolivar Point Lighthouse became a casualty of war ten years later. When the Civil War broke out, Confederate troops seized the lighthouse, pulled down the cast-iron tower, and reforged the metal. Then they iron-clad their ships or fired the federals' own back at them in the form of shot and shell.

Bolivar Point Light

Following the war, a yellow fever epidemic delayed reconstruction of the structure, which was sorely needed to guide ships into Galveston Bay. So severe was the outbreak that the government placed the Texas coast under quarantine. Crews finally completed the new 117-foot tower in 1872, constructing it of cast-iron plates according to the original plans, making it a twin to Louisiana's **Pass a l'Outre Lighthouse.** A second-order Fresnel lens provided the beacon. It originally was painted with black-and-white bands.

During the horrible Galveston hurricane and flood of 1900, dozens of storm refugees saved themselves by climbing the tower steps to avoid the rising waters. Many of those outside the tower were not so lucky. Thousands of Galveston residents drowned or had their necks literally broken by the wind.

In 1907 its Fresnel lens was changed out for a third order. Further, the light was darkened during the Great Depression and its service passed to the **Galveston Jetty Lighthouse.** Discontinued by the Coast Guard, the Bolivar Point Light has been dark now for more than half a century. Nonetheless, the historic tower, now privately owned, remains a favorite Texas landmark.

Travel information: The lighthouse can be seen from Route 87 on the Bolivar Peninsula. To reach the peninsula take the free ferry from the north end of Galveston Island. The ferry also provides an excellent view of the tower. Its third-order Fresnel lens is kept at the Smithsonian's National Museum of American History in Washington, D.C.

■ MATAGORDA ISLAND LIGHT ■
Matagorda Island (1852 and 1873)

The Lighthouse Board established several lights along the Texas coast in 1852, including those at Matagorda Island near Port O'Connor and Bolivar Point near Galveston. Built in cast-iron sections much like the Bolivar Point lighthouse, the Matagorda Island tower rose eighty feet above the island sands, placing the focal plane of its light at ninety feet above the waters of Matagorda Bay. Nineteenth-century sailors had no trouble distinguishing it from other coastal towers, since it was painted in red and white horizontal bands. Nowadays, however, the tower is black.

Matagorda Island Light

During the early 1860s Confederate soldiers removed the third-order Fresnel lens and buried it in the sand. They tried to blow up the tower with kegs of gunpowder but failed to topple it. The wounded structure remained precariously erect until well after the Civil War. Lighthouse Board workers finally dismantled it to keep it from falling over on its own and put a wooden tower into service with a fifth-order Fresnel lens in the interim. In 1873 they reassembled the original tower on a new site and returned the old lens, retrieved from the sand, to its place of honor in the lantern. The lighthouse was automated in 1959, and the original classic lens served the station—and ships entering Matagorda Bay—until 1977, when a solar-powered modern optic replaced the Fresnel. The light remains operational, shining some twenty-five miles

Halfmoon Reef Light

over the sea, thanks to the efforts of a friends group, which gave the tower a complete overhaul. It is within the boundaries of Matagorda Island State Park.

Travel information: The lighthouse is accessible only by boat or ferry. To find out how you can visit this lighthouse and for ferry schedules and reservations, call (361) 983-2215. The original Fresnel lens is on display at the Calhoun County Museum, 301 S. Ann, Port Lavaca, Texas 77979; call (361) 553-4689, or see http://calhouncountymuseum.org.

The **Halfmoon Reef Lighthouse** (1858), which once rested on pilings far out in Matagorda Bay, is now a well-loved landmark on Route 35 in Port Lavaca adjacent to the Bauer Community Center, named for the lighthouse's benefactors. Contact the Port Lavaca Chamber of Commerce, 2300 State Highway 35 N, Port Lavaca, TX 77979; call (361) 552-2959.

■ ARANSAS PASS (LYDIA ANN) LIGHT ■
Port Aransas (1857)

Breaking through an almost solid wall of barrier islands, Aransas Pass confronts navigators with rolling surf, uncharted shoals, and channels that seem to shift with every tide. Soon after Texas joined the Union in 1845, federal officials concluded that this strategic pass should be marked with a major navigational light, but no action was taken for more than a decade.

In 1855 the Lighthouse Board assigned the task of establishing the light station to Captain Danville Leadbetter, an army engineer. Leadbetter built a fifty-foot octagonal brick tower and an adjacent wood-frame keeper's dwelling. The station's light, focused by a fourth-order Fresnel lens, began to shine late in 1857.

During the Civil War Leadbetter served as a Confederate general, and the lighthouse he had built at Aransas Pass became the target of both armies. Confederate raiders removed the lens and tried to blow up the tower. Union warships used it for target practice. Despite this abuse, however, the lighthouse survived the conflict, as did General Leadbetter.

Its lens restored, the lighthouse was back in operation by 1867, after which it served mariners more or less without interruption for more than eighty years. In 1952 the Coast Guard replaced the light with an automated beacon located on the opposite shore of Aransas Pass. Now privately owned, the historical station remains in prime condition with modern-day keepers in attendance, and its light still serves mariners. The light is shown on charts as the **Lydia Ann Light,** after the Lydia Ann Channel that runs close to the northeastern shore of the pass.

Travel information: The lighthouse is not open to the public, but both the tower and its light—visible from about seven miles away—can be seen from boats in the nearby Lydia Ann Channel. The original Fresnel lens is on display in the Port Aransas Civic Center. Follow Route 35 north from Corpus Christi, then Route 361 toward Mustang Island. Contact the Port Aransas Chamber of Commerce and Tourist Bureau at 403 West Cotter Avenue, Port Aransas, TX 78373; call (361) 749-5919 or see www.portaransas.org.

Aransas Pass Light
US Coast Guard

■ POINT ISABEL LIGHT ■

South Padre Island (1852)

Built in 1852 on the site of an old army camp used by General Zachary Taylor and his troops during the Mexican War, the Point Isabel Lighthouse provided the backdrop for the last battle of America's Civil War. Northern forces used the tower as an observation post as the blue and gray armies fought the Battle of Palmito Ranch on May 13, 1865. Ironically, the Southerners won the battle, only to learn that they had already lost the war—Lee had surrendered at Appomattox the month before.

During the decades after the war, commerce and sea traffic along the south Texas coast fell off so dramatically that the Lighthouse Board discontinued the light in 1888. When the board reversed its decision a few years later, officials were unhappy to learn that the government no longer owned the

Point Isabel Light

station. The property had been turned over to private owners in settlement of a lawsuit. The board ended up having to buy back its own lighthouse for $6,000.

Permanently deactivated in 1905, the lighthouse now serves as the prime attraction of a state park. Even after nearly a century of disuse, the fifty-seven-foot brick tower remains in excellent condition along with its original third-order Fresnel lens.

Travel information: Follow Route 100 through Port Isabel to the Point Isabel State Historic Site. The lighthouse is operated by the City of Port Isabel. Contact the Port Isabel State Historic Site, 421 East Queen Isabella Boulevard, Port Isabel, TX 78578; call (800) 792-1112 or (956) 943-7602. The park is located on the Lower Laguna Madre in the City of Port Isabel, approximately twenty-six miles east of US Highway 77/83 on State Highway 100. It is open to the public for climbing on a self-guided tour basis.

WEST

East Brother Lighthouse

ALASKA
11 Lights

Anchorage •

Prince
William
Sound

Unimak
Island

Glacier • Juneau
Bay
National
Park

Cape Flattery • • Dungeness
WASHINGTON   25 Lights
• Seattle
Aberdeen • • Tacoma

Astoria •

Tillamook •

Newport •   OREGON
9 Lights

Coos Bay •

Crescent City •

Pacific
Ocean

Eureka •

Mendocino •

San Francisco •

CALIFORNIA
42 Lights

Monterey •

San Luis Obispo •

Santa Barbara •

Los Angeles •

San Diego •

Kauai

Oahu   Molokai
Maui
Lanai

Hawaii
5 Lights

CALIFORNIA

■ OLD POINT LOMA LIGHT ■
San Diego (1855)

Hundreds of years ago, when California was still part of Spain's colonial empire, residents of San Diego built fires on lofty Point Loma to help royal supply ships reach harbor safely. Following acquisition of California by the United States in 1848, the government chose the point as the site for one of the West's first lighthouses.

Built of locally quarried sandstone, the combination Cape Cod–style dwelling and forty-foot tower cost Uncle Sam a whopping $30,000. Despite its hefty price the structure was not constructed according to specifications. When its first-order Fresnel lens arrived by sailing ship from France, workers could not fit it into the lantern. Instead, they substituted a third-order lens.

Worse problems lay ahead for the lighthouse. Although the station's third-order lens was less powerful than the one intended for it, the 460-foot elevation of the light made it visible from distances of more than forty miles. That same extraordinary elevation, however, all too often placed the light above low-lying clouds and fog banks. In heavy weather mariners simply could not see it. So in 1891, only thirty-six years after its lamps were first lit, the Old Point Loma Light went dark. A skeleton tower, built at a lower, more practical elevation, took its place and is now maintained by the Coast Guard.

Old Point Loma Light

Travel information: Follow Route 209 to Cabrillo National Monument at the tip of Point Loma Peninsula, just west of San Diego. Having refitted it with a classic lens and furnished the dwelling much as it might have looked when its first keepers lived there, the Park Service maintains the Old Point Loma Lighthouse as a museum with exhibits that include a third-order Fresnel. Cabrillo National Monument, 1800 Cabrillo Memorial Drive, San Diego, CA 92106; call (619) 557-5450, or see www.nps.gov/cabr.

■ POINT LOMA LIGHT (NEW) ■
San Diego (1891)

The seventy-foot iron skeleton tower of the Point Loma Lighthouse places its light eighty-eight feet above the Pacific. A white cylinder centered between the tower's braced iron legs allows access to the lantern room. A horn at the base of the tower alerts vessels when fog shrouds the point. The original third-order Fresnel lens placed here in 1891 was removed in 2002, was restored, and is now on display in the reproduction keeper's quarters next to **Old Point Loma Lighthouse.**

New Point Loma Light

Travel information: Follow Route 209 to Cabrillo National Monument in San Diego. An active Coast Guard facility, the station is closed to the public, but it can be enjoyed from the road leading to the monument's popular tidal pools.

■ LONG BEACH HARBOR LIGHT ■
Los Angeles (1949)

One could hardly imagine a less romantic edifice than the blocky, concrete structure marking the San Pedro Middle Breakwater in Los Angeles, but believe it or not, this is a lighthouse. Built half a century ago at a time when modernist architects thought in terms of the purely functional, it is indeed a radical departure from the old stone dwellings and towers built by Winslow Lewis or Francis Gibbons. Ultramodern even by present-day standards, it looks a bit like a space invader from a low-budget, 1950s science-fiction movie. No doubt that is why Los Angeles children know it as the "Robot Light."

Long Beach Harbor Light
Bob and Sandra Shanklin

Supported by six cylindrical columns made of cement cast into huge molds, the forty-two-foot-high rectangular tower is designed to withstand both earthquakes and high winds. When the light went into operation in 1949, its functions were monitored and controlled electronically from the nearby **Los Angeles Harbor Lighthouse.** Nowadays computers keep tabs on the light and relay commands to its airport-style beacon.

Travel information: The Long Beach Harbor Lighthouse cannot be reached easily from shore. Its light can be seen, however, from numerous points along the coast. A second Long Beach Lighthouse was completed in 2000 at Rainbow Harbor. A sixty-five-foot conical steel tower, it was built by the Lions Club and serves as a private aid to navigation.

■ LOS ANGELES HARBOR LIGHT ■
Los Angeles (1913)

Rising more than seventy feet above the Pacific, the Romanesque Los Angeles Harbor Lighthouse has anchored the far end of the San Pedro Harbor Breakwater since 1913. Despite gales, earthquakes, and even a brush with a US Navy battleship, the old tower has remained solid and functional. Its distinctive vertical black stripes and flashing green light are a familiar sight to sailors entering the harbor and boaters enjoying the waters off Los Angeles.

Los Angeles Harbor Light

Keepers lived here full time until the station was automated in 1973. The Coast Guard replaced the original fourth-order Fresnel lens with a plastic optic when the facility was converted to solar power during the 1980s. The Los Angeles Maritime Museum in San Pedro now proudly displays the old six-hundred-pound classic lens.

Travel information: Somewhat resembling a column from an ancient temple, the Los Angeles Harbor Lighthouse can be seen from Pacific Avenue and from the Point Fermin Park, where visitors can also enjoy the **Point Fermin Lighthouse.** The ferry to Santa Catalina passes by these lighthouses; call (800) 360-1212. Located at the lower end of Sixth Street in San Pedro, the Los Angeles Maritime Museum features informative lighthouse exhibits and is well worth a visit. The museum is located at Berth 84, Foot of 6th Street, San Pedro, CA 90731; call (310) 548-7618, or see www.lamaritimemuseum.org.

■ POINT FERMIN LIGHT ■
Los Angeles (1874)

No longer in operation, the Point Fermin Lighthouse remains a venerable landmark. Built in 1874 with highly durable redwood, its Stick Style design embraces Victorian-era Italianate styling and decorative gingerbread, which makes it an architectural delight. The fourth-order Fresnel lens that previously shone here was removed during World War II, when the structure was pressed into service as a coastal watchtower. Deactivated in 1942, the lighthouse is now the centerpiece of a Los Angeles city park.

Point Fermin Light
Kim Andrews

Travel information: The lighthouse is open to the public with guided tours offered each day except Monday. The Point Fermin Lighthouse Historic Site and Museum is managed by the Department of Recreation and Parks, City of Los Angeles. For specific visitation details, contact the Point Fermin Lighthouse Historic Site and Museum, 807 W. Paseo Del Mar, San Pedro, CA 90731; call (310) 241-0684, or see www.pointferminlighthouse .org.

Located on Paseo Del Mar, west of Pacific Avenue, the park also offers an excellent place to view the **Los Angeles Harbor Lighthouse** (1913).

■ POINT VICENTE LIGHT ■
Los Angeles (1926)

Situated on a cliff high above the blue Pacific and surrounded by graceful palms, the sparkling-white Point Vicente tower fits everyone's romantic image of a Southern California lighthouse. In fact film crews have used it as the backdrop for countless movie and television scenes. Built in 1926 near the edge of a rocky cliff more than a hundred feet above the ocean, the sixty-seven-foot cylindrical tower is crowned by a handsome lantern with crosshatched windows. The original third-order Fresnel lens still shines each night, producing a powerful 1.1-million-candlepower flash every twenty seconds. It can be seen from twenty miles at sea.

Naturally, this quintessential lighthouse has a resident ghost. The ladylike phantom, who appears only on foggy nights, is said to be the

Point Vicente Light

former lover of a sailor who died in a shipwreck on Point Vincente. Skeptics, on the other hand, say she is nothing more than an optical illusion created by stray refractions of the station's lens.

Travel information: Point Vicente Lighthouse is within a US Coast Guard Station; it is open to the public on a very limited basis at the courtesy of the US Coast Guard Aids to Navigation Team Los Angeles and the US Coast Guard Auxiliary. The lighthouse is located north of Marineland at 31550 Palos Verdes Drive West, Rancho Palos Verdes, CA 90274; call (310) 541-0334 for a recorded message, or see www.vicentelight.org. A fine view of the light can also be had from the grounds of the nearby Palos Verdes Interpretive Center. Exhibits recount the history of the lighthouse and explore the natural history of the Palos Verdes Peninsula. Call (310) 377-5370.

■ POINT HUENEME LIGHT ■
Oxnard (1874 and 1941)

An identical twin of the ornate **Point Fermin Lighthouse** once stood in Oxnard, northwest of Los Angeles, marking the heavily traveled Santa Barbara Channel. Both structures consisted of a square fifty-two-foot redwood tower rising through the roof of an Italianate residence, also known as Stick Style architecture. Not only did these stations look exactly alike, but they came to life on the same day, showing their lights for the first time on December 1, 1874. A matched pair of fourth-order Fresnel lenses focused their beacons. Their lights were not identical, however. The Point Hueneme station flashed white, whereas the Point Fermin displayed alternate white and red flashes.

Point Hueneme Light as it once looked
US Coast Guard

Also unlike its twin, the original Point Hueneme Lighthouse did not survive the ravages of time. Deteriorating from repeated battering by storms, it was sold to private owners in 1941 and eventually torn down. A far less attractive, though effective, square fifty-foot concrete tower took its place.

Travel information: Like the **Point Vicente Lighthouse**, this light is located on an active Coast Guard installation, and the workaday Point Hueneme Light tower is open to the public on a limited basis. Its light remains active and can also be seen from many points along the nearby coast. Entrance to the lighthouse is via the Lighthouse Promenade near the intersection of Surfside Drive and Ventura Road in the city of Port Hueneme. The Promenade walk is approximately one-half-mile long to the lighthouse gate. For more information access a recorded message at (310) 541-0334, or see http://huenemelight.org.

∎ ANACAPA ISLAND LIGHT ∎
Anacapa Island (1912 and 1932)

From a distance Southern California's beautiful Channel Islands seem placid, but their jagged rocks have torn apart countless ships. The Spanish treasure ship *San Sebastian* wrecked here in 1784, dumping its shipment of gold doubloons into the surf. In 1853 the steamer *Winfield Scott* slammed into Anacapa Island, stranding 250 passengers for several weeks without food or shelter.

Government officials had long recognized the crying need for a light to warn mariners of the dangers here, but until the twentieth century few believed a lighthouse could be built on the island's rugged, almost perpendicular cliffs. In 1912 the project was finally attempted, and after considerable effort a light station was established on Anacapa Island. Equipped with an automated acetylene lamp, its iron skeleton tower stood near the spot where the *Winfield Scott* had run onto the rocks nearly sixty years earlier.

Ancapa Island Light
US Coast Guard

In 1932 the Lighthouse Service assigned resident keepers to the station and built a new thirty-nine-foot masonry tower. Although not as tall, the tower looks much like the one at Point Vicente near Los Angeles. The height of the cliffs placed its light 275 feet above the ocean, from which elevation its third-order beacon could be seen from twenty-five miles away. Always difficult to supply, especially with fresh water, the station was automated in 1969. A modern lens replaced the original Fresnel in 1991.

Travel information: The Anacapa Lighthouse is now part of Channel Islands National Park, one of the nation's foremost scenic wonders. Visits to Anacapa and other islands are available through park concessionaires in Ventura; call (805) 658-5700. Also highly recommended is a stop at the park's Ventura visitor center, where the old Anacapa third-order Fresnel lens is now on display. Contact the Robert J. Lagomarsino Visitor Center, Channel Islands National Park, 1901 Spinnaker Drive, Ventura, CA 93001; call (805) 658-5730, or see www.nps.gov/chis.

∎ SANTA BARBARA LIGHT ∎
Santa Barbara (1856 and 1926)

A simple white tower on a Coast Guard base just west of Santa Barbara now serves in place of the city's historic lighthouse, destroyed in a 1925 earthquake. Among the first lighthouses in the West, the combination tower and dwelling were built by contractor George Nagle for a modest $8,000. Julia Williams, one of America's most famous lighthouse keepers, tended the Santa Barbara Light for more than forty years. It is said she spent only two nights away from the station during all that time.

Travel information: The existing automated light tower is within a fenced Coast Guard compound and is closed to the public. It is visible from Shoreline Drive and the La Mesa Park pedestrian bridge.

Santa Barbara Light
National Archives

▪ POINT CONCEPTION LIGHT ▪
Point Conception (1856 and 1882)

At Point Conception ships headed along the California coast must change course, either northward toward San Francisco or eastward toward Los Angeles. Here colliding ocean currents generate some of the worst weather in America, causing experienced seamen to compare Point Conception to South America's notoriously stormy Cape Horn. And well they should. The crushed hulls of wrecked vessels—eighteenth-century Spanish sailing ships and more recent American steamers—litter the churning waters off this dramatic angle of land.

Aware of Point Conception's importance and nightmarish reputation, the US government chose its isolated cliff tops as the site for one of the West's earliest light stations. Built with great difficulty in 1854, the lighthouse was beset with problems from the start. Workmanship of the brick-and-mortar structure was shoddy, and the combination tower and dwelling began to fall apart almost as soon as it was finished. What was worse, the tower was too small for the first-order Fresnel lens

Point Conception Light
Bob and Sandra Shanklin

assigned to it. Finally, the contractors had to enlarge and modify the tower. Then, when lampists installed the big lens, they discovered that several key parts of the lighting apparatus were missing. New ones had to be ordered from France.

Once the station was finally operational in 1856, it quickly became apparent that the tower had been built too high on the cliffs. Fog and low-lying clouds frequently obscured the light. Weakened by repeated gales and earthquakes, the building was finally abandoned in 1882 in favor of a better-constructed lighthouse built at a more practical elevation, about 130 feet above sea level. The two-foot-thick, fifty-two-foot-high brick-and-granite walls of the replacement structure have aged well. The lighthouse remains as solid as ever; the station's original ten-foot-high first-order lens that flashed out its warning until around 2000 has been replaced by a modern optic.

> *Travel information:* Nearly impossible to approach from land or sea, as it is surrounded by a sprawling private ranch on one side and Vandenberg Air Force Base on another, the station is closed to the public. For anyone braving the trek, tides have to be planned perfectly and access to the tower is strictly controlled by the Coast Guard Headquarters in Long Beach.

■ POINT ARGUELLO ■
Point Arguello (1901 and 1934)

On the evening of September 8, 1923, seven destroyers slammed into fog-shrouded Point Arguello in one of the US Navy's worst peacetime disasters. Tragically, the lives of twenty-three sailors were lost along with the fighting ships. Flotilla commander Edward Watson had misjudged his position and ordered his destroyers to turn eastward, thinking they were about to enter the Santa Barbara Channel. Instead, they each came to a grinding halt on solid rock. Had Captain Watson seen the Point Arguello Light that night, the ships and lives might not have been lost.

The Point Arguello Lighthouse no doubt prevented many such calamities, but on that particular night its light could not be seen because of the fog. Completed in 1901, the station's squat twenty-eight-foot tower stood on a cliff more than a hundred feet above the sea. In good weather its fixed white beacon, produced by a fourth-order Fresnel lens, could be seen from many miles out in the Pacific.

Point Arguello Light
National Archives

Isolated and difficult to supply, Point Arguello was among the first Pacific coast lights to be automated. Decommissioned in 1934, the lighthouse was razed and replaced by an aeromarine beacon on an iron skeleton tower that is serviced by the Coast Guard.

Travel information: As part of Vandenburg Air Force Base, Point Arguello is closed to the public. The best way to see the light is from the sea. Rail passengers riding past Point Arguello, however, may catch a glimpse of this remote and rather unglamorous light station.

■ POINT SAN LUIS OBISPO (PORT HARTFORD) LIGHT ■
San Luis Obispo (1890)

Although the lovely old Spanish town of San Luis Obispo had one of the best harbors in Southern California, it was among the last West Coast ports to receive a lighthouse. Regional political squabbling blocked congressional appropriations until the late 1880s, when funds finally became available.

Built on an isolated point on the west side of San Luis Obispo Bay, the station was ready for service by June of 1890. It consisted of a distinctly Victorian two-story resi-

Point San Luis Obispo Light
Bob and Sandra Shanklin

dence with a square forty-foot tower rising from one corner and a fog-signal building with a ten-inch steam whistle. A fourth-order Fresnel lens produced the beacon, which had a focal plane 116 feet above sea level. Because there was no road leading to the point, Lighthouse Service supply steamers made regular calls at the San Luis Obispo station.

The light was automated in 1975, and two years later, the old lighthouse lost its job to a cylindrical structure built just to the east. The new, far less scenic tower boasts a pair of powerful, rotating airport-type beacons. The Fresnel lens that served so long in the lighthouse has been moved to a museum in town.

The lighthouse was purchased in 1992 by the Port San Luis Harbor District to open the area to the public as a historic and recreational park. The district partnered with the nonprofit Point San Luis Lighthouse Keepers to restore and operate the facilities. Volunteers also had a lane rebuilt to permit public access.

Travel information: Since the lighthouse is located near the Diablo Canyon Nuclear Power Plant, it has long been off-limits to visitors. However, thanks to community support and the efforts of volunteers, weekend tours are available; for reservations contact the Point San Luis Lighthouse Keepers, P.O. Box 13556, San Luis Obispo, CA 93406; call (805) 540-5771, or see www.sanluislighthouse.org The station's Fresnel lens can now be seen at the San Luis Obispo County History Museum at 696 Monterey Street; call (805) 543-0638, or go to www.historycenterslo.org.

▪ PIEDRAS BLANCAS LIGHT ▪
San Simeon (1875)

Piedras Blancas tower as it originally appeared
Piedras Blancas Light Station Collection

Automation has transformed this once-handsome lighthouse into an ugly duckling. During a 1949 renovation its lovely old lantern was lopped off and a rotating, airport-style beacon set atop the decapitated tower to do the work of the original first-order bivalve (clamshell shaped) Fresnel lens that once guided ships into the northern entrance of San Simeon Bay.

When completed in 1875 the cone-shaped brick tower stood 74 feet tall on a grassy knoll that boosted its light to an elevation of more than 140 feet. With its ornate gallery and crownlike lantern, the tower looked a bit like a giant elegantly carved ivory chess rook. The unattractive modern beacon that now serves here is no less powerful and can be seen from up to eighteen miles at sea. The Bureau of Land Management now owns the lighthouse.

Travel information: In general the station is closed to the public except for limited, scheduled interpretive programs. Because it resides in an environmentally sensitive area, there is no public access to any surrounding wetlands or intertidal zones. However, the light can be seen from Route 1. For information on the lighthouse or scheduled tours, contact Piedras Blancas Light Station, US Department of Interior, Bureau of Land Management, 15950 Cabrillo Hwy, P.O. Box 129, San Simeon, CA 93452; call (805) 927-7361, or see www.blm.gov/ca and choose the "Visit Us" and "Special Areas" links.

In the nearby town of Cambria, the station's restored first-order lens is housed in a handsome lanternlike structure. Lighthouse lovers traveling in California should not miss this unique opportunity to view a big classic lens up close.

Piedras Blancas tower as it appears today
Piedras Blancas Light Station Collection

■ POINT SUR LIGHT ■
Big Sur (1889)

At Big Sur the churning Pacific makes relentless war on a chain of coastal mountains. The same natural forces—weather and geology—responsible for this scenic spectacle have also made it a very dangerous place for ships. Countless seafaring vessels—and at least one dirigible—have been lost here. But since 1889 the powerful beacon of the Point Sur Lighthouse has warned mariners to keep away.

At one time it was thought impossible to build a light station on Big Sur's precipitous cliffs, but the Lighthouse Service took up the challenge during the late 1880s. Before construction could begin workers had to lay tracks for a special railroad to carry materials and supplies to the rugged sandstone mountain known as Point Sur. The project took two years of hard work and more than $100,000 to complete.

The station consisted of a 48-foot granite tower atop the cliffs and a collection of dwellings and other buildings nearer the water. The high-rise cliffs lifted the light's focal plane to 273 feet above the sea. Keepers found the lighthouse almost as hard to maintain as it had been to build. Every night they had to trudge up the 395 steps leading to the tower. The station was finally automated in 1972, eliminating the need for the long daily climb. At that time a rotating aerobeacon replaced the original first-order Fresnel lens.

In 1935 an unusual sea disaster took place just west of Point Sur and within sight of the lighthouse. Caught in a squall, the 780-foot dirigible USS *Macon* lost buoyancy and crashed into the Pacific, causing a loss of seventy-three lives.

> *Travel information:* The lighthouse can be seen from Route 1 along the way from Monterey to Big Sur. Point Sur State Historic Park and Lighthouse offer guided tours several times each week. For more information call the park at (831) 625-4419, or see www.pointsur.org, the official site of the Central Coast Lighthouse Keepers volunteers. The station's original first-order lens can now be seen at the Maritime Museum in Monterey; call (831) 373-2469.

Point Sur Light
Nancy A. Pizzo

■ POINT PINOS LIGHT ■
Pacific Grove (1855)

Now surrounded by a lush golf course, the West's oldest standing lighthouse is leased by the Coast Guard, which uses it as a maritime museum. Designed in a Cape Cod–integral style, the forty-three-foot tower rises from the center of the keeper's dwelling. Both the tower and dwelling were built during the 1850s by legendary lighthouse contractor Francis Gibbons. Originally granite, the structure was covered over with reinforced concrete following a severe shaking by the same earthquake that devastated San Francisco in 1906. The third-order Fresnel lens in place here since 1855 still shines.

Point Pinos Light

Counted among the West's historic treasures, the old lighthouse has played host to many notables, the likes of John Steinbeck and Robert Louis Stevenson. The station's first keeper, former gold-rush miner Charles Layton, died in a shoot-out with the notorious bandito Anastasio Garcia. Layton's wife, Charlotte, then took over as keeper. She was followed by several subsequent women keepers, including Mrs. Emily Fish, who served from 1893 to 1914; she was called the "Socialite Keeper" because she loved to entertain guests at the lighthouse.

Travel information: Owned by the City of Pacific Grove, the light continues as an active aid to navigation. A group of volunteers from the Central Coast Lighthouse Keepers maintains the lighthouse and offers tours. Located on Lighthouse Avenue between Sunset Drive and Asilomar Avenue in opulent Pacific Grove, the lighthouse is open to the public Thursday through Monday afternoons from 1:00 until 4:00 p.m. on a self-guided tour basis; call (831) 648-3176. Be sure to visit the Pacific Grove Museum of Natural History in town at the corner of Forest and Central Avenues; call (831) 648-5716, or see www.pgmuseum.org.

■ SANTA CRUZ LIGHT ■
Santa Cruz (1869)

Established in 1869, the Santa Cruz Light guided lumber and lime freighters in and out of the harbor. Laura Heacox, daughter of the station's first keeper, tended this light for nearly half a century. The original lighthouse was a one-and-one-half-story house with a pitched roof and a lantern room rising from its center. In 1878 it was moved about a football field's length away from eroding cliffs. The original fifth-order Fresnel

Santa Cruz Light

lens was replaced by a larger fourth order lens in 1913. Its beacon was darkened during World War II, and the wood-and-brick lighthouse was torn down in 1948 by the private owner who had bought the light from the Coast Guard.

The brick light tower seen here now was built in 1969 as a memorial to teenager Mark Abbott, who drowned in a nearby surfing accident. The building houses a surfing museum and is currently supported with private donations.

Travel information: Follow West Cliff Drive to Lighthouse Point. The free museum is open every afternoon except Tuesdays. Call (831) 420-6289, or see www.santacruzsurfingmuseum.org.

■ PIGEON POINT LIGHT ■
Pescadero (1872)

The Pigeon Point Light, some fifty miles south of San Francisco, shines out toward the Pacific from an elevation of nearly 160 feet. Little more than 40 feet of the height is provided by the point; the rest is from the 115-foot brick tower. One of the tallest light towers on the Pacific coast, it was built in 1872 with brick shipped around Cape Horn from the east. The land, lighthouse, and huge first-order Fresnel lens cost the government approximately $20,000. An aeromarine beacon replaced the big glass lens in 1972. Pigeon Point takes its name from the Yankee clipper *Carrier Pigeon*, wrecked here in 1853.

Travel information: Now open to the public as a hostelry, the station is located just off Route 1, south of Pescadero. The Pigeon Point Light Station State Historic Park grounds are open all year. Call the park's hotline for updates at (650) 879-2120, or see www.norcalhostels .org/pigeon. To the south is the **Ano Nuevo Lighthouse**

Pigeon Point Light

(1872), now part of a state nature preserve and closed to the public. Only ruins remain of the original station, deactivated in 1948.

■ POINT MONTARA LIGHT ■
Pacifica (1900 and 1928)

Over ninety wrecks in the vicinity did not move Congress to establish a lighthouse on this site. In 1868 the steamer *Colorado* ran aground on a ledge near Point Montara, and four years later the freighter *Acuelo* wrecked just below the point, spilling into the sea a cargo of coal and iron worth at least $150,000. The latter disaster finally led to the placement of a fog signal on Point Montara in 1875. Nearly three decades would pass before the Point Montara fog-signal station received a light.

A simple pole light, set up in 1900, served until 1912, when it was replaced by a wooden tower that housed a fourth-order Fresnel lens.

The existing thirty-foot cast-iron tower was built at the edge of the rocky point in 1928. This small light got around: It served on Cape Cod from 1881 to 1922, then was moved to Yerba Buena, and then to Point Montara. Its light shines out toward the Pacific from an elevation of seventy feet.

Point Montara Light

The station's fourth-order Fresnel lens gave way to a modern optic in 1970.

Travel information: Most of the station buildings, including the keeper's Victorian-style quarters, are now used as a youth hostel. Visitors are welcome to walk the grounds until sunset. Call (650) 728-7177 at the lighthouse, or see www.norcalhostels.org/montara. The lighthouse's fourth-order Fresnel lens is on display at the San Mateo County Museum, 2200 Broadway, Redwood City, CA 94063; call (650) 299-0104, or see www.historysmc.org.

■ FORT POINT LIGHT ■

San Francisco (1855 and 1864)

Completed in 1855, at about the same time as the original Alcatraz Island Lighthouse, the Fort Point Lighthouse stood empty for more than a year, waiting for its third-order Fresnel lens to arrive from France. This light had an important job to do, that of marking the channel through the Golden Gate and into San Francisco Bay, but the lens was never installed and the tower's lamps were never lit. Before the station could be placed into operation, the lighthouse was torn down to make way for the massive brick walls of Fort Winfield Scott. The Fresnel lens originally intended for Fort Point was given instead to Point Pinos Lighthouse on Monterey Bay, where it still shines after more than 140 years.

Fort Point Light
John W. Weil

While the three-story fortress was under construction, workers built a wooden light tower outside its walls. By 1864 storm-driven Pacific waves threatened to sweep it away and undermine the foundations of the fort. To make way for a protective seawall, the Fort Point Lighthouse had to be torn down for a second time. It was replaced by a twenty-seven-foot iron skeleton tower, perched atop the walls of the fort. The additional height made the light, focused by a rather modest-order lens, easier for approaching seamen to spot. The lens was upgraded to a fourth order in 1902.

The station served its purpose for more than seven decades, until construction of the Golden Gate Bridge made the old lighthouse obsolete. It was discontinued in 1934. Towering 740 feet above the sea, the bridge itself is a mammoth lighthouse. Mariners can see its lights and recognize the distinctive inverted arches of its supporting cables from many miles at sea. Completed in 1937, the bridge is one of the world's most recognizable landmarks and seamarks.

Travel information: Follow Lincoln Boulevard and Long Avenue to Fort Point National Historical Site, part of the Golden Gate National Recreational Area. Open daily except on major holidays, the old fort, with its tiny lighthouse, offers wonderful views of San Francisco and the Golden Gate Bridge. Call (415) 556-1693, or see www.nps.gov/fopo. Less scenic is the blocky, concrete **Lime Point Light** (1900), where only the fog-signal building still stands on the opposite side of the Golden Gate Strait. It can be viewed from behind a fence at the end of Sausalito's Fort Baker Road. The sun powers the **Mile Rocks Light** (1901), just outside the Golden Gate and well to the west of Fort Point, which is now a truncated structure painted with orange and white stripes.

■ ALCATRAZ ISLAND LIGHT ■
San Francisco (1854 and 1909)

Derived from *alcatraces*, the Spanish word for pelican, the name Alcatraz now has a cold and forbidding ring to it, and no wonder. For years Alcatraz Island in San Francisco Bay was the unhappy home of Al Capone and many other notorious criminals. Here they served "hard time" at a federal penitentiary made escape-proof by high concrete walls and the shark-infested waters of the bay.

In contrast mariners and lighthouse lovers have warm feelings toward the island, for it is home to the oldest major navigational light on the West Coast. Francis Gibbons built the island's original lighthouse, a Cape Cod–style dwelling with a short tower peeking just above its roof. Focused by a third-order Fresnel lens, its light first shone on the evening of June 1, 1854. At that time gold-hungry miners were still arriving by sea, and the Alcatraz Island Light guided them and their ships into San Francisco Bay and on toward their destiny—only a handful would ever find the riches they sought.

The great San Francisco earthquake of 1906 caused keeper B. F. Leeds to believe he was witnessing "the end of the world." Not so, but the shaking did end the career of the little Gibbons lighthouse. The severely damaged structure was soon replaced by an eighty-four-foot reinforced-concrete tower and adjacent bay-style dwelling. The height of the octagonal tower allowed its light to be seen above the high walls of the military prison then under construction.

For more than fifty years, the light station would share its rugged roost with prisons, both military and civilian. As a result keepers here endured many sleepless

Alcatraz Island Light
US Coast Guard

days as well as nights during major breakouts and riots. The worst incident came in 1946, when inmates took over the prison, holding police and US Marines at bay for nearly two days. Both the lighthouse and its keeper survived the battle. Ironically, the light was automated in 1963, not long before the doors of the federal penitentiary, first opened in 1934, slammed shut for the last time. The two-story keeper's residence was burned during a protracted demonstration by young Native Americans in 1969. A modern optic continues as an active aid to navigation.

Travel information: Alcatraz Island is part of the Golden Gate National Recreation Area. Tours of the island, prison, and around the base of the lighthouse are offered at Pier 41 in the Fisherman's Wharf district by Alcatraz Cruises, an official concessionaire to the National Park Service; call (415) 981-7625, or see Alcatraz Cruises. A museum on the island displays the fourth-order Fresnel lens formerly used here; the station now employs a modern optic. For more details call the ranger's office at (415) 561-4900, or see www.nps.gov/alca.

■ YERBA BUENA (GOAT ISLAND) LIGHT ■
San Francisco (1875)

This lighthouse at one time guided dozens of passenger ferries passing back and forth each day between San Francisco and Oakland. The Bay Bridge, opened in 1939, now carries most cross-bay traffic, but the light on Yerba Buena Island still shines. Nowadays, it mostly serves pleasure craft and as the US Coast Guard Group

Yerba Buena (Goat Island) Light
Kraig Anderson

San Francisco and Aids to Navigation Team San Francisco base, which takes up the entire lovely 140-acre island.

The original fifth-order Fresnel lens crowns the station's two-story octagonal tower. It displays a fixed white light. A Coast Guard admiral now lives in the old keeper's dwelling.

Travel information: Located on an active Coast Guard station, the lighthouse is not open to the public. Its light can be seen from the water and from a variety of points along the shore; for instance it can be seen to the right while driving from San Francisco on the Bay Bridge.

■ BLUNTS REEF LIGHTSHIP *WAL-605* ■
Oakland (1950)

Lightship *WAL-605* rode at anchor for nearly ten years at Blunts Reef, off Eureka. Launched in 1950 at a shipyard in East Boothbay, Maine, the *WAL-605* was assigned originally to Overfalls Station, near Cape May, New Jersey. In 1960 it was sent west for service at Blunts Reef. During its last years on active duty with the Coast Guard—it was retired in 1975—the *WAL-605* served as a relief lightship at San Francisco Station or wherever it might be needed.

Blunts Reef Lightship
US Coast Guard

Sold as surplus property by the Coast Guard, the *WAL-605* later functioned as a historical museum and even as a fishing boat. Currently, it is owned by the nonprofit US Lighthouse Society in Oakland, which is doing lighthouse lovers, students of maritime history, and the nation an enormous favor by restoring the old ship.

The *WAL-605* has a steel hull 108 feet long, with a thirty-foot beam. The mushroom anchor, which so often held it firmly on station, weighs seven thousand pounds. The lightship is berthed on the Oakland waterfront.

Travel information: The US Lighthouse Society is restoring this fine old vessel for use as a floating museum in the San Francisco Bay area. Open for group tours on weekends, the lightship is berthed at Jack London Square, Oakland, California; call (510) 272-0544. The lightship is adjacent to the former presidential yacht *Potomac*, used by President Franklin Delano Roosevelt. The society can also provide a wealth of facts and information on lighthouses and lightships throughout the United States and Canada and on general lighthouse history. You may want to join. Write to United States Lighthouse Society, 9005 Point No Point Road NE, Hansville, WA 98340; call (415) 362-7255, or see www.uslhs.org.

■ EAST BROTHER LIGHT ■
Richmond (1874)

Built in 1874, the classically Victorian East Brother Lighthouse now serves as both a navigational light, guiding vessels into San Pablo Bay, and as a popular bed-and-breakfast inn. Located on a small island just off San Pablo Point, the lighthouse marks the channel through the narrow and often treacherous San Pablo Straits that link the Sacramento River estuary to the open San Francisco Bay.

Unable to buy property on the mainland at an acceptable price, the government resorted to building the station on tiny East Brother Island. Construction crews had to blast away much of the one-third-acre island to level the site. There was hardly room on what remained to squeeze the combination two-story tower and dwelling and separate fog-signal building.

East Brother Light

In 1969 the Coast Guard decided to automate the station, place its light on a pole, and tear down the old buildings. Local preservationists managed to save the structure and over time to restore the station to its original Victorian charm. The fifth-order light is still in operation.

Travel information: For overnight reservations at the East Brother Lighthouse B&B, call (510) 233-2385, or see www.ebls.org. Day visits are also encouraged.

To the north, at 2000 Glenn Cove Drive in Vallejo, is the **Carquinez Strait Lighthouse** (1910),

Carquinez Strait Light
Bob and Sandra Shanklin

which once marked the western reaches of the San Pablo Bay. Located off Route 780, this retired lighthouse is now privately owned, but visitors are welcome to walk the grounds.

■ POINT BONITA LIGHT ■
San Francisco (1855 and 1877)

Seamen approaching San Francisco from the west often scan the horizon looking for the bright beacon of Point Bonita Lighthouse. It points the way to the Golden Gate and the bay while warning mariners to keep well away from Point Bonita and its deadly rocks.

Built in 1855 on a high ledge more than three hundred feet above the sea, the original station had a fifty-six-foot brick tower and a detached Cape Cod–style dwelling. Officials considered this lighthouse so important that they assigned it an exceptionally powerful second-order Fresnel lens. The light could be seen from up to twenty miles at sea, except in a heavy fog, which could make it completely invisible.

Since low-lying clouds frequently masked the beacon, the station needed an effective fog signal. Originally, it was equipped only with a surplus army cannon fired off with an ear-splitting roar by the keepers whenever fog rolled in, which it did nearly every day. The cannon was eventually replaced by a fifteen-hundred-pound bell.

Point Bonita Light

In time officials decided to build another lighthouse down closer to the water, where its beacon would be more effective. Construction got under way in 1872, but fitting the new station onto the only available site—a frightfully narrow ledge about 120 feet above the waves—was no simple matter. To bring materials to the site, a landing platform, derrick, and incline railway had to be built and a tunnel blasted through more than one hundred feet of solid rock. It took more than five years to complete the thirty-three-foot tower and associated structures. Equipped with the Fresnel lens from the original lighthouse and a pair of steam-driven fog sirens, the station was, at last, ready for service by the winter of 1877.

The lighthouse survived the earthquake that leveled much of San Francisco in 1906. During the 1940s, however, a landslide destroyed the land bridge that connected the tower and fog-signal building. The Coast Guard first replaced it with a wooden bridge, then with the attractive suspension bridge that still serves the station. In 1981 the Point Bonita Light became the last of California's lighthouses to be automated.

Travel information: Now part of the Golden Gate National Recreation Area, this extraordinarily scenic lighthouse is located off Highway 101, just north of San Francisco. From San Francisco cross the Golden Gate

Bridge, take the Alexander Avenue exit, and follow Conzelman Road to the lighthouse. The winding road to Point Bonita provides spectacular views of the city and the coast. You should bring sensible shoes, since reaching the lighthouse requires a hike of more than a mile. For updates on accessibility, ahead of your visit be sure to contact the Marin Headlands Visitor Center, Fort Barry, Building 948, Sausalito, CA 94965; call (415) 331-1540, or see www.nps.gov/goga/pobo.htm. For more information about the Golden Gate National Recreation Area, contact the Golden Gate National Parks, Building 201, Fort Mason, San Francisco, CA 94123; call (415) 561-4700, or see www.nps.gov/goga.

▪ POINT REYES LIGHT ▪
Inverness, Point Reyes National Seashore (1870)

In 1885 Point Reyes keeper E. G. Chamberlain wrote the following: "Solitude, where are your charms . . . better dwell in the midst of alarms than in this horrible place." It is not hard to understand keeper Chamberlain's melancholy when one considers that Point Reyes is socked in by fog more than 110 days a year. Keepers lived and worked on this isolated and frequently shrouded point for more than a century and must at times have thought they were on another planet. Established in 1870, the station was not automated until 1975, much to the relief of the no doubt lonely, wind-battered keeper.

Point Reyes Light

Considered one of the West Coast's most dangerous navigational obstacles, Point Reyes sweeps more than fifteen miles southwestward from the mostly southeastward-trending Northern California coast. With its fog, wind, and tricky currents, the mostly low-lying point has been tearing open the hulls of ships since the sixteenth century.

Clinging to a cliff more than 250 feet above the sea, the Point Reyes Lighthouse warns ships with its extraordinarily powerful first-order beacon. Its flashing light is still focused by the station's original two-ton Fresnel lens. The huge lens dominates the sixteen-sided brick tower, which, despite its lofty elevation, is only forty feet tall.

Travel information: The lighthouse is located in Point Reyes National Seashore, off Route 1 northwest of San Francisco. Visitors should stop first at the Bear Valley Visitors Center near the entrance. Winds above forty miles per hour will close the stairs down to the lighthouse. Special evening programs are offered; for more information, call (415) 669-1534, or see www.nps.gov/pore.

■ FARALLON ISLAND LIGHT ■
South Farallon Island (1856)

A toiling construction crew, consisting of failed gold-rush prospectors and a sea-sick mule, built the first lighthouse here in 1853. Then, almost immediately, they tore it down and started work on another. Like several other early western light-houses, the original structure had to be demolished when it proved too small to house its bulky Fresnel lens. The second tower was ready and its enormous first-order lens installed by January 1, 1856.

Farallon Island Light
National Archives

Early keepers at this station were caught in the middle of a bizarre "Egg War." Freebooting poachers made large profits stealing eggs from the millions of seabirds nesting on South Farallon and other nearby islands. So large and lucrative were their hauls that greedy poachers fought with one another—first with fists, then with pistols—for gathering rights. When people started getting shot, California lawmen stepped in and drove off the poachers.

One of the nation's most isolated lighthouses, the Southeast Farallon Island station was automated in 1972. At the same time the big first-order Fresnel was exchanged for a modern aerobeacon.

Travel information: Located some twenty-three miles west of San Francisco, the rugged, pristine islands are now part of the Farallon National Wildlife Refuge. Used primarily as a nature-study area, the light station is off-limits to the public. However, some Oceanic Society wildlife cruises provide views of the station; call (800) 326-7491 for details on weekend trips to the island.

■ POINT ARENA LIGHT ■
Point Arena (1870 and 1906)

Like much of the California coastline, Point Arena turns a hospitable face to trav-elers who come by land but bares its teeth to mariners. Jagged, saw-toothed rocks rise from the waves just offshore. Two and a half miles to the west, predatory Point Arena Rock rises from the sea, waiting to tear open the hulls of ships. Since 1870 the powerful flashing beacon of the Point Arena Lighthouse has warned vessels of these dangers.

The point's rugged topography was created by movement of the San Andreas Fault, which lies beneath the lighthouse. The legendary fault slipped and growled in 1906, flattening much of San Francisco and, not surprisingly, devastating the Point Arena Light station. Fatally cracked by the shaking, the original brick tower had to be replaced. To buttress the new 115-foot tower against future tremblers, builders gave it walls of reinforced concrete. A first-order Fresnel lens focused the powerful flashing beacon until 1977, when it was replaced by a modern optic.

The nonprofit Point Arena Lighthouse Keepers leased the light station in 1984 from the USCG, became the owner in 2000, and brought the lighthouse back to life.

Point Arena Light

Travel information: Take Lighthouse Road north from the town of Point Arena. Now beautifully restored, the lighthouse is open to the public daily. A museum has been established in the fog-signal building adjacent to the tower. Write the Point Arena Lighthouse Keepers Association, P.O. Box 11, 45500 Lighthouse Road, Point Arena, CA 95468; call the association at (877) 725-4448, or see www.point arenalighthouse.com.

▪ POINT CABRILLO LIGHT ▪
Mendocino (1909)

A small clapboard fog-signal building and attached octagonal wooden light tower have guarded lonely Point Cabrillo since 1909. The original third-order Fresnel lens still serves mariners, flashing white six times each minute. The light has a focal plane about fifty feet above sea level and can be seen from up to fifteen miles at sea. The fog signal that at one time blasted from the back of the main building is now sounded by an offshore buoy.

Restored in 2007 by the nonprofit Point Cabrillo Lightkeepers Association, the light is now part of the Point Cabrillo Light Station State Historic Park.

Point Cabrillo Light
Nancy A. Pizzo

Travel information: Located off Route 1 near Mendocino, the glorious old frame building can be viewed and photographed from the highway. The Point Cabrillo Lightkeepers Association (PCLK) is working to keep the park open during times of state economic cutbacks. To check the status of this site, write PCLK, 13800 Lighthouse Drive, Mendocino, CA 95460; call (707) 937-6122, or see www.pointcabrillo.org. For state park information write California State Parks, c/o Mendocino District, 12301 N. Highway 1, P.O. Box 1, Mendocino CA 95460; call (707) 937-5804, or see www.parks.ca.gov.

■ PUNTA GORDA LIGHT ■
Petrolia (1912)

A rounded, nearly treeless cape thrusting eight hundred feet above the sea, Punta Gorda rises above the Northern California coast like a fist waiting to smash vessels that venture too close to its jagged rocks. Eight ships were lost near Punta Gorda between 1899 and 1907. The last of these, the *Columbia*, took eighty-seven people down with her.

Punta Gorda Light
US Coast Guard

Prompted by these disasters, Congress funded a light station in 1908, but building the new lighthouse was not easy. Materials had to be landed well to the north of the site and then dragged down the beach on horse-drawn sleds. Nonetheless, by 1912 the tower's fourth-order-bulls-eye Fresnel lens began to cast its flashing light toward the sea.

Since it was as difficult to maintain as it had been to build, the lighthouse was abandoned by the Coast Guard as soon as it became practical to do so. The station was closed permanently in 1951. All that remains of it is a single-story concrete watch room with a spiral staircase leading to an iron lantern room overhead. Resting on a bluff forty-eight feet above the surf on California's isolated "Lost Coast," the entire structure stands only twenty-seven feet high.

> *Travel information:* From Highway 101 in Northern California, take the Honeydew/Dyerville exit in Humboldt Redwoods State Park. Travel west to Mattole Road in Honeydew to Lighthouse Road, almost a one-and-one-half-hour trip. Travel five miles to Mattole Campground. The three-and-a-half-mile trail leads to the lighthouse through bear country, where weather can be windy and cold year-round. Various volunteer groups including the Honeydew Volunteer Firemen have kept the small light in good condition. Before visiting, it is advisable to contact the Bureau of Land Management, Arcata Field Office, 1695 Heindon Road, Arcata, CA 95521; call (707) 825-2300, or see www.blm.gov/ca.

■ (OLD) CAPE MENDOCINO LIGHT ■
Capetown (1868 and 1951)

California's westernmost point is also one of its most imposing headlands. Cape Mendocino's soaring fourteen-hundred-foot cliffs drop almost vertically into the Pacific. Although the cape was among the West's best-known seamarks and most feared navigational obstacles, no light was placed here until the late 1860s.

Establishing a lighthouse on the cape proved a daunting challenge. The first ship bringing supplies to the construction site was wrecked on the merciless rocks to the south. When a second ship finally delivered the necessary materials, they had to be hoisted hundreds of feet up the cliffs with ropes. Laborers were forced to endure weeks of rain and fog and to camp out in howling winds. Despite the difficulties workers eventually completed a two-story brick dwelling and barn and erected a sixteen-sided, pyramidal cast-iron tower that had been prefabricated by machinists in San Francisco.

Focused by a first-order Fresnel lens, the light first shone on the night of December 1, 1868. With a focal plane more than four hundred feet above the Pacific, the light could be seen from more than twenty-five miles at sea. The Blunts Reef Lightship was stationed offshore for several years, denoting the danger of this area to mariners.

Cape Mendocino Light
Bob and Sandra Shanklin

In 1951 the historic lighthouse was deactivated and its job taken over by an automated light on a steel pole located farther up the cliffs. The deteriorating, original tower was dismantled in 1998, reassembled at Point Delgada in Mal Coombs Park in Shelter Cove, restored, and opened to the public in 2001, thanks to the efforts of Cape Mendocino Lighthouse Preservation Society.

Travel information: To reach Shelter Cove travel south on Highway 101 through Humboldt State Redwood Park. Take the Redway exit, and turn onto Briceland Road. At the west end of town is Shelter Cove road; continue west for about twenty-five miles. To reach Cape Mendocino take the coast road off Highway 101 through Ferndale and Capetown. Contact Mal Cooms Park, 181 Cove Point West, Shelter Cove, CA 95589. For more information on the preservation of this lighthouse, contact the Cape Mendocino Preservation Society–Shelter Cove, P.O. Box 454, Whitehorn, CA, 95589.

■ HUMBOLDT HARBOR/TABLE BLUFF LIGHTS ■
Humboldt Bay (1856 and 1892)

Completed in 1856, at a time when much of the US Pacific coast was still a wilderness, the Humboldt Harbor Lighthouse was among the first light stations in the West. Built at a cost of $15,000, it consisted of a Cape Cod–style dwelling with a twenty-one-foot tower rising through the middle section of its roof. The lantern room held a fourth-order Fresnel lens.

Built on a sandy foundation, the lighthouse was threatened by nature almost from the beginning. Wracked by earthquakes, storms, and beach erosion, the structure began to deteriorate. In 1885 a cyclone tore away its roof and drove floating logs against its walls. The building was repaired, but soon its masonry began to crack and fall apart. It eventually collapsed into a jumble of masonry on the beach.

By 1892 a new lighthouse, built high atop nearby Table Bluff, was ready for service. A Victorian-style structure with an attached, square tower, it was given the same fourth-order lens that had once shone from the tower of the Humboldt Harbor Lighthouse. Although the Table Bluff tower was only thirty-five feet tall, its elevation placed the light almost 190 feet above the bay. The light could be seen from up to twenty miles away.

After more than eighty years of service, the Table Bluff Lighthouse was decommissioned in 1975 and turned over to a private foundation. The tower section of the lighthouse was cut into two parts and trucked to Woodley Island, near Eureka, where it was reassembled, repaired, and refitted with the station's old Fresnel lens in 1987. It presently serves as a tourist attraction and a reminder of the area's rich maritime history.

Table Bluff Light
Bob and Sandra Shanklin

Travel information: The Table Bluff tower is on display at Woodley Island in the Eureka Inner Harbor area. Follow US Highway 101 into Eureka, turn toward the water on Route 255, and follow signs to the lighthouse. The nearby Humboldt Bay Maritime Museum in Samoa is also well worth a visit; call (707) 444-9440, or see http://humboldtbaymaritimemuseum.com. Nothing remains of the old Humboldt Harbor Lighthouse except, perhaps, a few chunks of stone on the beach.

■ TRINIDAD HEAD LIGHT ■
Trinidad (1871)

Set on a jagged cliff face almost two hundred feet above the Pacific surf, this little lighthouse has aided commercial fishermen and other mariners seeking the shelter of Trinidad Harbor for more than a century. Built in 1871 to guide schooners carrying lumber to San Francisco, the light helped close a gap of darkness between Crescent City and Humboldt Bay to the south. Although the station's fourth-order lens was small for a coastal light, the elevation of the tower, which was perched on a high cliff, made its beacon visible from up to twenty miles at sea. When the light was automated in 1947, its classic lens was replaced by an airport-style beacon. The old Trinidad Head light is still operational.

Travel information: Take the Trinidad exit from US Highway 101. Now automated, the Trinidad Head Lighthouse is closed to the general public, although Coast Guard presence has ended. Hiking trails lead to an overlook with a view of the old lighthouse, but less energetic visitors have another attractive option. For the benefit of tourists who constantly ask the locals how to get to the lighthouse, a reproduction of the tower has been built in the town as a "Memorial Lighthouse" by the Trinidad Civic Club. It is a near-perfect match to the original and now houses the antique Fresnel lens that served for so many years at the Trinidad Head station. The original 1898 fog bell resides beside it.

Trinidad Head Light
US Coast Guard

■ BATTERY POINT (CRESCENT CITY) LIGHT ■
Crescent City (1856)

Pressed by Northern California lumber interests during the 1850s, Congress designated Crescent City as a site for a lighthouse. Like many other early western light stations, this one consisted of a simple Cape Cod–style dwelling with a tower rising through the center of its roof. Beginning in 1856, the beacon focused by its fourth-order Fresnel lens guided freighters into the city's bustling harbor, then out again, bearing loads of redwood bound for San Francisco.

Captain John Jeffrey and his wife, Nellie, took over keeper's duties at the Battery Point Lighthouse

Battery Point Light

in 1875. They became near-permanent fixtures of the station. In all, they spent thirty-nine years in the lighthouse and raised four children there.

The thick stone walls of the lighthouse, built for a mere $15,000, outlasted several generations of keepers. They still stand, little changed from the station's earliest days. Except for a stroke of luck, however, the station's last night might have been that of March 27, 1964. The earthquake that hit Alaska on that date sent five titanic tidal waves hurtling toward the coast of Northern California, where they stormed ashore shortly after midnight. Keepers Clarence and Peggy Coons saw them coming but could do little but say their prayers. Fortunately, the enormous waves struck at such an extreme angle that the lighthouse and its keepers were spared.

Although discontinued in 1965, the light was reestablished in 1982 as a private aid to navigation. The building now serves as a history museum.

Travel information: The lighthouse and museum are located at Battery Point on the west side of the Crescent City harbor at the foot of "A" Street. Write to the Del Norte County Historical Society, P.O. Box 396, Crescent City, CA 95531; call (707) 464-3089 or (707) 464-3922 (museum), or see www.delnortehistory.org.

■ ST. GEORGE REEF LIGHT ■
Crescent City (1892)

Built on an exposed rock constantly pounded by the Pacific, the St. George Reef Light station cost the US government $704,633, making it the most expensive lighthouse in the nation's history. Mariners who long dreaded this deadly obstacle certainly thought the money was well spent. Over the centuries this notorious reef has ruined numerous ships, including the side-wheeler *Brother Jonathan*, wrecked here in 1865 with a loss of more than two hundred lives.

The hulking and costly stone tower was erected on a giant elliptical base of granite and concrete. Rising more than 140 feet above the waves, the tower held a first-order Fresnel lens, displaying an alternating red and white flashing light.

Because of the station's isolated and dangerous location, families were never housed here. The all-male crews who lived on the rock for months at a time found the tower damp, cold, and uncomfortable. Most keepers considered the St. George Reef station an unpleasant and undesirable posting. Mercifully, the light was discontinued in 1975 and replaced by a large buoy.

Travel information: The abandoned but spectacular lighthouse can be seen from the end of Crescent City's Washington Boulevard. The station's eighteen-foot-high first-order Fresnel lens is on display in the Del Norte County Historical Society Museum on Sixth Street in Crescent City. Progressing in restoration efforts, the St. George Reef Lighthouse Preservation Society (SGRLPS) is offering occasional tours of the lighthouse, weather permitting. Tours depart from the Crescent City Airport in a helicopter for a six-minute flight to the light. SGRLPS docents give a one-hour tour. Reservations are required; write SGRLPS–Tours, P.O. Box 577, Crescent City, CA 95531; call (707) 464-8299, or see www.stgeorgereeflighthouse.us.

St. George Reef Light
Rick Hiser

OREGON

■ CAPE BLANCO LIGHT ■
Port Orford (1870)

Cape Blanco and its light station take their names from the precipitous white cliffs that drop almost vertically down to the beaches nearly two hundred feet below the lighthouse. Oldest and southernmost of Oregon's major beacons, the light shines from atop a fifty-nine-foot conical tower erected in 1870. The considerable height of the cliffs raises the focal plane of the light to a lofty 245 feet above mean sea level. Focused by a second-order Fresnel lens, the light can be seen from up to twenty-two miles at sea. Unfortunately, vandals ravaged the classic lens in 1992, doing more than $500,000 in damage. However, a beautiful second-order Fresnel lens replacement was then given to this Oregon light station, which boasts these superlatives: the state's most westerly light station, the oldest continuously operating light, and the light with the highest focal plane above the sea.

Cape Blanco Light
John W. Weil

> *Travel information:* The lighthouse is located near Cape Blanco State Park, off US Highway 101 a few miles north of Port Orford. Visitors are welcome to walk the grounds when the light station is open. The lighthouse is open because of joint efforts of the Bureau of Land Management, Oregon State Parks, local Native American tribes, Curry County, and the Friends of Cape Blanco. For more tour information contact Coos Bay Bureau of Land Management at (541) 756-0100, or see www.portorfordoregon.com/blanco .html. Write Friends of Cape Blanco, P.O. Box 1178, Port Orford, Oregon 97465; call (541) 332-0248.

■ COQUILLE RIVER LIGHT ■
Bandon (1896)

Now an attraction of Bullards Beach State Park, this little lighthouse stood empty and ignored for nearly half a century—longer than it served as an active light station. Gutted by fire after the Coast Guard abandoned the structure in 1939, it was nearly destroyed by wind, weather, and vandals. Its story has a happy ending, however, as the old lighthouse has now been lovingly restored by the state.

When it was built in 1896, the forty-foot brick lighthouse tower was covered in a protective layer of stucco and was painted white. Given a fourth-order lens,

Coquille River Light

it served for more than four decades before it was discontinued and replaced by a series of buoys and a small jetty light.

To the delight of Bullards Beach visitors, the park has placed a light in the tower since 1991. Interestingly, since it is not an official coastal beacon, the light is blacked out on the ocean side.

Travel information: Bullards Beach State Park and its lighthouse are located off US Highway 101 near Bandon. The park is open year-round; the lighthouse is open generally from May through October. For updates call the park office at (541) 347-3501, or see www.oregonstateparks.org/park_71.php. The Lighthouse Bed and Breakfast in Bandon offers a fine view of the tower. For reservations, contact the Lighthouse Bed and Breakfast, 650 Jetty Rd. SW, Bandon, OR 97411; call (541) 347-9316, or see www.lighthouselodging.com.

■ CAPE ARAGO LIGHT ■
Charleston (1866, 1909, and 1934)

The prosperous lumber ports on Coos Bay have been served by several lighthouses. The first, completed in 1866, was established on a small, strategically placed island just north of the prominent headland known as Cape Arago. An octagonal iron tower on slender legs, it stood for more than four decades before erosion forced the Lighthouse Board to make improvements to the light station, including enclosing the iron tower in brick and giving it a stucco exterior. But just a few years later, in 1909,

Cape Arago Light

a wooden structure was built farther back from the rapidly weathering cliffs, and it served for twenty-five years before it, too, threatened to tumble into the Pacific.

One of the more recently completed of the West's lighthouses, the existing reinforced-concrete tower has proven more durable than its predecessors. The forty-foot octagonal concrete tower rises through the roof of a rectangular fog-signal building. The light's original fourth-order Fresnel lens shone from about one hundred feet above the Pacific and had a range of approximately sixteen miles. The Coast Guard removed the lens in 1993 and put it on display at the US Coast Guard Group/Air Station North Bend. Following years of debate, the lighthouse was transferred from the Coast Guard to the Confederated tribes of the Coos, Lower Umpqua, and Siuslaw Indians in 2008.

> *Travel information:* Cape Arago and its lighthouse are located about two miles south of Charleston on Cape Arago Highway near the entrance to Coos Bay. Turn west off US Highway 101 at the town of Coos Bay. The lighthouse is not open to the public, but it can be viewed from Sunset Bay State Park, just south of Charleston. There is a loop road with a viewpoint, but since the actual site is ten miles away, a telephoto lens or binoculars are needed. The Fresnel lens is on display in the main building of Group Air Station North Bend, 2000 Connecticut Ave., North Bend, OR 97459; call (541) 756-9220.

■ UMPQUA RIVER LIGHT ■
Winchester Bay (1857 and 1894)

The conical, plaster-covered masonry tower rises just above the treetops of a state park named in its honor. At night the flashing light, alternating red and white, can be seen from twenty-one miles away. The existing tower dates back to 1894, but a lighthouse stood here as early as 1857.

Erected under the constant threat of attack by Indians, the first Umpqua River tower stood for only four years. Floods quickly undercut its foundation, and in 1861 it collapsed into the river. Nothing was done to revive the station until the

1890s. Completed in 1894 from the same plans as the **Heceta Head Light,** the present sixty-seven-foot tower was crowned with a powerful first-order Fresnel lens and its characteristic ruby-glass red sector. The site, well above the river, raises the focal plane of the light 165 feet above the sea.

> *Travel information:* Managed by Douglas County, the light can be seen and enjoyed from the adjacent Umpqua River Lighthouse State Park, located off US Highway 101 just south of Winchester Bay. A fine visitor center with museum occupies the former Umpqua River Coast Guard station. For information about an arranged tour of the light, call the museum at (541) 271-4631.

Umpqua River Light

■ HECETA HEAD LIGHT ■
Florence (1894)

Before 1894 there was no light to guide ships along the ninety-mile stretch of coast between Cape Foulweather and Cape Argo. The crews of ships plying these waters were left to find their way in the dark. But in the spring of that year, a fifty-six-foot-tall white masonry tower was completed high up on the Heceta Head cliffs, and a bright light began to shine from its lantern.

To build the lighthouse in this remote location took nearly two years and $180,000—a fantastic sum at the time. Construction materials had to be brought in by ship to the nearby Suislaw River, then hauled by mule-drawn wagon to the construction site.

The new lighthouse was fitted with an exquisite first-order Fresnel lens with 640 individual prisms. Originally, the light came from a five-wick coal-oil lamp. A weighted cable powered the gears

Heceta Head Light
John W. Weil

that turned the lamp, causing the light to flash. Although the old lamp has given way to a million-candlepower electric bulb, the original classic lens still shines. Its beam flashes seaward from an elevation of more than two hundred feet and can be seen from a distance of up to twenty-one miles.

The station is now owned by the US Forest Service and operated as an interpretive center and bed-and-breakfast inn. The first innkeepers were chosen in 1995; innkeeping and restoration of the keeper's house have become multigenerational projects.

Travel information: One of the most scenic light stations in the West, Heceta Head Lighthouse is popular with photographers. It stands on a craggy point about eleven miles north of Florence. Turn off US Highway 101 at Devils Elbow State Park. Tours are given regularly during summer months; write 92072 Highway 101 South, Yachats, OR 97498; call for reservations at the inn or information on tours, (866) 547-3696, or see http://hecetalighthouse.com.

■ YAQUINA BAY LIGHT ■
Newport (1871)

Yaquina Bay Light

Built on the crest of a hill near the entrance to Yaquina Bay, the lamps in the little red lantern atop this wood-frame lighthouse first burned in November 1871. Fewer than three years later, they were permanently snuffed out. Due to an extraordinary bureaucratic bungle, a second lighthouse was mistakenly erected nearby, rendering the Yaquina Bay Light completely superfluous.

People might have supposed at the time that the abandoned, two-story lighthouse would soon be demolished, but not so. The building was eventually put to use as a crew station for the US Life-Saving Service. Later it was carefully restored and became an attractive historical museum.

Travel information: The Yaquina Bay Lighthouse is located near the north end of the Yaquina Bay Bridge in Yaquina Bay State Park. Filled with nineteenth-century furnishings and artifacts, it is open to the public daily. Together with the Friends of Yaquina Lighthouses, the US Forest Service maintains the structure as a museum. For further information write Friends of Yaquina Lighthouses, P.O. Box 410, Newport, OR 97365, or call about park tours, (541) 574-3100; the interpretive stores, (541) 574-3125, or see www.yaquinalights.org.

■ YAQUINA HEAD LIGHT ■
Newport (1873)

One of the most beautiful lighthouses in America, the Yaquina Head Light is a magnet for photographers and tourists, who can see it from US Highway 101, the Pacific Coast Highway. The magnificent outcropping of rock on which the tower stands is a more literal magnet. At its core is a rich vein of magnetized iron, which sends the compasses of passing ships into a crazy spin. For this reason and others, this headland is a formidable threat to shipping and, over the years, has claimed many fine vessels.

Yaquina Head Light

Interestingly, the ninety-three-foot conical tower built atop the cliffs here had been intended for Cape Foulweather, miles to the north. Construction crews, however, mistakenly landed their materials on Yaquina Head and built the tower there instead. Lighthouse officials detected the mistake soon after the station was completed in 1873. Rather than tear down the expensive masonry towers, they left it in service and deactivated the redundant Yaquina Bay Lighthouse.

A huge twelve-foot-high classic lens has graced the lantern room for more than a century. It still shines today, casting seaward a beam visible from nineteen miles away.

Travel information: Located about four miles north of Newport off US Highway 101, the station is open to the public. It is managed by the Bureau of Land Management, which offers interpretive tours; visitors may contact Friends of Yaquina Lighthouses, Yaquina Head Outstanding Natural Area, P.O. Box 410, Newport, OR 97365; call (541) 574-3125, or see www .yaquinalights.org.

■ CAPE MEARES LIGHT ■
Tillamook (1890)

As with the Yaquina Head Light well to the south, the lighthouse that now stands on Cape Meares was built in the wrong place. Originally intended for Cape Lookout, the station ended up on Cape Meares because of a mapmaker's error. The two names had been reversed on US Coast Survey charts, and dismayed officials did not discover the mistake until the station was almost complete. Rather than incur the cost of building an entirely new facility on Cape Lookout, the Lighthouse Service decided to leave well enough alone.

Only thirty-eight feet tall, the octagonal iron-sheathed brick tower stood at the edge of a cliff, placing the focal plane of its light 215 feet above the breakers. A huge first-order Fresnel lens, for many years illuminated by a coal-oil lamp, made the light visible from twenty-one miles at sea.

Deactivated in 1963, the old lighthouse is now a popular tourist attraction. Much to their discredit, vandals have damaged the magnificent lens on more than one occasion.

Travel information: Located in Cape Meares State Park, the lighthouse can be reached via Three Capes Loop Road, off US Highway 101 at Tillamook. Call (503) 842-3182. More information is also at Friends of Cape Meares Lighthouse & Wildlife Refuge, P.O. Box 262, Netarts, OR 97143, or see www.capemeares lighthouse.org.

Cape Meares Light

■ LIGHTSHIP *COLUMBIA* ■
Astoria (1951)

Among the last of America's lightships, the 128-foot *Columbia* was launched in Maine in 1951. For nearly three decades she rode the waves on station eight miles off the dangerous Columbia River bar. Retired in 1979, she has since served as the prime attraction of the Columbia River Maritime Museum in Astoria.

Travel information: The lightship is moored near the Columbia River Maritime Museum at 1792 Marine Drive, Astoria, OR 97103. For hours and tours call (503) 325-2323, or see www.crmm.org.

Photo at left is the original Columbia Lightship LV 50, *which went on station April 11, 1892. Here it is being put back on station after it had been blown ashore by a severe turn-of-the-century storm. At right is the last* Columbia Lightship *that went on station in 1951, was retired in 1979, and is now the prime attraction of the Columbia River Maritime Museum in Astoria, Oregon.*

Left: National Archives; Right: John W. Weil

■ CAPE DISAPPOINTMENT LIGHT ■

Ilwaco (1856)

This cape received its melancholy name from fur trader John Meares, who mistook the headland for another landfall farther south—the one now named for him—and sailed away in disappointment. The captains of many other ships have encountered another, more bitter form of disappointment at this cape. Countless vessels have foundered here and on the nearby Columbia River bar.

Federal surveyors recommended as early as 1848 that a lighthouse be erected on the cape, but eight years went by before one was finally completed. Constructing a station on the isolated cape proved far more difficult and expensive than anyone had imagined. During the fall of 1853, the bark *Oriole* foundered on the Columbia River bar while attempting to deliver materials for the tower. It took almost a year to bring in a second shipment. Once it arrived, downpours and deep mud further delayed the project. Finally, in 1856, the fifty-three-foot dressed-stone conical tower was finished, and the oil lamps inside its first-order Fresnel lens were lit on October 15 of that year.

Cape Disappointment Light
US Coast Guard

In 1898 the Cape Disappointment Lighthouse lost its classic first-order lens and much of its status to the recently completed light station on nearby North Head. A fourth-order Fresnel optic replaced the original lens in 1937; this lens was replaced by the present marine rotating beacon in 1998.

For many years the station's closest neighbor was Fort Canby. Bristling with artillery, the fort controlled access to the Columbia. The concussion of its huge guns sometimes shattered windows in the tower.

Travel information: From Ilwaco follow signs for Cape Disappointment State Park. Visitors can reach the lighthouse via a short hike from a well-marked parking area. The park's Lewis and Clark Interpretive Center offers exhibits that celebrate the famous explorers and their visit to the cape nearly two centuries ago as well as the Cape Disappointment first-order Fresnel lens. Call (360) 642-3078, or see www.parks.wa.gov/parks.

■ NORTH HEAD LIGHT ■
Ilwaco (1898)

Built in 1898 for $25,000, the North Head Light station was established to warn ships approaching the Columbia River from the north. The Columbia's extensive bar is very dangerous and has claimed many vessels.

The white tower is sixty-five feet tall and stands at the edge of a cliff almost 130 feet high. Originally fitted with a first-order classic lens removed from the nearby **Cape Disappointment Lighthouse,** it received a less powerful fourth-order lens in 1930. Nowadays, a rotating aeromarine beacon serves here.

North Head is said to be the windiest spot in the nation. Winds blast across the narrow

North Head Light
John W. Weil

peninsula at speeds that have been clocked at 150 miles per hour. Trees, chimneys, and fences have been flattened by these gale force winds. In 1932 a wild duck, blown off course by the wind, smashed into the lantern, shattering a window and chipping the glass prisms of the lens. The damaged equipment was repaired, but the unfortunate duck was beyond help.

> *Travel information:* From the town of Ilwaco off US Highway 101, follow the signs to Cape Disappointment State Park. Markers point the way to the lighthouse. The park's Lewis and Clark Interpretive Center houses what is claimed to be the enormous first-order classic lens that served at Cape Disappointment from 1856 to 1898 and North Head from 1898 until 1932. The lighthouse grounds are open free of charge year-round, from dawn until dusk. Call (360) 642-3078 or see www.parks.wa.gov/parks for details prior to your visit about tour schedules.

■ THE KENNEWICK (CLOVER ISLAND) LIGHT ■
Kennewick (2010)

Completed in 2010, this white flashing light reminds boaters that Clover Island juts several hundred yards into the Columbia River. The Kennewick Light is sixty-two-feet tall with its light source produced by a solar-powered LED (light-emitting diode).

The lighthouse contains a spiral staircase to provide maintenance access to the light, and there is a plaza along the restored waterfront with the lighthouse as a prominent feature. It is earning significance as the most recent American lighthouse to have been built since 1962. Lighthouse enthusiasts can get a United States

Kennewick Light on Clover Island
Kevin Cole

Lighthouse Society passport and stamp for this site. The light is owned and operated by the Port of Kennewick and is recognized by the US Coast Guard as a private aid to navigation.

Travel information: From I-90 West/US-395 South take exit 220 toward Pasco. Merge onto WA-397 South and continue to East Columbia Drive. Turn right onto Clover Island Drive; parking is available near the port across from Cedars Pier 1 Restaurant. For more information, contact the Port of Kennewick, 350 Clover Island Drive, Suite 200, Kennewick, WA 99336; call (509) 586-1186. Nearby is a 9/11 memorial at the Southridge Sport Complex at the corner of US-395 and 27th Avenue, a short drive from Clover Island, which contains part of the twisted steel from former New York's World Trade Center landmark twin towers.

■ GRAYS HARBOR (WESTPORT) LIGHT ■
Westport (1898)

Towering more than one hundred feet from base to lantern, the octagonal brick Grays Harbor Lighthouse is one of the tallest on the Pacific coast. The light, still focused by the station's original third-order Fresnel lens, serves as a major coastal light and guides vessels to the harbor and fishing town of Westport. The lens has three bull's-eyes, about eight inches in diameter, emitting white and red flashes. The light is visible from about twenty-one miles away.

Grays Harbor Light

Travel information: Photographers are especially fond of this tower, which rises like an empress above a lush forest of conifers. The lighthouse is closed to the public except on holiday weekends during the summer, but it can be viewed anytime from Ocean Avenue in the delightful seaside town of Westport or from the maritime museum within the former 1939 Grays Harbor Coast Guard Lifeboat Station. For museum hours and tours, contact the Westport Maritime Museum, 2201 Westhaven Drive, P.O. Box 1074, Westport, WA 98595; call (360) 268-0078, or see www .westportwa.com/museum. The restored first-order Fresnel lens from Destruction Island is handsomely displayed here.

■ DESTRUCTION ISLAND LIGHT ■
Destruction Island (1891)

During the eighteenth century an Indian war party killed several seamen who had gone ashore here to fill casks with fresh water. Afterward, this wilderness landfall would always be known as Destruction Island, and the name proved an apt one. Over the years the boulder-strewn island, often hidden under heavy blankets of fog, was to exact a heavy toll in ships and lives.

Destruction Island Light
US Coast Guard

As early as 1855 the Lighthouse Board saw the need for a powerful navigational light to warn ships away from Destruction Island. Building a dressed-stone, iron-plated lighthouse on this remote and extraordinarily rugged offshore site, however, was a daunting task. Although Congress set aside $45,000 for the project, it was deemed impractical, and the money was spent elsewhere.

Spurred on by a sharp increase in shipping along the Washington coast and the lengthening list of wrecks on the island's jagged rocks, work on the lighthouse finally got underway in 1888. Materials had to be brought ashore in small boats from a tender anchored in a cove near the construction site, and the tower, dwelling, and outbuildings took nearly three years to build on a plateau at least eighty feet above the water. At last the steam-driven fog signal began to sound in November 1891, and one month later keepers lit the lamps inside the station's first-order Fresnel lens. Although the Destruction Island station was automated in 1968—much to the relief of its lonely Coast Guard keepers—its classic lens was removed in 1995, was later restored, and is now on exhibit at the Westport Maritime Museum in a special lens-exhibit building. Even the modern optic was darkened in the tower by the Coast Guard in 2008, and the lighthouse now stands on isolated grounds and alone.

> *Travel information:* Destruction Island Lighthouse is off-limits to the public, but it can be seen from a parking area along US Highway 101, about a mile south of Ruby Beach. It lies about three miles offshore at about a midpoint between Grays Harbor and Cape Flattery (Tatoosh Island).

■ CAPE FLATTERY LIGHT ■
Cape Flattery (1857)

Situated at the far northwestern corner of the United States (not counting Alaska), the Cape Flattery Light beams out into the Pacific's Olympic Peninsula from barren Tatoosh Island at the entrance of the Strait of Juan de Fuca. Thirty miles across the stormy strait is Canada's Vancouver Island.

Not only is this the most northwesterly lighthouse in the lower forty-eight states, it is also one of the nation's most isolated light stations. The sixty-five-foot sandstone tower and Cape Cod–style dwelling stand as a testament to the hardiness of lighthouse keepers and their families who lived here for more than a century.

Cape Flattery Light
US Coast Guard

Among the West's first great navigational sentinels, this lighthouse was completed and placed in operation in 1857. The stone tower rose directly out of the keeper's dwelling so that station personnel could climb its steps and keep the light burning without braving the harsh weather. Tatoosh Island is a hundred feet high, which elevates the light's focal plane to 165 feet above the ocean.

The original first-order Fresnel lens had been intended for Old Point Loma, but it was brought to Cape Flattery instead, because the Point Loma tower proved too small to hold the lens's enormous frame. Automated in 1977, the station now employs a modern rotating optic on a thirty-foot-high skeletal tower owned and maintained by the Coast Guard.

Now part of the Makah Indian Reservation with no permanent residents, the island has a diverse rocky habitat and is a marine biologist's dream; it is now part of a marine sanctuary.

Travel information: Inaccessible from the land, the station can be seen from the water or from a trail on the Makah Reservation at the end of Route 112. The trail requires several steep climbs and moderate physical exertion.

■ NEW DUNGENESS LIGHT ■
Dungeness (1857)

The lighthouse that stands near the tip of the eight-mile-long Dungeness Spit is the same one built there in 1857, but nowadays the tower is only about half as tall as it was 140 years ago. Suffering from structural weakness, the original structure was in danger of collapse by the late 1920s. To save it engineers decided to take some of the strain off its walls by lopping thirty-seven feet off the top.

During its early years the light guided not only ships and fishing vessels but canoes paddled by Indian warriors prepared to do battle on the spit. Traditionally, tribes living on opposite sides of the Strait of Juan de Fuca would meet on the spit to settle their differences. After the lighthouse was built, they continued the practice, but now their meeting place was much easier to find. Apparently happy to have a light to guide them to their dark and bloody work, the war parties never molested the keepers—only one another.

The lighthouse and the spit on which it stands took their name from Dungeness Point in England, coincidentally famed for its magnificent lighthouse also. Like its British namesake, Dungeness Spit is a ship killer. The list of vessels wrecked on its sands is nearly endless. The New Dungeness Light, originally focused by a classic Fresnel lens, slowed the pace of the wrecks but did not stop them—nature's impenetrable Dungeness Spit defied all human efforts to warn mariners away from it. The beacon, now provided by a modern optic, remains in operation.

Travel information: The lighthouse is accessible only by boat or by means of an eight-mile hike along highly scenic Dungeness Spit, a major part of the Dungeness Wildlife Refuge. Carefully read tide tables if you plan to walk. Take US Highway 101 west of Sequim; then turn north and follow the signs to the Dungeness Wildlife Area. Boat transportation and tours of the Olympic Peninsula can be arranged with Captain Charles Martin at (360) 775-2288. For more information contact the volunteer group that maintains and operates the light station: New Dungeness Light Station Association, P.O. Box 1283, Sequim, WA 98382; call (360) 683-6638, or see www.newdungenesslighthouse.com. Lodging is available at the lighthouse, where guests serve as "keepers" and help maintain the property.

To the west of New Dungeness, near Port Angeles, the **Ediz Hook Light** (1865, 1908, and 1946) beams from a sixty-three-foot tower atop a hanger on a Coast Guard air station. Two earlier, more conventional lighthouses once stood on Ediz Hook, and their dwellings are now used as residences. The station is closed to the public.

New Dungeness Light
Chad Kaiser

Still farther west is the **Slip Point Light** (1906), located at the east end of Clallam Bay. During the 1950s the original lighthouse was torn down and replaced by a fifty-foot tower with an automated light. This station, too, is closed to the public.

Near the far eastern end of the Strait of Juan de Fuca is Smith Island, where a Cape Cod–style lighthouse stood for a century. Undercut by erosion, the **Smith Island Lighthouse** (1858) collapsed during the late 1950s. It was replaced by a modest light mounted on a steel tower. The station is closed to the public.

■ POINT WILSON LIGHT ■
Port Townsend (1879 and 1914)

Traditionally, sailing ships approached Port Townsend along the eastern shore of Admiralty Inlet. The **Admiralty Head Light,** established in 1861 on Whidbey Island, guided them into port. But steam-powered vessels, with their deeper drafts, favored the inlet's western side. As sail gave way to steam, shippers and citizens of Port Townsend lobbied for a light to mark the western shore.

Point Wilson Light

Eventually, the Lighthouse Board responded, and on December 15, 1879, keeper David Littlefield lit the new station's lamps for the first time. A fourth-order Fresnel lens focused the light, visible from any point along a sweeping 270 degrees of horizon.

In time erosion threatened to undercut the tower, and in 1914 a forty-six-foot octagonal masonry tower replaced the original wooden lighthouse. Set a safe distance from the water's edge, the 1914 lighthouse still stands. The station's classic fourth-order lens with its ruby-glass red sector remains in use, maintained remotely by the Coast Guard Air Station at Port Angeles.

Travel information: The lighthouse is adjacent to Fort Worden State Park, at the far northeastern end of the Olympic Peninsula. You must enter the park and pay a fee to reach the lighthouse. Take Route 20 to Port Townsend, then follow signs to the park, which is open all year during daylight hours. The lighthouse is open for tours generally from May through September on Saturday afternoons. Other tours are available by special arrangement with the Coast Guard Auxiliary; call (360) 908-4390. Or contact Fort Worden State Park, 200 Battery Way, Port Townsend, WA 98368; call (360) 344-4400, or see www.parks.wa.gov/fortworden.

On an island a few miles southeast of Point Wilson is the **Marrowstone Point Lighthouse** (1888 and 1918). Nearby is Fort Flagler, once an army base and now a state park. From Route 20 south of Port Townsend, follow the signs to Port Hadlock, the marine camping park at Fort Flagler State Park, and the lighthouse. For information on the park, contact Fort Flagler State Park, 10541 Flagler Road, Nordland, WA 98358; for camping reservations online, see www.stateparks.com/fort_flagler.html.

■ POINT NO POINT LIGHT ■
Hansville (1879)

The pilots of ships moving up from Puget Sound into Admiralty Inlet often notice a prominent headland sweeping up from the southwest. They may think they are seeing Foulweather Bluff at the far end of Washington's long central peninsula, but they are mistaken. This land feature is the appropriately named Point No Point.

A key navigational light has shone from Point No Point since 1879. Built on a forty-acre tract acquired by the Lighthouse Service for just $1,800, the Point No Point Light station is a near twin of its sister lighthouse on West Point, near Seattle. Both stations consist of a rectangular fog-signal building with a squat tower barely peeking through its roof and separate keeper's dwellings. The lanterns of both towers held a bull's-eye-type fourth-order Fresnel lens. The bull's-eye lenses focused the light into a series of flashes, which could be seen from about fifteen miles away.

Point No Point Light
Bob and Sandra Shanklin

Over the years the Point No Point Lighthouse saved many ships from disaster. One that it could not save was the small passenger liner *Admiral Sampson*, which sank off the point in 1914 after colliding with a second liner, the *Princess Victoria*. Eleven passengers and crew went down with the *Sampson*, including Captain Zimro Moore.

Travel information: From Port Gamble follow Highway 104 south, then Highway 305 east. Turn north onto Hansville Road Northeast, and follow it for approximately ten miles to the town of Hansville. Signs show the way to the lighthouse. Cooperative efforts among the US Lighthouse Society, Kitsap County Parks, and Friends of Point No Point have created the opportunity to rent rooms within the keeper's quarters, overlooking Puget Sound and its many islands, as vacation rentals. The light station is now headquarters for the US Lighthouse Society, 9005 Point No Point Road NE, Hansville, WA 98340; call (415) 362-7255 for more information or reservations, or see www.uslhs.org/vacation_rental.php.

■ POINT ROBINSON LIGHT ■
Tacoma (1887 and 1915)

Pilots of vessels plying the Puget Sound waters between Seattle and Tacoma keep a sharp eye out for the Point Robinson Light. Located on the eastern end of Maury Island, the light marks a key safe channel in this narrow but heavily trafficked waterway.

A fog signal was placed on the point in 1885 to protect ships against running aground on the island. Particularly threatening was a low, sandy spit extending several hundred yards out into Puget Sound. Lighthouse officials soon concluded that the fog signal alone was inadequate, and in 1887 a modest lantern and lens were added to the station.

As shipping increased in the lower Puget Sound, the station's importance grew. In 1915 a full-fledged lighthouse was established here. It consisted of a pair of keeper's dwellings and a thirty-eight-foot masonry and concrete tower, a twin of **Alki Point Lighthouse,** and a lantern room containing a fifth-order Fresnel lens. The cylindrical tower and fog-signal building stand approximately 150 yards out on the spit.

Point Robinson Light

With its peaceful, scenic location and proximity to Tacoma and Seattle, Point Robinson Lighthouse was once a very popular duty station for keepers and their families. Nowadays, the light is automated and does its job without the help of resident keepers.

Travel information: The lighthouse is located on the northeast corner of Maury Island, just across from the larger and more populous Vachon Island in Puget Sound. The station is open to the public as part of the Vashon Park District. Leased from the US Coast Guard, which maintains the original Fresnel lens, rentals are available in both keeper's quarters. Write the Vashon Park District (part of King County Parks) Headquarters, Ober Park, 17130 Vashon Highway SW, P.O. Box 1608, Vashon, WA 98070; call (206) 463-9602, or see www.vashonparkdistrict.org.

Other lights in the lower Puget Sound include the **Dofflemyer Point Lighthouse** (1887 and 1934) near Olympia, Washington's capital city, and **Browns Point Lighthouse** (1887), near Tacoma. The thirty-foot concrete tower on Dofflemyer Point is closed to the public. Its near twin at Browns Point is located in a public park, open year-round during daylight hours. Take Route 509 north from Tacoma, turn left on Le-Lou-Wa, and follow signs to Browns Point.

■ ALKI POINT LIGHT ■
Seattle (1887 and 1913)

Thrusting far out into the blue waters of Puget Sound, wedge-shaped Alki Point makes a notable impression on mariners, who must swing their ships wide to avoid it. Perhaps hoping it would develop into a burgeoning commercial center, early settlers called the point "New York," but it was not destined to become a West Coast

Manhattan. Overshadowed by bustling Seattle only a few miles to the northeast, the point languished, almost completely ignored by commercial interests. Disappointed landowners took to calling it "Alki" Point, after a Chinook Indian word meaning "by-and-by" or "all in good time."

Alki Point was of obvious importance to shipping, however, both as a daymark showing the way to Seattle and as a threat in fog and at night. Even so, no light was displayed here until the 1880s, when landowner Hans Martin Hanson hung up a small brass lantern as a humanitarian gesture on a barn. In 1887 the US Lighthouse Service improved the light, installing a small lantern and lens. Hanson was paid $15 per month to keep the lamp burning.

Alki Point Light

With shipping traffic between Seattle and Tacoma to the south on the increase, the government eventually decided to build a full-fledged lighthouse on Alki Point. Buying land from Hanson's heirs for $10,000, the Lighthouse Service built an octagonal, thirty-seven-foot-tall masonry tower, an attached fog-signal building, and a nearby keeper's dwelling. Originally, the station employed a fourth-order Fresnel lens, but now a modern optic serves here, flashing white every two seconds. The original lens took an adventurous trip after being stolen by an antique dealer; it was returned and is safely on display in the Coast Guard Museum in Seattle, while a reproduction lens resides at the lighthouse.

Travel information: Alki Point Lighthouse is located at 3201 Alki Avenue SW, just to the south of the public beach at Alki. To reach the beach and lighthouse from Seattle, follow Interstate 5 south, then the West Seattle Freeway to the Harbor Avenue exit. Turn right on Harbor Avenue, and follow it (Harbor Avenue eventually becomes Beach Drive) along the water to the lighthouse. Although an active District 13 Coast Guard facility and home to an admiral, the lighthouse is open to the public on Saturday and Sunday afternoons in June, July, and August, with tours conducted by auxiliary volunteers; see www.uscga-seattle.com/alki-tours.htm.

■ WEST POINT LIGHT ■
Seattle (1881)

Rising twenty-three feet above a low, sandy peninsula at the north entrance to Elliot Bay, West Point Lighthouse has welcomed ships to Seattle for more than a hundred years. Situated five miles from the city's thriving business core, the old lighthouse stands at the foot of Magnolia Bluff in Discovery Park.

West Point Light

The little lighthouse was built in 1881 at a cost to taxpayers of $25,000, a rather princely sum in those days. Fitted with a complex fourth-order Fresnel lens with twelve separate bull's-eyes, it began operation in November of 1881. According to a Coast Guard estimate, its flashing light has put in more than 400,000 hours of service. The beacon can be seen from fifteen miles away.

> *Travel information:* A popular attraction of Seattle's Discovery Park, the lighthouse is located about a mile and half from the entrance. A pleasant way to enjoy an exterior view of the lighthouse is with a relaxing stroll along West Point Beach, or call the park for further information at (206) 386-4236.

■ MUKILTEO LIGHT ■
Mukilteo (1906)

Centuries ago Indian tribes often gathered at the place we now call Mukilteo, a Native American word meaning "good spot for camping." Early in this century, the Lighthouse Service decided that Mukilteo was also a good location for a navigational light to guide vessels headed for Everett. Completed in 1906, the Victorian-style structure was fitted with a fourth-order Fresnels lens and equipped with a Daboll trumpet to warn ships plowing blindly through fog or heavy weather.

In 1960 the Coast Guard planned to replace the station's Fresnel lens with an aeromarine beacon. Residents of Mukilteo and other nearby communities protested, however, and the old Fresnel remains in operation to this day, flashing white every five seconds.

Mukilteo Light

The Mukilteo Historical Society works with the US Coast Guard and the City of Mukilteo for the preservation, maintenance, and accessibility of the light station.

Travel information: The lighthouse, located at 608 Front Street in Mukilteo, contains a photographic exhibit on the lights of the Puget Sound. Located near the Whidbey Island ferry landing, the wood-frame structure is open to the public on weekends. Contact the lighthouse and Mukilteo Historical Society at (425) 513-9602, or see http://mukilteohistorical.org.

■ ADMIRALTY HEAD LIGHT ■
Whidbey Island (1861 and 1903)

Completed during the months just prior to the Civil War, the ancestor of the Admiralty Head Lighthouse was among the West's earliest navigational markers. The frame structure was built atop a knob called Red Bluff. Its tower rose forty-one feet from base to lantern, and it had a fourth-order Fresnel lens. The station's fixed white light, which could be seen from about sixteen miles away, welcomed Puget Sound marine traffic into Admiralty Inlet.

Admiralty Head Light

During the Spanish-American War, the US Army built a fort on Red Bluff to protect the entrance to the inlet. To make room for Fort Casey, the old lighthouse was demolished. The present Spanish-style structure was ready for service in 1903. Its brick tower rose only a few feet higher than the attached two-story residence, but the elevation of Admiralty Head placed its light more than 120 feet above the water.

As it turned out the new lighthouse had a relatively short active life. It was discontinued in 1927, after which it became a residence for officers posted to Fort Casey. Nowadays, the carefully restored lighthouse serves as a museum.

The lighthouse is open to the public through a cooperative agreement between Fort Casey State Park and the Washington State University Island County Extension Office.

Travel information: The lighthouse is part of Fort Casey State Park, not far from the Keystone/Port Townsend ferry slip and a few miles from the historic island town of Coupeville. The park is open year-round for tours. For further information contact the lighthouse: Keepers of Admiralty Head Lighthouse, P.O. Box 5000, 1280 Engle Road, Coupeville, WA 98239; call (360) 240-5584, or see www.admiraltyhead.wsu.edu.

■ LIGHTS OF THE SAN JUAN ISLANDS ■

Turn Point Light (1893), Patos Island Light (1908)
Lime Kiln Light (1914), Burrows Island Light (1906)
Cattle Point Light (1935)

Pleasure boaters, yachtsmen, and ferry pilots who frequent the San Juans, an unspoiled chain of 172 islands in the straits between Washington State and Canada, know that navigation here can be difficult and dangerous. A tangle of narrow passages separates the islands, some of which are large enough for several towns and harbors, whereas others are no more than a scrap of exposed rock.

Several lighthouses mark the way for mariners. Built in 1893, **Turn Point Lighthouse** shines from a squat sixteen-foot concrete tower on the northwest end of Stuart Island. Restoration efforts continue in a cooperative effort between the Bureau of Land Management, the Coast Guard, and the Turn Point Lighthouse Preservation Society. For details, TPLPS, P.O. Box 243, Orcas, WA 98280, or see www.tplps.org.

Turn Point Light
Bob and Sandra Shanklin

The thirty-eight-foot wooden tower of **Patos Island Lighthouse,** completed in 1908, stands on the western side of a scenic, 260-acre islet in the northern part of the chain that is owned by the federal government and managed by the Bureau of Land Management; for more information see www.parks.wa.gov/parks.

The octagonal tower of **Lime Kiln Lighthouse** dates from 1914 and marks the key shipping channel through Haro Strait. It is now part of a state park and also known as Whale Watch Park. For more information see www.thesanjuans.com.

Built in 1906, the thirty-four-foot wood-frame **Burrows Island Lighthouse,** marking the southern entrance to Rosario Strait, has served well for more than ninety years. Since 1972 the light station has been abandoned, but restoration efforts are ongoing. More information is available from the Northwest Schooner Club at www.nwschooner.org.

Cattle Point Lighthouse marks the southern end of San Juan Island and is within the Cattle Point Interpretive Area. It can be accessed by trail; it is not open to the public, but there is a nearby interpretive center.

Travel information: Access to the San Juan Islands and their lighthouses is by boat or ferry. For information and schedules contact the Washington State Ferry Service at (206) 464-6400.

Patos Island Light
Bob and Sandra Shanklin

Lime Kiln Light
Bob and Sandra Shanklin

Burrows Island Light
Bob and Sandra Shanklin

Cattle Point Light
US Coast Guard

ALASKA

■ LINCOLN ROCK LIGHT ■
Clarence Strait (1903)

Few light stations proved as difficult to establish and maintain as the one on Lincoln Rock, a tiny, barren island near the western end of the Clarence Strait, some fifty-four miles northwest of Ketchikan, Alaska. Funded in 1902, the project got off to a shaky start when the construction contractor lost a small steamer, a barge, and a large load of lumber in a gale. No doubt financially strapped, the contractor tried to recoup his losses by using substandard materials and was eventually fired by the Lighthouse Service.

Purchasing its own materials, the Lighthouse Service hired laborers and completed the station in time for an official lighting on December 1, 1903. A short, square tower pushed through the roof of the two-story wooden keeper's dwelling. The lantern room contained a fourth-order Fresnel lens, which displayed a fixed white light.

Much of the tiny island is submerged at high tide, so the lighthouse was built atop a concrete pier to protect it from the waves. As it turned out, however, the building was much more exposed than was at first thought. Large storm-driven waves often broke over the

Lincoln Rock Light
US Coast Guard

pier, smashing into the side of the dwelling. By 1909 the lighthouse had been so badly damaged by wave action that it had to be abandoned. It was never completely rebuilt.

In 1911 a manned fog-signal station went into service about a quarter of a mile from the old pier. An automated acetylene light took the place of the original beacon. The Lincoln Rock Station was permanently discontinued in 1968.

Travel information: The site of the Lincoln Rock Lighthouse is not accessible to the public. To the south of Lincoln Rock is **Guard Islands Lighthouse** (1904). The square wooden structure displays a fixed white light that marks the entrance to Tongass Narrows, a few miles north of Ketchikan.

■ CAPE DECISION LIGHT ■

Cape Decision (1932)

The appropriately named Cape Decision, located on the far southeastern end of Kuiu Island about sixty miles from the old Russian settlement of Sitka, presents mariners with a difficult choice. Here they must choose between several likely routes. Here, too, they face an assortment of dangers, including strong tides, hidden rocks, and unpredictable weather, as well as the ubiquitous coastal fog.

During the early twentieth century, seamen near the cape had to rely for guidance on an unwatched acetylene light that shone from one of the nearby Spanish Islands, but most mariners considered it woefully inadequate. Their pleas for a better, more powerful light fell on deaf ears in the tight-fisted Congress of the 1920s. Finally, only a few months before the Stock Market Crash of 1929 and the beginning of the Great Depression, Congress relented and approved partial funding for a lighthouse on Cape Decision.

The isolation of the site, funding shortages during the early years of the Depression, and the cape's notoriously foul weather all hindered progress. After three years of start-and-stop construction, the lighthouse was finally completed in 1932 at a total cost of $158,000 and placed in service on March 15 of that year.

The station's square forty-foot tower rises from the flat roof of the main reinforced-concrete building. Its flashing, 350,000-candlepower light reaches out to mariners from an elevation of ninety-six feet. During the fogs and heavy weathers that frequently blanket the cape, an especially powerful fog signal warns vessels away from nearby rocks. A radio beacon

Cape Decision Light
US Coast Guard

helps guide ships in from the open Pacific. Automated in 1974, the Cape Decision Light was formerly fully staffed around the clock by keepers and assistants. After a year of service, station crewmen received a ninety-day leave.

In 1997 the US Coast Guard leased the structure to the Cape Decision Lighthouse Society, which has refurbished the station. The keeper's quarters are open to overnight guests.

Travel information: The Cape Decision Lighthouse is accessible only by boat or float plane. The old Cape Decision third-order Fresnel lens is now on display at the Clausen Museum in Petersburg; call (907) 772-3598.
For further information, write the Cape Decision Lighthouse Society, 224 Katlian Street, Sitka, AK 99835; call for reservations to stay overnight, (907) 747-7803, or see http://capedecisionlight.org.

■ FIVE FINGER ISLANDS LIGHT ■
Five Finger Islands (1902 and 1935)

One of Alaska's first two official lighthouses, the Five Finger Islands Light station was established just after the turn of the twentieth century to guide ships through the Inside Passage to Juneau. Located on a craggy island in the northern section of Frederick Sound north of Petersburg, its beacon first shone on March 1, 1902, the same night the **Sentinel Island Light** was placed in service.

A two-story combination dwelling and tower, the original Five Finger Islands Lighthouse displayed a fixed white light focused by a fourth-order Fresnel lens. The lantern room peeked through the roof of the structure, its light shining from a point sixty-eight feet above high water. A wooden structure, the lighthouse served for more than thirty years before it burned to the ground in December of 1933.

The government moved quickly to restore this vital Inside Passage light station, and a new lighthouse was completed and in operation by late in 1935. This one was built to last and to this day continues to guide ships, ferries, and fishing boats plying the waters of the passage. Standing on a hefty concrete pier, the forty-foot-square main building is built of reinforced concrete. It serves as a platform for the sixty-eight-foot tower, which places the station's light more than eighty feet above the water.

The Five Fingers Island station remained fully staffed longer than any other Alaskan lighthouse. For months at a time, the keepers shared the building with boilers, batteries, and a jumble of other equipment. The last full-time keepers left the station in 1984, bringing to a close a unique era in lighthouse history.

Travel information: The light can be seen from the decks of the ferries that travel the extraordinarily scenic Inside Passage. Otherwise, like most other Alaskan lighthouses, it is accessible only by boat or float plane. The Juneau Lighthouse Society now leases the station and hopes to open it to visitors. For current status write to the society at P.O. Box 22163, Juneau, AK 99802.

Five Finger Islands Light
Bob and Sandra Shanklin

◾ SENTINEL ISLAND LIGHT ◾
Frederick Sound (1902 and 1935)

Sentinel Island Light
US Coast Guard

Among Alaska's earliest light stations, the Sentinel Island Lighthouse was established in 1902 to guide vessels into the Lynn Canal, northwest of Juneau. During the 1930s, many original wooden Alaskan lighthouses were replaced with rugged art-deco concrete structures, as was the case on Sentinel Island in 1935. The residence, where keepers lived a rustic and solitary existence for a year or more at a time, was torn down after the light was automated in 1966. The station remains in operation but needs little human assistance. Solar panels help charge the batteries that supply electric power for the light and fog signal.

Travel information: The station is accessible only by boat. The light has been leased by the Gastineau Channel Historical Society. Limited overnight accommodations are occasionally available. Contact the society at P.O. Box 21264, Juneau, AK 99802; call (907) 586-5338, or see http://gastineau channel.blogspot.com.

◾ POINT RETREAT LIGHT ◾
Northern end of Admiralty Island (1904 and 1924)

Point Retreat Light
Bob and Sandra Shanklin

Located at the northern tip of Admiralty Island, Point Retreat Lighthouse marks a watery crossroads where key shipping channels converge to link Alaska's capital city of Juneau with the Inside Passage and the Pacific. The station was established in 1904 and was rebuilt of concrete in 1924 with an adjoining fog signal building. Until it was automated in 1973, its light was focused by a giant first-order clamshell (bivalve) Fresnel lens. The beacon still shines from the relatively short twenty-five-foot tower, but nowadays, it is provided by a solar-powered modern optic. The Coast Guard has leased the station buildings and other property to the Alaska Lighthouse Association. The organization has undertaken a complete restoration of the lighthouse and hopes to open it to the public as a maritime museum.

Travel information: The station is accessible only by air or boat. Contact the Alaska Lighthouse Association at 2116-B Second Street, Juneau, AK 99801, or see www.aklighthouse.org/newsite.

■ CAPE SPENCER LIGHT ■
Cape Spencer (1912 and 1925)

The keepers of Cape Spencer Lighthouse must have thought they were living at the end of the earth. Located on a barren, rocky island at the entrance to Cross Sound on the northern end of the Alaska Panhandle, this duty station placed keepers a half-day round-trip journey from mail or other services of any kind. The nearest town, Juneau, was more than seventy miles away.

Cape Spencer Light
US Coast Guard

As early as 1906 commercial maritime interests had pressed the Lighthouse Service for a light to mark the cape and the route through Icy Strait, which was often followed by vessels trying to avoid the stormy Outside Passage. At that time, however, service resources were stretched to the limit, and it was not until 1912 that a small, automated acetylene beacon was placed on the cape.

Construction of a fully operational light station began in 1923 atop a precipitous, exposed rock just off the tip of the cape. The isolation and ruggedness of the site drove the cost of the facility to more than $175,000. Completed in 1925, it consisted of a fourteen-foot-wide square tower rising twenty-five feet above the flat roof of a reinforced-concrete fog-signal building, which also served as a residence for the keepers. A steel derrick and gasoline-powered hoist lifted supplies from a small landing to the lighthouse, which stood at the top of the rock, about eighty feet above the sea.

The lantern displays a flashing white light with a focal plane 105 feet above the water. The station's exceptionally powerful radio beacon, often received by ships as far as two hundred miles from shore, also guides vessels. The Cape Spencer Light has been automated since 1974.

Travel information: The Cape Spencer Lighthouse can be reached only by boat or helicopter. Often it can be seen from a distance by passengers on cruise ships visiting Glacier Bay National Park. Planes offering scenic tours of Glacier Bay operate out of Juneau during warmer-weather months and occasionally fly near the lighthouse. Contact Glacier Bay National Park at P.O. Box 140, Gustavas, AK 99826; call (907) 697-2230. The station's original third-order lens is now on display at the Alaska State Museum in Juneau, 395 Whittier Street, Juneau, AK 99801; call (907) 465-2901.

■ ELDRED ROCK LIGHT ■
Haines (1906)

This unusual octagonal lighthouse stands on Eldred Rock, south of Haines and Skagway at the northwestern end of the Alaska Panhandle. The fifty-six-foot tower rises through the roof of the dwelling. The elevation of Eldred Rock places the focal plane of the light more than ninety feet above the water. The light guides ships along the strategic Lynn Canal.

In 1898, eight years before the light went into service, the steamer *Clara Nevada* was wrecked and burned not far from Eldred Rock. Lost with the vessel were $100,000 in gold dust and more than a hundred passengers, most of them miners returning from the Klondike.

Travel information: The light station can be reached only by boat or helicopter. Contact the Sheldon Museum and Cultural Center, P.O. Box 269, Haines, AK 99827; call (907) 766-2366, or see www.sheldonmuseum.org. The station's original fourth-order Fresnel lens is on display at the museum.

■ CAPE ST. ELIAS LIGHT ■
Cape St. Elias (1916)

The monumentlike, seventeen-hundred-foot peak soaring above the rock-strewn beaches of Cape St. Elias makes this one of the most spectacular landfalls in all of North America. It is also among the most dangerous. As if to warn against the threat, mysterious colored lights are said to play along the shores here. Some especially imaginative mariners say a sea monster lurks in the bays and inlets near the mountain.

Funds for a lighthouse to guide ships through the perilous waters off Cape St. Elias were not approved until 1913. One year earlier the lighthouse tender *Armeria* had been wrecked while on route to place a buoy here. By the fall of 1916, the embarrassed Lighthouse Service had completed a permanent light station on the cape. It consisted of a fifty-five-foot-tall reinforced-concrete tower rising from the corner of a fog-signal building, a two-story keeper's dwelling, a boathouse, and storage buildings.

So isolated was the station that supply ships arrived only once a year. Usually, only men served here, and some keepers considered this the "worst lighthouse posting in America." The storms that blew in off the cape were often so powerful that rocks, kelp, and small fish were thrown up into the lantern room. The mountain behind the station posed other dangers as, occasionally, huge boulders came tumbling down its precipitous slopes, crashing through the trees. No doubt, few of the keepers who had served at Cape St. Elias were sorry to hear that the station was decommissioned in 1974 and replaced by an automated light.

Despite its considerable power the light at Cape St. Elias has never been particularly effective. The beacon is often obscured by fog, and the relatively low eighty-five-foot elevation of its focal plane limited its range to only about fifteen miles. To help guide mariners a radio beacon was installed here in 1927. Today the light station is listed with the honored title of National Historic Landmark.

Cape St. Elias Light
US Coast Guard

Travel information: The lighthouse is accessible only by boat or helicopter. Contact the Cape St. Elias Lighthouse Keepers, P.O. Box 1023, Cordova, AK 99574; call (907) 424-5182, or see http://kayakisland.org. For more travel information see Alaska Marine Highway System (ferry routes and schedules) at www.dot.state.ak.us/amhs.

■ CAPE HINCHINBROOK LIGHT ■
Hinchinbrook Island (1910 and 1934)

Hinchinbrook Island and its southwestward-thrusting cape have been recognized as key seamarks for as long as oceangoing vessels have visited Alaska—Russian ships started coming here in the 1740s. The Lighthouse Service considered placing a light on the cape as early as 1900 but could not coax the necessary $125,000 from a reluctant Congress until 1909.

In April of 1909 contractor A. B. Lewis of Seattle brought a crew of forty men to Hinchinbrook Island, hoping to complete the station that same year. But as was often the case with construction projects in Alaska, the weather played havoc with the schedule. Rain and wind halted work at Cape Hinchinbrook for weeks at a time. An especially powerful storm washed away a scow loaded with supplies valued at $12,000. Not until the following fall were the tower and other structures in place. The station's lamps were first lit on November 15, 1910.

The light and fog signal were housed in an octagonal concrete building more than fifty feet in diameter. Equipped with a third-order Fresnel lens of an advanced design said to provide the same power as a first-order lens, the lantern stood atop the two-story roof. Shining from an elevation of almost two hundred feet, its light could be seen from as far as twenty-five miles at sea.

The lighthouse was of such advanced design and so solidly built that some thought it to be "indestructible." Not so. In 1927 and again in 1928, earthquakes rocked the station, cracking concrete walls, breaking up the foundation, and threatening to dump the entire structure into the Pacific.

Alarmed by the damage, the Lighthouse Service decided to build another light tower on Cape Hinchinbrook, this time on a more stable foundation of solid rock. Completed in 1934, the reinforced-concrete structure rises sixty-seven feet above the cliff and displays a powerful light supplied by the station's original third-order lens. Along with several other Alaskan lights, this one was automated in 1974.

Cape Hinchinbrook Light
US Coast Guard

Travel information: The lighthouse is inaccessible to the public. It can sometimes be seen, however, from the deck of cruise ships, ferries, and other vessels entering or exiting Prince William Sound. The station's original third-order lens can be seen at the Valdez Museum at 217 Egan Drive, P.O. Box 8, Valdez, AK 99686; call (907) 835-2764, or see www.valdezmuseum.org.

■ SCOTCH CAP LIGHT ■
Unimak Island (1903, 1940, and 1950)

The original Scotch Cap Lighthouse was an octagonal wooden structure located on the side of a cliff about ninety feet above the sea. Built for a total of $76,571 by a team of thirty workers brought from Seattle, the tower and other station facilities took more than a year to complete. Placed in operation on July 15, 1903, it displayed a flashing white light produced by a third-order Fresnel lens.

In 1940 the old wooden lighthouse was replaced by a reinforced-concrete structure. Ironically, it was this new, much sturdier build-

Scotch Cap Light
US Coast Guard

ing that was smashed and swept away by the great tsunami of 1946. Several keepers lost their lives in the disaster.

A replacement facility was ready for duty by 1950. Built far up on the cliff to keep it safe from future tidal waves, the new lighthouse bore little resemblance to its predecessors. A rugged, rectangular concrete building, it looks more like a storage building than a lighthouse. A rotating aeromarine beacon shines from atop its flat roof 116 feet above the sea. Since the facility is fully automated, no personnel are stationed at Scotch Cap today.

Travel information: Located in one of the most remote and inhospitable places on the planet, the Scotch Cap Lighthouse is, of course, inaccessible to the public.

■ CAPE SARICHEF LIGHT ■
Unimak Island (1904 and 1950)

Clinging to what the Aleuts sometimes describe as the "Roof of Hell," on bleak Unimak Island in the Aleutians, Cape Sarichef Lighthouse is the most westerly lighthouse in North America; indeed, it is twenty-one hundred miles farther west on the map than San Francisco. Automated since 1950, the station was established in 1904 to guide ships through Unimak Pass, which links the Pacific Ocean with the Bering Sea.

The original lighthouse had a thirty-five-foot octagonal tower, which rose through the roof of a fog-signal building. Its third-order Fresnel lens displayed a fixed light with a focal plane more than 125 feet above the sea.

In 1950 the lighthouse was replaced by a concrete structure built higher on the cliffs to protect it from tsunamis, like the one that destroyed the nearby Scotch Gap station. Automated in 1979, the light remains in service.

Travel information: The station is inaccessible to the public.

Cape Sarichef Light
US Coast Guard

HAWAII

■ MAKAPUU POINT LIGHT ■
East of Honolulu (1909)

This huge twelve-foot-high hyperradial Fresnel at Makapuu is the largest lighthouse lens in the United States. Ironically, it is housed in a relatively small tower only forty-six feet tall, but what the station lacks in stature it more than makes up for in the power of its beacon—visible from more than twenty-eight miles at sea to serve as a landfall light. Unlike the tower itself, the station's surroundings are Olympian in scale. When the Makapuu Lighthouse was built in the early twentieth

Makapuu Point light
Bob and Sandra Shanklin

century, workers had to blast a site from a solid wall of lava several hundred feet high. Perched on an artificial ledge more than three hundred feet above the waves, the stone and steel tower still serves mariners. The Coast Guard continues to maintain this light as an active aid to navigation.

> *Travel information:* Located off Highway 72 (Kalaniana'ole Highway) in the easternmost corner of Oahu, the lighthouse can be reached only by means of a moderately strenuous uphill climb. Bring your hiking shoes to explore the Makapuu Point Lighthouse Trail.

■ DIAMOND HEAD LIGHT ■
Honolulu (1899 and 1917)

Certainly among Hawaii's most important navigational aids, the Diamond Head Light guides vessels headed toward the busy mid-Pacific port of Honolulu. Built in 1899, the lighthouse had to be completely rebuilt after severe cracks appeared in its foundation. The new tower, completed in 1917, was given reinforced-concrete walls and fitted with the station's original third-order Fresnel lens. Essentially unchanged in more than ninety years, the lighthouse remains in operation, its automated beacon shining out over the ocean from an elevation of 147 feet. The light shows a red sector to warn vessels away from the reefs off Waikiki Beach. Nowadays, the station dwelling serves as residence for the commander of the US Coast Guard 14th District.

Travel information: Located southeast of Waikiki, the station is part of an active Coast Guard base and is not open to the public but can be viewed from Diamond Head Road. Be sure to explore the Diamond Head State Park Monument, with a trail that requires a strenuous hike of well over an hour, round trip. For directions and general visitors information, call (808) 587-0300, or see www.hawaiistateparks.org.

Diamond Head Light
Bob and Sandra Shanklin

■ LAHAINA LIGHT ■
Lahaina on Maui (1840 and 1916)

Having unified the islands through conquest during the 1790s, Hawaii's King Kamehameha I established his royal capital at Lahaina. Its harbor became an important port of call for diplomats, merchants, and missionaries who came here to ask favors of Kamehameha and his descendants. Beginning in 1840, Lahaina's harbor was marked by a lighthouse, perhaps the first in all of what is now the western United States. Unfortunately, nothing is left of that early lighthouse, which was replaced in 1916 by the existing concrete tower. Maintained by the Coast Guard, the simple pyramidal structure still guides vessels in and out of the harbor with a modest beacon.

Lahaina Light
Bob and Sandra Shanklin

Travel information: The tower is located just off Front Street near the center of Lahaina. Call (808) 667-9193.

■ KALAUPAPA LIGHT ■
Kalaupapa Peninsula on Molokai (1908)

Once the site of a notorious leper colony, the Kalaupapa Peninsula on Molokai is backed by the highest sea cliffs in the world—some soaring more than two thousand feet above the waves. To help mariners keep their distance from these rugged shores, the government established a lighthouse on Kalaupapa Point in 1908. The exceptional remoteness of the peninsula made getting materials and construction crews to this faraway site unusually difficult and expensive. Building the station cost $60,000, but it has proven invaluable to mariners and their vessels. The 138-foot tower is the tallest on the Pacific and remains an active aid to navigation under the care of the Coast Guard.

Travel information: Reaching the remote Kalaupapa Peninsula is not much easier today than it was a century ago. Since there is no direct road access, visitors climb down from the cliffs on foot or ride down on the backs of sure-footed mules, but these options are not recommended for the faint of heart. Some flights are available. Contact Kalaupapa National Historical Park, Kalaupapa, HI 96742. For tours, call (808) 567-6171.

Kalaupapa Light
Bob and Sandra Shanklin

■ KILAUEA POINT LIGHT ■
Kilauea Point on Kauai (1913)

Established in 1913, the Kilauea Point Lighthouse guided several generations of mariners, its beacon focused by one of the largest clamshell (bivalve) lenses in the world. A light here still marks the far northwestern edge of the Hawaiian chain, but it no longer emanates from the lighthouse or the giant Fresnel that still graces the fifty-two-foot tower. Instead, it shines from a much smaller structure nearby. The old lighthouse and lens are now a key attraction at the Kilauea Point National Wildlife Refuge, a natural wonderland alive with frigate birds, albatrosses, and other seabirds.

Travel information: Kilauea Point National Wildlife Refuge and its lighthouse are located about ten miles northwest of Anahola off Highway 56 on Kauai. Call (808) 828-1413, or see www.fws.gov/kilaueapoint.

Kilauea Point Light
Bob and Sandra Shanklin

GREAT LAKES

Baileys Harbor Rear Range Light, Door County, WI
Rick Polad

CANADA

Kingston

Lake
Ontario

Oswego

Rochester

NEW YORK
12 Lights

Toronto

Buffalo

PENNSYLVANIA
2 Lights

Erie

Lake
Erie

Cleveland

OHIO
9 Lights

Sault Ste. Marie

Lake
Huron

Port
Huron

Toledo

Mackinaw
City

Presque
Isle

Muskegon

MICHIGAN
Lower Peninsula
36 Lights

Michigan
City

INDIANA
2 Lights

Grand Marais

Marquette

MICHIGAN
Upper Peninsula
4 Lights

Sturgeon
Bay

Lake
Michigan

Milwaukee

Chicago

WISCONSIN
23 Lights

ILLINOIS
3 Lights

Lake
Superior

MICHIGAN
Isle Royale
4 Lights

Thunder
Bay

Bayfield

Apostle Islands
7 Lights

Duluth

MINNESOTA
6 Lights

CANADA

NEW YORK

■ ROCK ISLAND LIGHT ■
Rock Island (1848)

From the mid-1800s until after World War II, ships coming up the St. Lawrence River from the Atlantic used the Rock Island Lighthouse to help them navigate their way safely to Lake Ontario. Built in 1848 as one of six lighthouses commissioned to help ships negotiate this important passage, the Rock Island signal actually sits just off the island—a stone walkway connects the concrete foundation

Rock Island Light
US Coast Guard

to the land. When the station was deactivated following World War II, its sixth-order Fresnel lens was removed.

> *Travel information:* You can see the lighthouse from Thousand Island Park on Wellesley Island or from Fisher's Landing, a community not far from the Thousand Island Bridge. There is no public transportation to Rock Island, but enough private boats make the trip to warrant summer visiting hours. The Rock Island Lighthouse Historical & Memorial Association formed to facilitate restoration of the lighthouse and visits to the island; see http://rockislandlighthouse.org.

■ TIBBETTS POINT LIGHT ■
Cape Vincent (1827 and 1854)

Lighthouses are nearly always strategically located, but this is especially true of Tibbetts Point Lighthouse. Its beacon marks the entrance to the St. Lawrence River and the beginning of the last leg of any journey from the Great Lakes to the Atlantic. Originally, the stone tower stood fifty-eight feet high and employed a whale-oil lamp and reflector beacon. A major renovation in 1854 raised the tower's height by ten feet, and the addition of a fourth-order Fresnel lens dramatically improved the light's performance. A steam-powered fog signal was added in 1896. Automated in 1981, the station now serves as a youth hostel and is a popular destination for photographers and history buffs.

Travel information: Take Lighthouse Road off Highway 12E. The grounds are open daily, but the hostel operates only from mid-May to mid-October. For hostel reservations call (315) 654-3450.

To the southwest, near Sackets Harbor, is the sixty-foot tower of the **Stony Point Lighthouse** (1838). From New York Route 3, turn onto Lighthouse Road and follow it to Stony Point.

Tibbetts Point Light

■ SELKIRK LIGHT (POINT ONTARIO) ■
Selkirk (Pulaski) (1838)

One of the more fascinating and historic structures on the Great Lakes, the Selkirk Lighthouse guided Lake Ontario sailors from 1838 until 1859. Taken out of service shortly before the Civil War, it remained dark for more than 130 years, but it is once again guiding mariners.

Produced by a fourteen-inch parabolic reflector-and-oil-lamp system, the original beacon could be seen from fourteen miles out in the lake. A sixth-order Fresnel lens replaced the outmoded reflector system shortly before the shrinking local economy caused lighthouse officials to snuff out the light.

The unique two-story fieldstone tower and dwelling would later be used as a hotel. At present the building, recognized for both its architectural and historic significance,

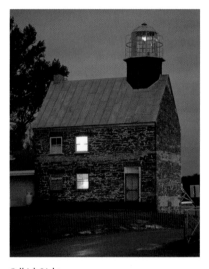

Selkirk Light

is privately owned. Although not open to the public, it is sometimes rented out to overnight visitors. The lighthouse is privately owned, has been restored, and serves as a private aid to navigation.

Travel information: Take Route 3 to Port Ontario; then follow Lake Road to its end. The lighthouse stands near the mouth of the Salmon River. Overnight stays are available. Contact the Salmon River Lighthouse Marina, 6 Lake Extension Road, Pulaski, NY 13142; call (315) 298-6688, or see www.salmonriverlighthousemarina.com.

■ OSWEGO WEST PIERHEAD LIGHT ■
Oswego (1822, 1836, and 1934)

Several lighthouses have served Oswego. The first, a simple stone tower and keeper's dwelling completed in 1822, stood beside strategic Fort Ontario on the east bank of the Oswego River. But the booming shipping and fishing port of Oswego soon outgrew this modest beacon, and in 1836 a new tower was erected at the end of a long pier on the west side of the harbor. Its light, focused by a fine third-order Fresnel lens, could be seen from at least fifteen miles out in Lake Ontario.

Oswego West Pierhead Light

The hearts of Lake Ontario sailors and Oswego old-timers were saddened when the Oswego Lighthouse was pulled down by wreckers in 1930, some ninety-four years after its lamps first burned. But the city's harbor would not go unmarked for long. By 1934 a new pier light was in service. It beamed from a square metal tower attached to a small dwelling at the far end of a long stone breakwater. Colored red by tinted windows, its light still shines.

The City of Oswego now owns the lighthouse.

Travel information: The public is not allowed to visit the lighthouse while the tower and attached keeper's house await restoration, but its white walls and red roof are visible from several places in Oswego, including Breitbeck Park. To reach the park from Route 104, turn toward the lake on West First Street, then left onto Van Buren, then right onto Lake Street. The park is just beyond Wright's Landing. While in the area, take time to visit historic Fort Ontario, where the keeper's residence of the original 1822 lighthouse can still be seen.

■ SODUS POINT LIGHT ■
Sodus Point (1825 and 1871)

In the early 1800s ship captains and residents of Sodus Point petitioned Congress for a light to mark the entrance of Sodus Bay. In 1825 Congress allocated funds, and a rough split-stone tower and dwelling went up. By the end of the Civil War, however, these structures were in a sad state of disrepair.

In 1871 a new forty-five-foot square stone tower took over the job of warning sailors. The new station served until 1903, when its light was extinguished and the still-operating **Sodus Point Pierhead Lighthouse** took over. The original 1871 structure remains, however. It now houses a maritime museum run by the Sodus

Sodus Point Light

Sodus Point Pierhead Light

Bay Historical Society. Visitors climbing the tower stairs can examine the three-and-a-half-order Fresnel lens (a type often seen on the Great Lakes) and catch a spectacular view of Sodus Bay and the lake beyond. The 1903 pierhead lighthouse, a simple square tower that resembles a chess rook, stands at the end of a nearby concrete pier.

The Sodus Bay Historical Society manages and maintains the lighthouse.

Travel information: Take Route 104, then Route 14 north to the village of Sodus Point and turn left onto Ontario Street (at the fire hall). The Old Sodus Point Lighthouse is open daily from May through October. For hours contact the Sodus Bay Lighthouse Museum, 7606 N. Ontario Street, P.O. Box 94, Sodus Point, NY 14555; call (315) 483-4936, or see www.sodus pointlighthouse.org.

■ CHARLOTTE-GENESEE LIGHT ■
Rochester (1822)

In 1822, the same year the **Oswego Lighthouse** went up near Fort Ontario, the Genesee beacon was first seen by sailors on Lake Ontario. It shone from atop a forty-foot octagonal limestone tower on a bluff overlooking the juncture of the Genesee River and the lake. David Denman, the first keeper, lived in an adjacent small limestone cottage and tended the station's old lamp-and-reflector system (ten Argand lamps and a set of reflectors to concentrate the light).

A more powerful and efficient fourth-order Fresnel lens replaced the reflectors in 1852. That same year, a second, smaller lighthouse was built on a nearby pier. In 1884 the Genesee Lighthouse was discontinued, leaving the pier light to guard the shore alone. Having deteriorated over the years, the old lighthouse was slated to be torn down in 1965. To save it students at nearby Charlotte High School circulated petitions and, in time, convinced the government to hand the building over to the Charlotte-Genesee Lighthouse Historical Society. Today the handsomely restored station is counted among the Great Lakes' most historic structures.

Travel information: In Rochester take Seaway Trail (Lakeshore Boulevard); then follow Lake Avenue north to Holy Cross Church, or take the Lake Ontario State Parkway to Lake Avenue. The lighthouse parking lot is behind the church. Grounds are open daily, and the Charlotte-Genesee Lighthouse Historical Society opens the tower and dwelling to the public on weekends. Special tours can

Charlotte-Genesee Light

be arranged by appointment. Call (585) 621-6179, or see www.geneseelighthouse.org.

To the west of Rochester is the site of the **Braddock Point Lighthouse** (1896). Much of the tower, nearly lost over many decades, is now rebuilt in tribute to the original lighthouse and is functional. The Victorian-style dwelling is now a private residence but is open for overnight stays on a limited basis. Contact the innkeepers at Braddock Point Lighthouse, 585 State Road 559, Auburndale, FL 33823, where mail is answered year-round.

Braddock Point Light
Braddock Point Bed & Breakfast

▪ THIRTY MILE POINT LIGHT ▪
Somerset (1876)

Thirty Mile Point Light

This light station marks a noted headland some thirty miles east of the Niagara River. Built in 1876 at the top of Golden Hill above Thirty Mile Point, the station was constructed of squared-off gray limestone blocks shipped in from Chaumont Bay, near the St. Lawrence River. The station cost the government $90,000, but in time it proved well worth this hefty price, as the sixty-one-foot tower served without interruption for more than eighty years.

The beacon, produced by a classic third-order Fresnel lens, had a focal plane seventy-one feet above Lake Ontario and could be seen from eighteen miles out in the lake. Originally, oil or kerosene powered the lamp, but in 1885 the government installed an electric bulb—one of the first ever used in a lighthouse. Lighthouse officials were impressed with the results and noted that, with its newfangled electric bulb, Thirty Mile Point now had the strongest light on Lake Ontario and the fourth strongest on the Great Lakes.

The lighthouse served the area until 1959, when a slender steel tower with an automated signal took over its duties. The stately old lighthouse is now part of Golden Hill State Park. Self-guided tours as well as docent-led tours of the well-preserved structures are a popular attraction at this historically rich site.

The striking lighthouse was chosen as one of five to represent the Great Lakes in a postage series in the mid-1990s. In celebration, the Friends of Thirty Mile Point Lighthouse restored a light in the tower.

Travel information: To reach Golden Hill State Park, take Route 18 to Route 269 north; then turn west on Lower Lake Road. The park offers campsites, picnic tables, a marina, and an engaging nature trail in addition to the self-guided lighthouse tour. For details on tours of the lighthouse and museum, call the park at (716) 795-3885. Rooms within the "Lighthouse Cottage" are available for overnight accommodations. Contact Reserve America at www.reserveamerica.com; call (800) 456-2267, or see http://friendsofthirtymilepointlighthouse.com.

▪ FORT NIAGARA LIGHT ▪
Youngstown (1781, 1823, and 1872)

Around 1781 the British built a stone light tower atop Fort Niagara, which they had captured in 1759, near the end of the French and Indian War. The fort was a natural place for a navigational light, as it overlooked the strategic juncture of the Niagara River and Lake Ontario and marked the site of overland portages around Niagara

Falls. Following the American Revolution, the US Army took possession of the fort but by 1796 had quit using the lighthouse. The tower was dismantled sometime between 1803 and 1806.

In 1823 a light once again shone from Fort Niagara, this time from a wooden tower. The light did not signal a revival of the old fort's commercial significance, however, for within two years the Erie Canal began diverting most of the river's east-west traffic away from the old Niagara Portage. When Canada opened its Welland Canal in 1829, Buffalo, on Lake Erie, became a booming commercial center overnight, whereas Fort Niagara settled into the life of a minor trading port.

In 1872 a new fifty-foot octagonal stone tower was completed on the lake shoreline just south of the fort, and the signal at Fort

Fort Niagara Light

Niagara was extinguished. This new tower had eleven feet added to its height in 1900, enabling its beacon to shine out some twenty-five miles over Lake Ontario. The refurbished tower included a watch room, complete with a built-in desk for the keeper. A lamp-oil shed sat at the tower's base. This new tower served lake vessels until fairly recently. The deactivated lighthouse is one of many exhibits in Old Fort Niagara State Park, where it placidly watches over the park's numerous military reenactments. Maintenance is assisted by the Old Fort Niagara Historic Site, within the state park.

Travel information: From Niagara, New York, take the Robert Moses Parkway to the Old Fort Niagara State Park entrance. Once inside the park, follow signs to the lighthouse. Visitors should set aside plenty of time to enjoy this historic site, which is a gold mine for history buffs. Living-history exhibits and military reenactments are part of the park's summer offerings. The fort and lighthouse grounds are open year-round except on January 1. Contact the Old Fort Niagara Association, P.O. Box 169, Youngstown, NY 14174; call (716) 745-7611, or see http://oldfortniagara.org.

■ BUFFALO MAIN LIGHT ■
Buffalo (1818 and 1833)

In 1805 the US government designated the then village of Buffalo a port of entry and made plans to build a lighthouse there. Political squabbling delayed construction, and when British troops burned Buffalo during the War of 1812, it began to look as if the lighthouse might never be built. Buffalo recovered, however, and in 1818 the tower was finally completed.

With the opening of the Erie Canal in 1825, Buffalo became one of the fastest growing cities in America and its port one of the busiest in the world. In 1833 a new

Buffalo Main Light
Mike Vogel

octagonal limestone tower signaled Buffalo's growing importance as a commercial center. This tower stood at the end of a fourteen-hundred-foot-long pier, its beam shining lakeward from a lantern some sixty-eight feet above the lake.

The **Buffalo Breakwater Lighthouse** went up in 1872 and was rebuilt in 1914. Built at the far end of a four-thousand-foot-long breakwater, the tower gained the third-order Fresnel lens that was moved from the main light. This lens is on display at the Buffalo and Erie County Historical Society.

The old 1833 (main light) tower stood empty and neglected for many years, but during the early 1960s citizens began raising money to restore it. In 1987 the beacon, focused by a rare fourth-order bivalve Fresnel lens, was relit to help celebrate Buffalo's first International Friendship Festival and remains active, albeit as a purposely dim light. The tower is highlighted akin to lighting designed for the Statue of Liberty and is open on special occasions.

Travel information: The Buffalo Main Lighthouse is on the grounds of a Coast Guard station, but acreage was relinquished to establish a promenade to the main and breakwater lights. Nearby is the rather extraordinary **Buffalo Bottle Light** (early 1900s), which looks like a cross between a buoy and a light tower. Take Interstate 190 to the Church Street exit; then turn right at the first traffic signal onto Lower Terrace. Follow signs to the Erie

Basin Marina and Buffalo Main Lighthouse. The lighthouse can also be viewed from the Naval and Military Park, across the river near downtown Buffalo on Buffalo Place at the foot of Pearl and Main streets. For more information on the lighthouse and available tours, contact the Buffalo Lighthouse Association, 1 Fuhrman Boulevard, Buffalo, NY 14203; call (716) 947-9126, or see www.buffalohistoryworks.com.

▪ DUNKIRK (POINT GRATIOT) LIGHT ▪
Point Gratiot (1829 and 1875)

The original 1829 Point Gratiot Lighthouse was the work of Buffalo contractor Jesse Peck. Like most lighthouses at the time, its lamps were fueled by whale oil. Several attempts were made to convert the station to natural gas, but the innovative experiments failed. The light was nonetheless powerful. Fitted with a third-order Fresnel lens in 1857, it produced a fifteen-thousand-candlepower beam visible from seventeen miles offshore; this same lens continues to shine today.

Dunkirk Light

After almost half a century of service, this lighthouse was replaced by the existing sixty-one-foot tower. The tower stands on a twenty-foot-high bluff. Unfortunately, its guiding light could not always prevent wrecks, and several vessels have sunk within site of the tower. In 1893 the *Dean Richmond* sank nearby, along with a cargo of bagged meal and flour, copper sheets, $50,000 worth of pig zinc, and $141,000 in gold and silver bullion. In 1897 the *Idaho* went down with a load of merchandise intended to be sold as Christmas presents. Afterward, large slabs of chocolate washed up on shore.

Currently, the light station at Point Gratiot serves as a military memorial, and the seven-room keeper's home now houses one of the best lighthouse museums on the Great Lakes.

Travel information: The lighthouse complex is in Dunkirk, just off Route 5, which parallels the lakeshore northwest of the New York State Thruway (Interstate 90). The complex is owned and operated by the nonprofit Dunkirk Lighthouse & Veterans Park Association; it is open daily except Wednesdays from May through October and at other times upon request. Contact the association ahead to find out about lighthouse tours as well as special events, such as War of 1812 reenactments, craft shows, and outdoor concerts at P.O. Box 69, 1 Lighthouse Point Drive, Dunkirk, NY 14048; call (716) 366-5050, or see www.dunkirklighthouse.com.

■ BARCELONA LIGHT ■
Barcelona (1829)

The Barcelona Lighthouse's claim to fame is its distinction as the first public build-ing in the United States—and perhaps the only lighthouse in the world—to be illu-minated by gas. The structure stands near a gas-emitting spring, so the experiment in using this alternative fuel source was a natural.

The lighthouse, built in 1829 on a bluff in Portland Harbor, as it was then called, had conventional oil lamps and a fourteen-inch reflector. Three years after it began operating, residents of this community made an astonishing discovery: a pool of water that would, on occasion, catch fire. This "burning spring" produced natural gas, which was soon piped to the tower and put to work guiding ships. The gas, burned in a specially designed lamp, pro-duced a flame so intense that sailors on Lake Erie sometimes reported that the whole lighthouse seemed on fire. Some-time after 1838 the gas ran out and the Bar-celona keeper had to replace the tower's origi-nal oil lamps.

Barcelona Light

In 1859 the light-house achieved another distinction, this one embarrassing. Government inspectors discovered that the station had been a mistake from the first. The light had been built to guide vessels into Barcelona's harbor, but Barcelona, as it turned out, had no harbor. The light was immediately discontinued.

Despite its short career the lighthouse survived and still stands today. Now a private residence, the forty-foot conical tower and its keeper's cottage are so attrac-tive that they are often depicted on postcards. The lantern was removed long ago, but a wooden framework at the top suggests the tower's original function.

Travel information: Located just off Interstate 90 on East Lake Road (Route 5) in Barcelona, the lighthouse is a private residence not open to the public. The structure can be seen from the public right-of-way, but visitors are asked to please not trespass on the private property.

PENNSYLVANIA

■ PRESQUE ISLE LIGHT ■

Erie (1819 and 1873)

In French *presque isle* means "almost an island." A port town that grew up on the shore of Lake Erie apparently used the term to refer to their long, narrow peninsula. The peninsula came close to also being "almost Pennsylvania," for, originally, Pennsylvania had no shore frontage on Lake Erie. Recognizing the strategic importance of access to the new country's inland seas, the state bought a forty-five-mile stretch of beaches and inlets immediately after the Revolutionary War. Included in the purchase was a fine harbor at a place that later would become Erie, Pennsylvania.

Here, during the War of 1812, Lieutenant Oliver Hazard Perry built the fleet of American warships that defeated the British in the famous Battle of Lake Erie. A few

Presque Isle Light

years later the government acknowledged Erie's strategic importance and growth as a port by erecting one of the first Great Lakes lighthouses here. Built in 1819 with large blocks of sandstone, on the sandy lakeshore across from Presque Isle, the **Erie Land Lighthouse** operated until the late 1890s.

In 1873 a brick lighthouse was built at the end of Presque Isle, a seven-mile-long finger of sand stretching into the lake on the northern side of the peninsula. The lantern at the top of its sixty-eight-foot tower held a fourth-order Fresnel lens, which displayed a fixed white light. This light station is still active, but these days the Fresnel is gone, replaced by an automated airport-style beacon.

Travel information: The current Presque Isle Light-house and the **Presque Isle North Pier Head Light** (1857) are in Presque Isle State Park. From Interstate 79 take Pennsylvania Alternate Route 5 west. At the fourth streetlight turn right onto Route 832 (Peninsula Drive), and continue north to the park entrance. The current Presque Isle Light-house is located about three miles from the entrance. The restored Old Presque Isle Light, also known as the **Erie Land Lighthouse** (1818 and 1867) is in Land Lighthouse Park. The site is open year-round and is open occasionally for tours as a fund-raiser, sponsored by the Erie Port Authority. To

Erie Land Lighthouse
Bob and Sandra Shanklin

reach the park follow Lake Road East about half a mile beyond East Avenue, then turn toward Lake Erie onto Lighthouse Street.

OHIO

■ ASHTABULA LIGHT ■
Ashtabula (1836, 1876, and 1905)

The squat Ashtabula Light sits on the end of a long breakwater, where it marks the entrance to the harbor at Ashtabula, Ohio. Lighthouses have guided ships from this location since 1836; a ramp connected the wooden crib on which the tower was built to the Ashtabula River's east pier. A new light was built on the west pier in 1876 to serve new dock facilities. It housed a fourth-order Fresnel lens.

The current light has been in operation since 1905, when a new tower was built a half mile north, again to serve newer docks after the river was widened. The tower was moved and the station enlarged in 1916 to its present position; additionally, in 1959 the tower was fitted with a new fourth-order Fresnel lens. Automated in 1973 by the Coast Guard, it was the last manned light on Lake Erie. Nearby is the Ashtabula Maritime Museum, which is in the former lighthouse keeper's quarters and specializes in the history of commerce, life-saving, and lighthouses on the lakes.

Ashtabula Light
Mike Adley

Travel information: Visitors can view the lighthouse from Point Park, near the intersection of Walnut and Hulbert Streets, in the Ashtabula waterfront district. Ashtabula Lighthouse Restoration and Preservation Society took ownership of the lighthouse in 2007, and restoration continues by the society's efforts. See www.ashtabulalighthouse.com for dates of lighthouse tours. The maritime museum, open weekends and holiday afternoons from Memorial Day through September, is across from the park. For more information call the museum (440) 964-6847, or see www.ashtabulamarinemuseum.org.

■ FAIRPORT HARBOR LIGHT ■
Fairport (1825 and 1871)

The original Fairport Harbor Light began its long career of welcoming immigrants to the American Midwest in 1825, the same year the Erie Canal opened. Fairport served as an important refueling and supply port for passenger and freight steamers bound westward from Buffalo, New York.

The original 1825 brick tower at Fairport was thirty feet high, had supporting walls three feet thick at ground level, and was capped with an octagonal iron lantern. Its two-story keeper's house had spacious rooms, each with plastered walls, three windows, and a fireplace.

Fairport Harbor Light

But by midcentury the tower and keeper's cottage were badly deteriorated, and in 1869 Congress appropriated $30,000 to replace them. Two years later a new sandstone tower, fitted with a third-order Fresnel lens, was ready to begin operating. The lighthouse served until 1925, when a combination light and foghorn station took over. The federal government planned to raze the old lighthouse, but local citizens launched a campaign to save the historic structure. In 1941 Fairport leased the lighthouse from the Coast Guard. Presently, the Fairport Harbor Historical Society maintains the lighthouse and keeper's dwelling as a marine museum.

Travel information: The lighthouse and museum—noted for its collection of artifacts from the early days of the Lighthouse Service—are at the northwest corner of Second and High streets in the village of Fairport Harbor. From US Highway 20 at Painesville, follow either Route 283 or Route 535 to the village. The museum is open from 1:00 to 6:00 p.m. on Wednesday, Saturday, Sunday, and legal holidays from Memorial Day through the third weekend in September. For information or to schedule a special tour, call (440) 354-4825, or go to www.ncweb.com/org/fhlh. Across the harbor is the **Fairport West Breakwater Lighthouse** (1925).

■ CLEVELAND HARBOR WEST PIERHEAD LIGHT ■
Cleveland (1910)

A pair of lighthouses, the West Pierhead Light and the East Pierhead Light, marked either side of Cleveland's harbor. Both towers date back to 1910, although an earlier pier light originally marked the entrance as early as 1831. The west light marks the entrance to the navigable Cuyahoga River, as well as the entrance to the inner harbor. Its sixty-seven-foot cast-iron tower and connected steel foghorn building are painted white with green trim. At night floodlights make the light station a landmark attraction of the harborscape.

The West Pierhead beacon, visible from ten miles away, passed through a fourth-order Fresnel lens and had a focal plane sixty-three feet above the lake surface. This lens is now on display at the Great Lakes Science Center. The station's foghorn was originally operated by steam. The deep-throated horn, the story goes, sounded so animal-like that the horn became known locally as "the cow." Despite its peculiar sound the horn was effective. On foggy nights its warning could be heard up to twelve miles out.

The **East Pierhead Light** stands about half a mile across the harbor from its counterpart. The small tower sits on a circular platform protected by a low wall of steel and stone, which marks the tip of an extensive breakwater that forms the Cleveland inner harbor and helps protect the shoreline from storm-driven waves.

Recently, the West Pierhead Light was declared excess property by the Coast Guard, but at time of printing, no one has stepped up to buy and maintain the old light, which still warns mariners of the pierhead. However, the small East Pierhead was bought by an individual and is planned to become a rental to boaters wanting a different view of the city's skyline.

Travel information: From Interstate 90 in downtown Cleveland, take the Ohio Highway 2 exit, drive west about 1 mile to the Ninth Street exit, and turn right. Then follow Ninth Street for about two blocks, and park in the lot beside the harbor. You can see both lighthouses from many points along the waterfront, but harbor cruises may offer the best views. Call (216) 861-5110. Near the parking area are two museum ships, the steam freighter *William G. Mather* and the USS *Cod,* a World War II submarine. The *Cod* sank forty Japanese ships on seven combat missions in the Pacific. To

Cleveland Harbor West Pierhead Light
Kraig Anderson

see the Fresnel lens, contact the Great Lakes Science Center, 601 Erieside Avenue, Cleveland, OH 44114; call (216) 694-2000.

■ LORAIN LIGHT ■
Lorain (1837 and 1917)

The original navigational light at Lorain, Ohio, was a lantern hung from the end of a pole on the Lake Erie shoreline, but by 1837 a full-fledged lighthouse had taken over. The new light, however, was not much of an improvement. The tower, built at the end of a pier, was wooden, and its lamps burned soot-producing lard oil; it had to be rebuilt at least twice over an eighty-year span. In contrast the present light tower is a monument to lighthouse technology. Its 1917 builders, the Army Corps of Engineers, used hundreds of tons of concrete and fill to form a foundation massive enough to resist Lake Erie's awesome storm waves. They constructed concrete-and-steel walls ten inches thick to protect keepers from gale-force winds.

Interestingly, although built like a fortress, the structure has the appearance of an old-fashioned, two-story town home. The chimney, rising from one end of its red-tiled pitched roof, gives the building a domestic air. But the short, square tower, which protruded a few feet from one corner of the roof, and the small cast-iron lantern room perched atop it made clear that this was no ordinary residence, as indeed it wasn't. For almost half a century, a rotating fourth-order Fresnel lens flashed its light from the lantern room's diamond-shaped windows every ten seconds. Mariners could see the beam fifteen miles out on the lake.

Lorain Light
David Kramer

By 1965 times had caught up with the Lorain Lighthouse. A small, fully automated light tower at the tip of a recently constructed breakwater took over navigational duties, and the old building was scheduled for demolition. Lorain citizens began mobilizing to save their town's landmark. Eventually, a five-year struggle with government officials to save the lighthouse ended in success. Saving the old tower was no easy—or inexpensive—task, however. Five hundred cubic yards of grout and $850,000 were required to keep it from falling into the lake.

Travel information: From US Highway 6, turn north onto Oberlin Avenue, and drive about three blocks to the parking area at the municipal pier. The lighthouse, known as the "Jewel of the Port," can be viewed from the north end of the parking area and from several other points along the Lake Erie shore. For more information and reservations for June through August weekend boat tours to the lighthouse, contact the Port of Lorain Foundation, Inc. at (440) 204-2269, or see www.lorainlighthouse.com.

▪ VERMILION LIGHT ▪
Vermilion (1847, 1859, 1877
and 1992 [reproduction])

The perky red, white, and black lighthouse that visitors see at Vermilion today has never been a commissioned light station. Rather, this is a 1992 reproduction of the 1877 Vermilion Lighthouse. A light guarded this site as early as 1847 and was rebuilt twice. The third lighthouse had a long record of service—it operated until 1929. But its many years of pounding by Lake Erie storms left both tower and foundation in such a state of deterioration that the Lighthouse Service was

Vermilion Light

afraid the structure would collapse. Rather than risk this, they had the structure dismantled and replaced by an eighteen-foot skeleton tower.

Sixty years later construction of the reproduction began. At present this monument to local history is one of the featured exhibits of the Inland Seas Maritime Museum in Vermilion. It resides in front of the museum and the home of the Great Lakes Historical Society.

> *Travel information:* The lighthouse and museum are at the end of Main Street, about three blocks north of US Highway 6 in Vermilion. For more information contact the Great Lakes Historical Society and its Inland Seas Maritime Museum, 480 Main Street, Vermilion, OH 44089; call (440) 967-3467, or see www.inlandseas.org.

■ MARBLEHEAD LIGHT ■
Bay Point (1821)

Marblehead is home to the oldest active light tower on the Great Lakes. Its beacon has faithfully served mariners since the station began operating in 1821. The old stone tower has changed very little over the last one hundred seventy years, although ten feet were added to the height of the original fifty-five-foot tower in the late nineteenth century. The station's three-and-a-half-order Fresnel lens that displayed a flashing green light over Lake Erie is now on display at the Marblehead Lighthouse Museum.

Marblehead Light

The lighthouse has stood silent witness to a lot of history; for instance, a nearly successful attempt by Confederate partisans to rescue prisoners of war on nearby Johnson Island. The would-be rescuers commandeered a passenger steamer and headed toward the island, only to encounter the mighty Union gunboat *Michigan*, which guarded the approach. No match for the *Michigan*'s heavy cannon, the Confederates' first and only Great Lakes warship fled for Canadian waters, where it was scuttled.

The lighthouse still watches over history from its strategic location at the entrance to Sandusky Bay. Although it remains an active light station, its 1880 keeper's dwelling has been converted to the museum run by the Marblehead Lighthouse Historical Society.

> *Travel information:* From US Highway 2 at Port Clinton, take Route 163 to Marblehead. A convenient parking area offers a good view of the light. For details on June through Labor Day tours of the keeper's museum and lighthouse, contact the Marblehead Lighthouse State Park at (419) 734-4424, ext. 2, or see www.marbleheadlighthouseohio.org. Or you may write to the Marblehead Lighthouse Historical Society at P.O. Box 144, Marblehead, OH 43440.

■ TOLEDO HARBOR LIGHT ■
Toledo (1904)

Toledo's turn-of-the-century light station is surely one of the architectural wonders of the Great Lakes. With its chocolate-colored brick walls, Romanesque arches, and bulging round-edge roof, it has been described as a cross between a Victorian palace and a Russian Orthodox church. Its outward appearance belies the solidness of its construction. The station sits on a massive concrete-and-stone crib that rises almost twenty feet above the water, and its three-story thick brick walls are topped with a light tower, which pushes it even higher, to eighty-five feet.

Toledo Harbor Light
David Kramer

The lighthouse was situated well offshore in 1904 to mark a channel the Army Corps of Engineers dredged from Lake Erie into the Maumee River. This channel opened Toledo's harbor to an influx of deep-water freighter traffic. Together, channel and lighthouse helped the city capture its share of Great Lakes commerce.

Some say that the lighthouse is haunted, whereas others maintain that the US Coast Guard began rumors of a ghost to discourage vandals. Another source of ghost stories may be the mannequin that occupies the still-active lighthouse. This fully uniformed inhabitant took up residence in 1965, when the light became automated and the last keeper came ashore for good. The station's original three-and-a-half-order Fresnel lens has been replaced by a modern optic.

Travel information: The only way to get a good look at the Toledo Harbor Lighthouse is from a boat. The active station is off-limits to visitors, but its distinctive red and white flashing light is visible from many points along the Toledo shoreline, including through a viewer in front of the lodge at Maumee Bay State Park. The lighthouse's original lens is on display at the lodge. Contact the Toledo Harbor Lighthouse Preservation Society, 1750 Park Road #2, Toledo, OH 43618; or see www.toledolighthouse.org.

MICHIGAN

Lower Peninsula

■ LIGHTSHIP *HURON* ■
Port Huron (1921)

Commissioned in 1921 as *Lightship No. 103*, the vessel known today as the *Huron* was used as a relief ship for Lake Michigan's Twelfth Lighthouse District. The *103* would replace lightships temporarily out of service while under repair. After fourteen years of filling in for others, the *103* took over a station of its own at Gray's Reef, Michigan. Later it served at Manitou Shoals on northern Lake Michigan, then in 1935 at Corsica Shoals in Lake Huron. Here its beacon helped guide traffic in and out of

the narrow dredged channel that allowed large vessels to navigate the St. Clair River and lower Lake Huron.

The ninety-seven-foot lightship came equipped with a fifty-two-and-a-half-foot lantern mast and a five-thousand-pound mushroom anchor. It originally was steam powered, but in 1949 it received a diesel engine, radar, and a radio beacon.

The *Huron* was the last lightship to serve on the Great Lakes.

Lightship Huron

When it was finally decommissioned in 1970, the city of Port Huron bought the ship. Two years later *Lightship No. 103* began a new era of service, this time as a part of the Port Huron Museum and National Historic Landmark.

> *Travel information:* The lightship rests in Pine Grove Park in Port Huron and near **Fort Gratiot Light.** From Interstate 94 drive south onto Pine Grove Street (M–25), turn left onto Prospect Street, and follow it one block to the parking area. The lightship and museum are open five days weekly, closed Tuesday and Wednesday, from mid-June to early September. Call (810) 984-9768, or see www.phmuseum.org.

■ FORT GRATIOT LIGHT ■
Port Huron (1825 and 1829)

In addition to the *Huron*, the last lightship to serve the Great Lakes, Port Huron can also boast of having Michigan's oldest light station. The Fort Gratiot Light station dates back to 1825, well before Michigan became a state in 1837. After almost one and three-quarter centuries of service, the station still marks the Lake Huron entrance to the St. Clair River.

The original tower did not last long. The materials and workmanship were so shoddy that the tower collapsed within four years. A new tower went up in 1829, this one more sturdily constructed, with thick, conical

Fort Gratiot Light

walls of stone overlaid with brick. It still stands and remains in operation. Automated in 1933, its eighty-two-foot height gives the beacon a focal plane eighty-six feet above Lake Michigan. The white tower, red-brick keeper's cottage, and fog-whistle house were once an active Coast Guard facility and rarely open to the public; however, the County of St. Clair purchased the property in recent years, and the site is undergoing restoration. Soon, it is hoped, visitors can view Michigan's oldest lighthouse up close and personal.

Travel information: From Interstate 94 take Pine Grove Street (M–25) north. Turn right onto Garfield Street, and follow it to Gratiot Avenue. Parking is available in the area. For the status on this light, ask at the nearby *Huron* lightship, part of the Port Huron Museum; call (810) 984-9768, or see www.phmuseum.org. For more information, contact the Friends of the Fort Gratiot Light, 1115 Sixth Street, Port Huron, MI 48060; call the Port Huron Museum at (810) 982-0891, or see www.phmuseum.org.

■ PORT SANILAC LIGHT ■
Port Sanilac (1886)

Once a vital link in a three-hundred-mile chain of navigational lights guiding vessels along Michigan's eastern shores, the Port Sanilac beacon was the first light mariners saw as they exited the St. Clair River and steamed northward into Lake Huron. Although its importance as a navigational aid has diminished with time, the light remains in operation. The fourth-order Fresnel lens atop the sixty-nine-foot octagonal tower remains in use. The station's unusual step-sided brick keeper's dwelling is now a private residence.

Travel information: Now a private home, the lighthouse is not open to the public. However, it can be viewed from the end of a breakwater off Cherry Street in Port Sanilac.

▪ POINTE AUX BARQUES LIGHT ▪

Port Austin (1848 and 1857)

This lighthouse is located on a strategic headland near the spot where Saginaw Bay opens into Lake Huron. French traders called the place Pointe Aux Barques or "Point of Little Boats," because of many canoes that used to gather here during fur-trading season. A town grew up here and, after Michigan became part of the United States, grew into a prime shipping port.

In 1848 the federal government approved $5,000 to build a lighthouse at Pointe Aux Barques. It proved far less than adequate, and nine years later it was replaced by the eighty-nine-foot conical brick tower that still stands here. Originally fitted with a state-of-the-art third-order Fresnel lens, the station now employs an automated optic. Its powerful flashing white light is visible from eighteen miles out on Lake Huron.

Travel information: To reach the lighthouse take M–25 to Lighthouse Road. The county park, where the lighthouse stands, is about ten miles east of Port Austin and six miles north of Port Hope. The park offers camping and picnicking facilities. The museum and gift shop are open daily from

Pointe Aux Barques Light

10:00 a.m. to 8:00 p.m., Memorial Day through Labor Day. For further information about the lighthouse, send a request via www.pointauxbarques lighthouse.org, or call the Pointe Aux Barques Lighthouse Society for special lighthouse tour dates at Lighthouse County Park: (989) 428-4749.

▪ TAWAS (OTTAWA) POINT LIGHT ▪

East Tawas (1852 and 1876)

Built in 1852 to mark the northern entrance to Saginaw Bay, the first lighthouse on Tawas Point, then known as the **Ottawa Point Lighthouse,** served for only twenty years. By the 1870s the rapidly shifting shoreline had placed the light more than a mile from the water, rendering it useless; subsequently, the light was taken down. The Lighthouse Board appealed to Congress for funds to build a new structure, and in 1876 a sixty-seven-foot brick tower, fitted with the Ottawa Point's fourth-order Fresnel lens, began operating on a site closer to the bay. In 1891 the lens was upgraded to a fifth order, and in 1902 the name changed to Tawas Point. Its light can still be seen as the Fresnel lens continues to emit a bright light and serves as an active aid to navigation.

The Tawas Point Lighthouse now sits on the grounds of Tawas Point State Park, managed by the Michigan Department of Natural Resources; the area has been referred to as "the Cape Cod of the Midwest." Tours of the tower are available during summer.

Travel information: Take US Highway 23
to about a mile and a half west of Tawas
City; then turn right onto Tawas Beach Road,
which will take you to Tawas Point State
Park, approximately two-and-a-half miles
southeast of East Tawas. Drive to the beach
parking area at the end of the road, and follow the walking path to the lighthouse. The
museum store and tower are open generally
from Memorial Day until Labor Day. A fee is
charged for park entry and lighthouse admission. For more information or to apply for a
resident keeper's position, contact the Tawas
Point Lighthouse, 686 Tawas Beach Road,
East Tawas, MI 48730; call (989) 362-5658, or
the park at (989) 362-5041, or see www
.michigan.gov/tawaslighthouse. *Note*: For
in-state residents at all Michigan state parks,
a Recreation Passport is required; for out-of-state visitors, a day pass is available. Both permits are available at each state park.

Tawas Point Light

■ STURGEON POINT LIGHT ■
Alcona (1870)

Not far from Sturgeon Point on Lake Huron, a potentially deadly reef lies in wait
for unwary vessels. Built in 1870 to warn mariners to steer clear of this dangerous
obstacle, the Sturgeon Point Light has prevented countless accidents. Even so, many
vessels have been wrecked practically in the shadow of its seventy-foot-tall tower.
On the station grounds sits a big rudder salvaged from the wooden steamer *Marine
City*, which burned near here in an 1880
disaster just off Sturgeon Point. Also
lost nearby were the 233-ton schooner
Venus in 1887, the three-masted schooner *Ispeming* in 1903, the *Clifton* in a 1924
gale, and many other vessels.

The Alcona County Historical Society owns the station, and the old keeper's
residence houses museum exhibits. The
light, automated since 1936, remains
active. Visitors are allowed to climb the
tower's eighty-five steps to the lantern
room, where the station's 1889 three-
and-a-half-order Fresnel lens sits ready
to beam its warning out across the lake.

Sturgeon Point Light

Travel information: To reach the lighthouse take US Highway 23 north
from Harrisville, then follow Lakeshore Drive and Point Road to Sturgeon

Point. The parking lot is less than a mile down the road. The museum, housed in the keeper's quarters, is open daily from Memorial Day through Labor Day weekend. During the fall-color season, the museum is open weekends, and the grounds remain open year-round. For hours contact the Sturgeon Point Lighthouse, P.O. Box 174, Alcona Historical Society, Harrisville, MI 48740; call the lighthouse (989) 724-6297, or see www.alconahistorical society.com.

■ MIDDLE ISLAND LIGHT ■
North of Alpena (1905)

Established in 1905, the Middle Island Light station was automated and abandoned by the Coast Guard years ago. However, thanks to a hardworking group of lighthouse preservationists, this handsome seventy-seven-foot island tower north of Alpena is being restored to tip-top condition. Known as the Middle Island Light Keepers Association, the group has opened the station to guests as a bed-and-breakfast inn.

Middle Island Light
Lighthouse Digest

Travel information: The lighthouse is accessible only by boat. Contact the Middle Island Light Keepers Association, 5671 Rockport Road, Alpena, MI 49707. Boat tours of the island and reservations can be made with Captain Mike Theut at (989) 884-2722. The same group helps sponsor and organize the Great Lakes Lighthouse Festival, held each October in Alpena. Across the Thunder Bay River from Alpena is the spindly legged, red metal tower of the **Alpena Lighthouse** (1914), known affectionately to some locals as "Sputnik."

■ NEW PRESQUE ISLE LIGHT ■
Presque Isle (1871)

A treasure trove of lighthouses awaits visitors at Presque Isle, home to no fewer than four light towers. The oldest, a thirty-eight-foot stone-and-brick structure now known as **Old Presque Isle Lighthouse,** served the peninsula from 1840 to 1871. During the Civil War a pair of range lights were built to mark the channel for vessels bound in and out of the harbor. In addition, President Abraham Lincoln authorized construction of a new, higher light tower at the main light station. The New Presque Isle Lighthouse took several years to complete and finally went into service in 1871. The beacon from the 113-foot tower, one of the highest on the Great Lakes, was visible twenty-five miles away.

Old Presque Isle Light

New Presque Isle Lighthouse

The Old and New Presque Isle Light towers and the two peninsula range lights now stand in neighborly proximity. The New Presque Isle Light sits amid a scenic one-hundred-acre park; both lighthouses and museums are maintained by the Presque Isle Township Museum Society. All four lighthouses are easily accessible and together give visitors an unusually complete look at the history of a light station.

Travel information: From Presque Isle, follow Grand Lake Road past the intersection of Highway 638, or from US Highway 23 take Highway 638 to Grand Lake Road and turn left. The Old Presque Isle Lighthouse and Museum are just over half a mile to the north. The front- and rear-range light towers stand nearby. From the museum continue north about one mile on Grand Lake Road to New Presque Isle Lighthouse, where you'll find a second museum and gift shop. For hours of operation and climbing, contact the New Presque Isle Lighthouse Park and Museum, 4500 E. Grand Lake Road, Presque Isle, MI 49777; call (989) 595-9917. For the Old Presque Isle Lighthouse located at 5245 E. Grand Lake Road, call (989) 595-6979; for the 1905 keeper's dwelling and museum, call (989) 595-5419, or see www.presqueislelighthouses.org.

■ 40 MILE POINT LIGHT ■
Rogers City (1897)

One of the last dark stretches facing ships navigating the Great Lakes was finally lit when the 40 Mile Point Lighthouse beacon began to flash in 1897. Shining from a square brick tower equipped with a fourth-order Fresnel lens, the light still guides vessels passing between Cheboygan and Presque Isle.

The architecturally interesting dwelling features two gables, one on either side of the light tower. A brick oil house and fog-signal building complete the station. Well maintained, the tower, dwelling, and other structures are open to the public within Presque Isle County's Lighthouse Park. The keeper's quarters houses a museum run by volunteers of the 40 Mile Point Lighthouse Society. The grounds, open year-round, and buildings are lovely, and the beach below the lighthouse features the hulk of a wooden ship that was wrecked here long ago.

40 Mile Point Light

Travel information: Drive about six miles north of Rogers City on US Highway 23. Look for a sign pointing the way to Presque Isle County Lighthouse Park. Turn right onto an otherwise unmarked road, and follow it to the lighthouse (do not take 40 Mile Point Road). The museum and gift shop are open from Memorial Day weekend to mid-October. For more information, including the Guest Keeper program, contact the 40 Mile Point Lighthouse Society at P.O. Box 205, Rogers City, MI 49779, or see www.40milepointlighthouse.org.

■ MICHIGAN REEF LIGHTS ■
Northwestern Lake Huron

During the late nineteenth century, the growth of shipping on the Great Lakes focused attention on the dangers of the Straits of Mackinac, the link connecting Lake Huron to Lake Michigan. Here Huron narrows to a mere few miles in width, forcing ships to run a gauntlet of treacherous shallows and killer reefs. Some believed this stretch of water to be the most dangerous in all the Great Lakes. To make navigation safer the government marked the most threatening obstacles with lighthouses, some of them built in open water directly over the shoals. They were all part of the network of markers that evolved to help vessels maneuver safely through these waters.

After the submerged claws of Spectacle Reef hooked a pair of large schooners in 1867, Congress approved funds to mark the shoal with a lighthouse. The job took $406,000 and two hundred men working nearly four years, but by 1874 the **Spectacle Reef Lighthouse** was at last complete. Its beacon, produced by a massive second-order Fresnel lens, was removed in 1982 and is on display at the Inland Seas Maritime Museum (see *Travel information* for **Vermilion Light**). Today it hosts one of the newest genres of beacons with its solar-powered Vega LED light, which still warns ships.

The **Round Island Lighthouse** (1895), **Poe Reef Lighthouse** (1893), and **DeTour Reef Lighthouse** (1931) remain in operation, but all are now automated. These reef lighthouses are generally not open to the public, and most are difficult to view from land.

Spectacle Reef Light

Kraig Anderson

Round Island Light

Poe Reef Light

Kraig Anderson

Cheboygan Crib Light

The **Cheboygan Crib Lighthouse** (1884), at one time located offshore on a concrete-and-stone crib, was decommissioned when its foundation settled into the lake. The town of Cheboygan salvaged the structure and gave it a new home at the end of a short pier in a park.

Travel information: Michigan's reef lighthouses are generally off-limits to the public. The Round Island Lighthouse Preservation Society joined efforts with the US Forest Service and Boy Scout Troop 323 to restore this historic tower; the society holds an annual open house in July; see http://roundisland lightmichigan.com. Shepler's Ferry Service out of Mackinaw City offers summer lighthouse cruises, which include views of Round Island and Poe Reef Lights; call (800) 828-6157.

The **DeTour Reef Light** is at the busy St. Marys River entrance to Lake Superior. It is maintained and operated by the DeTour Reef Light Preservation Society, declared a Preserve America Steward by First Lady Michelle Obama. For more information on lighthouse cruises and the summer weekend resident Lighthouse Keeper Program, contact Lighthouse Keeper Program, P.O. Box 307, Drummond Island, MI 49726; call (906) 493-6609 or (906) 493-6303, or see www.drlps.com.

DeTour Reef Light
Hallie Wilson

The **Cheboygan Crib Lighthouse** (1884) resides in Gordon Turner Park at the end of Huron Street, off US Highway 23. It was relocated onshore in 1984 and is owned and maintained by the City of Cheboygan. Tours of the lighthouse can be arranged with volunteer keepers at the **Cheboygan River Front Range Light** during open hours. This light, which acted as a range with the Crib Light, was transferred to the Great Lakes Lighthouse Keepers Association (GLLKA) in 2006 and continues to undergo restoration. Both lights remain active aids to navigation. GLLKA volunteers has a keeper program at the front-range light and opens the lighthouse to the public on weekends and holidays from Memorial Day through Labor Day. For information call (231) 436-5580 or see www.gllka .com.

Offshore near the Cheboygan Crib Light is the **Fourteen Foot Shoal Light** (1930).

◼ OLD MACKINAC POINT LIGHT ◼
Mackinaw City (1892)

In 1957 a bridge over Mackinac Straits opened, making the Old Mackinac Point Light obsolete. Vessels began taking bearings from the long string of bridge lights, and the beacon at the top of the forty-foot-tall, turn-of-the-century station was soon turned off. Within three years the building had been converted into a maritime museum.

Old Mackinac Point Light

The original Mackinaw City station opened in 1890 as a fog-signal station. It was, obviously, much needed. During one amazingly foggy two-week stretch, hardworking stokers burned fifty-two cords of wood to keep its boilers filled with steam.

By late 1892 a lighthouse was ready to supplement the fog signal, and the forty-foot tower, equipped with a fourth-order lens, began a stint of service that ended only after the 1957 bridge opened up. Today the buff-colored station, with its bright red roof, is part of a historical park run by the Mackinac Island State Park Commission.

Travel information: Take Interstate 75 to exit 336. From this exit follow Nicolet Avenue through Mackinaw City, and turn right onto Huron Avenue. The Old Mackinac Point Lighthouse parking area is about two blocks down Huron Avenue. The lighthouse sits in Michilimackinac Maritime Park that overlooks the Mackinac Bridge. Picnic tables and lovely surroundings will tempt you to make this a leisurely stop. The lighthouse has been restored to its 1910 appearance, and the station's fourth-order Fresnel lens has been returned to the tower.

The lighthouse is open seasonally from early May until early October. For more details on exhibits and tower tours led by a costumed, historic interpreter, call (231) 436-8705, or see www.mackinacparks.com. The Great Lakes Lighthouse Keepers Association (GLLKA) operates a gift shop across the street from the lighthouse. Headquartered in the same building, GLLKA answers questions year-round about Great Lakes lighthouses. See Travel information for **St. Helena Lighthouse.**

◼ SOUTH MANITOU ISLAND LIGHT ◼
South Manitou Island (1839, 1858, and 1872)

Among the most impressive structures on the Great Lakes is the white conical tower of South Manitou Island Lighthouse. Replacing two earlier, less sturdy lights, it is the third light to guard this point. Its purpose is to guide ships through the narrow Manitou Passage between South Manitou Island and Sleeping Bear Point. It was a favorite route, as it provided a shorter shipping course between Michigan's southern shores and the Straits of Mackinac. Soaring 104 feet into the skies over Lake Michigan, its stark white walls now seem a natural part of the pristine island that surrounds them. The tower and keeper's dwelling have been empty since

South Manitou Island Light

1958, when the Coast Guard decommissioned the station. These buildings have been stabilized, and the tower has been handsomely restored by the National Park Service and its contributing partners; they are now part of the Sleeping Bear Dunes National Lakeshore.

The 1872 tower's powerful beacon could be seen from a distance of eighteen miles, produced by third-order Fresnel lens. After fifty years of darkness, a reproduction third-order lens was relit in a grand ceremony in 2008. The tower is open seasonally for climbing, and ranger-guided tours of the light station are scheduled each summer day.

Travel information: To reach the South Manitou Island Lighthouse between June and August, take the ferry from Leland, on the mainland. For schedules to North and South Manitou Islands, call Manitou Island Transit at (231) 256-9061. Reservations are recommended. Passengers can get a good view of the **North Manitou Island Shoals Lighthouse Crib** (1935) during the passage. The South Manitou Lighthouse is a short hike from the ferry slip. The Sleeping Bear Dunes National Lakeshore offices can be reached at (231) 326-5134, or see www.nps.gov/slbe/planyourvisit/smilighthouse.htm.

■ BEAVER ISLAND (HEAD) LIGHT ■
Beaver Island (1858)

Well north of the Manitou Islands and demarking the approach to Mackinac Straits is historic Beaver Island, where radical Mormon James Jesse Strang at one time reigned as a self-styled king. He had already been deposed by 1858, when the island became the home of the forty-six-foot-high, yellow-brick Beaver Island Lighthouse and its attached two-story keeper's dwelling.

The Beaver Island station was once a popular destination for picnickers, who rode sleighs over the winter ice from Charlevoix, on the mainland. Occasionally, even cars made the trip. In 1929 three Model T Fords set out for the island, only to get lost in the fog. The resident keeper finally guided them to safety with the station's fog bell. The Coast Guard kept the light in operation until 1970, but at present the building serves a different use: It is now an education center for Charlevoix County public schools.

Beaver Island Light
US Coast Guard

Travel information: A ferry from Charlevoix provides access to Beaver Island, known as a great family vacation area overlooking Lake Michigan. The three-hour ride can be expensive. For schedules and prices call the Beaver Island Boat Company, (231) 547-2311. For information on the lighthouse or marine museum, contact the Beaver Island Chamber of Commerce at (231) 448-2505, or see www.beaverisland.org. At the north end of the island is the St. James Lighthouse, also known as the **Beaver Harbor Lighthouse,** owned by St. James Township. Both island lights are accessible and frequently open to visitors. Contact St. James Township, P.O. Box 85, Beaver Island, MI 49782; call (231) 448-2834, or see www.charlevoixcounty.org.

■ ST. HELENA ISLAND LIGHT ■
St. Helena Island (1871)

Established in 1871, the St. Helena Light served ships passing through the Mackinac Straits. Automated in 1922, the seventy-one-foot brick tower and attached dwelling suffered greatly from neglect and vandalism. It might have fallen into ruin, but believing it deserved a better fate, the Great Lakes Lighthouse Keepers Association has been handling the formidable task of repairing and caring for the structure for many years. Michigan Boy Scouts can earn Eagle Scout badges by helping with restoration work.

St. Helena Island Light

Travel information: St. Helena Island can be reached by boat from St. Ignace. For information on the lighthouse restoration project and all the wide-ranging programs offered by this preservation group, write to Great Lakes Lighthouse Keepers Association, 707 N. Huron Street, P.O. Box 219, Mackinaw City, MI 49701; call (231) 436-5580, or see www.gllka.com.

■ CHARLEVOIX SOUTH PIERHEAD LIGHT ■
Charlevoix (1885 and 1948)

A narrow, mile-long channel links the pristine waters of Lake Charlevoix to Lake Michigan at the mouth of Pine River leading to Round Lake. Ferries, Coast Guard patrol boats, and other vessels are guided in and out of the channel by the red flash of the Charlevoix Lighthouse beacon, once focused by a fifth-order Fresnel lens. Established in 1885, this light first served on the outer end of the north pier. Various improvements were made to this light over the years, culminating in its relocation to the South Pierhead in 1914, while a steel skeleton light took its place on the north pierhead. The existing steel tower on the south pier replaced the old wooden tower in 1948 after many years of wear and tear. It is now owned by the City of Charlevoix and maintained by a nonprofit historical society.

Charlevoix South Pierhead Light

Travel information: Charlevoix is located on US Highway 31 about fifty miles north of Traverse City. A parking area off Grant Street provides a good view of the lighthouse.

Contact the Charlevoix Historical Society, P.O. Box 525, Charlevoix, MI 49720; call (231) 547-0373, or see www.chxhistory.com/lighthouse.htm.

■ OLD MISSION POINT LIGHT ■
Near Traverse City (1870)

Interestingly, this light station is located on the forty-fifth parallel, exactly halfway between the North Pole and the equator. Most of the mariners who depended on this light, however, were more likely interested in the fact that the Mission Point beacon marked the far end of the slender—and sometimes dangerous—peninsula that divides Traverse Bay. Established in 1870, the station was deactivated in 1933. Nowadays, the combination wooden tower and dwelling serve as the central attraction of Peninsula Township Park. Although the light is no longer active, the Coast Guard loaned a fifth-order Fresnel lens for an exhibit.

Old Mission Point Light
Rick Polad

Travel information: From Traverse City follow M–37 north to its end to the inviting historical Peninsula Township Park, which surrounds the lighthouse. Opened to the public in 2008, the lighthouse is open from April through October. To check hours and programs offered, write to 13235 Center Road, Traverse City, MI 49686; call (231) 223-7324 or (231) 645-0759. To apply for the resident keeper's program, contact Mission Point Lighthouse Manager, P.O. Box 98, Old Mission, MI 49673; call (231) 645-0759, or see www.missionpointlighthouse.com.

■ GRAND TRAVERSE LIGHT ■
North Port (1853 and 1858)

Grand Traverse Light

Built in 1853 on strategic Cat Head Point, this lighthouse commanded the entrance to Grand Traverse Bay, guiding ships with a beacon produced by a relatively small fourth-order Fresnel lens. In 1858 the Lighthouse Board built a second tower in a more visible spot nearby. In 1900 it was converted to a two-family structure, proving its continued value as a guide for mariners. The light beamed out into the lake from atop a square tower that rose just above the roofline of a large, two-story brick dwelling. After serving mariners for over a century, the old lighthouse was retired in 1972, its duties taken over by a nearby skeleton tower. The structure currently houses an excellent lighthouse museum. Among its exhibits is a fourth-order Fresnel lens.

> *Travel information:* The lighthouse is located in Leelanau State Park, at the end of a long peninsula pointing northward into Lake Michigan. From Traverse City follow M–22 to Northport, then County Road 201 to the park. For more information on hours of operation and programs offered, including a resident keeper program, contact the Grand Traverse Lighthouse Museum, P.O. Box 43, 15500 N. Lighthouse Point Road, Northport, MI 49670; call (231) 386-7195, or see www.grandtraverselighthouse.com. The museum and gift shop are open from May through October.

■ POINT BETSIE LIGHT ■
Frankfort (1858)

Built in 1858 to mark a key turning place for ships moving in or out of the strategic Manitou Passage, the Point Betsie Lighthouse marks the southern entrance and has long been considered among the most important navigational aids on the Great Lakes. The original thirty-seven-foot tower and attached two-story dwelling still stand, and the light still shines each night.

The Point Betsie Lighthouse was among the last light stations on the Great Lakes to be automated. Resident keepers operated the light until 1983, when electronic machinery took over the job. In 2004 the light station was transferred to Benzie County and is managed and maintained by a nonprofit organization that has restored and opened the lighthouse to the public. It has become a popular destination for visitors as well as a picturesque spot for weddings.

Point Betsie Light

Travel information: Once used as a private residence, the lighthouse is now open to the public but also can be viewed from Point Betsie Road, off M–22 just south of Sleeping Bear Dunes National Lakeshore and about five miles north of Frankfort.

For further information contact the stewards, Friends of Point Betsie Lighthouse, P.O. Box 601, Frankfort, MI 49635; call (231) 352-7666, or see www.pointbetsie.org.

■ BIG SABLE POINT LIGHT ■
Ludington (1867)

The construction of the 107-foot Big Sable Point Lighthouse in 1867 helped fill one of the last dark stretches along the western Michigan shore. The light, produced by a third-order Fresnel lens, helped coast-hugging vessels avoid the point and reach Ludington safely. So did the station's powerful foghorn, which proved quite a bit more efficient than its predecessor. Previously, local citizens had warned ships away from the point by firing up an old steam engine and giving a blast on its whistle.

Wind and weather hammered away at the tower's brick walls, and by the 1920s the lighthouse was in danger of collapse. To protect it officials had the tower encased in a shell of riveted iron plates. Painted in broad white and black bands, the Big Sable Point tower is one of the

Big Sable Point Light

most distinctive structures on the Great Lakes. Now part of Ludington State Park, the station remains in operation.

Travel information: From US Highway 10 in Ludington, turn right onto Lakeshore Drive, and follow it for approximately six miles to Ludington

State Park. The lighthouse can be reached via a half-mile walk up the beach from the parking lot. Also in the area is the **Ludington North Breakwater Light,** which can be reached by following Ludington Avenue to Stearns Park. Built early in the twentieth century, it stands on a concrete base that looks something like the bow of a ship. Big Sable is open from May through October and Ludington from May through September. For more information on hours of operation and climbing, contact the stewards of these lights, Sable Points Lighthouse Keepers Association, P.O. Box 673, Ludington, MI 49431; call (231) 845-7417, or see www.splka.org.

■ LITTLE SABLE POINT LIGHT ■
Mears (1874)

When completed in 1874 the tower at Little Sable Point was nearly a twin of its sister lighthouse at Big Sable Point. Both towers stood 107 feet tall, both were constructed of brick, and both were fitted with third-order Fresnel lenses. But unlike its neighbor, which was eventually covered in steel plates, the Little Sable tower still looks much the way it did nearly one and a quarter centuries ago.

The keeper's dwelling was demolished when the station was automated during the 1950s, leaving the tower to stand a solitary vigil. It is one of the loveliest lighthouses on the lakes, and its red-brick walls offer a handsome contrast to the white dunes of Silver Lake State Park. The station's original Fresnel lens remains in use.

Little Sable Point Light

Travel information: From US Highway 31 near Mears, turn west on Shelby Road, and follow the signs to Silver Lake State Park. This light is owned by the Friends of Sable Points Lighthouse Keepers Association, which opens this site from the end of May through September. See Travel information for **Big Sable Point Light.** For the nearby **White River Lighthouse** (1875), turn west off US Highway 31 on White Lake Road, then follow South Shore Road and Murray Road. Discontinued in 1941, the restored combination tower and dwelling houses the delightful Great Lakes Marine Museum. Inside, visitors will find on display the station's original fourth-order Fresnel lens. Contact the White River Light Station Museum, 6199 Murray Road, Whitehall, MI 49461; call (231) 894-8265, or see www.white riverlightstation.org.

White River Light

■ MUSKEGON SOUTH PIER LIGHT ■
Muskegon (1903)

The eastern shores of Lake Michigan are marked by several of the most beautiful and distinctive pier lighthouses in America. Located on often lengthy stone or concrete piers that place them well out in the lake, these towers guide vessels in and out of harbors and warn them away from the piers and other dangerous obstacles. Many of the Michigan pier lighthouses were built during a flurry of construction in the early 1900s.

As is the case with several of these offshore towers, the Muskegon South Pier Lighthouse is painted bright red for better daytime visibility. Built in 1903, the tower is forty-eight feet high, and its lantern holds a fourth-order Fresnel lens. The tower and its light guide vessels through the passage that links Muskegon Lake with the open waters of Lake Michigan.

Muskegon South Pier Light

Travel information: In Muskegon take Lakeshore Drive to Beach Street, and follow it to Pere Marquette Park. The pier and lighthouse are located just north of the park, which offers excellent swimming and picnicking. Nearby is the 70-foot Muskegon **South Breakwater Light,** built in 1930. The red, square tapered-steel tower sits on the south breakwater, also along the Lake Michigan shore at the mouth of Muskegon Lake. The Michigan Lighthouse Conservancy owns both these lights. Contact the group at P.O. Box 973, Fenton, MI 48430; call (810) 750-9236, or see www.michigan lights.com.

■ GRAND HAVEN PIER LIGHTS ■
Grand Haven (1905)

Among the most striking of Michigan's pier lighthouses are those that mark the entrance to Grand Haven River, which offers one of the state's best deep-water harbors. Known as the **Grand Haven South Pierhead Inner Light** and **Pier Light,** they stand several hundred feet apart on a long stone pier. The inner tower, which was built in 1905, consists of a fifty-one-foot steel cylinder topped by a small lantern.

The squat pierhead tower was originally the station's fog-signal building and was moved several times as the pier was extended over the years; its present location marks when the pier was extended in 1905. A tiny lantern nestles on the roof. According to the Maritime Initiative Inventory of Lighthouses, the pierhead tower has been sheathed in steel since 1922 to protect it from the lake's destructive storm-driven waves.

Grand Haven Pier Light

Grand Haven South Pier Light

Travel information: From US Highway 31 in Grand Haven, follow Franklin Avenue and South Harbor Drive to Grand Haven State Park. The pier is open to the public and attracts droves of fishermen. The park also offers picnicking and swimming.

To the south are the **Holland Harbor (Black Lake) Lighthouse** (1936) and **South Haven South Pier Lighthouse** (1903). Both are painted bright red for visibility and sheathed in steel to protect them from the elements. In Holland follow Ottawa Beach Road to Holland State Park. In South Haven follow Phoenix and Water Streets to the South Beach parking area. The light can be photographed and enjoyed from a nearby public park.

▪ HOLLAND HARBOR (BLACK LAKE) SOUTH PIERHEAD LIGHT ▪
Holland (1872 and 1907)

When it was completed in 1907, the existing Holland Harbor Lighthouse was sheathed in steel, and no wonder. Located at the end of a long pier and situated at the south side of the entrance to Lake Macatawa from Lake Michigan, the thirty-two-foot structure takes a tremendous pounding during heavy weather. Originally, a wooden tower stood here in 1872 but had to be replaced over time. The current tower rises through the slate roof of the main station building. It is painted bright red, and locals know it as "Big Red." The lighthouse is now owned by the Holland Harbor Lighthouse Historical Commission.

Holland Harbor Light

Travel information: In Holland turn west onto Douglas Avenue, and drive approximately six miles to Holland State Park. Visitors can walk out on the pier and view the light up close. For information on the Greater Holland, Michigan area, contact the Holland Area Convention and Visitors Bureau, 76 E. 8th Street, Holland, MI 49423; call (616) 394-0000, or see http://holland.org.

■ SOUTH HAVEN LIGHT ■
South Haven (1872 and 1903)

South Haven seems just the sort of place to shop for antiques, and not surprisingly, this quaint lakeside community can boast its own antique lighthouse. Located at the far end of one of two protective harbor piers at the mouth of the Black River, the red cast-iron tower is still an active aid to navigation. Like other Michigan pier lights, this tower was relocated in 1901 after the piers were widened and extended to accommodate more river traffic.

A new cylindrical steel structure, the one we know today, was built on one of the new pierheads in 1903; subsequently, it was moved after the final extension to the piers in 1913. A rear range light was added in 1916, but it no longer exists. At some point during recent years, the lighthouse gained its distinctive red exterior. Its original fifth-order Fresnel lens was replaced by a sixth-order lens that still warns mariners with a flashing red light. The long and dramatic catwalk allowed keepers to reach the light above waters that were often rough or even frozen. At night, the catwalk's lights are nearly as dramatic as the red flashing light emanating from the tower. The Historical Association of South Haven plans acquisition and future maintenance of this light while the city of South Haven gained ownership of the keepers' house, which will become part of the Michigan Maritime Museum complex.

Travel information: From US Highway 31 follow Route 196 West, then Phoenix and Water Streets to South Haven's sandy beach. The lighthouse can be reached by walking a long concrete pier, but do not chance it in rough weather. For more information, contact the Michigan Maritime Museum, 260 Dyckman Avenue, South Haven, MI 49090; call (269) 637-8078, or see www.michiganmaritimemuseum.org.

■ ST. JOSEPH NORTH PIER LIGHTS ■
St. Joseph (1907)

Among the best known and loved of the Michigan pier lights are the **St. Joseph Inner** and **Outer Pier Lighthouses,** which function in tandem as range lights. As with all range lights, they are located some distance apart and are meant to be seen one atop the other. Mariners on the lake who see them in perpendicular alignment may rest assured that they are sailing in safe water.

A much earlier federal lighthouse, built on the mainland in 1859, served St. Joseph until it was discontinued during the 1920s; it was eventually demolished. The St. Joseph Pier Lights, established in 1907, still stand. The forward, or front-range light, is a cylindrical structure. The one closest to shore, or rear-range light, is octagonal. An elevated walkway links the two towers.

Travel information: From US Highway 31 in St. Joseph, follow Marina Drive south to Tiscornia Park. The park offers an excellent view of both lights. Visitors who want a close look can walk out on the pier.

St. Joseph North Pier Light

INDIANA

■ MICHIGAN CITY LIGHT ■
Michigan City (1837 and 1858)

Despite its name Michigan City is in Indiana, not Michigan. Located on the Lake Michigan shore just a few miles west of South Bend, it has been an important shipping point for the better part of two centuries. A lighthouse has served its busy harbor since 1837.

Michigan City Light

The city's first lighthouse, a simple brick-and-stone tower, was replaced by a more elaborate structure in 1858. Built with wood and brick at a cost of $8,000, it had a large central gable with a squat tower and lantern perched on the roof. At present the old lighthouse looks more like a schoolhouse or library building than a navigational aid. Out of service since 1904, when it was replaced by a nearby pier light, it was eventually handed over to the Michigan City Historical Society for use as a maritime museum. One exhibit portrays the story of Harriet Colfax, loyal keeper from 1861 until 1904.

> *Travel information:* In Michigan City take Heisman Harbor Road to Washington Park and the Michigan City Lighthouse Museum. Among many other fascinating exhibits, visitors will find the station's original fifth-order Fresnel lens that also served at the **Michigan City East Pier Light.** For more information contact The Old Lighthouse Museum, Michigan City Historical Society, Inc., P.O. Box 512, Michigan City, IN 46361; call (219) 872-6133, or see www.oldlighthousemuseum.org.

■ MICHIGAN CITY EAST PIER LIGHT ■
Michigan City (1904)

The Michigan City East Pier Lighthouse has guided vessels since the early twentieth century. Built on a square concrete platform, the structure has a pyramidal roof. An octagonal tower thrusts through the roof, raising the focal plane of the light more than fifty feet above the lake waters. Like many similar pier lighthouses, this one is encased in steel to protect it from storms.

It is said that during the 1920s keeper Ralph Moore hurried his three daughters indoors whenever he saw a certain speedboat roaring through the channel. "Get in the house!" he shouted. "That damn fool is coming." The particular "damn fool"

Michigan City East Pier Light

the keeper had in mind was none other than Al Capone, the Chicago gangster. Capone had a house on nearby Long Beach and reached it by boat rather than driving and chancing an ambush by rival bad guys.

Travel information: In Michigan City take Heisman Harbor Road to Washington Park. The pier and its lighthouse can be reached from the parking area. The nearby Michigan City Lighthouse Museum contains exhibits and information on the pier light. Call (219) 872-6133, or see www.oldlight housemuseum.org.

ILLINOIS

■ CHICAGO HARBOR LIGHT ■
Chicago (1832, 1859, and 1893)

One of the earliest lighthouses on the Great Lakes was built at the mouth of the Chicago River in 1832. Even then, the city sprouting along the lakefront was showing signs of the unrestrained growth and spirit that would turn it into one of the world's great metropolises. This first tower was not able to withstand the bashing weather of the river and harbor areas, and it was replaced in 1859. As the city grew, a series of lighthouses, built both on the mainland and on piers out in the harbor,

Chicago Harbor Light
Rick Polad

guided a tremendous volume of shipping to its wharves. Because the St. Lawrence Seaway makes Chicago a seaport, ships from every nation have docked here.

The Harbor Lighthouse seen here today originally stood on the mainland near the mouth of the river and the site of the city's first light tower—long since demolished. Built in 1893, the Harbor Lighthouse was given an especially fine third-order Fresnel lens, which had been intended for the **Point Loma Lighthouse** in Southern California. The lens had been a popular attraction of the Chicago Columbian Exposition. As a public relations gesture at the end of the big show, lighthouse officials placed the lens in the recently completed Chicago tower instead. In 1917, just before the United States entered World War I, the forty-eight-foot brick-and-steel tower was moved to the end of a harbor breakwater. Declared excess property by the US Coast Guard in 2005, ownership was transferred in 2009 to the City of Chicago. A museum is planned at this site, in spite of the difficulty of accessing the lighthouse far out into Chicago Harbor.

> *Travel information:* The lighthouse, declared a Chicago Landmark in 2003, is currently closed to the public but can be seen from many points along the Chicago waterfront. Perhaps the best viewpoint, although distant, is from the far end of the Navy Pier, which can be reached easily from Lakeshore Drive. Be sure to enjoy one of the city's famous piled-high hotdogs while visiting Navy Pier. The pier is also a good place to view the thirty-foot steel tower of the **Chicago Harbor Southeast Guidewall Lighthouse** (1938). For more information, see http://webapps.cityofchicago.org/landmarksweb.

■ GROSSE POINT LIGHT ■
Evanston (1873)

Among the most beautiful buildings on the Great Lakes, the Grosse Point Lighthouse is in many ways a superlative structure. Its 113-foot tower is among the tallest on the lakes, and its second-order Fresnel lens is more powerful than that of any other lake lighthouse. The conical brick tower, painted light yellow and trimmed in dark red, is exceptionally graceful. It was built to be the leading light to steer vessels into Chicago Harbor, then brimming with industrial lake traffic headed in and out of the port. Electricity powered an incandescent bulb within the huge lens beginning in 1935 when it was automated.

Although decommissioned by the Coast Guard in 1941, the Grosse Point Light continues to serve lake sailors as a private aid to navigation. Built during the 1870s for approximately $50,000, the station was meant to serve primarily as a coastal light. It was given a double-size keeper's dwelling and several outbuildings to house the fog signal and other equipment. The tower bricks deteriorated over the years, and in 1914 the walls received a protective layer of concrete. The striking sentinel has been designated a National Historic Landmark.

Travel information: Operated by the Evanston Parks Department as the key attraction of that city's lovely Lighthouse Park, the Grosse Point Lighthouse can be reached via Sheridan Road. The lighthouse and park are located near Central Avenue and the Evanston Art Museum. The grounds are open to the public daily. Contact Lighthouse Park District, 2601 Sheridan Road, Evanston, IL 60201; call (847) 328-6961, or see www.grossepoint lighthouse.net.

Grosse Point Light
Rick Polad

WISCONSIN

Lake Michigan

■ OLD SOUTHPORT (KENOSHA) LIGHT ■
Simmons Island, Kenosha (1866)

Kenosha's Simmons Island Park is home to "Old" Southport Lighthouse, so designated because it has been out of service for nearly a century. Built in 1866, just after the Civil War, the sixty-foot brick tower marked Kenosha Harbor for more than forty years. It replaced other lights that once marked the entrance to the harbor within protective Pike Creek, but only this light has endured time and the elements. It was decommissioned in 1906 after construction of the Kenosha North Pier Lighthouse. The Kenosha County Historical Society restored the tower and adjacent dwelling.

> *Travel information:* In Kenosha follow Fiftieth Street to Simmons Island Park, then take Fourth Avenue and Simmons Island Road to the lighthouse. Just down the beach from the Old Southport Lighthouse is the **Kenosha North Pier Lighthouse** (1906), now used as part of a range-light system. Accessible by foot, the pier lighthouse retains its original fourth-order Fresnel lens. For more information and days/hours of operation, contact the Kenosha County Historical Society, 220 51st Place, Kenosha, WI 53140; call (262) 654-5770, or see www.kenosha historycenter.org.

■ WIND POINT LIGHT ■
Racine (1866 and 1880)

Immediately after the Civil War, a pier light was built to guide ships into Racine Harbor. The beacon was never totally satisfactory, however, since Wind Point blocked the light from the view of mariners on vessels approaching from the north. To correct this problem, Congress appropriated $100,000 for construction of a true lighthouse on the point.

Begun in 1877 and completed three years later, the Wind Point Lighthouse was fitted with a pair of lenses. Its third-order Fresnel lens displayed a flashing white light, while a smaller fifth-order lens marked the dangerous Racine Shoals with a red light. The station is now automated, and its lenses have been replaced by an aeromarine beacon. The brick tower is 108 feet tall and attached by a passageway to its two-story dwelling.

> *Travel information:* From Route 32 south of Milwaukee, follow Three Mile Road and Lighthouse Drive to the station in the village of Wind Point. The grounds are open to the public, and the tower is open once a

month in summer. A friends group has turned the fog-signal building into a museum that interprets the maritime history of Racine County. It is generally open on weekends through October. For hours of operation and reservations for lighthouse tours, contact the Friends of Wind Point Lighthouse, 5110 Wind Point Road, Racine, WI 53402; to arrange a summer tour, call (262) 639-2026 or call the lighthouse, (262) 639-3777, or see www.windpoint-lighthouse.com.

Wind Point Light
Rick Polad

From Racine's Lake Festival Park, visitors can see the forty-foot tower of the old **Racine North Breakwater Light** (1872 and 1910) and the skeleton tower of the **Racine South Breakwater Light** (1903). From Route 32 turn toward the lake on Fourth Street.

■ NORTH POINT LIGHT ■
Milwaukee (1855, 1888, and 1912)

Milwaukee's first lighthouse, built several years before the Civil War, served for more than thirty years before erosion undercut the structure. A second tower, erected alongside the first, was ready for service in 1888. These early towers were similar in design—octagonal and made of cast iron or steel.

The 1888 tower was only thirty-five feet tall, and within two decades spreading tree limbs began to obscure its beacon. In 1912 three lighthouse engineers came up with a novel way to solve this problem. Rather than build an entirely new tower, they constructed a broad octagonal base, about forty feet

North Point Light
John Enright

high, and then placed the original tower on top of it. In this way the overall height was raised to seventy-four feet.

The lantern contains a fourth-order Fresnel lens, and its beacon helps mark the entrance to the Milwaukee River. The flashing light has a range of about twenty-one miles. The spacious keeper's dwelling, adjacent to the tower, is the original, dating from about 1855. Today the station has been beautifully restored and is maintained by the North Point Lighthouse Friends, Inc., which leases the property from Milwaukee County and opens the light station to the public.

Travel information: The lighthouse is located in historic Lake Park, at 2650 North Wahl Avenue in Milwaukee. Follow Lincoln Memorial Drive to McKinley Park, then North Terrace to North Wahl. For information on the maritime museum, events, and lighthouse tours (generally year-round on Saturday afternoons), contact the North Point Lighthouse Friends, Inc., at 2650 N. Wahl Avenue, Milwaukee, WI 53211; call (414) 332-6754, or see www.northpointlighthouse.org.

Near downtown Milwaukee are the **Milwaukee Breakwater Lighthouse** (1926) and **Milwaukee Pierhead Lighthouse** (1907). The Pierhead Light can be reached by walking along the harbor pier, reached via North Harbor, Polk, and East Erie streets. The blocky Breakwater Lighthouse cannot be reached from land but can be seen from the pier.

■ PORT WASHINGTON LIGHT ■
Port Washington (1860 and 1935)

Established shortly before the Civil War, the Old Port Washington Lighthouse dates from a time when the western shore of Lake Michigan was still partly wilderness. Shining from a bluff overlooking the lake, the light marked a busy little harbor a few miles north of Milwaukee. After nearly seventy-five years of service, the light was removed from the rooftop lantern at the original station and placed in a concrete tower at the end of a harbor

Port Washington Light

breakwater. The wishbone-shaped breakwater tower remains an active aid to navigation, while the earlier lighthouse on the bluff now serves as a museum. The Port Washington Historical Society hopes to restore the old lighthouse to its original appearance.

Travel information: The first Port Washington Lighthouse—now a museum—is located at Johnson and Power Streets atop St. Mary's Hill. The lighthouse and museum are open weekends from May through October or by appointment. Contact the Port Washington Historical Society, P.O. Box 491, Port Washington, WI 53074; call (262) 284-7240, or see www.portwashingtonhistoricalsociety.org. Generally, the lighthouse is open on summer weekends; however, to schedule a special group tour year-round, call the light station at (262) 284-7240 and leave a message, or see www.portwashingtonhistoricalsociety.org. The breakwater light can be seen from the Port Washington waterfront but is best viewed from a boat. About thirty miles north of Port Washington is the **Sheboygan Breakwater Light** (1915), a conical cast-iron tower that can be seen from Deland Park in downtown Sheboygan.

■ MANITOWOC BREAKWATER LIGHT ■
Manitowoc (1840 and 1918)

Manitowoc Breakwater Light

Still an active port today, Manitowoc had its own lighthouse as early as 1840. The present breakwater lighthouse—a steel tower at the end of a long concrete pier—dates from 1918. For many years this light guided the hefty steamers that ferried railroad cars back and forth across Lake Michigan. Nowadays, it guides the automobile and passenger ferries that link the lake's Wisconsin shores with the Michigan port of Ludington. It is being bid for by the executive director of the Wisconsin Maritime Museum and is slated for restoration.

Travel information: For a close-up view of the lighthouse, from Interstate 43 southwest of Manitowoc, take exit 148 and follow Highway 151 to downtown Manitowoc. Highway 151 will eventually become Washington Street, from which you will turn left onto 8th Street and cross the Manitowoc River. Just after the river, turn right onto Maritime Drive, and follow it to the marina. Walk to the end of the breakwater on the north side of the Manitowoc Harbor. A more romantic view of the old tower can be had from the decks of the Lake Michigan ferry; call (800) 841-4243. While in Manitowoc, don't miss the Wisconsin Maritime Museum, where you'll find the fifth-order Fresnel lens that once graced the lantern room of the Manitowoc tower. For the status on this lighthouse, contact the museum at 75 Maritime Drive, Manitowoc, WI 54220; call (866) 724-2356, or see www.wisconsinmaritime.org.

■ RAWLEY POINT LIGHT ■
Two Rivers (1853 and 1894)

A deadly shoal reaches nearly a mile from Rawley Point into Lake Michigan. After several tragic wrecks a light was finally placed on the point to warn ships of the danger. Beaming from a small tower perched on the roof of the keeper's dwelling, it served well until 1894, when the current, soaring tower was completed. More than 110 feet tall, the present tower is a steel skeleton structure with a central cylinder braced by eight legs. At the top is a three-level lantern complex equipped with an unusually powerful aeromarine beacon. Its light can be seen from twenty-eight miles away.

Rawley Point Light

Travel information: The tower and adjacent two-and-one-half-story dwelling, once a Coast Guard residence, are available to the public for rental. The station is surrounded by lush and beautiful Point Beach State Park, which offers camping, picnicking, hiking, and a wonderful opportunity to view the lighthouse.

From Two Rivers follow County Road O and Sandy Bay Road to the park. For reservations at the light station, contact the Coast Guard Station Two Rivers, 13 East Street, Two Rivers, WI; call (414) 747-7185, or see www.uscg.mil/mwr/lodging/RawleyPoint Cottage.asp. For park information call (414) 794-7480.

Off Twenty-second and Jackson streets in Two Rivers is the upper portion of the old **Two Rivers Pierhead Lighthouse** (1883). It stands adjacent to the Rogers Street Fishing Village Museum; call (920) 793-5905.

Two Rivers Pierhead Light
Rick Polad

■ KEWAUNEE PIERHEAD LIGHT ■
Kewaunee (1891 and 1931)

A forty-three-foot square tower attached to a breakwater fog-signal building, the existing Kewaunee Pierhead Lighthouse has stood since 1931, near the height of the Great Depression. An earlier tower had guided vessels in and out of Kewaunee's harbor since 1891. Still in use, the beacon is focused by the station's original fifth-order Fresnel lens.

Kewaunee Pierhead Light

Travel information:
Located at the end of the pier on the north side of the Kewaunee River entrance, the lighthouse is difficult to reach from land and is best seen from a boat. A few miles to the north is the **Algoma Pierhead Light** (1932), a red conical steel tower at the end of a breakwater defining the Ahnapee River entrance near Algoma. The light, produced by a fifth-order Fresnel lens, remains in operation. The tower has been transferred to the City of Kewaunee.

■ STURGEON BAY SHIP CANAL LIGHT ■
Sturgeon Bay (1899)

Lighthouse Service engineers designed an experimental tower for the Sturgeon Bay Lighthouse, completed in 1899. Held erect by latticework buttresses, it proved unequal to the strong winds howling in off Lake Michigan. With the slender central column its only support, the tower became a tuning fork, vibrating constantly. Various methods were used to steady the tower; finally, major modifications to the ninety-eight-foot steel-cylinder tower in 1903 allowed for evenly distributed weight of the structure and the cessation of severe vibration. The station's third-order Fresnel lens remains in operation.

Travel information: Take Highway 42/57 north across Ship Canal; turn right (east) onto Utah Street, and follow signs to the Coast Guard Station. As part of an active Coast Guard station, the lighthouse is closed. Visitors may walk the path through the station, or it can be photographed and enjoyed from a nearby pier. The same pier offers a view of the **Sturgeon Bay Ship Canal North Pierhead Lighthouse** (1882 and 1899) with its metal catwalk, octagonal lantern, and striking red roof. In Sturgeon Bay follow Canal Drive to Lake Forest Park Road, and park near the station entrance.

■ BAILEYS HARBOR REAR RANGE LIGHT ■
Baileys Harbor (1870)

To guide vessels into Baileys Harbor, near the far end of the peninsula that forms Door County, Wisconsin, the government established a pair of range lights in 1870. These lights replaced an older, single-lens lighthouse located on a small island far out in the harbor. The front-range light was housed in a squat, twenty-one-foot wooden tower down beside the lake. The rear-range light shone from a gablelike extension on the roof of a clapboard dwelling about one thousand feet from the water. Automated in 1930, the station was afterward cared for by Lutheran ministers, who used the dwelling as a parsonage right up until the lights were discontinued in the 1960s.

Baileys Harbor Rear Range Light
Rick Polad

Travel information: Although out of service for many years, the Baileys Harbor Range Lighthouses remain in excellent condition. From Highway 57 in Baileys Harbor, take Ridge Drive. The schoolhouselike rear-range lighthouse stands on the right. The **Baileys Harbor Front Range Lighthouse** (1870), which looks much like a big chess pawn, is located about one-fifth of a mile away. The ruins of **Old Baileys Harbor Lighthouse** (1851) are located on a privately owned island out in the harbor. The old tower, with its tall birdcage-style lantern, can be seen from the shore near the far end of Ridge Drive. For information on Door County lighthouses, including **Cana Island, Chambers Island, Eagle Bluff, Pottawatomie, Pilot Island, Plum Island, Baileys Harbor Range Lights,** and **Sherwood Point,** contact the Door County Maritime Museum & Lighthouse Preservation Society, Inc., 120 N. Madison Avenue, Sturgeon Bay, WI 54235; call the museum at (920) 743-5958, or see or www.dcmm.org; call the historical society at (920) 743-4945, or see www.doorcountyhistoricalsociety.org.

■ CANA ISLAND LIGHT ■
Baileys Harbor (1870)

On a clear night the impressive Cana Island Lighthouse throws its beam seventeen miles out into Lake Michigan. Established in 1870, the light marks the northern approaches to Baileys Harbor. To help the eighty-six-foot tower and adjacent one-and-a-half-story dwelling withstand the lake's prodigious storms, construction crews built them with brick. The light yellow bricks, however, weathered more rapidly than had been expected, and after a few decades the tower had begun to crumble. In 1902, to protect it lighthouse officials had it encased in a protective cocoon made of individual steel plates riveted together and then painted white. The station's original third-order Fresnel lens remains in operation.

Travel information: With its pristine island setting, the Cana Island station is among the most beautiful lighthouses in America. Take County Road Q north from Baileys Harbor; then follow Cana Island Road and Cana Cove Road to the lighthouse. The Door County Maritime Museum leases the station from the US Coast Guard, and it is open to the public until 5:00 p.m. daily during warm-weather months from May through October. Call the museum at (920) 743-5958. Please be mindful of the quiet residential area surrounding the light; watch for children playing, and be courteous by parking only in designated areas. For more information contact the Door County Maritime Museum & Lighthouse Preservation Society, Inc.; call (920) 743-4945, or see www.dcmm.org/canaisland.html.

■ POTTAWATOMIE (ROCK ISLAND) LIGHT ■
Gills Rock (1836 and 1858)

A chain of rock-strewn islands forms a lakeward extension of the long, daggerlike peninsula of Door County. The jagged shores of these islands and the shoals that lie between them have claimed countless vessels. To guide ships safely around these formidable obstacles and toward Green Bay, the government established on Rock Island, at the end of the chain, one of the first light stations in the western Great Lakes. Completed in 1836, the original Pottawatomie Lighthouse—named for an Indian tribe—served until 1858, when a hurricanelike storm swept it into the lake. Given massive walls of stone, the combination keeper's residence and light tower that replaced it still stands. Unfortunately, the lantern was removed after the station was discontinued during the 1920s.

The lighthouse has been restored to its 1910 appearance; live-in docents conduct tours of the historic light during summer, which includes a visit to the tower and the replica fourth-order Fresnel lens.

Travel information: The lighthouse is located in Wisconsin's Rock Island State Park. Visitors must take a ferry from Northport, at the northern end of Highway 42, to Washington Island, then a second ferry to Rock Island. Contact Washington Island Ferry, Washington Island, WI 54246; for ferry schedules call (920) 847-2546 or (800) 223-2094. The ferry provides excellent views of the **Plum Island Range Lighthouse** (1897), a white skeleton

Cana Island Light
Rick Polad

tower, and the **Pilot Island Lighthouse** (1858), a historic brick combination tower and dwelling. Tours of the Pottawatomie Lighthouse are offered by the Friends of Rock Island State Park, which operates and maintains the lighthouse, from Memorial Day through Columbus Day; call (715) 823-6873. For information on Rock Island State Park, call (920) 847-2235 or the Newport State Park (920) 854-2500, or see http://uniontel.net.

■ EAGLE BLUFF LIGHT ■
Ephraim (1868)

Marking a safe channel from Lake Michigan into Green Bay, the Eagle Bluff Light first shone in 1868, the same year that U. S. Grant was elected president. Its square forty-three-foot brick tower was set at a diagonal into the side of the one-and-a-half-story dwelling. This made it easier for keepers to reach the tower when cold winds blew in off the lake. Ironically, there has been no full-time keeper here since 1909, as this was among the first American lighthouses to be automated. Still active, the lighthouse has done its work alone now for almost nine decades.

Eagle Bluff Light

The old keeper's residence, which has been attractively restored, is used as a museum by the Door County Historical Society. The lighthouse and museum are among the many attractions of Peninsula State Park, which also offers hiking, fishing, swimming, and golf.

Travel information: Follow Highway 42 to Fish Creek and the entrance to Peninsula State Park. Once inside the park, follow Shore Drive for about four miles to the lighthouse; for more information or tour schedules, call the Door County Historical Society at (920) 743-4945, or the lighthouse at (920) 421-3636. Several miles to the west is the boarded-up **Chambers Island Lighthouse** (1867) in Gibraltar Township Park overlooking Green Bay. Replaced by a steel tower in 1961, the octagonal brick tower and attached gabled dwelling have been obtained by a private individual who continues to work on improvements. Visitors are welcome when a caretaker is present, but the best way to see this and all of Door County's historic lighthouses is during the Annual Door County Lighthouse Festival every summer. For more information see www.dcmm.org/lighthouses.html or http://eagleblufflighthouse.doorcountyhistoricalsociety.org.

■ SHERWOOD POINT LIGHT ■
Sturgeon Bay (1883)

Completed in 1883, the square thirty-seven-foot brick tower is attached to its residence. Although the Coast Guard still uses the handsome, though small, keeper's dwelling as a residence, the light is automated. This was the last lighthouse on the Great Lakes with a full-time staff, and it was not automated until 1983. The station's fourth-order Fresnel lens was removed in 2001, but at one time its light could be seen from up to eighteen miles away. A small, pyramidal fog-signal building stands

Sherwood Point Light
Rick Polad

near the tower. During its heyday, the light teamed with the Sturgeon Bay Lighthouse to guide ships hauling lumber through the passage between Green Bay and Lake Michigan.

Travel information: As part of an active Coast Guard station, the lighthouse is off-limits to the public except during the Annual Door County Lighthouse Festival in the summer; see Travel information for **Eagle Bluff Lighthouse.** It is best viewed from the water. The original fourth-order Fresnel lens is on display at the Door County Maritime Museum, 120 N. Madison Street, Sturgeon Bay, WI 54235; call (920) 743-5958, or see www.dcmm.org/sherwood.html.

Built on a caisson in open water across the bay is the **Pestigo Reef Lighthouse** (1934) that warned mariners of the three-mile-long reef in shallow waters, an extension of Prestigo Point, which presented great danger to ships plying in and out of southern Green Bay. This light is accessed and maintained only by the Coast Guard.

MICHIGAN

Upper Peninsula

■ SAND POINT LIGHT ■
Escanaba (1868)

Vessels approaching Escanaba must take care to avoid Sand Point and a cluster of nearby shoals. To warn mariners away from these dangers, the government established a lighthouse on Sand Point in 1868. A fixed red light shone from the square brick tower, beaming toward the lake from just over forty feet above the water.

Sand Point Light
Rick Polad

The Coast Guard discontinued the light in 1939, after channel dredging rendered it obsolete, and converted the building into a residence, including removal of the lantern room, and used it as a residence until 1985, when it was turned over to the Delta County Historical Society. Since then the society has restored the Sand Point Lighthouse to its original appearance, new lantern and all. The beacon, focused by a fourth-order Fresnel lens, is once again operational.

> *Travel information:* The lighthouse is located in Ludington Park, just off US Highways 2 and 41 and is now a museum. Contact the Delta County Historical Society, 16 Water Plant Road, Escanaba, MI 49829; call (906) 789-6790, or http://deltahistorical.org.

■ SEUL CHOIX POINT LIGHT ■
Gulliver (1895)

One of only a few safe harbors on the north shore of Lake Michigan, Seul Choix was given its name, meaning "only choice," by early French explorers. Seul Choix Point stands guard over this inviting harbor. Even so, it did not receive a lighthouse until late in the nineteenth century. Congress finally appropriated money for the project in 1886, but partly because of its remote location, the lighthouse was not completed and operational until 1895.

The conical brick tower, seventy feet tall, was topped by a ten-sided, cast-iron lantern, giving its third-order Fresnel lens a focal plane just over eighty feet above the lake. When the Coast Guard automated the lighthouse in 1972, the Fresnel lens was removed and replaced by an airport-style beacon, visible from about seventeen miles out in the lake.

The two-story brick keeper's dwelling still stands and is attached to the tower by an enclosed brick passageway. Although the structure and the grounds are now the property of the State of Michigan, this is still an operating light station. The lighthouse has been beautifully restored and the keeper's quarters are furnished with antiques donated by keepers' families.

Seul Choix Point Light

Travel information: Turn off US Highway 2 at Gulliver and follow Port Inland Road and then County Road 431 to the lighthouse. The tower and dwelling are open daily to the public from May through September with guided tours offered. There is a small but worthy museum in the old fog-signal building. Contact the Gulliver Historical Society at R.R. 1, P.O. Box 79, 672N West Gulliver Lake Road, Gulliver, MI 49840; call (906) 283-3183; for operational hours or to arrange a special tour see www.great lakelighthouse.com.

■ POINT IROQUOIS LIGHT ■
Brimley (1856 and 1871)

Point Iroquois gets its name from a massacre that took place here in 1662. A war party sent westward by the Iroquois Confederation was set upon and slaughtered on this point by an army of Ojibwas.

Ships passing by the point are also in danger of ambush. On their port side are the reefs near Gros Cap in Canada, while on their starboard side are the ship-killing rocks near Point Iroquois. The St. Marys River became a heavily trafficked thoroughfare

Point Iroquois Light

after the Soo Locks connected Superior to the other lakes in 1856, and since that time many vessels have been lost while approaching the river. Often, an otherwise minor navigational error can be fatal here.

To help captains enter the river safely, a small lighthouse was built on Point Iroquois not long after the locks opened. Fitted with a fourth-order Fresnel lens, this modest wooden structure served until 1871, when it was replaced by an impressive sixty-five-foot brick tower and dwelling that still stand today.

Its beacon discontinued in 1965, the lighthouse is now part of the Hiawatha National Forest, which maintains and operates the lighthouse, museum, and gift shop here.

Travel information: From Interstate 75 take Highway 28 for about 8 miles to the town of Brimley. Then follow Six Mile Road and Lakeshore Drive to the Lighthouse. For more information, contact the Point Iroquois Lighthouse, 12942 West Lakeshore Drive, Brimley, MI; call (906) 437-5272, or see www.fs.usda.gov. The tower is open to the public during summer months through October and has a fourth-order Fresnel lens on loan for display although the original lens resides in the Smithsonian National Museum of American History. Original Lighthouse Service fixtures and nineteenth-century furnishings are on display.

■ WHITEFISH POINT LIGHT ■
Whitefish Point, Sault Ste. Marie (1848 and 1861)

Whitefish Point Light

On the evening of November 16, 1975, the huge iron-ore freighter *Edmund Fitzgerald* plowed through a powerful storm, heading for the relatively safe waters just beyond Whitefish Point. She never made it. The enormous ship, longer than two football fields, disappeared, along with twenty-nine crewmen, a few miles north of the point. The sinking of the *Edmund Fitzgerald* gave rise to a legend and a popular ballad by Gordon Lightfoot.

Ironically, on the night the "Big Fitz" met her end, the lighthouse on Whitefish Point was out of service. The storm had cut the power supply to the station. On thousands of other nights, however—almost continuously since 1848—mariners have been able to rely on the guidance of the station's beacon.

Recognizing the strategic nature of the point and its importance to shipping, the government established a light station here in 1848. Its masonry tower gave way to an iron-pile skeleton structure shortly before the Civil War. Built during President Lincoln's administration, the structure is braced by a network of iron supports, and the tower's central iron cylinder is more than eighty feet tall and topped by a metal lantern. The open design was intended to take stress off the building during high winds and storms like the one that sank the *Fitzgerald*.

Automated in 1970, the tower now hosts one of the new genres of LED lights. The station now serves as home to the Great Lakes Shipwreck Museum and the Great Lakes Shipwreck Historical Society. Here imaginative visitors can relive the last moments of the *Fitz* and many other ill-fated ships claimed forever by the lakes. The lighthouse is open for climbing during summer months.

Travel information: The lighthouse and its museum, housed in the former keeper's residence, can be reached from the Mackinac Bridge by taking Interstate 75 north to M–123 at exit 352 and the town of Paradise. From Paradise follow Wire Road to North Whitefish Point Road. Contact the Whitefish Point Great Lakes Shipwreck Museum, 18335 N. Whitefish Point Road, Paradise, MI 49768; call (888) 492-3747 or the museum's administrative office (906) 635-1742, or see www.shipwreckmuseum.com.

▪ CRISP POINT LIGHT ▪
West of Paradise (1904)

Veteran of over a century of service to mariners, the Crisp Point Lighthouse on Michigan's sparsely settled Upper Peninsula very nearly succumbed to the fate of far too many historic light towers. More or less abandoned by the government in 1989, it was all but destroyed by weather and erosion. Over the last couple of decades, however, an idealistic couple, the late Don and Nellie Ross, cofounders of the Crisp Point Historical Society, made

Crisp Point Light

saving the tower a personal crusade, and they attained notable success that continues today through volunteers. The advance of Lake Superior has been checked by a stone breakwater, and the lighthouse has been restored.

Travel information: Located eighteen miles from the main road, a trip to Crisp Point is something of an adventure, but for those prepared to make the effort, it is a worthwhile one. The tower is open occasionally when volunteers are present during summer months; the grounds remain open year-round. For more information, contact the Crisp Point Historical Society, 450 W Marr Road, Howell, MI 48855. The group has an informative website at www.crisppointlighthouse.org.

■ AU SABLE POINT LIGHT ■
Grand Marais (1874)

For many years sailors dreaded the eighty miles of dark shoreline that stretched westward from Whitefish Point. Unmarked by any navigational light, these dangerous shores claimed dozens of ships. To fill the gap and save lives, a lighthouse was placed on Au Sable Point in 1874.

Au Sable Point Light

The eighty-seven-foot brick tower was built on a rise, placing the beacon 107 feet above the surface of the lake. Its third-order Fresnel lens displayed a fixed white light. The attached, two-story dwelling was spacious, but the keepers who lived in it knew theirs was one of the most remote light stations in America. The nearest town, Grand Marais, lay more than twelve miles away, and there was no road. Keepers either hiked in or came by boat.

Perhaps because of its isolation, the Coast Guard automated the station in 1958, turning the property and buildings over to the National Park Service for inclusion in Pictured Rocks National Lakeshore. A museum here exhibits artifacts formerly at the Grand Marais Maritime Museum.

> *Travel information:* Just as keepers once did, visitors today must walk to this lighthouse, located in Pictured Rocks National Lakeshore on the Michigan Upper Peninsula. From Highway 28 take Highway 77 north for about twenty-five miles to Grand Marais. Then follow the gravel-surfaced Alger County Road H–58 for another twelve miles to the Hurricane Campground. A trail provides access to the shore and the lighthouse. Tours are offered daily except Monday and Tuesday during June through August. Write to Pictured Rocks National Lakeshore, N8391 Sand Point Road, P.O. Box 40, Munsing, MI 49862; call the Pictured Rocks National Lakeshore/Hiawatha National Forest Interagency Visitor Center at (906) 387-3700, or see www .nps.gov/piro/historyculture/ausablelightstation.htm.

■ MUNISING RANGE LIGHTS ■
Munising (1908)

For nearly a century the narrow, safe channel through Munising Bay has been marked by two extraordinary lighthouses. Unlike most range-light structures, where the rear tower is taller, here the forward tower is by far the taller and more impressive of the two. The fifty-eight-foot steel front-range tower stands near the lakeshore, while the squat rear-range tower is located on a hillside some distance away. At night, both make their presence known with locomotive-style headlamps.

Travel information: The Munising Front Range tower can be found just west of town off Route 28 at 604 West Munising Avenue. The rear-range tower is two blocks south at the end of Hemlock Street. Both lights are part of Pictured Rocks National Lakeshore. See Travel information for **Au Sable Point Light.**

Munising Rear Range Lights

■ MARQUETTE HARBOR LIGHT ■
Marquette (1853 and 1866)

With the discovery of copper and iron in the mountains of the Michigan Upper Peninsula, Marquette became an important port. A lighthouse built here in 1853 guided ships into the city's harbor. Of poor construction quality, however, it lasted only a few years. The square masonry tower that replaced it in 1866 proved very much more durable, even withstanding an added second story in 1909, and still serves to this day. A fourth-order classic lens at one time shone from atop the forty-foot tower, but an automated aeromarine beacon has taken its place.

In 2002 the Marquette Maritime Museum leased the lighthouse and acreage from the Coast Guard.

Marquette Harbor Light

Travel information: From US Highway 41 in Marquette, follow Lake Street to the lighthouse. The tower is located on an active Coast Guard station; however, museum guides take visitors through the station to the nearby Marquette Maritime Museum beginning in May. For complete tour schedules contact the museum at 300 Lakeshore Boulevard, Marquette, MI 49855; call (906) 226-2006, or see http://mqtmaritimemuseum.com.

■ BIG BAY LIGHT ■
Big Bay (1896)

Many ships have foundered in the treacherous waters just to the north of the famed Huron Mountains. To help mariners find their way safely, the government established a major light at Big Bay in 1896. It shone from a square brick tower attached to a two-story dwelling. The light was automated shortly before World War II, and in 1961 it was moved to a nearby steel skeleton tower. The old lighthouse was then converted for use as a private residence and later as a bed-and-breakfast inn that offers stunning views out over vast Lake Superior.

Travel information: The inn is located on Lighthouse Road, about three miles north of Big Bay. Write to Big Bay Point Lighthouse, 3 Lighthouse Road, Big Bay, MI 49808, or call (906) 345-9957, or see www.bigbaylight house.com.

Big Bay Light

■ SAND HILLS LIGHT ■
Near Eagle River (1919)

An imposing brick edifice with a square tower, the Sand Hills Lighthouse reflects the modernist style prevalent during the early twentieth century. The design is similar to that of Alaska's **Scotch Cap Lighthouse,** which was destroyed by a tsunami during the 1940s. The lighthouse replaced the discontinued Eagle River Light. After seeing action during World War II as a barracks, it was decommissioned by the Coast Guard during the 1950s and its fourth-order Fresnel lens removed. The building stood empty for decades, its interior all but gutted by time. Its walls remained solid, however, and a local lighthouse lover eventually bought the property. Handsomely restored, it is now an attractive lakeside inn.

Travel information: Located off Five Mile Point Road to the west of Highway 41, the Sand Hills Lighthouse Inn has eight delightful guest rooms. Contact the inn at Five Mile Point Road, P.O. Box 298, Ahmeek, MI 49901. Reservations should be made far in advance; call (906) 337-1744, or see www.sandhillslighthouseinn.com.

Sand Hills Light

■ COPPER HARBOR LIGHT ■
Copper Harbor (1849 and 1866)

Winters on Michigan's Upper Peninsula are notoriously severe, but the weather did not deter the rapid development of mining when deposits of copper were found during the 1840s. The richest copper veins were located on the Keweenaw Peninsula, which thrusts to the northeast toward the center of Lake Superior. Ship traffic in and out of Copper Harbor expanded rapidly to carry the ore to markets in the east.

Copper Harbor Light

Shippers and government officials soon saw the need for a lighthouse to guide the big freighters in and out of the harbor.

A stone tower with detached dwelling, it was located on a point near the harbor entrance. Upgraded and given a Fresnel lens in 1856, it was replaced with an entirely new structure shortly after the Civil War. A square stone tower with a small attached dwelling, this second Copper Harbor Lighthouse still stands, although its duties have been taken over by a beacon displayed from a nearby skeleton tower.

Travel information: The town of Copper Harbor is located at the far northern end of Route 26 or Route 41. The lighthouse is now part of Fort

Wilkins State Park. The park and lighthouse are generally open from mid-May through Labor Day. For park and lighthouse hours see www.michigan.gov/ftwilkins. Public access to the lighthouse is via ferry service from Copper Harbor Municipal Marina; see http://marinas.com. Call the park at (906) 289-4215.

Also in the area is the wooden **Copper Harbor Rear Range Lighthouse** (1869). Far to the east of Copper Harbor, off the tip of the Keweenaw Peninsula, is the iron-pile skeleton tower **Manitou Island Lighthouse** (1861). Its light, once produced by a third-order Fresnel lens, is now a modern optic that remains active. The Coast Guard maintains the iron skeleton tower.

■ EAGLE HARBOR LIGHT ■
Eagle Harbor (1851 and 1871)

Like Copper Harbor to the east, Eagle Harbor became a busy ore-shipping point during the copper-and-iron boom years of the nineteenth and early twentieth centuries. From 1851 onward this important Keweenaw Peninsula port was marked by a key navigational light. During its first few years of service, the station was equipped with an outmoded lamp and reflector optic but received a Fresnel lens in 1857.

Lake Superior's notorious weather took a heavy toll on the lighthouse, and it lasted less than twenty years. The forty-foot octagonal tower and attached dwelling seen here today date back to 1871. For many years the tower had a fourth-order Fresnel lens, but it was replaced by a modern aerobeacon in 1968 and later automated in 1980.

Eagle Harbor Light

The Keweenaw Historical Society now owns and maintains four museums at the light station.

Travel information: Follow Route 26 down the Keweenaw Peninsula and turn left toward the lake just before entering Eagle Harbor. The Keweenaw Historical Society, which has restored the station to its early-twentieth-century appearance, maintains a nautical museum in one of the outer buildings and offers the Light Keeper's Cottage for rent. The complex is open generally from mid-June until early October, weather permitting. Contact the society at Eagle Harbor Lighthouse Complex and Museum, 670 Lighthouse Road, Eagle Harbor, MI 49950; for reservations, call (906) 289-4613, or see www.keweenawhistory.org.

WISCONSIN

Lake Superior

■ APOSTLE ISLANDS LIGHTS ■

Apostle Islands National Lakeshore: Michigan Island Light (1857 and 1930); Raspberry Island Light (1863); Outer Island Light (1874); Sand Island Light (1881); Devils Island Light (1891); La Pointe Light (1858 and 1896); Chequamegon Point Light (1897)

According to the National Park Service, "There are two light towers at Michigan Island. One was supposed to be built somewhere else, and the second originally was elsewhere!"

To explain: Built in 1857, **Michigan Island Lighthouse** is the oldest of the six light stations in the Apostle Islands. Like many other lights in the upper Midwest, this one went into operation not long after the Soo Locks opened Lake Superior to shipping from the other lakes. The whitewashed tower and dwelling, with pitched roof and dormers, give this station the look of a New England lighthouse.

The Michigan Island Light guided vessels by focusing a light through an impressive three-and-a-half-order Fresnel lens, long since removed, along the eastern side of the Apostles for more than seventy years. Its duties were taken over in 1930 by a skeleton-style tower moved here from Schooner Ledge in Maine. The 102-foot tower

Michigan Island Light

was originally built in 1880 and consists of a central steel cylinder braced by six legs. The light, known as "New" Michigan Light remains active and can be seen from up to sixteen miles out in Lake Superior.

Originally, the Michigan Island Light station had been intended for nearby Long Island. Once the mistake became apparent, officials commissioned a lighthouse for the correct location. Completed in 1858, the wood-frame "Old" **La Pointe Lighthouse** on Long Island served until 1896, when it was completely remodeled

Raspberry Island Light

Outer Island Light

Sand Island Light

Devils Island Light

into living quarters for the keepers. Nearby, the "New" La Pointe cast-iron skeleton tower began operation in 1896 to serve maritime traffic among Michigan, Madeleine, and Long Islands. That same year, the **Chequamegon Lighthouse** was also built toward the southern end of Long Island. Both lights survive, but only "New" **La Pointe Lighthouse** remains an active aid to navigation.

In addition to the Old and New Michigan Island and the Old and New La Pointe Lights, the Apostle Islands National Lakeshore in Wisconsin can boast five other historic light towers including the **Raspberry Island Lighthouse** (1863), **Outer Island Lighthouse** (1874), **Sand Island Lighthouse** (1881), **Devils Island Lighthouse** (1891), and **Chequamegon Point** (1897). Together, these excellently maintained structures continue to undergo restoration and compose one of the nation's finest collections of lighthouses and form what is, in effect, an outdoor nautical/lighthouse museum. Special programs are offered at Raspberry Island Lighthouse. Devils Island Light is the only one of the group to retain its original Fresnel lens; visitors—many come by personal boat or kayak—will find a volunteer light keeper during summer months to give tower tours twice daily.

Travel information: Visitors should stop first at the lakeshore headquarters, located in the Old Courthouse in Bayfield, Wisconsin. Write to Apostle Islands National Lakeshore, Chief of Interpretation, Route 1, P.O. Box 4, Bayfield, WI 54814; call (715) 779-3397. Apostle Island Cruise Service passes by these lights during warm-weather months. Trips regularly go past all Apostle Island lights except Outer Island. Being the most remote of the light stations, it is visited only during special trips during September as part of their lighthouse celebration activities; call the cruise service at (715) 779-3925.

MINNESOTA

■ DULUTH BREAKWATER LIGHTS ■
Duluth (1901)

Built just after the turn of the twentieth century, these three lighthouses mark the breakwaters that define the channel connecting the Duluth Inner Harbor with Lake Superior. The **South Breakwater Outer Lighthouse** consists of a thirty-five-foot tower rising from the corner of a squat brick fog-signal building. Its fourth-order Fresnel lens remains in service.

Erected at the same time was the **South Breakwater Inner Lighthouse,** a steel-cylinder tower with supporting skeleton framework. This lighthouse, somewhat shorter than its neighbor, displays a flashing light produced by a fourth-order bull's-eye lens.

The **Duluth North Breakwater Lighthouse** entered service during the spring of 1910. Its metal frame is enclosed by riveted steel plates. The lantern atop its thirty-seven-foot tower contained a fifth-order Fresnel lens.

Travel information: From Interstate 35 North take the Highway 61 exit 256-B and follow signs to the Duluth waterfront area and Canal Park Drive. The park is located beside the famous Aerial Bridge, only a few blocks from

Duluth Breakwater Lights

downtown Duluth. The lighthouses are on piers beside the ship canal. Adjacent to the canal and near the bridge is Lake Superior Maritime Visitor Center, which contains many fascinating exhibits on the history of Lake Superior and its lighthouses. For more information, contact the Lake Superior Maritime Marine Museum and Historic Canal Park, 600 South Lake Avenue, Duluth, MN 55802; call (218) 727-2497, or see www.lsmma.com.

▪ TWO HARBORS LIGHT ▪
Two Harbors (1892)

Built in 1892 to guide iron-ore freighters and other vessels to the busy loading docks nearby, the Two Harbors Lighthouse remains an active aid to navigation. The light emanates from a fifty-foot square tower set into the southwest corner of a two-story brick dwelling. Situated on a grassy knoll, the tower places the focal plane of its light almost eighty feet above the lake surface.

Two Harbors Light

The lantern room once contained a fourth-order Fresnel lens, but it was replaced with a matched pair of aeromarine beacons in 1970. The Coast Guard automated the station in 1981 and later turned it over to the Lake County Historical Society for use as a museum.

Travel information: From Highway 61 turn toward the lake on First Street, then right on First Avenue and left onto Third Street. A parking area at the end of Third Street provides access to the lighthouse and its excellent museum. Visitors will find a broad array of maritime and lighthouse exhibits; call (218) 834-4898. Several guest rooms are available at the Lighthouse; call (888) 832-5606. Nearby is the **Two Harbors East Breakwater Lighthouse,** a spindly metal structure with a small lantern room only twenty-five feet above the water.

▪ SPLIT ROCK LIGHT ▪
Two Harbors (1910)

An octagonal, yellow-brick structure, the Split Rock tower is only fifty-four feet tall, but the cliff beneath it soars more than 120 feet above the lake. This makes Split Rock, with its focal plane nearly 170 feet above the water, one of the loftiest lighthouses on the Great Lakes. It also makes this one of the most spectacular and frequently photographed lighthouses in America—or the world. Ironically, Split Rock is no longer an active aid to navigation, but rather a highly popular maritime museum.

Built in 1910, the lighthouse owes its existence to a hurricanelike blizzard that struck the Great Lakes in November of 1905. This mighty storm drove more than

Split Rock Light

thirty sizable ore boats and freighters onto Lake Superior's rocky shores. The calamity convinced officials that the system of navigation aids on Lake Superior must be improved. The most important improvement undertaken was construction of a lighthouse on Split Rock near where the freighter *William Edenborn* had met its end during the storm. In all, the project cost taxpayers some $72,000.

The station's flashing light, seen from up to twenty-two miles out in the lake, was produced by a third-order bivalve-style Fresnel lens—still in place—that looks something like a huge clamshell. It served until 1969, when the Coast Guard decommissioned the lighthouse and handed it over to the state of Minnesota for use as a park and museum.

Travel information: The Split Rock Park and Lighthouse are located about twenty miles northeast of Two Harbors on Highway 61. Open year-round, the park offers a fascinating history center as well as camping facilities, hiking trails, and picnicking areas. The lighthouse is open mid-May through mid-September. Contact Split Rock Lighthouse Park at 3713 Split Rock Lighthouse Road, Two Harbors, MN 55616; call (218) 226-6372. The Minnesota Historical Society owns and manages the lighthouse as one of more than two dozen historic sites. Call Minnesota Historical Society at the lighthouse: (218) 226-6372, or write the society at 345 W. Kellogg Boulevard, St. Paul, MN 55102, or see www.mnhs.org.

■ GRAND MARAIS LIGHT ■
Grand Marais (1886 and 1922)

This four-legged steel structure, which stands thirty-five feet above the lake, marks the end of the Grand Marais breakwater. In addition to warning mariners away from the low breakwater, it guides vessels into the town's harbor. Built in 1922, the relatively diminutive existing light replaced the larger tower that had stood on the shore since 1886. The light, produced by a classic lens, can be seen from up to sixteen miles away.

Grand Marais Light

Travel information: Follow Highway 61 to Grand Marais, near the far northeastern corner of Minnesota. The lighthouse stands at the end of the town's primary breakwater. Contact the Cook County Historical Society, 8 South Broadway, Grand Marais, WI 55604; call (218) 387-2883, or see www.cookcountyhistory.org.

Isle Royale

■ ROCK OF AGES LIGHT ■
Near Isle Royale (1908)

Built in 1908 on an open-water caisson atop a notoriously dangerous shoal, the Rock of Ages Lighthouse was one of the most isolated manned light stations in America, if not the world. Keepers had to sail more than fifty miles across the often stormy waters of Lake Superior to spend a day in town, see a doctor, visit friends, or pick up food and supplies. For much of the year, the five-level, 130-foot-tall steel tower was their entire world.

Rock of Ages Light

In 1933 keepers had unexpected company when the freighter *George Cox* slammed into a nearby reef and sank. Rescued by the keeper and his assistant from the frigid waters of the lake, 125 survivors huddled in the lighthouse. They sat one atop the other on the tower's staircase until a ship arrived to take them to shore.

Anyone stranded on the rock nowadays would find nobody at home. The lighthouse has been automated since 1978, much to the relief, no doubt, of the lonely keepers. Following automation, the station lost its second-order classic lens—at one time the most powerful optic on the Great Lakes. A modern, strong beacon shines here today. It is now part of Isle Royale National Park.

Travel information: The Rock of Ages Lighthouse is, of course, closed to the public. It can sometimes be seen from the decks of ferries approaching Isle Royale.

■ ROCK HARBOR LIGHT ■
Isle Royale (1855)

Now a pristine wilderness visited primarily by backpackers and outdoor enthusiasts, Isle Royale was, in the past, a thriving mining center. The discovery of copper here during the late 1840s led to construction of the Rock Harbor Lighthouse in 1855 to guide ore freighters to the island through Middle Island Passage. The station consisted of a fifty-foot brick tower with attached stone dwelling.

The Isle Royale copper veins played out within a few years, and by the late 1870s mining ceased all together. This made the Rock Harbor Light unnecessary, and it was closed permanently in 1878. The tower and dwelling still stand.

The work of guiding vessels and visitors to Isle Royale is handled nowadays by **Isle Royale Lighthouse,** located on a barren rock near the entrance to Siskit Bay. The stone tower, completed in 1875, still displays its white light, produced by a fourth-order Fresnel lens. Also still in operation is the **Passage Island Lighthouse** (1882), which marks the channel just off the northeastern tip of Isle Royale.

Passage Island Light
Bob and Sandra Shanklin

Travel information: For nature lovers—and lighthouse aficionados as well—a visit to Isle Royale National Park can be the experience of a lifetime. As many travelers can attest, however, reaching Isle Royale is no easy task. Usually, it requires a lengthy ferry ride from Copper Harbor or other departure points on the Michigan Upper Peninsula, and visitors must have prior reservations for camping or accommodations on the island. For

Isle Royale Light
Bob and Sandra Shanklin

reservations on Isle Royale or for further information, contact Isle Royale National Park, 87 North Ripley Street, Houghton, MI 49931; call (906) 487-7151, or see www.nps.gov/isro.

There are several ways to reach these outlying, pristine areas and see the lights: For reservations on the *Ranger III*: Isle Royale National Park, Reservation Office, 800 East Lakeshore Drive, Houghton, MI 49931; call (906) 482-0984. For reservations on the *Voyageur II* and the *Sea Hunter*: P.O. Box 10529, White Bear Lake, MN 55110; call (651) 653-5872 or (218) 475-0024, or see www.grand-isle-royale.com. For reservations on the *Isle Royale Queen IV* out of Copper Harbor, MI: call (906) 289-4437, or see www.isleroyale .com. For reservations to go by seaplane: Royale Air Service, Houghton County Memorial Airport, 23810 Airpark Boulevard, Laurium, MI 49913; call (877) 359-4753, or see www.royaleairservice.com. All reservations for this national park should be made well in advance.

Rock Harbor Light
Bob and Sandra Shanklin

INDEX

T

U

ABOUT THE AUTHORS

Bruce Roberts and his wife, Cheryl, live on North Carolina's Outer Banks, not far from the Cape Lookout Lighthouse. For many years Bruce was senior travel photographer for *Southern Living* magazine. He started his career working as a photographer for newspapers in Tampa, Florida, and Charlotte, North Carolina. He is the recipient of many photography awards, and some of his photos are in the permanent collection of the Smithsonian Institution.

Cheryl Shelton-Roberts has done extensive research on American lighthouses for two decades and has written numerous maritime-themed books including *Lighthouse Families,* named best lighthouse history book by The Foundation for Coast Guard History in 2007, and most recently *North Carolina Lighthouses: Stories of History and Hope* in 2011. She wrote the interpretive book *Moving Hatteras: Relocating the Cape Hatteras Lighthouse to Safety* for the National Park Service after working with move engineers for six months prior to the move. She was awarded the American Lighthouse Foundation's Keeper of the Light award in 2001 and saluted as the US Lighthouse Society's Keeper of the Quarter in 2012. She is cofounder of the Outer Banks Lighthouse Society (1995) and creates the society's *The Lighthouse News,* now in its eighteenth year.

Ray Jones is a historian, author, and publishing consultant living in Pebble Beach, California. He has written more than thirty books on subjects ranging from dinosaurs to country stores but is probably best known for his lighthouse travel guides and histories. Published by Globe Pequot Press in 2004, his award-winning *Lighthouse Encyclopedia* is widely regarded to be the best and most informative volume on the subject. He has also written a number of PBS companion books, including *Niagara Falls: An Intimate Portrait,* published in 2006, also by Globe Pequot Press.